BUSINESS ADVENTURES

TWELVE CLASSIC TALES FROM THE WORLD OF WALL STREET

JOHN BROOKS

OPEN ROAD

INTEGRATED MEDIA

NEW YORK

All of the material in this book has appeared in the *New Yorker* in slightly different form.

Cover design by Andrea Worthington

978-1-4976-4489-2

This edition published in 2014 by Open Road Integrated Media, Inc.
345 Hudson Street
New York, NY 10014
www.openroadmedia.com

CONTENTS

CONTENTS

BUSINESS ADVENTURES

1

THE FLUCTUATION

THE STOCK MARKET—the daytime adventure serial of the well-to-do—would not be the stock market if it did not have its ups and downs. Any board-room sitter with a taste for Wall Street lore has heard of the retort that J. P. Morgan the Elder is supposed to have made to a naïve acquaintance who had ventured to ask the great man what the market was going to do. "It will fluctuate," replied Morgan dryly. And it has many other distinctive characteristics. Apart from the economic advantages and disadvantages of stock exchanges—the advantage that they provide a free flow of capital to finance industrial expansion, for instance, and the disadvantage that they provide an all too convenient way for the unlucky, the imprudent, and the gullible to lose their money—their development has created a whole pattern of social behavior, complete with customs, language, and predictable responses to given events. What is truly extraordinary is the speed with which this pattern emerged full blown following the establishment, in 1611, of the world's first important stock exchange—a roofless courtyard in Amsterdam—and the degree to which it persists (with variations, it is true) on the New York Stock Exchange in the nineteen-sixties. Present-day stock trading in the United States—a bewilderingly vast enterprise, involving millions of miles of private telegraph wires, computers that can read and copy the Manhattan Telephone Directory in three minutes, and over twenty million stockholder participants—would seem to be a far cry from a handful of seventeenth-century Dutchmen haggling in the rain. But the field marks are much the same. The first stock exchange was, inadvertently, a laboratory in which new human reactions were revealed. By the same token, the New York Stock Exchange is also a sociological test tube, forever contributing to the human species' self-understanding.

The behavior of the pioneering Dutch stock traders is ably documented in a book entitled "Confusion of Confusions," written by a plunger on the Amsterdam market named Joseph de la Vega; originally published in 1688, it was reprinted in English translation a few years ago by the Harvard Business School. As for the behavior of present-day American investors and brokers—whose traits, like those of all stock traders, are exaggerated in times of crisis—it may be clearly revealed through a consideration of their activities during the last week of May, 1962, a time when the stock market fluctuated in a startling way. On Monday, May 28th, the Dow-Jones average of thirty leading industrial stocks, which has been computed every trading day since 1897, dropped 34.95 points, or more than it had dropped on any other day except October 28, 1929, when the loss was 38.33 points. The volume of trading on May 28th was 9,350,000 shares—the seventh-largest one-day turnover in Stock Exchange history. On Tuesday, May 29th, after an alarming morning when most stocks sank far below their Monday-afternoon closing prices, the market suddenly changed direction, charged upward with astonishing vigor, and finished the day with a large, though not record-breaking, Dow-Jones gain of 27.03 points. Tuesday's record, or near record, was in trading volume; the 14,750,000 shares that changed hands added up to the greatest one-day total ever except for October 29, 1929, when trading ran just over sixteen million shares. (Later in the sixties, ten, twelve, and even fourteen-million share days became commonplace; the 1929 volume record was finally broken on April 1st, 1968, and fresh records were set again and again in the next few months.) Then, on Thursday, May 31st, after a Wednesday holiday in observance of Memorial Day, the cycle was completed; on a volume of 10,710,000 shares, the fifth-greatest in history, the Dow-Jones average gained 9.40 points, leaving it slightly above the level where it had been before all the excitement began.

The crisis ran its course in three days, but, needless to say, the post-mortems took longer. One of de la Vega's observations about the Amsterdam traders was that they were "very clever in inventing reasons" for a sudden rise or fall in stock prices, and the Wall Street pundits certainly needed all the cleverness they could muster to explain why, in the middle of an excellent business year, the market had suddenly taken its second-worst nose dive ever up to that moment. Beyond these explanations—among which President Kennedy's April crackdown on the steel industry's planned price increase ranked high—it was inevitable that the postmortems should often compare May, 1962, with October, 1929. The figures for price movement and trading volume alone would have forced the parallel, even if the worst panic days of the two months—the twenty-eighth and the twenty-ninth—had not mysteriously and, to some people, ominously coincided. But it was generally conceded that the contrasts were more persuasive than the similarities. Between 1929 and 1962, regulation of trading practices and limitations on the amount of credit extended to customers for the purchase of stock had made it difficult, if not actually impossible, for a man to lose *all* his money on the Exchange. In short, de la Vega's epithet

for the Amsterdam stock exchange in the sixteen-eighties—
he called it "this gambling hell," although he obviously loved
it—had become considerably less applicable to the New York
exchange in the thirty-three years between the two crashes.

The 1962 crash did not come without warning, even though
few observers read the warnings correctly. Shortly after the
beginning of the year, stocks had begun falling at a pretty consistent rate, and the pace had accelerated to the point where
the previous business week—that of May 21st through May
25th—had been the worst on the Stock Exchange since June,
1950. On the morning of Monday, May 28th, then, brokers
and dealers had reason to be in a thoughtful mood. Had the
bottom been reached, or was it still ahead? Opinion appears,
in retrospect, to have been divided. The Dow-Jones news service, which sends its subscribers spot financial news by tele-
printer, reflected a certain apprehensiveness between the time
it started its transmissions, at nine o'clock, and the opening
of the Stock Exchange, at ten. During this hour, the broad
tape (as the Dow-Jones service, which is printed on vertically
running paper six and a quarter inches wide, is often called,
to distinguish it from the Stock Exchange price tape, which
is printed horizontally and is only three-quarters of an inch
high) commented that many securities dealers had been busy
over the weekend sending out demands for additional collateral to credit customers whose stock assets were shrinking in
value; remarked that the type of precipitate liquidation seen
during the previous week "has been a stranger to Wall Street
for years;" and went on to give several items of encouraging
business news, such as the fact that Westinghouse had just
received a new Navy contract. In the stock market, however,
as de la Vega points out, "the news [as such] is often of little
value;" in the short run, the mood of the investors is what
counts.

This mood became manifest within a matter of minutes

after the Stock Exchange opened. At 10:11, the broad tape reported that "stocks at the opening were mixed and only moderately active." This was reassuring information, because "mixed" meant that some were up and some were down, and also because a falling market is universally regarded as far less threatening when the amount of activity in it is moderate rather than great. But the comfort was short-lived, for by 10:30 the Stock Exchange tape, which records the price and the share volume of every transaction made on the floor, not only was consistently recording lower prices but, running at its maximum speed of five hundred characters per minute, was six minutes late. The lateness of the tape meant that the machine was simply unable to keep abreast of what was going on, so fast were trades being made. Normally, when a transaction is completed on the floor of the Exchange, at 11 Wall Street, an Exchange employee writes the details on a slip of paper and sends it by pneumatic tube to a room on the fifth floor of the building, where one of a staff of girls types it into the ticker machine for transmission. A lapse of two or three minutes between a floor transaction and its appearance on the tape is normal, therefore, and is not considered by the Stock Exchange to be "lateness;" that word, in the language of the Exchange, is used only to describe any additional lapse between the time a sales slip arrives on the fifth floor and the time the hard-pressed ticker is able to accommodate it. ("The terms used on the Exchange are not carefully chosen," complained de la Vega.) Tape delays of a few minutes occur fairly often on busy trading days, but since 1930, when the type of ticker in use in 1962 was installed, big delays had been extremely rare. On October 24, 1929, when the tape fell two hundred and forty-six minutes behind, it was being printed at the rate of two hundred and eighty-five characters a minute; before May, 1962, the greatest delay that had ever occurred on the new machine was thirty-four minutes.

Unmistakably, prices were going down and activity was

going up, but the situation was still not desperate. All that had been established by eleven o'clock was that the previous week's decline was continuing at a moderately accelerated rate. But as the pace of trading increased, so did the tape delay. At 10:55, it was thirteen minutes late; at 11:14, twenty minutes; at 11:35, twenty-eight minutes; at 11:58, thirty-eight minutes; and at 12:14, forty-three minutes. (To inject at least a seasoning of up-to-date information into the tape when it is five minutes or more in arrears, the Exchange periodically interrupted its normal progress to insert "flashes," or current prices of a few leading stocks. The time required to do this, of course, added to the lateness.) The noon computation of the Dow-Jones industrial average showed a loss for the day so far of 9.86 points.

Signs of public hysteria began to appear during the lunch hour. One sign was the fact that between twelve and two, when the market is traditionally in the doldrums, not only did prices continue to decline but volume continued to rise, with a corresponding effect on the tape; just before two o'clock, the tape delay stood at fifty-two minutes. Evidence that people are selling stocks at a time when they ought to be eating lunch is always regarded as a serious matter. Perhaps just as convincing a portent of approaching agitation was to be found in the Times Square office (at 1451 Broadway) of Merrill Lynch, Pierce, Fenner & Smith, the undisputed Gargantua of the brokerage trade. This office was plagued by a peculiar problem: because of its excessively central location, it was visited every day at lunchtime by an unusual number of what are known in brokerage circles as "walk-ins"—people who are securities customers only in a minuscule way, if at all, but who find the atmosphere of a brokerage office and the changing prices on its quotation board entertaining, especially in times of stock-market crisis. ("Those playing the game merely for the sake of entertainment and not because of greediness are easily to be distinguished." —de la Vega.) From long experience, the office manager, a calm Georgian named Samuel Mothner, had learned to recognize a close correlation between the current degree of public concern about the market and the number of walk-ins in his office, and at midday on May 28th the mob of them was so dense as to have, for his trained sensibilities, positively albatross-like connotations of disaster ahead.

Mothner's troubles, like those of brokers from San Diego to Bangor, were by no means confined to disturbing signs and portents. An unrestrained liquidation of stocks was already well under way; in Mothner's office, orders from customers were running five or six times above average, and nearly all of them were orders to sell. By and large, brokers were urging their customers to keep cool and hold on to their stocks, at least for the present, but many of the customers could not be persuaded. In another midtown Merrill Lynch office, at 61 West Forty-eighth Street, a cable was received from a substantial client living in Rio de Janeiro that said simply, "Please sell out everything in my account." Lacking the time to conduct a long-distance argument in favor of forbearance, Merrill Lynch had no choice but to carry out the order. Radio and television stations, which by early afternoon had caught the scent of news, were now interrupting their regular programs with spot broadcasts on the situation; as a Stock Exchange publication has since commented, with some asperity, "The degree of attention devoted to the stock market in these news broadcasts may have contributed to the uneasiness among some investors." And the problem that brokers faced in executing the flood of selling orders was by this time vastly complicated by technical factors. The tape delay, which by 2:26 amounted to fifty-five minutes, meant that for the most part the ticker was reporting the prices of an hour before, which in many cases were anywhere from one to ten dollars a share higher than the current prices. It was almost impossible for a broker accepting a selling order to tell his customer what price he might expect to get. Some brokerage firms were try-

ing to circumvent the tape delay by using makeshift reporting systems of their own; among these was Merrill Lynch,
whose floor brokers, after completing a trade, would—if they
remembered and had the time—simply shout the result into a
floorside telephone connected to a "squawk box" in the firm's
head office, at 70 Pine Street. Obviously, haphazard methods
like this were subject to error.

On the Stock Exchange floor itself, there was no question
of any sort of rally; it was simply a case of all stocks' declining rapidly and steadily, on enormous volume. As de la Vega
might have described the scene—as, in fact, he *did* rather flam-
boyantly describe a similar scene—"The bears [that is, the
sellers] are completely ruled by fear, trepidation, and nervous-
ness. Rabbits become elephants, brawls in a tavern become
rebellions, faint shadows appear to them as signs of chaos."
Not the least worrisome aspect of the situation was the fact
that the leading bluechip stocks, representing shares in the
country's largest companies, were right in the middle of the
decline; indeed, American Telephone & Telegraph, the largest
company of them all, and the one with the largest number of
stockholders, was leading the entire market downward. On a
share volume greater than that of any of the more than fifteen
hundred other stocks traded on the Exchange (most of them
at a tiny fraction of Telephone's price), Telephone had been
battered by wave after wave of urgent selling all day, until
at two o'clock it stood at 104¾—down 6⅞ for the day—
and was still in full retreat. Always something of a bellwether,
Telephone was now being watched more closely than ever,
and each loss of a fraction of a point in its price was the signal
for further declines all across the board. Before three o'clock,
I.B.M. was down 17½ points; Standard Oil of New Jersey,
often exceptionally resistant to general declines, was off 3¼;
and Telephone itself had tumbled again, to 101⅛. Nor did the
bottom appear to be in sight.

Yet the atmosphere on the floor, as it has since been

described by men who were there, was not hysterical—or, at least, any hysteria was well controlled. While many brokers were straining to the utmost the Exchange's rule against running on the floor, and some faces wore expressions that have been characterized by a conservative Exchange official as "studious," there was the usual amount of joshing, horseplay, and exchanging of mild insults. ("Jokes . . . form a main attraction to the business." —de la Vega.) But things were not entirely the same. "What I particularly remember is feeling physically exhausted," one floor broker has said. "On a crisis day, you're likely to walk ten or eleven miles on the floor—that's been measured with pedometers—but it isn't just the distance that wears you down. It's the physical contact. You have to push and get pushed. People climb all over you. Then, there were the sounds—the tense hum of voices that you always get in times of decline. As the rate of decline increases, so does the pitch of the hum. In a rising market, there's an entirely different sound. After you get used to the difference, you can tell just about what the market is doing with your eyes shut. Of course, the usual heavy joking went on, and maybe the jokes got a little more forced than usual. Everybody has commented on the fact that when the closing bell rang, at three-thirty, a cheer went up from the floor. Well, we weren't cheering because the market was down. We were cheering because it was over."

But was it over? This question occupied Wall Street and the national investing community all the afternoon and evening. During the afternoon, the laggard Exchange ticker slogged along, solemnly recording prices that had long since become obsolete. (It was an hour and nine minutes late at closing time, and did not finish printing the day's transactions until 5:58.) Many brokers stayed on the Exchange floor until after five o'clock, straightening out the details of trades, and then went to their offices to work on their accounts. What the price tape had to tell, when it finally got around to telling it, was a uniformly sad tale. American Telephone had closed at 100⅝, down 11 for the day. Philip Morris had closed at 71½, down 8¼ Campbell Soup had closed at 81, down 10¾. I.B.M. had closed at 361, down 37½. And so it went. In brokerage offices, employees were kept busy—many of them for most of the night—at various special chores, of which by far the most urgent was sending out margin calls. A margin call is a demand for additional collateral from a customer who has borrowed money from his broker to buy stocks and whose stocks are now worth barely enough to cover the loan. If a customer is unwilling or unable to meet a margin call with more collateral, his broker will sell the margined stock as soon as possible; such sales may depress other stocks further, leading to more margin calls, leading to more stock sales, and so on down into the pit. This pit had proved bottomless in 1929, when there were no federal restrictions on stock-market credit. Since then, a floor had been put in it, but the fact remains that credit requirements in May of 1962 were such that a customer could expect a call when stocks he had bought on margin had dropped to between fifty and sixty per cent of their value at the time he bought them. And at the close of trading on May 28th nearly one stock in four had dropped as far as that from its 1961 high. The Exchange has since estimated that 91,700 margin calls were sent out, mainly by telegram, between May 25th and May 31st; it seems a safe assumption that the lion's share of these went out in the after-noon, in the evening, or during the night of May 28th—and not just the early part of the night, either. More than one customer first learned of the crisis—or first became aware of its almost spooky intensity—on being awakened by the arrival of a margin call in the pre-dawn hours of Tuesday.

If the danger to the market from the consequences of margin selling was much less in 1962 than it had been in 1929, the danger from another quarter—selling by mutual funds—

was immeasurably greater. Indeed, many Wall Street professionals now say that at the height of the May excitement
the mere thought of the mutual-fund situation was enough
to make them shudder. As is well known to the millions of
Americans who have bought shares in mutual funds over the
past two decades or so, they provide a way for small investors
to pool their resources under expert management; the small
investor buys shares in a fund, and the fund uses the money
to buy stocks and stands ready to redeem the investor's shares
at their current asset value whenever he chooses. In a serious stock-market decline, the reasoning went, small investors
would want to get their money out of the stock market and
would therefore ask for redemption of their shares; in order
to raise the cash necessary to meet the redemption demands,
the mutual funds would have to sell some of their stocks;
these sales would lead to a further stock-market decline, causing more holders of fund shares to demand redemption—and
so on down into a more up-to-date version of the bottomless
pit. The investment community's collective shudder at this
possibility was intensified by the fact that the mutual funds'
power to magnify a market decline had never been seriously
tested; practically nonexistent in 1929, the funds had built up
the staggering total of twenty-three billion dollars in assets
by the spring of 1962, and never in the interim had the market declined with anything like its present force. Clearly, if
twenty-three billion dollars in assets, or any substantial fraction of that figure, were to be tossed onto the market now,
it could generate a crash that would make 1929 seem like a
stumble. A thoughtful broker named Charles J. Rolo, who
was a book reviewer for the *Atlantic* until he joined Wall
Street's literary coterie in 1960, has recalled that the threat
of a fund-induced downward spiral, combined with general
ignorance as to whether or not one was already in progress,
was "so terrifying that you didn't even mention the subject."
As a man whose literary sensibilities had up to then survived

the well-known crassness of economic life, Rolo was perhaps a good witness on other aspects of the downtown mood at dusk on May 28th. "There was an air of unreality," he said later. "No one, as far as I knew, had the slightest idea where the bottom would be. The closing Dow-Jones average that day was down almost thirty-five points, to about five hundred and seventy-seven. It's now considered elegant in Wall Street to deny it, but many leading people were talking about a bottom of four hundred—which would, of course, have been a disaster. One heard the words 'four hundred' uttered again and again, although if you ask people now, they tend to tell you they said 'five hundred.' And along with the apprehensions there was a profound feeling of depression of a very personal sort among brokers. We knew that our customers— by no means all of them rich—had suffered large losses as a result of our actions. Say what you will, it's extremely disagreeable to lose other people's money. Remember that this happened at the end of about twelve years of generally rising stock prices. After more than a decade of more or less constant profits to yourself and your customers, you get to think you're pretty good. You're on top of it. You can make money, and that's that. This break exposed a weakness. It subjected one to a certain loss of self-confidence, from which one was not likely to recover quickly." The whole thing was enough, apparently, to make a broker wish that he were in a position to adhere to de la Vega's cardinal rule: "*Never give anyone the advice to buy or sell shares*, because, where perspicacity is weakened, the most benevolent piece of advice can turn out badly."

It was on Tuesday morning that the dimensions of Monday's debacle became evident. It had by now been calculated that the paper loss in value of all stocks listed on the Exchange amounted to $20,800,000,000. This figure was an all-time record; even on October 28, 1929, the loss had been a mere

$9,600,000,000, the key to the apparent inconsistency being the fact that the total value of the stocks listed on the Exchange was far smaller in 1929 than in 1962. The new record also represented a significant slice of our national income—specifically, almost four per cent. In effect, the United States had lost something like two weeks' worth of products and pay in one day. And, of course, there were repercussions abroad. In Europe, where reactions to Wall Street are delayed a day by the time difference, Tuesday was the day of crisis; by nine o'clock that morning in New York, which was toward the end of the trading day in Europe, almost all the leading European exchanges were experiencing wild selling, with no apparent cause other than Wall Street's crash. The loss in Milan was the worst in eighteen months. That in Brussels was the worst since 1946, when the bourse there reopened after the war. That in London was the worst in at least twenty-seven years. In Zurich, there had been a sickening thirty-per-cent selloff earlier in the day, but some of the losses were now being cut as bargain hunters came into the market. And another sort of backlash—less direct, but undoubtedly more serious in human terms—was being felt in some of the poorer countries of the world. For example, the price of copper for July delivery dropped on the New York commodity market by forty-four one-hundredths of a cent per pound. Insignificant as such a loss may sound, it was a vital matter to a small country heavily dependent on its copper exports. In his recent book "The Great Ascent," Robert L. Heilbroner had cited an estimate that for every cent by which copper prices drop on the New York market the Chilean treasury lost four million dollars; by that standard, Chile's potential loss on copper alone was $1,760,000.

Yet perhaps worse than the knowledge of what had happened was the fear of what might happen now. The *Times* began a queasy lead editorial with the statement that "something resembling an earthquake hit the stock market yesterday," and then took almost half a column to marshal its forces for the reasonably ringing affirmation "Irrespective of the ups and downs of the stock market, we are and will remain the masters of our economic fate." The Dow-Jones news ticker, after opening up shop at nine o'clock with its customary cheery "Good morning," lapsed almost immediately into disturbing reports of the market news from abroad, and by 9:45, with the Exchange's opening still a quarter of an hour away, was asking itself the jittery question "When will the dumping of stocks let up?" Not just yet, it concluded; all the signs seemed to indicate that the selling pressure was "far from satisfied." Throughout the financial world, ugly rumors were circulating about the imminent failure of various securities firms, increasing the aura of gloom. ("The expectation of an event creates a much deeper impression . . . than the event itself." —de la Vega.) The fact that most of these rumors later proved false was no help at the time. Word of the crisis had spread overnight to every town in the land, and the stock market had become the national preoccupation. In brokerage offices, the switchboards were jammed with incoming calls, and the customers' areas with walk-ins and, in many cases, television crews. As for the Stock Exchange itself, everyone who worked on the floor had got there early, to batten down against the expected storm, and additional hands had been recruited from desk jobs on the upper floors of 11 Wall to help sort out the mountains of orders. The visitors' gallery was so crowded by opening time that the usual guided tours had to be suspended for the day. One group that squeezed its way onto the gallery that morning was the eighth-grade class of Corpus Christi Parochial School, of West 121st Street; the class's teacher, Sister Aquin, explained to a reporter that the children had prepared for their visit over the previous two weeks by making hypothetical stock-market investments with an imaginary ten thousand dollars each. "They lost all their money," said Sister Aquin.

The Exchange's opening was followed by the blackest ninety minutes in the memory of many veteran dealers, including some survivors of 1929. In the first few minutes, comparatively few stocks were traded, but this inactivity did not reflect calm deliberation; on the contrary, it reflected selling pressure so great that it momentarily paralyzed action. In the interests of minimizing sudden jumps in stock prices, the Exchange requires that one of its floor officials must personally grant his permission before any stock can change hands at a price differing from that of the previous sale by one point or more for a stock priced under twenty dollars, or by two points or more for a stock priced above twenty dollars. Now sellers were so plentiful and buyers so scarce that hundreds of stocks would have to open at price changes as great as that or greater, and therefore no trading in them was possible until a floor official could be found in the shouting mob. In the case of some of the key issues, like I.B.M., the disparity between sellers and buyers was so wide that trading in them was impossible even *with* the permission of an official, and there was nothing to do but wait until the prospect of getting a bargain price lured enough buyers into the market. The Dow-Jones broad tape, stuttering out random prices and fragments of information as if it were in a state of shock, reported at 11:30 that "at least seven" Big Board stocks had still not opened; actually, when the dust had cleared it appeared that the true figure had been much larger than that. Meanwhile, the Dow-Jones average lost 11.09 more points in the first hour, Monday's loss in stock values had been increased by several billion dollars, and the panic was in full cry.

And along with panic came near chaos. Whatever else may be said about Tuesday, May 29th, it will be long remembered as the day when there was something very close to a complete breakdown of the reticulated, automated, mind-boggling complex of technical facilities that made nationwide stock-trading possible in a huge country where nearly one out of six adults was a stockholder. Many orders were executed at prices far different from the ones agreed to by the customers placing the orders; many others were lost in transmission, or in the snow of scrap paper that covered the Exchange floor, and were never executed at all. Sometimes brokerage firms were prevented from executing orders by simple inability to get in touch with their floor men. As the day progressed, Monday's heavy-traffic records were not only broken but made to seem paltry; as one index, Tuesday's closing-time delay in the Exchange tape was two hours and twenty-three minutes, compared to Monday's hour and nine minutes. By a heaven-sent stroke of prescience, Merrill Lynch, which handled over thirteen per cent of all public trading on the Exchange, had just installed a new 7074 computer—the device that can copy the Telephone Directory in three minutes—and, with its help, managed to keep its accounts fairly straight. Another new Merrill Lynch installation—an automatic teletype switching system that occupied almost half a city block and was intended to expedite communication between the firm's various offices—also rose to the occasion, though it got so hot that it could not be touched. Other firms were less fortunate, and in a number of them confusion gained the upper hand so thoroughly that some brokers, tired of trying in vain to get the latest quotations on stocks or to reach their partners on the Exchange floor, are said to have simply thrown up their hands and gone out for a drink. Such unprofessional behavior may have saved their customers a great deal of money.

But the crowning irony of the day was surely supplied by the situation of the tape during the lunch hour. Just before noon, stocks reached their lowest levels—down twenty-three points on the Dow-Jones average. (At its nadir, the average reached 553.75—a safe distance above the 500 that the experts now claim was their estimate of the absolute bottom.) Then they abruptly began an extraordinarily vigorous recovery. At 12:45, by which time the recovery had become a mad scramble to buy, the tape was fifty-six minutes late; therefore, apart from fleeting intimations supplied by a few "flash" prices, the ticker was engaged in informing the stock-market community of a selling panic at a moment when what was actually in progress was a buying panic.

The great turnaround late in the morning took place in a manner that would have appealed to de la Vega's romantic nature—suddenly and rather melodramatically. The key stock involved was American Telephone & Telegraph, which, just as on the previous day, was being universally watched and was unmistakably influencing the whole market. The key man, by the nature of his job, was George M. L. La Branche, Jr., senior partner in La Branche and Wood & Co., the firm that was acting as floor specialist in Telephone. (Floor specialists are broker-dealers who are responsible for maintaining orderly markets in the particular stocks with which they are charged. In the course of meeting their responsibilities, they often have the curious duty of taking risks with their own money against their own better judgment. Various authorities, seeking to reduce the element of human fallibility in the market, have lately been trying to figure out a way to replace the specialists with machines, but so far without success. One big stumbling block seems to be the question: If the mechanical specialists should lose their shirts, who would pay their losses?) La Branche, at sixty-four, was a short, sharp-featured, dapper, peppery man who was fond of sporting one of the Exchange floor's comparatively few Phi Beta Kappa keys; he had been a specialist since 1924, and his firm had been the specialist in Telephone since late in 1929. His characteristic habitat— indeed, the spot where he spent some five and a half hours almost every weekday of his life—was immediately in front of Post 15, in the part of the Exchange that is not readily visible from the visitors' gallery and is commonly called the Garage; there, feet planted firmly apart to fend off any sudden surges of would-be buyers or sellers, he customarily stood with pencil poised in a thoughtful way over an unprepossessing loose-leaf ledger, in which he kept a record of all outstanding orders to buy and sell Telephone stock at various price levels. Not surprisingly, the ledger was known as the Telephone book. La Branche had, of course, been at the center of the excitement all day Monday, when Telephone was leading the market downward. As specialist, he had been rolling with the punch like a fighter—or to adopt his own more picturesque metaphor, bobbing like a cork on ocean combers. "Telephone is kind of like the sea," La Branche said later. "Generally, it is calm and kindly. Then all of a sudden a great wind comes and whips up a giant wave. The wave sweeps over and deluges everybody; then it sucks back again. You have to give with it. You can't fight it, any more than King Canute could." On Tuesday morning, after Monday's drenching eleven-point drop, the great wave was still rolling; the sheer clerical task of sorting and matching the orders that had come in overnight—not to mention finding a Stock Exchange official and obtaining his permission—took so long that the first trade in Telephone could not be made until almost an hour after the Exchange's opening. When Telephone did enter the lists, at one minute before eleven, its price was 98½—down 2⅛ from Monday's closing. Over the next three-quarters of an hour or so, while the financial world watched it the way a sea captain might watch the barometer in a hurricane, Telephone fluctuated between 99, which it reached on momentary minor rallies, and 98⅛, which proved to be its bottom. It touched the lower figure on three separate occasions, with rallies between—a fact that La Branche has spoken of as if it had a magical or mystical significance. And perhaps it had; at any rate, after the third dip buyers of Telephone began to turn up at Post 15, sparse and timid at first, then more numerous and aggressive. At 11:45, the stock sold at 98¾; a few minutes later, at 99; at 11:50, at 99⅜; and finally, at 11:55, it sold at 100.

Many commentators have expressed the opinion that that first sale of Telephone at 100 marked the exact point at which the whole market changed direction. Since Telephone is among the stocks on which the ticker gives flashes during periods of tape delay, the financial community learned of the transaction almost immediately, and at a time when everything else it was hearing was very bad news indeed; the theory goes that the hard fact of Telephone's recovery of almost two points worked together with a purely fortuitous circumstance—the psychological impact of the good, round number 100—to tip the scales. La Branche, while agreeing that the rise of Telephone did a lot to bring about the general upturn, differs as to precisely which transaction was the crucial one. To him, the first sale at 100 was insufficient proof of lasting recovery, because it involved only a small number of shares (a hundred, as far as he remembers). He knew that in his book he had orders to sell almost twenty thousand shares of Telephone at 100. If the demand for shares at that price were to run out before this two-million-dollar supply was exhausted, then the price of Telephone would drop again, possibly going as low as 98⅛ for a fourth time. And a man like La Branche, given to thinking in nautical terms, may have associated a certain finality with the notion of going down for a fourth time.

It did not happen. Several small transactions at 100 were made in rapid succession, followed by several more, involving larger volume. Altogether, about half the supply of the stock at that price was gone when John J. Cranley, floor partner of Dreyfus & Co., moved unobtrusively into the crowd at Post 15 and bid 100 for ten thousand shares of Telephone—just enough to clear out the supply and thus pave the way for a further rise. Cranley did not say whether he was bidding on behalf of his firm, one of its customers, or the Dreyfus Fund, a mutual fund that Dreyfus & Co. managed through one of its subsidiaries; the size of the order suggests that the principal was the Dreyfus Fund. In any case, La Branche needed only to say "Sold," and as soon as the two men had made notations of it, the transaction was completed. Where-upon Telephone could no longer be bought for 100.

There is historical precedent (though not from de la Vega's day) for the single large Stock Exchange transaction that turns the market, or is intended to turn it. At half past one on October 24, 1929—the dreadful day that has gone down in financial history as Black Thursday—Richard Whitney, then acting president of the Exchange and probably the best-known figure on its floor, strode conspicuously (some say "jauntily") up to the post where U.S. Steel was traded, and bid 205, the price of the last sale, for ten thousand shares. But there are two crucial differences between the 1929 trade and the 1962 one. In the first place, Whitney's stagy bid was a calculated effort to create an effect, while Cranley's, delivered without fanfare, was apparently just a move to get a bargain for the Dreyfus Fund. Secondly, only an evanescent rally followed the 1929 deal— the next week's losses made Black Thursday look no worse than gray—while a genuinely solid recovery followed the one in 1962. The moral may be that psychological gestures on the Exchange are most effective when they are neither intended nor really needed. At all events, a general rally began almost immediately. Having broken through the 100 barrier, Telephone leaped wildly upward: at 12:18, it was traded at 101¼; at 12:41, at 103½; and at 1:05, at 106¼. General Motors went from 45½ at 11:46 to 50 at 1:38. Standard Oil of New Jersey went from 46¾ at 11:46 to 51 at 1:28. U.S. Steel went from 49½ at 11:40 to 52⅜ at 1:28. I.B.M. was, in its way, the most dramatic case of the lot. All morning, its stock had been kept out of trading by an overwhelming preponderance of selling orders, and the guesses as to its ultimate opening price varied from a loss of ten points to a loss of twenty or thirty; now such an avalanche of buying orders appeared that when it was at last technically possible for the stock to be traded, just before two o'clock, it opened *up* four points, on a huge block of thirty thousand shares. At 12:28, less than half an hour after the big Telephone trade, the Dow-Jones news service was sure enough of what was happening to state flatly, "The market has turned strong."

And so it had, but the speed of the turnaround produced more irony. When the broad tape has occasion to transmit an extended news item, such as a report on a prominent man's speech, it customarily breaks the item up into a series of short sections, which can then be transmitted at intervals, leaving time in the interstices for such spot news as the latest prices from the Exchange floor. This was what it did during the early afternoon of May 29th with a speech delivered to the National Press Club by H. Ladd Plumley, president of the United States Chamber of Commerce, which began to be reported on the Dow-Jones tape at 12:25, or at almost exactly the same time that the same news source declared the market to have turned strong. As the speech came out in sections on the broad tape, it created an odd effect indeed. The tape started off by saying that Plumley had called for "a thoughtful appreciation of the present lack of business confidence." At this point, there was an interruption for a few minutes' worth of stock prices, all of them sharply higher. Then the tape returned to Plumley, who was now warming to his task and blaming the stock-market plunge on "the coincidental impact of two confidence-upsetting factors—a dimming of profit expectations and President Kennedy's quashing of the steel price increase." Then came a longer interruption, chockfull of reassuring facts and figures. At its conclusion, Plumley was back on the tape, hammering away at his theme, which had now taken on overtones of "I told you so." "We have had an awesome demonstration that the 'right business climate' cannot be brushed off as a Madison Avenue cliché but is a reality much to be desired," the broad tape quoted him as saying. So it went through the early afternoon; it must have been a heady time for the Dow-Jones subscribers, who could alternately nibble at the caviar of higher stock prices and sip the champagne of Plumley's jabs at the Kennedy administration.

It was during the last hour and a half on Tuesday that the pace of trading on the Exchange reached its most frantic. The official count of trades recorded after three o'clock (that is, in the last half hour) came to just over seven million shares—in normal times as they were reckoned in 1962, an unheard-of figure even for a whole day's trading. When the closing bell sounded, a cheer again arose from the floor—this one a good deal more full-throated than Monday's, because the day's gain of 27.03 points in the Dow-Jones average meant that almost three-quarters of Monday's losses had been recouped; of the $20,800,000,000 that had summarily vanished on Monday, $13,500,000,000 had now reappeared. (These heart-warming figures weren't available until hours after the close, but experienced securities men are vouchsafed visceral intuitions of surprising statistical accuracy; some of them claim that at Tuesday's closing they could feel in their guts a Dow-Jones gain of over twenty-five points, and there is no reason to dispute their claim.) The mood was cheerful, then, but the hours were long. Because of the greater trading volume, tickers ticked and lights burned even farther into the night than they had on Monday; the Exchange tape did not print the day's last transaction until 8:15—four and three-quarters hours after it had actually occurred. Nor did the next day, Memorial Day, turn out to be a day off for the securities business. Wise old Wall Streeters had expressed the opinion that the holiday, falling by happy chance in the middle of the crisis and thus providing an opportunity for the cooling of overheated emotions, may have been the biggest factor in preventing the crisis from becoming a disaster. What it indubitably did provide was a chance for the Stock Exchange and its member organizations—all of whom had been directed to remain at their battle stations over the holiday—to begin picking up the pieces.

The insidious effects of a late tape had to be explained to thousands of naïve customers who thought they had bought U.S. Steel at, say, 50, only to find later that they had paid 54 or 55. The complaints of thousands of other customers could not be so easily answered. One brokerage house discovered that two orders it had sent to the floor at precisely the same time—one to buy Telephone at the prevailing price, the other to sell the same quantity at the prevailing price—had resulted in the seller's getting 102 per share for his stock and the buyer's paying 108 for his. Badly shaken by a situation that seemed to cast doubt on the validity of the law of supply and demand, the brokerage house made inquiries and found that the buying order had got temporarily lost in the crush and had failed to reach Post 15 until the price had gone up six points. Since the mistake had not been the customer's, the brokerage firm paid him the difference. As for the Stock Exchange itself, it had a variety of problems to deal with on Wednesday, among them that of keeping happy a team of television men from the Canadian Broadcasting Corporation who, having forgotten all about the United States custom of observing a holiday on May 30th, had flown down from Montreal to take pictures of Wednesday's action on the Exchange. At the same time, Exchange officials were necessarily pondering the problem of Monday's and Tuesday's scandalously laggard ticker, which everyone agreed had been at the very heart of—if not, indeed, the cause of—the most nearly catastrophic technical snarl in history. The Exchange's defense of itself, later set down in detail, amounts, in effect, to a complaint that the crisis came two years too soon. "It would be inaccurate to suggest that all investors were served with normal speed and efficiency by existing facilities," the Exchange conceded, with characteristic conservatism, and went on to say that a ticker with almost twice the speed of the present one was expected to be ready for installation in 1964. (In fact, the new ticker and various other automation devices, duly installed more or less on time, proved to be so heroically effective that the fantastic trading pace of April, 1968 was handled with only negligible tape delays.) The fact that the 1962 hurricane hit while the shelter was under construction was characterized by the Exchange as "perhaps ironic."

There was still plenty of cause for concern on Thursday morning. After a period of panic selling, the market has a habit of bouncing back dramatically and then resuming its slide. More than one broker recalled that on October 30, 1929—immediately after the all-time-record two-day decline, and immediately before the start of the truly disastrous slide that was to continue for years and precipitate the great depression—the Dow-Jones gain had been 28.40, representing a rebound ominously comparable to this one. In other words, the market still suffers at times from what de la Vega clinically called "antiperistasis"—the tendency to reverse itself, then reverse the reversal, and so on. A follower of the antiperistasis system of security analysis might have concluded that the market was now poised for another dive. As things turned out, of course, it wasn't. Thursday was a day of steady, orderly rises in stock prices. Minutes after the ten-o'clock opening, the broad tape spread the news that brokers everywhere were being deluged with buying orders, many of them coming from South America, Asia, and the Western European countries that are normally active in the New York stock market. "Orders still pouring in from all directions," the broad tape announced exultantly just before eleven. Lost money was magically reappearing, and more was on the way. Shortly before two o'clock, the Dow-Jones tape, having proceeded from euphoria to insouciance, took time off from market reports to include a note on plans for a boxing match between Floyd Patterson and Sonny Liston. Markets in Europe, reacting to New York on the upturn just as they had on the downturn, had risen sharply. New York copper futures had recovered over eighty per cent of their Monday and Tuesday-morning losses, so Chile's treasury was mostly bailed out. As for the Dow-Jones industrial average at closing, it figured out to 613.36, meaning that the week's losses had been wiped out *in toto*, with a little bit to spare. The crisis was over. In Morgan's terms, the market had fluctuated; in de la Vega's terms, antiperistasis had been demonstrated.

All that summer, and even into the following year, security analysts and other experts cranked out their explanations of what had happened, and so great were the logic, solemnity, and detail of these diagnoses that they lost only a little of their force through the fact that hardly any of the authors had had the slightest idea what was *going* to happen before the crisis occurred. Probably the most scholarly and detailed report on who did the selling that caused the crisis was furnished by the New York Stock Exchange itself, which began sending elaborate questionnaires to its individual and corporate members immediately after the commotion was over. The Exchange calculated that during the three days of the crisis rural areas of the country were more active in the market than they customarily are; that women investors had sold two and a half times as much stock as men investors; that foreign investors were far more active than usual, accounting for 5.5 per cent of the total volume, and, on balance, were substantial sellers; and, most striking of all, that what the Exchange calls "public individuals"—individual investors, as opposed to institutional ones, which is to say people who would be described anywhere but on Wall Street as *private* individuals—played an astonishingly large role in the whole affair, accounting for an unprecedented 56.8 per cent of the total volume. Breaking down the public individuals into income categories, the Exchange calculated that those with family incomes of over twenty-five thousand dollars a year were the heaviest and most insistent sellers, while those with incomes under ten thousand dollars, after selling on Monday and early on Tuesday, bought so many shares on Thursday that they actually became net buyers over the three-day period. Furthermore, according to the Exchange's calculations, about a million shares—or 3.5 per cent of the total volume during the three days—were sold as a result of margin calls. In sum, if there was a villain, it appeared to have been the relatively rich investor not connected with the securities business—and, more often than might have been expected, the female, rural, or foreign one, in many cases playing the market partly on borrowed money.

The role of the hero was filled, surprisingly, by the most frightening of untested forces in the market—the mutual funds. The Exchange's statistics showed that on Monday, when prices were plunging, the funds bought 530,000 more shares than they sold, while on Thursday, when investors in general were stumbling over each other trying to buy stock, the funds, on balance, *sold* 375,000 shares; in other words, far from increasing the market's fluctuation, the funds actually served as a stabilizing force. Exactly how this unexpectedly benign effect came about remains a matter of debate. Since no one has been heard to suggest that the funds acted out of sheer public-spiritedness during the crisis, it seems safe to assume that they were buying on Monday because their managers had spotted bargains, and were selling on Thursday because of chances to cash in on profits. As for the problem of redemptions, there were, as had been feared, a large number of mutual-fund shareholders who demanded millions of dollars of their money in cash when the market crashed, but apparently the mutual funds had so much cash on hand that in most cases they could pay off their shareholders without selling substantial amounts of stock. Taken as a group, the funds proved to be so rich and so conservatively managed that they not only could weather the storm but, by happy inadvertence, could do something to decrease its violence.

Whether the same conditions would exist in some future storm was and is another matter.

In the last analysis, the cause of the 1962 crisis remains unfathomable; what is known is that it occurred, and that something like it could occur again. As one of Wall Street's aged, ever-anonymous seers put it recently, "I was concerned, but at no time did I think it would be another 1929. I never said the Dow-Jones would go down to four hundred. I said *five* hundred. The point is that now, in contrast to 1929, the government, Republican or Democratic, realizes that it must be attentive to the needs of business. There will never be apple-sellers on Wall Street again. As to whether what happened that May can happen again—of course it can. I think that people may be more careful for a year or two, and then we may see another speculative buildup followed by another crash, and so on until God makes people less greedy."

Or, as de la Vega said, "It is foolish to think that you can withdraw from the Exchange after you have tasted the sweetness of the honey."

2

THE FATE OF THE EDSEL

RISE AND FLOWERING

IN THE CALENDAR OF AMERICAN ECONOMIC LIFE, 1955 was the Year of the Automobile. That year, American automobile makers sold over seven million passenger cars, or over a million more than they had sold in any previous year. That year, General Motors easily sold the public $325 million worth of new common stock, and the stock market as a whole, led by the motors, gyrated upward so frantically that Congress investigated it. And that year, too, the Ford Motor Company decided to produce a new automobile in what was quaintly called the medium-price range—roughly, from $2,400 to $4,000—and went ahead and designed it more or less in conformity with the fashion of the day, which was for cars that were long, wide, low, lavishly decorated with chrome, liberally supplied with gadgets, and equipped with engines of a power just barely insufficient to send them into orbit. Two years later, in September, 1957, the Ford Company put its new car, the

Edsel, on the market, to the accompaniment of more fanfare than had attended the arrival of any other new car since the same company's Model A, brought out thirty years earlier. The total amount spent on the Edsel before the first specimen went on sale was announced as a quarter of a billion dollars; its launching—as *Business Week* declared and nobody cared to deny—was more costly than that of any other consumer product in history. As a starter toward getting its investment back, Ford counted on selling at least 200,000 Edsels the first year.

There may be an aborigine somewhere in a remote rain forest who hasn't yet heard that things failed to turn out that way. To be precise, two years two months and fifteen days later Ford had sold only 109,466 Edsels, and, beyond a doubt, many hundreds, if not several thousands, of those were bought by Ford executives, dealers, salesmen, advertising men, assembly-line workers, and others who had a personal interest in seeing the car succeed. The 109,466 amounted to considerably less than one per cent of the passenger cars sold in the United States during that period, and on November 19, 1959, having lost, according to some outside estimates, around $350 million on the Edsel, the Ford Company permanently discontinued its production.

How could this have happened? How could a company so mightily endowed with money, experience, and, presumably, brains have been guilty of such a monumental mistake? Even before the Edsel was dropped, some of the more articulate members of the car-minded public had come forward with an answer—an answer so simple and so seemingly reasonable that, though it was not the only one advanced, it became widely accepted as the truth. The Edsel, these people argued, was designed, named, advertised, and promoted with a slavish adherence to the results of public-opinion polls and of their younger cousin, motivational research, and they concluded that when the public is wooed in an excessively calculated manner, it tends to turn away in favor of some gruffer but more spontaneously attentive suitor. Several years ago, in the face of an understandable reticence on the part of the Ford Motor Company, which enjoys documenting its boners no more than anyone else, I set out to learn what I could about the Edsel debacle, and my investigations have led me to believe that what we have here is less than the whole truth.

For, although the Edsel was *supposed* to be advertised, and otherwise promoted, strictly on the basis of preferences expressed in polls, some old-fashioned snake-oil-selling methods, intuitive rather than scientific, crept in. Although it was *supposed* to have been named in much the same way, science was curtly discarded at the last minute and the Edsel was named for the father of the company's president, like a nineteenth-century brand of cough drops or saddle soap. As for the design, it was arrived at without even a pretense of consulting the polls, and by the method that has been standard for years in the designing of automobiles—that of simply pooling the hunches of sundry company committees. The common explanation of the Edsel's downfall, then, under scrutiny, turns out to be largely a myth, in the colloquial sense of that term. But the facts of the case may live to become a myth of a symbolic sort—a modern American antisuccess story.

The origins of the Edsel go back to the fall of 1948, seven years before the year of decision, when Henry Ford II, who had been president and undisputed boss of the company since the death of his grandfather, the original Henry, a year earlier, proposed to the company's executive committee, which included Ernest R. Breech, the executive vice-president, that studies be undertaken concerning the wisdom of putting on the market a new and wholly different medium-priced car. The studies were undertaken. There appeared to be good reason for them. It was a well-known practice at the time for low-income owners of Fords, Plymouths, and Chevrolets to turn in their symbols of inferior caste as soon as their earnings rose above five thousand dollars a year, and "trade up" to a medium-priced car. From Ford's point of view, this would have been all well and good except that, for some reason, Ford owners usually traded up not to Mercury, the company's only medium-priced car, but to one or another of the medium-priced cars put out by its big rivals— Oldsmobile, Buick, and Pontiac, among the General Motors products, and, to a lesser extent, Dodge and De Soto, the Chrysler candidates. Lewis D. Crusoe, then a vice-president of the Ford Motor Company, was not overstating the case when he said, "We have been growing customers for General Motors."

The outbreak of the Korean War, in 1950, meant that Ford had no choice but to go on growing customers for its competitors, since introducing a new car at such a time was out of the question. The company's executive committee put aside the studies proposed by President Ford, and there matters rested for two years. Late in 1952, however, the end of the war appeared sufficiently imminent for the company to pick up where it had left off, and the studies were energetically resumed by a group called the Forward Product Planning Committee, which turned over much of the detailed work to the Lincoln-Mercury Division, under the direction of Richard Krafve (pronounced Kraffy), the division's assistant general manager. Krafve, a forceful, rather saturnine man with a habitually puzzled look, was then in his middle forties. The son of a printer on a small farm journal in Minnesota, he had been a sales engineer and management consultant before joining Ford, in 1947, and although he could not have known it in 1952, he was to have reason to look puzzled. As the man directly responsible for the Edsel and its fortunes, enjoying its brief glory and attending it in its mortal agonies, he had a rendezvous with destiny.

In December, 1954, after two years' work, the Forward Product Planning Committee submitted to the executive committee a six-volume blockbuster of a report summarizing its findings. Supported by copious statistics, the report predicted the arrival of the American millennium, or something a lot like it, in 1965. By that time, the Forward Product Planning Committee estimated, the gross national product would be $535 billion a year—up more than $135 billion in a decade. (As a matter of fact, this part of the millennium arrived much sooner than the Forward Planners estimated. The G. N. P. passed $535 billion in 1962, and for 1965 was $681 billion.) The number of cars in operation would be seventy million— up twenty million. More than half the families in the nation would have incomes of over five thousand dollars a year, and more than 40 percent of all the cars sold would be in the medium-price range or better. The report's picture of America in 1965, presented in crushing detail, was of a country after Detroit's own heart—its banks oozing money, its streets and highways choked with huge, dazzling medium-priced cars, its newly rich, "upwardly mobile" citizens racked with longings for more of them. The moral was clear. If by that time Ford had not come out with a second medium-priced car—not just a new model, but a new make—and made it a favorite in its field, the company would miss out on its share of the national boodle.

On the other hand, the Ford bosses were well aware of the enormous risks connected with putting a new car on the market. They knew, for example, that of the 2,900 American makes that had been introduced since the beginning of the Automobile Age—the Black Crow (1905), the Averageman's Car (1906), the Bug-mobile (1907), the Dan Patch (1911), and the Lone Star (1920) among them—only about twenty were still around. They knew all about the automotive casualties that had followed the Second World War—among them Crosley, which had given up altogether, and Kaiser Motors, which, though still alive in 1954, was breathing its last. (The members of the Forward Product Planning Committee must have glanced at each other uneasily when, a year later, Henry J. Kaiser wrote, in a valediction to his car business, "We expected to toss fifty million dollars into the automobile pond, but we didn't expect it to disappear without a ripple.") The Ford men also knew that neither of the other members of the industry's powerful and well-heeled Big Three—General Motors and Chrysler—had ventured to bring out a new standard-size make since the former's La Salle in 1927, and the latter's Plymouth, in 1928, and that Ford itself had not attempted to turn the trick since 1938, when it launched the Mercury.

Nevertheless, the Ford men felt bullish—so remarkably bullish that they resolved to toss into the automobile pond five times the sum that Kaiser had. In April, 1955, Henry Ford II, Breech, and the other members of the executive committee officially approved the Forward Product Planning Committee's findings, and, to implement them, set up another agency, called the Special Products Division, with the star-crossed Krafve as its head. Thus the company gave its formal sanction to the efforts of its designers, who, having divined the trend of events, had already been doodling for several months on plans for a new car. Since neither they nor the newly organized Krafve outfit, when it took over, had an inkling of what the thing on their drawing boards might be called, it became known to everybody at Ford, and even in the company's press releases, as the E-Car—the "E," it was explained, standing for "Experimental."

The man directly in charge of the E-Car's design—or, to use the gruesome trade word, "styling"—was a Canadian, then not yet forty, named Roy A. Brown, who, before taking on the

---

* The word "styling" is a weed deeply embedded in the garden of automobilia. In its preferred sense, the verb "to style" means to name; thus the Special Products Division's epic efforts to choose a name for the E-Car, which will be chronicled presently, were really the styling program, and what Brown and his associates were up to was something else again. In its second sense, says Webster, "to style" means "to fashion in . . . the accepted style"; this was just what Brown, who hoped to achieve originality, was trying not to do, so Brown's must have been the antistyling program.

E-Car (and after studying industrial design at the Detroit Art Academy), had had a hand in the designing of radios, motor cruisers, colored-glass products, Cadillacs, Oldsmobiles, and Lincolns.* Brown recently recalled his aspirations as he went to work on the new project. "Our goal was to create a vehicle which would be unique in the sense that it would be readily recognizable in styling theme from the nineteen other makes of cars on the road at that time," he wrote from England, where at the time of his writing he was employed as chief stylist for the Ford Motor Company, Ltd., manufacturers of trucks, tractors, and small cars. "We went to the extent of making photographic studies from some distance of all nineteen of these cars, and it became obvious that at a distance of a few hundred feet the similarity was so great that it was practically impossible to distinguish one make from the others. . . . They were all 'peas in a pod.' We decided to select [a style that] would be 'new' in the sense that it was unique, and yet at the same time be familiar."

While the E-Car was on the drawing boards in Ford's styling studio—situated, like its administrative offices, in the company's barony of Dearborn, just outside Detroit—work on it progressed under the conditions of melodramatic, if ineffectual, secrecy that invariably attend such operations in the automobile business: locks on the studio doors that could be changed in fifteen minutes if a key should fall into enemy hands; a security force standing round-the-clock guard over the establishment; and a telescope to be trained at intervals on nearby high points of the terrain where peekers might be roosting. (All such precautions, however inspired, are doomed to fail, because none of them provide a defense against Detroit's version of the Trojan horse—the job-jumping stylist, whose cheerful treachery makes it relatively easy for the rival companies to keep tabs on what the competition is up to. No one, of course, is better aware of this than the rivals themselves, but the cloak-and-dagger stuff is thought to pay for itself in publicity value.) Twice a week or so, Krafve—head down, and sticking to low ground—made the journey to the styling studio, where he would confer with Brown, check up on the work as it proceeded, and offer advice and encouragement. Krafve was not the kind of man to envision his objective in a single revelatory flash; instead, he anatomized the styling of the E-Car into a series of laboriously minute decisions—how to shape the fenders, what pattern to use with the chrome, what kind of door handles to put on, and so on and on. If Michelangelo ever added the number of decisions that went into the execution of, say, his "David," he kept it to himself, but Krafve, an orderly-minded man in an era of orderly-functioning computers, later calculated that in styling the E-Car he and his associates had to make up their minds on no fewer than four thousand occasions. He reasoned at the time that if they arrived at the right yes-or-no choice on every one of those occasions, they ought, in the end, to come up with a stylistically perfect car—or at least a car that would be unique and at the same time familiar. But Krafve concedes today that he found it difficult thus to bend the creative process to the yoke of system, principally because many of the four thousand decisions he made wouldn't stay put. "Once you get a general theme, you begin narrowing down," he says. "You keep modifying, and then modifying your modifications. Finally, you *have* to settle on something, because there isn't any more time. If it weren't for the deadline you'd probably go on modifying indefinitely."

Except for later, minor modifications of the modified modifications, the E-Car had been fully styled by midsummer of 1955. As the world was to learn two years later, its most striking aspect was a novel, horse-collar-shaped radiator grille, set vertically in the center of a conventionally low, wide front end—a blend of the unique and the familiar that was there for all to see, though certainly not for all to admire. In two prominent respects, however, Brown or Krafve, or both, lost sight entirely of the familiar, specifying a unique rear end, marked by widespread horizontal wings that were in bold contrast to the huge longitudinal tail fins then captivating the market, and a unique cluster of automatic-transmission push buttons on the hub of the steering wheel. In a speech to the public delivered a while before the public had its first look at the car, Krafve let fall a hint or two about its styling, which, he said, made it so "distinctive" that, externally, it was "immediately recognizable from front, side, and rear," and, internally, it was "the epitome of the push-button era without wild-blue-yonder Buck Rogers concepts." At last came the day when the men in the highest stratum of the Ford Hierarchy were given their first glimpse of the car. It produced an effect that was little short of apocalyptic. On August 15, 1955, in the ceremonial secrecy of the styling center, while Krafve, Brown, and their aides stood by smiling nervously and washing their hands in air, the members of the Forward Product Planning Committee, including Henry Ford II and Breech, watched critically as a curtain was lifted to reveal the first full-size model of the E-Car—a clay one, with tinfoil simulating aluminum and chrome. According to eyewitnesses, the audience sat in utter silence for what seemed like a full minute, and then, as one man, burst into a round of applause. Nothing of the kind had ever happened at an intracompany first showing at Ford since 1896, when old Henry had bolted together his first horseless carriage.

One of the most persuasive and most frequently cited explanations of the Edsel's failure is that it was a victim of the time lag between the decision to produce it and the act of putting it on the market. It was easy to see a few years later, when smaller and less powerful cars, euphemistically called "compacts," had become so popular as to turn the old automobile status-ladder upside down, that the Edsel was a giant step in the wrong direction, but it was far from easy to see that in fat, tail-finny 1955. American ingenuity—which has produced the electric light, the flying machine, the tin Lizzie, the atomic bomb, and even a tax system that permits a man, under certain circumstances, to clear a profit by making a charitable donation*—has not yet found a way of getting an automobile on the market within a reasonable time after it comes off the drawing board; the making of steel dies, the alerting of retail dealers, the preparation of advertising and promotion campaigns, the gaining of executive approval for each successive move, and the various other gavotte-like routines that are considered as vital as breathing in Detroit and its environs usually consume about two years. Guessing future tastes is hard enough for those charged with planning the customary annual changes in models of established makes; it is far harder to bring out an altogether new creation, like the E-Car, for which several intricate new steps must be worked into the dance pattern, such as endowing the product with a personality and selecting a suitable name for it, to say nothing of consulting various oracles in an effort to determine whether, by the time of the unveiling, the state of the national economy will make bringing out *any* new car seem like a good idea.

Faithfully executing the prescribed routine, the Special Products Division called upon its director of planning for market research, David Wallace, to see what he could do about imparting a personality to the E-Car and giving it a name. Wallace, a lean, craggy-jawed pipe puffer with a soft, slow, thoughtful way of speaking, gave the impression of being the Platonic idea of the college professor—the very steel die from which the breed is cut—although, in point of fact, his background was not strongly academic. Before going to Ford, in 1955, he had worked his way through Westminster College, in Pennsylva-

---

* For details on this product of the national creativity, see Chapter 3.

nia, ridden out the depression as a construction laborer in New York City, and then spent ten years in market research at *Time*. Still, impressions are what count, and Wallace has admitted that during his tenure with Ford he consciously stressed his professorial air for the sake of the advantage it gave him in dealing with the bluff, practical men of Dearborn. "Our department came to be regarded as a semi-Brain Trust," he says, with a certain satisfaction. He insisted, typically, on living in Ann Arbor, where he could bask in the scholarly aura of the University of Michigan, rather than in Dearborn or Detroit, both of which he declared were intolerable after business hours. Whatever the degree of his success in projecting the image of the E-Car, he seems, by his small eccentricities, to have done splendidly at projecting the image of Wallace. "I don't think Dave's motivation for being at Ford was basically economic," his old boss, Krafve, says. "Dave is the scholarly type, and I think he considered the job an interesting challenge." One could scarcely ask for better evidence of image projection than that.

Wallace clearly recalls the reasoning—candid enough—that guided him and his assistants as they sought just the right personality for the E-Car. "We said to ourselves, 'Let's face it—there is no great difference in basic mechanism between a two-thousand-dollar Chevrolet and a six-thousand-dollar Cadillac,'" he says. "'Forget about all the ballyhoo,' we said, 'and you'll see that they are really pretty much the same thing. Nevertheless, there's something—there's *got* to be something—in the makeup of a certain number of people that gives them a yen for a Cadillac, in spite of its high price, or maybe because of it.' We concluded that cars are the means to a sort of dream fulfillment. There's some irrational factor in people that makes them want one kind of car rather than another—something that has nothing to do with the mechanism at all but with the car's personality, as the customer imagines it. What we wanted to do, naturally, was to give the E-Car the personality that would make the greatest number of people want it. We figured we had a big advantage over the other manufacturers of medium-priced cars, because we didn't have to worry about changing a pre-existent, perhaps somewhat obnoxious personality. All we had to do was create the exact one we wanted—from scratch."

As the first step in determining what the E-Car's exact personality should be, Wallace decided to assess the personalities of the medium-priced cars already on the market, and those of the so-called low-priced cars as well, since the cost of some of the cheap cars' 1955 models had risen well up into the medium-price range. To this end, he engaged the Columbia University Bureau of Applied Social Research to interview eight hundred recent car buyers in Peoria, Illinois, and another eight hundred in San Bernardino, California, on the mental images they had of the various automobile makes concerned. (In undertaking this commercial enterprise, Columbia maintained its academic independence by reserving the right to publish its findings.) "Our idea was to get the reaction in cities, among clusters of people," Wallace says. "We didn't want a cross section. What we wanted was something that would show interpersonal factors. We picked Peoria as a place that is Midwestern, stereotyped, and not loaded with extraneous factors—like a General Motors glass plant, say. We picked San Bernardino because the West Coast is very important in the automobile business, and because the market there is quite different—people tend to buy flashier cars."

The questions that the Columbia researchers fared forth to ask in Peoria and San Bernardino dealt exhaustively with practically everything having to do with automobiles except such matters as how much they cost, how safe they were, and whether they ran. In particular, Wallace wanted to know the respondents' impressions of each of the existing makes. Who, in their opinion, would naturally own a Chevrolet or a Buick or whatever? People of what age? Of which sex? Of what social status? From the answers, Wallace found it easy to put together a personality portrait of each make. The image of the Ford came into focus as that of a very fast, strongly masculine car, of no particular social pretensions, that might character-istically be driven by a rancher or an automobile mechanic. In contrast, Chevrolet emerged as older, wiser, slower, a bit less rampantly masculine, and slightly more distingué—a clergy-man's car. Buick jelled into a middle-aged lady—or, at least, more of a lady than Ford, sex in cars having proved to be rela-tive—with a bit of the devil still in her, whose most felicitous mate would be a lawyer, a doctor, or a dance-band leader. As for the Mercury, it came out as virtually a hot rod, best suited to a young-buck racing driver; thus, despite its higher price tag, it was associated with persons having incomes no higher than the average Ford owner's, so no wonder Ford owners had not been trading up to it. This odd discrepancy between image and fact, coupled with the circumstance that, in sober truth all four makes looked very much alike and had almost the same horsepower under their hoods, only served to bear out Wallace's premise that the automobile fancier, like a young man in love, is incapable of sizing up the object of his affections in anything resembling a rational manner.

By the time the researchers closed the books on Peoria and San Bernardino, they had elicited replies not only to these questions but to others, several of which, it would appear, only the most abstruse sociological thinker could relate to medium-priced cars. "Frankly, we dabbled," Wallace says. "It was a dragnet operation." Among the odds and ends that the dragnet dredged up were some that, when pieced together, led the researchers to report:

> By looking at those respondents whose annual incomes range from $4,000 to $11,000, we can make an . . . obser-vation. A considerable percentage of these respondents [to a question about their ability to mix cocktails] are

in the "somewhat" category on ability to mix cocktails. . . . Evidently, they do not have much confidence in their cocktail-mixing ability. We may infer that these respondents are aware of the fact that they are in the learning process. They may be able to mix Martinis or Manhattans, but beyond these popular drinks they don't have much of a repertoire.

Wallace, dreaming of an ideally lovable E-Car, was delighted as returns like these came pouring into his Dearborn office. But when the time for a final decision drew near, it became clear to him that he must put aside peripheral issues like cocktail-mixing prowess and address himself once more to the old problem of the image. And here, it seemed to him, the greatest pitfall was the temptation to aim, in accordance with what he took to be the trend of the times, for extremes of masculinity, youthfulness, and speed; indeed, the following passage from one of the Columbia reports, as he interpreted it, contained a specific warning against such folly.

Offhand we might conjecture that women who drive cars probably work, and are more mobile than non-owners, and get gratifications out of mastering a traditionally male role. But . . . there is no doubt that whatever gratifications women get out of their cars, and whatever social imagery they attach to their automobiles, they do want to appear as women. Perhaps more worldly women, but women.

Early in 1956, Wallace set about summing up all of his department's findings in a report to his superiors in the Special Products Division. Entitled "The Market and Personality Objectives of the E-Car" and weighty with facts and statistics—though generously interspersed with terse sections in italics or capitals from which a hard-pressed executive could get the gist of the thing in a matter of seconds—the report first indulged in some airy, skippable philosophizing and then got down to conclusions:

> What happens when an owner sees his make as a car which a woman might buy, but is himself a man? Does this apparent inconsistency of car image and the buyer's own characteristics affect his trading plans? The answer quite definitely is Yes. When there is a conflict between owner characteristics and make image, there is greater planning to switch to another make. In other words, when the buyer is a different kind of person from the person he thinks would own his make, he wants to change to a make in which he, inwardly, will be more comfortable.
>
> It should be noted that "conflict," as used here, can be of two kinds. Should a make have a strong and well-defined image, it is obvious that an owner with strong opposing characteristics would be in conflict. But conflict also can occur when the make image is diffuse or weakly defined. In this case, the owner is in an equally frustrating position of not being able to get a satisfactory identification from his make.

The question, then, was how to steer between the Scylla of a too definite car personality and the Charybdis of a too weak personality. To this the report replied, "Capitalize on imagery weakness of competition," and went on to urge that in the matter of age the E-Car should take an imagery position neither too young nor too old but right along-side that of the middling Olds-mobile; that in the matter of social class, not to mince matters, "the E-Car might well take a status position just below Buick and Oldsmobile"; and that in the delicate matter of sex it should try to strad-dle the fence, again along with the protean Olds. In sum (and in Wallace typography):

The most advantageous personality for the E-Car might well be THE SMART CAR FOR THE YOUNGER EXECUTIVE OR PROFESSIONAL FAMILY ON ITS WAY UP.

Smart car: recognition by others of the owner's good style and taste.

Younger: appealing to spirited but responsible adventurers.

Executive or professional: millions pretend to this status, whether they can attain it or not.

Family: not exclusively masculine; a wholesome "good" role.

On Its Way Up: "The E-Car has faith in you, son; we'll help you make it!"

Before spirited but responsible adventurers could have faith in the E-Car, however, it had to have a name. Very early in its history, Krafve had suggested to members of the Ford family that the new car be named for Edsel Ford, who was the only son of old Henry; the president of the Ford Motor Company from 1918 until his death, in 1943; and the father of the new generation of Fords—Henry II, Benson, and William Clay. The three brothers had let Krafve know that their father might not have cared to have his name spinning on a million hubcaps, and they had consequently suggested that the Special Products Division start looking around for a substitute. This it did, with a zeal no less emphatic than it displayed in the personality crusade. In the late summer and early fall of 1955, Wallace hired the services of several research outfits, which sent interviewers, armed with a list of two thousand possible names, to canvass sidewalk crowds in New York, Chicago, Willow Run, and Ann Arbor. The interviewers did not ask simply what the respondent thought of some such name as Mars, Jupiter, Rover, Ariel, Arrow, Dart, or Ovation. They asked what free associations each name brought to mind, and having got an answer to this one, they asked what word or words was considered the opposite of each name, on the theory that, subliminally speaking, the opposite is as much a part of a name as the tail is of a penny. The results of all this, the Special Products Division eventually decided, were inconclusive. Meanwhile, Krafve and his men held repeated sessions in a darkened room, staring, with the aid of a spotlight, at a series of cardboard signs, each bearing a name, as, one after another, they were flipped over for their consideration. One of the men thus engaged spoke up for the name Phoenix, because of its connotations of ascendancy, and another favored Altair, on the ground that it would lead practically all alphabetical lists of cars and thus enjoy an advantage analogous to that enjoyed in the animal kingdom by the aardvark. At a certain drowsy point in one session, somebody suddenly called a halt to the card-flipping and asked, in an incredulous tone, "Didn't I see 'Buick' go by two or three cards back?" Everybody looked at Wallace, the impresario of the sessions. He puffed on his pipe, smiled an academic smile, and nodded.

The card-flipping sessions proved to be as fruitless as the sidewalk interviews, and it was at this stage of the game that Wallace, resolving to try and wring from genius what the common mind had failed to yield, entered into the celebrated car-naming correspondence with the poet Marianne Moore, which was later published in *The New Yorker* and still later, in book form, by the Morgan Library. "We should like this name . . . to convey, through association or other conjuration, some visceral feeling of elegance, fleetness, advanced features and design," Wallace wrote to Miss Moore, achieving a certain feeling of elegance himself. If it is asked who among the gods of Dearborn had the inspired and inspiriting idea of enlisting Miss Moore's services in this cause, the answer, according to Wallace, is that it was no god but the wife of one of his junior assistants—a young lady who had recently graduated from Mount Holyoke, where she had heard Miss Moore lecture. Had her husband's superiors gone a step further and actually adopted one of Miss Moore's many suggestions—Intelligent Bullet, for instance, or Utopian Turtletop, or Bullet Cloisonné, or Pastelogram, or Mongoose Civique, or Andante con Moto ("Description of a good motor?" Miss Moore queried in regard to this last)—there is no telling to what heights the E-Car might have risen, but the fact is that they didn't. Dissatisfied with both the poet's ideas and their own, the executives in the Special Products Division next called in Foote, Cone & Belding, the advertising agency that had lately been signed up to handle the E-Car account. With characteristic Madison Avenue vigor, Foote, Cone & Belding organized a competition among the employees of its New York, London, and Chicago offices, offering nothing less than one of the brand-new cars as a prize to whoever thought up an acceptable name. In no time at all, Foote, Cone & Belding had eighteen thousand names in hand, including Zoom, Zip, Benson, Henry, and Drof (if in doubt, spell it backward). Suspecting that the bosses of the Special Products Division might regard this list as a trifle unwieldy, the agency got to work and cut it down to six thousand names, which it presented to them in executive session. "There you are," a Foote, Cone man said triumphantly, flopping a sheaf of papers on the table. "Six thousand names, all alphabetized and cross-referenced."

A gasp escaped Krafve. "But we don't want six thousand names," he said. "We only want one."

The situation was critical, because the making of dies for the new car was about to begin and some of them would have to bear its name. On a Thursday, Foote, Cone & Belding canceled all leaves and instituted what is called a crash program, instructing its New York and Chicago offices to set about independently cutting down the list of six thousand names to ten and to have the job done by the end of the week-end. Before the weekend was over, the two Foote, Cone offices presented their separate lists of ten to the Special Products Division, and by an almost incredible coincidence, which all hands insist *was* a coincidence, four of the names on the two lists were the same; Corsair, Citation, Pacer, and Ranger had miraculously survived the dual scrutiny. "Corsair seemed to be head and shoulders above everything else," Wallace says. "Along with other factors in its favor, it had done splendidly in the sidewalk interviews. The free associations with Corsair were rather romantic—'pirate,' 'swashbuckler,' things like that. For its opposite, we got 'princess,' or something else attractive on that order. Just what we wanted."

Corsair or no Corsair, the E-Car was named the Edsel in the early spring of 1956, though the public was not informed until the following autumn. The epochal decision was reached at a meeting of the Ford executive committee held at a time when, as it happened, all three Ford brothers were away. In President Ford's absence, the meeting was conducted by Breech, who had become chairman of the board in 1955, and his mood that day was brusque, and not one to linger long over swashbucklers and princesses. After hearing the final choices, he said, "I don't like any of them. Let's take another look at some of the others." So they took another look at the favored rejects, among them the name Edsel, which, in spite of the three Ford brothers' expressed interpretation of their father's probable wishes, had been retained as a sort of anchor to windward. Breech led his associates in a patient scrutiny of the list until they came to "Edsel." "Let's call it that," Breech said with calm finality. There were to be four main models of the E-Car, with varia-tions on each one, and Breech soothed some of his colleagues by adding that the magic four—Corsair, Citation, Pacer, and Ranger—might be used, if anybody felt so inclined, as the subnames for the models. A telephone call was put through to Henry II, who was vacationing in Nassau. He said that if Edsel was the choice of the executive committee, he would abide by its decision, provided he could get the approval of the rest of his family. Within a few days, he got it.

As Wallace wrote to Miss Moore a while later: "We have chosen a name. . . . It fails somewhat of the resonance, gaiety, and zest we were seeking. But it has a personal dignity and meaning to many of us here. Our name, dear Miss Moore, is—Edsel. I hope you will understand."

It may be assumed that word of the naming of the E-Car spread a certain amount of despair among the Foote, Cone & Belding backers of more metaphorical names, none of whom won a free car—a despair heightened by the fact that the name "Edsel" had been ruled out of the competition from the first. But their sense of disappointment was as nothing compared to the gloom that enveloped many employees of the Special Products Division. Some felt that the name of a former president of the company, who had sired its current president, bore dynastic connotations that were alien to the American temper; others, who, with Wallace, had put their trust in the quirks of the mass unconscious, believed that "Edsel" was a disastrously unfortunate combination of syllables. What were its free associations? Pretzel, diesel, hard sell. What was its opposite? It didn't seem to have any. Still, the matter was settled, and there was nothing to do but put the best possible face on it. Besides, the anguish in the Special Products Division was by no means unanimous, and Krafve himself, of course, was among those who had no objection to the name. He still has none, declining to go along with those who contend that the decline and fall of the Edsel may be dated from the moment of its christening.

Krafve, in fact, was so well pleased with the way matters had turned out that when, at eleven o'clock on the morning of November 19, 1956, after a long summer of thoughtful silence, the Ford Company released to the world the glad tidings that the E-Car had been named the Edsel, he accompanied the announcement with a few dramatic flourishes of his own. On the very stroke of that hour on that day, the telephone operators in Krafve's domain began greeting callers with "Edsel Division" instead of "Special Products Division"; all stationery bearing the obsolete letterhead of the division vanished and was replaced by sheaves of paper headed "Edsel Division"; and outside the building a huge stainless-steel sign reading "EDSEL DIVISION" rose ceremoniously to the rooftop. Krafve himself managed to remain earthbound, though he had his own reasons for feeling buoyant; in recognition of his leadership of the E-Car project up to that point, he was given the august title of Vice-President of the Ford Motor Company and General Manager, Edsel Division.

From the administrative point of view, this off-with-the-old-on-with-the-new effect was merely harmless window dressing. In the strict secrecy of the Dearborn test track, vibrant, almost full-fledged Edsels, with their name graven on their superstructures, were already being road-tested; Brown and his fellow stylists were already well along with their designs for the *next* year's Edsel; recruits were already being signed up for an entirely new organization of retail dealers to sell the Edsel to the public; and Foote, Cone & Belding, having been relieved of the burden of staging crash programs to collect names and crash programs to get rid of them again, was already deep in schemes for advertising the Edsel, under the personal direction of a no less substantial pillar of his trade than Fairfax M. Cone, the agency's head man. In planning his campaign, Cone relied heavily on what had come to be called the "Wallace prescription"; that is, the formula for the Edsel's personality as set forth by Wallace back in the days before the big naming bee—"The smart car for the younger executive or professional family on its way up." So enthusiastic was Cone about the prescription that he accepted it with only one revision—the substitution of "middle-income" family for "younger executive," his hunch being that there were more middle-income families around than young executives, or even people who *thought* they were young executives. In an expansive mood, possibly induced by his having landed an account that was expected to bring billings of well over ten million dollars a year, Cone described to reporters on several occasions the kind of campaign he was plotting for the Edsel—quiet, self-assured, and avoiding as much as possible the use of the adjective "new," which, though it had an obvious application to the product, he considered rather lacking in cachet. Above all, the campaign was to be classic in its calmness. "We think it would be awful for the advertising to compete with the car," Cone told the press. "We hope that no one will ever ask, 'Say, did you see that Edsel ad?' in any newspaper or magazine or on television, but, instead, that hundreds of thousands of people will say, and say again, 'Man, did you read about that Edsel?' or 'Did you see that car?' This is the difference between advertising and selling." Evidently enough, Cone felt confident about the campaign and the Edsel. Like a chess master who has no doubt that he will win, he could afford to explicate the brilliance of his moves even as he made them.

Automobile men still talk, with admiration for the virtuosity displayed and a shudder at the ultimate outcome, of the Edsel Division's drive to round up retail dealers. Ordinarily, an established manufacturer launches a new car through dealers who are already handling his other makes and who, to begin with, take on the upstart as a sort of sideline. Not so in the case of the Edsel; Krafve received authorization from on high to go all out and build up a retail-dealer organization by making raids on dealers who had contracts with other manufacturers, or even with the other Ford Company divisions— Ford and Lincoln-Mercury. (Although the Ford dealers thus corralled were not obliged to cancel their old contracts, all the emphasis was on signing up retail outlets exclusively dedicated to the selling of Edsels.) The goal set for Introduction Day—which, after a great deal of soul-searching, was finally established as September 4, 1957—was twelve hundred Edsel dealers from coast to coast. They were not to be just any dealers, either; Krafve made it clear that Edsel was interested in signing up only dealers whose records showed that they had a marked ability to sell cars without resorting to the high-pressure tricks of borderline legality that had lately been giving the automobile business a bad name. "We simply have to have quality dealers with quality service facilities," Krafve said. "A customer who gets poor service on an established brand blames the dealer. On an Edsel, he will blame the car." The goal of twelve hundred was a high one, for no dealer, quality or not, can afford to switch makes lightly. The average dealer has at least a hundred thousand dollars tied up in his agency, and in large cities the investment is much higher. He must hire salesmen, mechanics, and office help; buy his own tools, technical literature, and signs, the latter costing as much as five thousand dollars a set; and pay the factory spot cash for the cars he receives from it.

The man charged with mobilizing an Edsel sales force along these exacting lines was J. C. (Larry) Doyle, who, as general sales-and-marketing manager of the division, ranked second to Krafve himself. A veteran of forty years with the Ford Company, who had started with it as an office boy in Kansas City and had spent the intervening time mainly selling, Doyle was a maverick in his field. On the one hand, he had an air of kindness and consideration that made him the very antithesis of the glib, brash denizens of a thousand automobile rows across the continent, and, on the other, he did not trouble to conceal an old-time salesman's skepticism about such things as analyzing the sex and status of automobiles, a pursuit he characterized by saying, "When I play pool, I like to keep one foot on the floor." Still, he knew how to sell cars, and that was what the Edsel Division needed. Recalling how he and his sales staff brought off the unlikely trick of persuading substantial and reputable men who had already achieved success in one of the toughest of all businesses to tear up profitable franchises in favor of a risky new one, Doyle said not long ago, "As soon as the first few new Edsels came through, early in 1957, we put a couple of them in each of our five regional sales offices. Needless to say, we kept those offices locked and the blinds drawn. Dealers in every make for miles around wanted to see the car, if only out of curiosity, and that gave us the leverage we needed. We let it be known that we would show the car only to dealers who were really interested in coming with us, and then we sent our regional field managers out to surrounding towns to try to line up the No. 1 dealer in each to see the cars. If we couldn't get No. 1, we'd try for No. 2. Anyway, we set things up so that no one got in to see the Edsel without listening to a complete one-hour pitch on the whole situation by a member of our sales force. It worked very well." It worked so well that by midsummer, 1957, it was clear that Edsel was going to have a lot of quality dealers on Introduction Day. (In fact, it missed the goal of twelve hundred by a couple of dozen.) Indeed, some dealers in other makes were apparently so confident of the Edsel's success, or so bemused by the Doyle staff's pitch, that they were entirely willing to sign up after hardly more than a glance at the Edsel itself. Doyle's people urged them to study the car closely, and kept reciting the litany of its virtues, but the prospective Edsel dealers would wave such protestations aside and demand a contract without further ado. In retrospect, it would seem that Doyle could have given lessons to the Pied Piper.

Now that the Edsel was no longer the exclusive concern of Dearborn, the Ford Company was irrevocably committed to going ahead. "Until Doyle went into action, the whole program could have been quietly dropped at any time at a word from top management, but once the dealers had been signed up, there was the matter of honoring your contract to put out a car," Krafve has explained. The matter was attended to with dispatch. Early in June, 1957, the company announced that of the $250 million it had set aside to defray the advance costs of the Edsel, $150 million was being spent on basic facilities, including the conversion of various Ford and Mercury plants to the needs of producing the new cars; $50 million on special Edsel tooling; and $50 million on initial advertising and promotion. In June, too, an Edsel destined to be the star of a television commercial for future release was stealthily transported in a closed van to Hollywood, where, on a locked sound stage patrolled by security guards, it was exposed to the cameras in the admiring presence of a few carefully chosen actors who had sworn that their lips would be sealed from then until Introduction Day. For this delicate photographic operation the Edsel Division cannily enlisted the services of Cascade Pictures, which also worked for the Atomic Energy Commission, and, as far as is known, there were no unintentional leaks. "We took all the same precautions we take for our A.E.C. films," a grim Cascade official has since said.

Within a few weeks, the Edsel Division had eighteen hundred salaried employees and was rapidly filling some fifteen thousand factory jobs in the newly converted plants. On July 15th, Edsels began rolling off assembly lines at Somerville, Massachusetts; Mahwah, New Jersey; Louisville, Kentucky; and San Jose, California. The same day, Doyle scored an important coup by signing up Charles Kreisler, a Manhattan dealer regarded as one of the country's foremost practitioners in his field, who had represented Oldsmobile—one of Edsel's self-designated rivals—before heeding the siren song from Dearborn. On July 22nd, the first advertisement for the Edsel appeared—in *Life*. A two-page spread in plain black-and-white, it was impeccably classic and calm, showing a car whooshing down a country highway at such high speed that it was an indistinguishable blur. "Lately, some mysterious automobiles have been seen on the roads," the accompanying text was headed. It went on to say that the blur was an Edsel being road-tested, and concluded with the assurance "The Edsel is on its way." Two weeks later, a second ad appeared in *Life*, this one showing a ghostly-looking car, covered with a white sheet, standing at the entrance to the Ford styling center. This time the headline read, "A man in your town recently made a decision that will change his life." The decision, it was explained, was to become an Edsel dealer. Whoever wrote the ad cannot have known how truly he spoke.

During the tense summer of 1957, the man of the hour at Edsel was C. Gayle Warnock, director of public relations, whose duty was not so much to generate public interest in the forthcoming product, there being an abundance of that, as to keep the interest at white heat, and readily convertible into a desire to buy one of the new cars on or after Introduction Day—or, as the company came to call it, Edsel Day. Warnock, a dapper, affable man with a tiny mustache, is a native of Converse, Indiana, who, long before Krafve drafted him from the Ford office in Chicago, did a spot of publicity work for county fairs—a background that has enabled him to spice the honeyed smoothness of the modern public-relations man with a touch of the old carnival pitchman's uninhibited spirit. Recalling his summons to Dearborn, Warnock says, "When Dick Krafve hired me, back in the fall of 1955, he told me, 'I want you to program the E-Car publicity from now to Introduction Day.' I said, 'Frankly, Dick, what do you mean by "program"?' He said he meant to sort of space it out, starting at the end and working backward. This was something new to me—I was used to taking what breaks I could get when I could get them—but I soon found out how right Dick was. It was almost too easy to get publicity for the Edsel. Early in

1956, when it was still called the E-Car, Krafve gave a little talk about it out in Portland, Oregon. We didn't try for anything more than a play in the local press, but the wire services picked the story up and it went out all over the country. Clippings came in by the bushel. Right then I realized the trouble we might be headed for. The public was getting to be hysterical to see our car, figuring it was going to be some kind of dream car—like nothing they'd ever seen. I said to Krafve, 'When they find out it's got four wheels and one engine, just like the next car, they're liable to be disappointed.'"

It was agreed that the safest way to tread the tightrope between overplaying and underplaying the Edsel would be to say nothing about the car as a whole but to reveal its individual charms a little at a time—a sort of automotive strip tease (a phrase that Warnock couldn't with proper dignity use himself but was happy to see the *New York Times* use for him). The policy was later violated now and then, purposely or inadvertently. For one thing, as the pre-Edsel Day summer wore on, reporters prevailed upon Krafve to authorize Warnock to show the Edsel to them, one at a time, on what Warnock called a "peekaboo," or "you've-seen-it-now-forget-it," basis. And, for another, Edsels loaded on vans for delivery to dealers were appearing on the highways in ever-increasing numbers, covered fore and aft with canvas flaps that, as if to whet the desire of the motoring public, were forever blowing loose. That summer, too, was a time of speechmaking by an Edsel foursome consisting of Krafve, Doyle, J. Emmet Judge, who was Edsel's director of merchandise and product planning, and Robert F. G. Copeland, its assistant general sales manager for advertising, sales promotion, and training. Ranging separately up and down and across the nation, the four orators moved around so fast and so tirelessly that Warnock, lest he lose track of them, took to indicating their whereabouts with colored pins on a map in his office. "Let's see, Krafve goes from Atlanta to New Orleans, Doyle from

Council Bluffs to Salt Lake City," Warnock would muse of a morning in Dearborn, sipping his second cup of coffee and then getting up to yank the pins out and jab them in again.

Although most of Krafve's audiences consisted of bankers and representatives of finance companies who it was hoped would lend money to Edsel dealers, his speeches that summer, far from echoing the general hoopla, were almost statesman-like in their cautious—even somber—references to the new car's prospects. And well they might have been, for developments in the general economic outlook of the nation were making more sanguine men than Krafve look puzzled. In July, 1957, the stock market went into a nose dive, marking the beginning of what is recalled as the recession of 1958. Then, early in August, a decline in the sales of medium-priced 1957 cars of all makes set in, and the general situation worsened so rapidly that, before the month was out, *Automotive News* reported that dealers in all makes were ending their season with the second-largest number of unsold new cars in history. If Krafve, on his lonely rounds, ever considered retreating to Dearborn for consolation, he was forced to put that notion out of his mind when, also in August, Mercury, Edsel's own stablemate, served notice that it was going to make things as tough as possible for the newcomer by undertaking a million-dollar, thirty-day advertising drive aimed especially at "price-conscious buyers"—a clear reference to the fact that the 1957 Mercury, which was then being sold at a discount by most dealers, cost less than the new Edsel was expected to. Mean-while, sales of the Rambler, which was the only American-made small car then in production, were beginning to rise ominously. In the face of all these evil portents, Krafve fell into the habit of ending his speeches with a rather downbeat anecdote about the board chairman of an unsuccessful dog-food company who said to his fellow directors, "Gentlemen, let's face facts—dogs don't like our product." "As far as we're concerned," Krafve added on at least one occasion, driving home the moral with admirable clarity, "a lot will depend on whether people like our car or not."

But most of the other Edsel men were unimpressed by Krafve's misgivings. Perhaps the least impressed of all was Judge, who, while doing his bit as an itinerant speaker, specialized in community and civic groups. Undismayed by the limitations of the strip-tease policy, Judge brightened up his lectures by showing such a bewildering array of animated graphs, cartoons, charts, and pictures of parts of the car—all flashed on a CinemaScope screen—that his listeners usually got halfway home before they realized that he hadn't shown them an Edsel. He wandered restlessly around the auditorium as he spoke, shifting the kaleidoscopic images on the screen at will with the aid of an automatic slide changer—a trick made possible by a crew of electricians who laced the place in advance with a maze of wires linking the device to dozens of floor switches, which, scattered about the hall, responded when he kicked them. Each of the "Judge spectaculars," as these performances came to be known, cost the Edsel Division five thousand dollars—a sum that included the pay and expenses of the technical crew, who would arrive on the scene a day or so ahead of time to set up the electrical rig. At the last moment, Judge would descend melodramatically on the town by plane, hasten to the hall, and go into his act. "One of the greatest aspects of this whole Edsel program is the philosophy of product and merchandising behind it," Judge might start off, with a desultory kick at a switch here, a switch there. "All of us who have been a part of it are real proud of this background and we are anxiously awaiting its success when the car is introduced this fall. . . . Never again will we be associated with anything as gigantic and full of meaning as this particular program. . . . Here is a glimpse of the car which will be before the American public on September 4, 1957 [at this point, Judge would show a provocative slide of a hubcap or section of fender]. . . . It is a different car in every respect, yet it has an element of conservatism which will give it maximum appeal. . . . The distinctiveness of the frontal styling integrates with the sculptured patterns of the side treatment. . . ." And on and on Judge would rhapsodize, rolling out such awesome phrases as "sculptured sheet metal," "highlight character," and "graceful, flowing lines." At last would come the ringing peroration. "We are proud of the Edsel!" he would cry, kicking switches right and left. "When it is introduced this fall, it will take its place on the streets and highways of America, bringing new greatness to the Ford Motor Company. This is the Edsel story."

The drum-roll climax of the strip tease was a three-day press preview of the Edsel, undraped from pinched-in snout to flaring rear, that was held in Detroit and Dearborn on August 26th, 27th, and 28th, with 250 reporters from all over the country in attendance. It differed from previous automotive jamborees of its kind in that the journalists were invited to bring their wives along—and many of them did. Before it was over, it had cost the Ford Company ninety thousand dollars. Grand as it was, the conventionality of its setting was a disappointment to Warnock, who had proposed, and seen rejected, three locales that he thought would provide a more offbeat *ambiance*—a steamer on the Detroit River ("wrong symbolism"); Edsel, Kentucky ("inaccessible by road"); and Haiti ("just turned down flat"). Thus hobbled, Warnock could do no better for the reporters and their wives when they converged on the Detroit scene on Sunday evening, August 25th, than to put them up at the discouragingly named Sheraton-Cadillac Hotel and to arrange for them to spend Monday afternoon hearing and reading about the long-awaited details of the entire crop of Edsels—eighteen varieties available, in four main lines (Corsair, Citation, Pacer, and Ranger), differing mainly in their size, power, and trim. The next morning, specimens of the models themselves were revealed to the reporters in the styling center's rotunda, and Henry II offered a few words of tribute to his father. "The wives were not asked to the unveiling," a Foote, Cone man who helped plan the affair recalls. "It was too solemn and businesslike an event for that. It went over fine. There was excitement even among the hardened newspapermen." (The import of the stories that most of the excited newspapermen filed was that the Edsel seemed to be a good car, though not so radical as its billing had suggested.)

In the afternoon, the reporters were whisked out to the test track to see a team of stunt drivers put the Edsel through its paces. This event, calculated to be thrilling, turned out to be hair-raising, and even, for some, a little unstringing. Enjoined not to talk too much about speed and horsepower, since only a few months previously the whole automobile industry had nobly resolved to concentrate on making cars instead of delayed-action bombs, Warnock had decided to emphasize the Edsel's liveliness through deeds rather than words, and to accomplish this he had hired a team of stunt drivers. Edsels ran over two-foot ramps on two wheels, bounced from higher ramps on all four wheels, were driven in crisscross patterns, grazing each other, at sixty or seventy miles per hour, and skidded into complete turns at fifty. For comic relief, there was a clown driver parodying the daredevil stuff. All the while, the voice of Neil L. Blume, Edsel's engineering chief, could be heard on a loudspeaker, purring about "the capabilities, the safety, the ruggedness, the maneuverability and performance of these new cars," and skirting the words "speed" and "horsepower" as delicately as a sandpiper skirts a wave. At one point, when an Edsel leaping a high ramp just missed turning over, Krafve's face took on a ghastly pallor; he later reported that he had not known the daredevil stunts were going to be so extreme, and was concerned both for the good name of the Edsel and the lives of the drivers. Warnock, noticing his boss's distress, went over and asked Krafve if he was enjoying the show. Krafve replied tersely that he would answer when it was over and all hands safe. But everyone else seemed to be having a grand time. The Foote, Cone man said, "You looked over this green Michigan hill, and there were those glorious Edsels, performing gloriously in unison. It was beautiful. It was like the Rockettes. It was exciting. Morale was high."

Warnock's high spirits had carried him to even wilder extremes of fancy. The stunt driving, like the unveiling, was considered too rich for the blood of the wives, but the resourceful Warnock was ready for them with a fashion show that he hoped they would find at least equally diverting. He need not have worried. The star of the show, who was introduced by Brown, the Edsel stylist, as a Paris *couturière*, both beautiful and talented, turned out at the final curtain to be a female impersonator—a fact of which Warnock, to heighten the verisimilitude of the act, had given Brown no advance warning. Things were never again quite the same since between Brown and Warnock, but the wives were able to give their husbands an extra paragraph or two for their stories.

That evening, there was a big gala for one and all at the styling center, which was itself styled as a night club for the occasion, complete with a fountain that danced in time with the music of Ray McKinley's band, whose emblem, the letters "GM"—a holdover from the days of its founder, the late Glenn Miller—was emblazoned, as usual, on the music stand of each musician, very nearly ruining the evening for Warnock. The next morning, at a windup press conference held by Ford officials. Breech declared of the Edsel, "It's a husky youngster, and, like most other new parents, we're proud enough to pop our buttons." Then seventy-one of the reporters took the wheels of as many Edsels and set out for home—not to drive the cars into their garages but to deliver them to the showrooms of their local Edsel dealers.

Let Warnock describe the highlights of this final flourish: "There were several unfortunate occurrences. One guy simply miscalculated and cracked up his car running into something. No fault of the Edsel *there*. One car lost its oil pan, so naturally the motor froze. It can happen to the best of cars. Fortunately, at the time of this malfunction the driver was going through a beautiful-sounding town—Paradise, Kansas, I think it was—and that gave the news reports about it a nice little positive touch. The nearest dealer gave the reporter a new Edsel, and he drove on home, climbing Pikes Peak on the way. Then one car crashed through a tollgate when the brakes failed. That was bad. It's funny, but the thing we were most worried about—other drivers being so eager to get a look at the Edsels that they'd crowd our cars off the road—happened only once. That was on the Pennsylvania Turnpike. One of our reporters was tooling along—no problems—when a Plymouth driver pulled up alongside to rubberneck, and edged so close that the Edsel got sideswiped. Minor damage."

Late in 1959, immediately after the demise of the Edsel, *Business Week* stated that at the big press preview a Ford executive had said to a reporter, "If the company weren't in so deep, we never would have brought it out now." However, since *Business Week* neglected to publish this patently sensational statement for over two years, and since to this day all the former ranking Edsel executives (Krafve included, notwithstanding his preoccupation with the luckless dog-food company) firmly maintained that right up to Edsel Day and even for a short time thereafter they expected the Edsel to succeed, it would seem that the quotation should be regarded as a highly suspect archaeological find. Indeed, during the period between the press preview and Edsel Day the spirit of everybody associated with the venture seems to have been one of wild optimism. "Oldsmobile, Goodbye!" ran the headline on an ad, in the Detroit *Free Press*, for an agency that was switching from Olds to Edsel. A dealer in Portland, Oregon, reported that he had already sold two Edsels, sight unseen. Warnock dug up a fireworks company in Japan willing to make him, at nine dollars apiece, five thousand rockets that, exploding in mid-air, would release nine-foot scale-model Edsels made of rice paper that would inflate and descend like parachutes; his head reeling with visions of filling America's skies as well as its highways with Edsels on Edsel Day, Warnock was about to dash off an order when Krafve, looking something more than puzzled, shook his head.

On September 3rd—E Day-minus-one—the prices of the various Edsel models were announced; for cars delivered to New York they ran from just under $2,800 to just over $4,100. On E Day, the Edsel arrived. In Cambridge, a band led a gleaming motorcade of the new cars up Massachusetts Avenue; flying out of Richmond, California, a helicopter hired by one of the most jubilant of the dealers lassoed by Doyle spread a giant Edsel sign above San Francisco Bay; and all over the nation, from the Louisiana bayous to the peak of Mount Rainier to the Maine woods, one needed only a radio or a television set to know that the very air, despite Warnock's setback on the rockets, was quivering with the presence of the Edsel. The tone for Edsel Day's blizzard of publicity was set by an ad, published in newspapers all over the country, in which the Edsel shared the spotlight with the Ford Company's President Ford and Chairman Breech. In the ad, Ford looked like a dignified young father, Breech like a dignified gentleman holding a full house against a possible straight, the Edsel just looked like an Edsel. The accompanying text declared that the decision to produce the car had been "based on what we knew, guessed, felt, believed, suspected—about you," and added, "YOU are the reason behind the Edsel." The tone was calm and confident. There did not seem to be much room for doubt about the reality of that full house.

Before sundown, it was estimated, 2,850,000 people had seen the new car in dealers' showrooms. Three days later, in North Philadelphia, an Edsel was stolen. It can reasonably be argued that the crime marked the high-water mark of public acceptance of the Edsel; only a few months later, any but the least fastidious of car thieves might not have bothered.

DECLINE AND FALL

The most striking physical characteristic of the Edsel was, of course, its radiator grille. This, in contrast to the wide and horizontal grilles of all nineteen other American makes of the time, was slender and vertical. Of chromium-plated steel, and shaped something like an egg, it sat in the middle of the car's front end, and was embellished by the word "EDSEL" in aluminum letters running down its length. It was intended to suggest the front end of practically any car of twenty or thirty years ago and of most contemporary European cars, and thus to look at once seasoned and sophisticated. The trouble was that whereas the front ends of the antiques and the European cars were themselves high and narrow—consisting, indeed, of little more than the radiator grilles—the front end of the Edsel was broad and low, just like the front ends of all its American competitors. Consequently, there were wide areas on either side of the grille that had to be filled in with something, and filled in they were—with twin panels of entirely conventional horizontal chrome grillwork. The effect was that of an Oldsmobile with the prow of a Pierce-Arrow implanted in its front end, or, more metaphorically, of the chairwoman trying on the duchess' necklace. The attempt at sophistication was so transparent as to be endearing.

But if the grille of the Edsel appealed through guilelessness, the rear end was another matter. Here, too, there was a marked departure from the conventional design of the day. Instead of the notorious tail fin, the car had what looked to its fanciers like wings and to others, less ethereal-minded, like eyebrows. The lines of the trunk lid and the rear fenders, swooping upward and outward, did somewhat resemble the wings of a gull in flight, but the resemblance was marred by two long, narrow tail lights, set partly in the trunk lid and partly in the fenders, which followed those lines and created the startling illusion, especially at night, of a slant-eyed grin. From the front, the Edsel seemed, above all, anxious to please, even at the cost of being clownish; from the rear it looked crafty, Oriental, smug, one-up—maybe a little cynical and contemptuous, too. It was as if, somewhere between grille and rear fenders, a sinister personality change had taken place.

In other respects, the exterior styling of the Edsel was not far out of the ordinary. Its sides were festooned with a bit less than the average amount of chrome, and distinguished by a gouged-out bullet-shaped groove extending forward from the rear fender for about half the length of the car. Midway along this groove, the word "EDSEL" was displayed in chrome letters, and just below the rear window was a small grille-like decoration, on which was spelled out—of all things—"EDSEL." (After all, hadn't Stylist Brown declared his intention to create a vehicle that would be "readily recognizable"?) In its interior, the Edsel strove mightily to live up to the prediction of General Manager Krafve that the car would be "the epitome of the push-button era." The push-button era in medium-priced cars being what it was, Krafve's had been a rash prophecy indeed, but the Edsel rose to it with a devilish assemblage of gadgets such as had seldom, if ever, been seen before. On or near the Edsel's dashboard were a push button that popped the trunk lid open;

a lever that popped the hood open; a lever that released the parking brake; a speedometer that glowed red when the driver exceeded his chosen maximum speed; a single-dial control for both heating and cooling; a tachometer, in the best racing-car style; buttons to operate or regulate the lights, the height of the radio antenna, the heater-blower, the windshield wiper, and the cigarette lighter; and a row of eight red lights to wink warnings that the engine was too hot, that it wasn't hot enough, that the generator was on the blink, that the parking brake was on, that a door was open, that the oil pressure was low, that the oil level was low, and that the gasoline level was low, the last of which the skeptical driver could confirm by consulting the gas gauge, mounted a few inches away. Epitomizing this epitome, the automatic-transmission control box—arrestingly situated on top of the steering post, in the center of the wheel—sprouted a galaxy of five push buttons so light to the touch that, as Edsel men could hardly be restrained from demonstrating, they could be depressed with a toothpick.

Of the four lines of Edsels, both of the two larger and more expensive ones—the Corsair and the Citation—were 219 inches long, or two inches longer than the biggest of the Oldsmobiles; both were eighty inches wide, or about as wide as passenger cars ever get; and the height of both was only fifty-seven inches, as low as any other medium-priced car. The Ranger and the Pacer, the smaller Edsels, were six inches shorter, an inch narrower, and an inch lower than the Corsair and the Citation. The Corsair and the Citation were equipped with 345-horsepower engines, making them more powerful than any other American car at the time of their debut, and the Ranger and the Pacer were good for 303 horsepower, near the top in their class. At the touch of a toothpick to the "Drive" button, an idling Corsair or Citation sedan (more than two tons of car, in either case) could, if properly skippered, take off with such abruptness that in ten and three-tenths seconds it would be doing a mile a minute, and in seventeen and a half seconds it would be a quarter of a mile down the road. If anything or anybody happened to be in the way when the toothpick touched the push button, so much the worse.

When the wraps were taken off the Edsel, it received what is known in the theatrical business as a mixed press. The automotive editors of the daily newspapers stuck mostly to straight descriptions of the car, with only here and there a phrase or two of appraisal, some of it ambiguous ("The difference in style is spectacular," noted Joseph C. Ingraham in the *New York Times*) and some of it openly favorable ("A handsome and hard-punching newcomer," said Fred Olmstead, in the Detroit *Free Press*). Magazine criticism was generally more exhaustive and occasionally more severe. *Motor Trend*, the largest monthly devoted to ordinary automobiles, as distinct from hot rods, devoted eight pages of its October, 1957, issue to an analysis and critique of the Edsel by Joe H. Wherry, its Detroit editor. Wherry liked the car's appearance, its interior comfort, and its gadgets, although he did not always make it clear just why; in paying his respects to the transmission buttons on the steering post, he wrote, "You need not take your eyes off the road for an instant." He conceded that there were "untold opportunities for more . . . unique approaches," but he summed up his opinion in a sentence that fairly peppered the Edsel with honorific adverbs: "The Edsel performs fine, rides well, and handles good." Tom McCahill, of *Mechanix Illustrated*, generally admired the "bolt bag," as he affectionately called the Edsel, but he had some reservations, which, incidentally, throw some interesting light on an automobile critic's equivalent of an aisle seat. "On ribbed concrete," he reported, "every time I shot the throttle to the floor quickly, the wheels spun like a gone-wild Waring Blendor. . . . At high speeds, especially through rough corners, I found the suspension a little too horsebacky. . . . I couldn't help but wonder what this salami would really do if it had enough road adhesion."

By far the most downright—and very likely the most damaging—panning that the Edsel got during its first months appeared in the January, 1958, issue of the Consumers Union monthly, *Consumer Reports*, whose 800,000 subscribers probably included more potential Edsel buyers than have ever turned the pages of *Motor Trend* or *Mechanix Illustrated*. After having put a Corsair through a series of road tests, *Consumer Reports* declared:

> The Edsel has no important basic advantages over other brands. The car is almost entirely conventional in construction. . . . The amount of shake present in this Corsair body on rough roads—which wasn't long in making itself heard as squeaks and rattles—went well beyond any acceptable limit. . . . The Corsair's handling qualities—sluggish, over-slow steering, sway and lean on turns, and a general detached-from-the-road feel—are, to put it mildly, without distinction. As a matter of, simple fact, combined with the car's tendency to shake like jelly, Edsel handling represents retrogression rather than progress. . . . Stepping on the gas in traffic, or in passing cars, or just to feel the pleasurable surge of power, will cause those big cylinders really to lap up fuel. . . . The center of the steering wheel is not, in CU's opinion, a good pushbutton location. . . . To look at the Edsel buttons pulls the driver's eyes clear down off the road. [Pace Mr. Wherry.] The "luxury-loaded" Edsel—as one magazine cover described it—will certainly please anyone who confuses gadgetry with true luxury.

Three months later, in a roundup of all the 1958-model cars, *Consumer Reports* went at the Edsel again, calling it "more uselessly overpowered . . . more gadget bedecked, more hung with expensive accessories than any car in its price class," and giving the Corsair and the Citation the bottom position in its competitive ratings. Like Krafve, *Consumer Reports* considered the Edsel an epitome; unlike Krafve, the magazine concluded that the car seemed to "epitomize the many excesses" with which Detroit manufacturers were "repulsing more and more potential car buyers."

And yet, in a way, the Edsel wasn't so bad. It embodied much of the spirit of its time—or at least of the time when it was designed, early in 1955. It was clumsy, powerful, dowdy, gauche, well-meaning—a de Kooning woman. Few people, apart from employees of Foote, Cone & Belding, who were paid to do so, have adequately hymned its ability, at its best, to coax and jolly the harried owner into a sense of well-being. Furthermore, the designers of several rival makes, including Chevrolet, Buick, and Ford, Edsel's own stablemate, later flattered Brown's styling by imitating at least one feature of the car's much reviled lines—the rear-end wing theme. The Edsel was obviously jinxed, but to say that it was jinxed by its design alone would be an oversimplification, as it would be to say that it was jinxed by an excess of motivational research. The fact is that in the short, unhappy life of the Edsel a number of other factors contributed to its commercial downfall. One of these was the scarcely believable circumstance that many of the very first Edsels—those obviously destined for the most glaring public limelight—were dramatically imperfect. By its preliminary program of promotion and advertising, the Ford Company had built up an overwhelming head of public interest in the Edsel, causing its arrival to be anticipated and the car itself to be gawked at with more eagerness than had ever greeted any automobile before it. After all that, it seemed, the car didn't quite work. Within a few weeks after the Edsel was introduced, its pratfalls were the talk of the land. Edsels were delivered with oil leaks, sticking hoods, trunks that wouldn't open, and push buttons that, far from yielding to a toothpick, couldn't be budged with a hammer. An obviously distraught man staggered into a bar up the Hudson River, demanding a double shot without delay and exclaiming that the dashboard of his new Edsel had just burst into flame. *Automotive News* reported that in general the earliest Edsels suffered from poor paint, inferior sheet metal, and faulty accessories, and quoted the lament of a dealer about one of the first Edsel convertibles he received: "The top was badly set, doors cockeyed, the header bar trimmed at the wrong angle, and the front springs sagged." The Ford Company had the particular bad luck to sell to Consumers Union—which buys its test cars in the open market, as a precaution against being favored with specially doctored samples—an Edsel in which the axle ratio was wrong, an expansion plug in the cooling system blew out, the power-steering pump leaked, the rear-axle gears were noisy, and the heater emitted blasts of hot air when it was turned off. A former executive of the Edsel Division has estimated that only about half of the first Edsels really performed properly.

A layman cannot help wondering how the Ford Company, in all its power and glory, could have been guilty of such a Mack Sennett routine of buildup and anticlimax. The wan, hard-working Krafve explains gamely that when a company brings out a new model of any make—even an old and tested one—the first cars often have bugs in them. A more startling theory—though only a theory—is that there may have been sabotage in some of the four plants that assembled the Edsel, all but one of which had previously been, and currently also were, assembling Fords or Mercurys. In marketing the Edsel, the Ford Company took a leaf out of the book of General Motors, which for years had successfully been permitting, and even encouraging, the makers and sellers of its Oldsmobiles, Buicks, Pontiacs, and the higher-priced models of its Chevrolet to fight for customers with no quarter given; faced with the same sort of intramural competition, some members of the Ford and Lincoln-Mercury Divisions of the Ford Company openly hoped from the start for the Edsel's downfall. (Krafve, realizing what might happen, had asked that the Edsel be assembled in plants of its own, but his superiors turned him down.) However, Doyle, speaking with the authority of a veteran of the automobile business as well as with that of Krafve's second-in-command, pooh-poohs the notion that the Edsel was the victim of dirty work at the plants. "Of course the Ford and Lincoln-Mercury Divisions didn't want to see another Ford Company car in the field," he says, "but as far as I know, anything they did at the executive and plant levels was in competitive good taste. On the other hand, at the distribution and dealer level, you got some rough infighting in terms of whispering and propaganda. If I'd been in one of the other divisions, I'd have done the same thing." No proud defeated general of the old school ever spoke more nobly.

It is a tribute of sorts to the men who gave the Edsel its big buildup that although cars tending to rattle, balk, and fall apart into shiny heaps of junk kept coming off the assembly lines, things didn't go badly at first. Doyle says that on Edsel Day more than 6,500 Edsels were either ordered by or actually delivered to customers. That was a good showing, but there were isolated signs of resistance. For instance, a New England dealer selling Edsels in one showroom and Buicks in another reported that two prospects walked into the Edsel showroom, took a look at the Edsel, and placed orders for Buicks on the spot.

In the next few days, sales dropped sharply, but that was to be expected once the bloom was off. Automobile deliveries to dealers—one of the important indicators in the trade—are customarily measured in ten-day periods, and during the first ten days of September, on only six of which the Edsel was on sale, it racked up 4,095; this was lower than Doyle's first-day figure because many of the initial purchases were of models and color combinations not in stock, which had to be factory-assembled to order. The delivery total for the second ten-day period was off slightly, and that for the third was down to just under 3,600. For the first ten days of October, nine of which were business days, there were only 2,751 deliveries—an average of just over three hundred cars a day. In order to sell the 200,000 cars per year that would make the Edsel operation profitable the Ford Company would have to move an average of between six and seven hundred each business day—a good many more than three hundred a day. On the night of Sunday, October 13th, Ford put on a mammoth television spectacular for Edsel, pre-empting the time ordinarily allotted to the Ed Sullivan show, but though the program cost $400,000 and starred Bing Crosby and Frank Sinatra, it failed to cause any sharp spurt in sales. Now it was obvious that things were not going at all well.

Among the former executives of the Edsel Division, opinions differ as to the exact moment when the portents of doom became unmistakable. Krafve feels that the moment did not arrive until sometime late in October. Wallace, in his capacity as Edsel's pipe-smoking semi-Brain Truster, goes a step further by pinning the start of the disaster to a specific date— October 4th, the day the first Soviet sputnik went into orbit, shattering the myth of American technical pre-eminence and precipitating a public revulsion against Detroit's fancier baubles. Public Relations Director Warnock maintains that his barometric sensitivity to the public temper enabled him to call the turn as early as mid-September; contrariwise, Doyle says he maintained his optimism until mid-November, by which time he was about the only man in the division who had not concluded it would take a miracle to save the Edsel. "In November," says Wallace, sociologically, "there was panic, and its concomitant—mob action." The mob action took the form of a concerted tendency to blame the design of the car for the whole debacle; Edsel men who had previously had nothing but lavish praise for the radiator grille and rear end now went around muttering that any fool could see they were ludicrous. The obvious sacrificial victim was Brown, whose stock had gone through the roof at the time of the regally accoladed debut of his design, in August, 1955. Now, without having done anything further, for either better or worse, the poor fellow became the company scapegoat. "Beginning in November, nobody talked to Roy," Wallace says. On November 27th, as if things weren't bad enough, Charles Kreisler, who as the only Edsel dealer in Manhattan provided its prize showcase, announced that he was turning in his franchise because of poor sales, and it was rumored that he added, "The Ford Motor Company has laid an egg." He thereupon signed up with American Motors to sell its Rambler, which, as the only domestic small car then on the market, was already the possessor of a zooming sales curve. Doyle grimly commented that the Edsel Division was "not concerned" about Kreisler's defection.

By December, the panic at Edsel had abated to the point where its sponsors could pull themselves together and begin casting about for ways to get sales moving again. Henry Ford II, manifesting himself to Edsel dealers on closed-circuit television, urged them to remain calm, promised that the company would back them to the limit, and said flatly, "The Edsel is here to stay." A million and a half letters went out over Krafve's signature to owners of medium-priced cars, asking them to drop around at their local dealers and test-ride the Edsel; everyone doing so, Krafve promised, would be given an eight-inch plastic scale model of the car, whether he bought a full-size one or not. The Edsel Division picked up the check for the scale models—a symptom of desperation indeed, for under normal circumstances no automobile manufacturer would make even a move to outfumble its dealers for such a tab. (Up to that time, the dealers had paid for everything, as is customary.) The division also began offering its dealers what it called "sales bonuses," which meant that the dealers could knock anything from one hundred to three hundred dollars off the price of each car without reducing their profit margin. Krafve told a reporter that sales up to then were about what he had expected them to be, although not what he had hoped they would be; in his zeal not to seem unpleasantly surprised, he appeared to be saying that he had expected the Edsel to fail. The Edsel's advertising campaign, which had started with studied dignity, began to sound a note of stridency. "Everyone who has seen it knows—with us—that the Edsel is a success," a magazine ad declared, and in a later ad this phrase was twice repeated, like an incantation: "The Edsel is a success. It is a new idea—a YOU idea—on the American Road. . . . The Edsel is a success." Soon the even less high-toned but more dependable advertising themes of price and social status began to intrude, in such sentences as "They'll know you've *arrived* when you drive up in an Edsel" and "The one that's really new is the lowest-priced, too!" In the more rarefied sectors of Madison Avenue, a resort to rhymed slogans is usually regarded as an indication of artistic depravity induced by commercial necessity.

From the frantic and costly measures the Edsel Division took in December, it garnered one tiny crumb: for the first ten-day period of 1958, it was able to report, sales were up 18.6 percent over those of the last ten days of 1957. The catch, as the *Wall Street Journal* alertly noted, was that the latter period embraced one more selling day than the earlier one, so, for practical purposes, there had scarcely been a gain at all. In any case, that early-January word of meretricious cheer turned out to be the Edsel Division's last gesture. On January 14, 1958, the Ford Motor Company announced that it was consolidating the Edsel Division with the Lincoln-Mercury Division to form a Mercury-Edsel-Lincoln Division, under the management of James J. Nance, who had been running Lincoln-Mercury. It was the first time that one of the major automobile companies had lumped three divisions into one since General Motors' merger of Buick, Oldsmobile, and Pontiac back in the depression, and to the people of the expunged Edsel Division the meaning of the administrative move was all too clear. "With that much competition in a division, the Edsel wasn't going anywhere," Doyle says. "It became a stepchild."

For the last year and ten months of its existence, the Edsel was very much a stepchild—generally neglected, little advertised, and kept alive only to avoid publicizing a boner any more than necessary and in the forlorn hope that it *might* go somewhere after all. What advertising it did get strove quixotically to assure the automobile trade that everything was dandy; in mid-February an ad in *Automotive News* had Nance saying,

> Since the formation of the new M-E-L Division at Ford Motor Company, we have analyzed with keen interest the sales progress of the Edsel. We think it is quite significant that during the five months since the Edsel was introduced, Edsel sales have been greater than the first five months' sales for any other new make of car ever introduced on the American Road. . . . Edsel's steady progress can be a source of satisfaction and a great incentive to all of us.

Nance's comparison, however, was almost meaningless, no new make ever having been introduced anything like so grandiosely, and the note of confidence could not help ringing hollow.

It is quite possible that Nance's attention was never called to an article by S. I. Hayakawa, the semanticist, that was published in the spring of 1958 in *ETC: A Review of General Semantics*, a quarterly magazine, under the title, "Why the Edsel Laid an Egg." Hayakawa, who was both the founder and the editor of *ETC*, explained in an introductory note that he considered the subject within the purview of general semantics because automobiles, like words, are "important . . . symbols in American culture," and went on to argue that the Edsel's flop could be attributed to Ford Company executives who had been "listening too long to the motivation-research people" and who, in their efforts to turn out a car that would satisfy customers' sexual fantasies and the like, had failed to supply reasonable and practical transportation, thereby neglecting "the reality principle." "What the motivation researchers failed to tell their clients . . . is that *only* the psychotic and the gravely neurotic *act out* their irrationalities and their compensatory fantasies," Hayakawa admonished Detroit briskly, and added, "The trouble with selling symbolic gratification via such expensive items as . . . the Edsel Hermaphrodite . . . is the competition offered by much cheaper forms of symbolic gratification, such as *Playboy* (fifty cents a copy), *Astounding Science Fiction* (thirty-five cents a copy), and television (free)."

Notwithstanding the competition from *Playboy*, or possibly because the symbol-motivated public included people who could afford both, the Edsel kept rolling—but just barely. The car moved, as salesmen say, though hardly at the touch of a toothpick. In fact, as a stepchild it sold about as well as it had sold as a favorite son, suggesting that all the hoopla, whether about symbolic gratification or mere horsepower, had had little effect one way or the other. The new Edsels that were registered with the motor-vehicle bureaus of the various states during 1958 numbered 34,481—considerably fewer than new cars of any competing make, and less than one-fifth of the 200,000 a year necessary if the Edsel was to show a profit, but still representing an investment by motorists of over a hundred million dollars. The picture actually brightened in November, 1958, with the advent of the Edsel's second-year models. Shorter by up to eight inches, lighter by up to five hundred pounds, and with engines less potent by as much as 158 horsepower, they had a price range running from five hundred to eight hundred dollars less than that of their predecessors. The vertical grille and the slant-eyed rear end were still there, but the modest power and proportions persuaded *Consumer Reports* to relent and say, "The Ford Motor Company, after giving last year's initial Edsel model a black eye, has made a respectable and even likable automobile of it." Quite a number of motorists seemed to agree; about two thousand more Edsels were sold in the first half of 1959 than had been sold in the first half of 1958, and by the early summer of 1959 the car was moving at the rate of around four thousand a month. Here, at last, was progress; sales were at almost a quarter of the minimum profitable rate, instead of a mere fifth.

On July 1, 1959, there were 83,849 Edsels on the country's roads. The largest number (8,344) were in California, which is perennially beset with far and away the largest number of cars of practically all makes, and the smallest number were in Alaska, Vermont, and Hawaii (122, 119, and 110, respectively). All in all, the Edsel seemed to have found a niche for itself as an amusingly eccentric curiosity. Although the Ford Company, with its stockholders' money still disappearing week after week into the Edsel, and with small cars now clearly the order of the day, could scarcely affect a sentimental approach to the subject, it nonetheless took an outside chance and, in mid-October of 1959, brought out a third series of annual models. The 1960 Edsel appeared a little more than a month after the Falcon, Ford's first—and instantly successful—venture into the small-car field, and was scarcely an Edsel at all; gone were both the vertical grille and the horizontal rear end, and what remained looked like a cross between a Ford Fairlane and a Pontiac. Its initial sales were abysmal; by the middle of November only one plant—in Louisville, Kentucky—was still turning out Edsels, and it was turning out only about twenty a day. On November 19th, the Ford Foundation, which was planning to sell a block of its vast holdings of stock in the Ford Motor Company, issued the prospectus that is required by law under such circumstances, and stated therein, in a footnote to a section describing the company's products, that the Edsel had been "introduced in September 1957 and discontinued in November 1959." The same day, this mumbled admission was confirmed and amplified by a Ford Company spokesman, who did some mumbling of his own. "If we knew the reason people aren't buying the Edsel, we'd probably have done something about it," he said.

The final quantitative box score shows that from the beginning right up to November 19th, 110,810 Edsels were produced and 109,466 were sold. (The remaining 1,344, almost all of them 1960 models, were disposed of in short order with the help of drastic price cuts.) All told, only 2,846 of the 1960 Edsels were ever produced, making models of that year a potential collector's item. To be sure, it will be generations before 1960 Edsels are as scarce as the Type 41 Bugatti, of which no more than eleven specimens were made, back in the late twenties, to be sold only to bona-fide kings, and the 1960 Edsel's reasons for being a rarity are not exactly as acceptable, socially or commercially, as the Type 41 Bugatti's. Still, a 1960-Edsel Owners' Club may yet appear.

The final fiscal box score on the Edsel fiasco will probably never be known, because the Ford Motor Company's public reports do not include breakdowns of gains and losses within the individual divisions. Financial buffs estimate, however, that the company lost something like $200 million on the Edsel after it appeared; add to this the officially announced expenditure of $250 million before it appeared, subtract about a hundred million invested in plant and equipment that were salvageable for other uses, and the net loss is $350 million. If these estimates are right, every Edsel the company manufactured cost it in lost money about $3,200, or about the price of another one. In other, harsher words, the company would have saved itself money if, back in 1955, it had decided not to produce the Edsel at all but simply to give away 110,810 specimens of its comparably priced car, the Mercury.

The end of the Edsel set off an orgy of hindsight in the press. *Time* declared, "The Edsel was a classic case of the wrong car for the wrong market at the wrong time. It was also a prime example of the limitations of market research, with its 'depth interviews' and 'motivational' mumbo-jumbo." *Business Week*, which shortly before the Edsel made its bow had described it with patent solemnity and apparent approval, now pronounced it "a nightmare" and appended a few pointedly critical remarks about Wallace's research, which was rapidly achieving a scapegoat status equal to that of Brown's design. (Jumping up and down on motivational research was, and is, splendid sport, but, of course, the implication that it dictated, or even influenced, the Edsel's design is entirely false, since the research, being intended only to provide a theme for advertising and promotion, was not undertaken until after Brown had completed his design.) The *Wall Street Journal's* obituary of the Edsel made a point that was probably sounder, and certainly more original.

> Large corporations are often accused of rigging markets, administering prices, and otherwise dictating to the consumer [it observed]. And yesterday Ford Motor Company announced its two-year experiment with the medium-priced Edsel has come to an end . . . for want of buyers. All this is quite a ways from auto makers being able to rig markets or force consumers to take what they want them to take. . . . And the reason, simply, is that there is

no accounting for tastes. . . . When it comes to dictating,
the consumer is the dictator without peer.

The tone of the piece was friendly and sympathetic; the Ford
Company, it seemed, had endeared itself to the *Journal* by
playing the great American situation-comedy role of Daddy
the Bungler.

As for the post-mortem explanations of the debacle that
have been offered by former Edsel executives, they are notable
for their reflective tone—something like that of a knocked-out
prize fighter opening his eyes to find an announcer's microphone pushed into his face. In fact, Krafve, like many a flattened
pugilist, blames his own bad timing; he contends that if he had
been able to thwart the apparently immutable mechanics and
economics of Detroit, and had somehow been able to bring out
the Edsel in 1955, or even 1956, when the stock market and the
medium-priced-car market were riding high, the car would have
done well and would still be doing well. That is to say, if he had
seen the punch coming, he would have ducked. Krafve refuses to
go along with a sizable group of laymen who tend to attribute
the collapse to the company's decision to call the car the Edsel
instead of giving it a brisker, more singable name, reducible to
a nickname other than "Ed" or "Eddie," and not freighted with
dynastic connotations. As far as he can see, Krafve still says, the
Edsel's name did not affect its fortunes one way or the other.

Brown agrees with Krafve that bad timing was the chief
mistake. "I frankly feel that the styling of the automobile had
very little, if anything, to do with its failure," he said later,
and his frankness may pretty safely be left unchallenged. "The
Edsel program, like any other project planned for future markets, was based on the best information available at the time
in which decisions were made. The road to Hell is paved with
good intentions!"

Doyle, with the born salesman's intensely personal feeling
about his customers, talks like a man betrayed by a friend—

the American public. "It was a buyers' strike," he says. "People weren't in the mood for the Edsel. Why not is a mystery to me. What they'd been buying for several years encouraged the industry to build exactly this kind of car. We gave it to them, and they wouldn't take it. Well, they shouldn't have acted like that. You can't just wake up somebody one day and say, 'That's enough, you've been running in the wrong direction.' Anyway, *why* did they do it? Golly, how the industry worked and worked over the years—getting rid of gear-shifting, providing interior comfort, providing plus performance for use in emergencies! And now the public wants these little beetles. I don't get it!"

Wallace's sputnik theory provides an answer to Doyle's question about why people weren't in the mood, and, furthermore, it is sufficiently cosmic to befit a semi-Brain Truster. It also leaves Wallace free to defend the validity of his motivational-research studies as of the time when they were conducted. "I don't think we yet know the depths of the psychological effect that that first orbiting had on us all," he says. "Somebody had beaten us to an important gain in technology, and immediately people started writing articles about how crummy Detroit products were, particularly the heavily ornamented and status-symbolic medium-priced cars. In 1958, when none of the small cars were out except the Rambler, Chevy almost ran away with the market, because it had the simplest car. The American people had put themselves on a self-imposed austerity program. Not buying Edsels was their hair shirt."

To any relics of the sink-or-swim nineteenth-century days of American industry, it must seem strange that Wallace can afford to puff on his pipe and analyze the holocaust so amiably. The obvious point of the Edsel's story is the defeat of a giant motor company, but what is just as surprising is that the giant did not come apart, or even get seriously hurt in the fall, and neither did the majority of the people who went down with him. Owing largely to the success of four of its other cars—the Ford, the Thunderbird, and, later on the small Falcon and Comet and then the Mustang—the Ford Company, as an investment, survived gloriously. True, it had a bad time of it in 1958, when, partly because of the Edsel, net income per share of its stock fell from $5.40 to $2.12, dividends per share from $2.40 to $2.00, and the market price of its stock from a 1957 high of about $60 to a 1958 low of under $40. But all these losses were more than recouped in 1959, when net income per share was $8.24, dividends per share were $2.80, and the price of the stock reached a high of around $90. In 1960 and 1961, things went even better. So the 280,000 Ford stockholders listed on the books in 1957 had had little to complain about unless they had sold at the height of the panic. On the other hand, six thousand white-collar workers were squeezed out of their jobs as a result of the Mercury-Edsel-Lincoln consolidation, and the average number of Ford employees fell from 191,759 in 1957 to 142,076 the following year, climbing back to only 159,541 in 1959. And, of course, dealers who gave up profitable franchises in other makes and then went broke trying to sell Edsels weren't likely to be very cheerful about the experience. Under the terms of the consolidation of the Lincoln-Mercury and Edsel Divisions, most of the agencies for the three makes were consolidated, too. In the consolidation, some Edsel dealers were squeezed out, and it can have been small comfort to those of them who went bankrupt to learn later that when the Ford Company finally discontinued making the car, it agreed to pay those of their former colleagues who had weathered the crisis one-half of the original cost of their Edsel signs, and was granting them substantial rebates on all Edsels in stock at the time of discontinuance. Still, automobile dealers, some of whom work on credit margins as slim as those of Miami hotel operators, occasionally go broke with even the most popular cars. And among those who earn their living in the rough-and-tumble world of automobile salesrooms, where Detroit is not always spoken of with affection, many will concede that the Ford Company, once it had found itself stuck with a lemon, did as much as it reasonably could to bolster dealers who had cast their lot with Edsel. A spokesman for the National Automobile Dealers Association has since stated, "So far as we know, the Edsel dealers were generally satisfied with the way they were treated."

Foote, Cone & Belding also ended up losing money on the Edsel account, since its advertising commissions did not entirely compensate for the extraordinary expense it had gone to of hiring sixty new people and opening up a posh office in Detroit. But its losses were hardly irreparable; the minute there were no more Edsels to advertise, it was hired to advertise Lincolns, and although that arrangement did not last very long, the firm has happily survived to sing the praises of such clients as General Foods, Lever Brothers, and Trans World Airways. A rather touching symbol of the loyalty that the agency's employees have for its former client is the fact that for several years after 1959, on every workday its private parking lot in Chicago was still dotted with Edsels. These faithful drivers, incidentally, are not unique. If Edsel owners have not found the means to a dream fulfillment, and if some of them for a while had to put up with harrowing mechanical disorders, many of them more than a decade later cherish their cars as if they were Confederate bills, and on Used Car Row the Edsel is a high-premium item, with few cars being offered.

By and large, the former Edsel executives did not just land on their feet, they landed in clover. Certainly no one can accuse the Ford Company of giving vent to its chagrin in the old-fashioned way, by vulgarly causing heads to roll. Krafve was assigned to assist Robert S. McNamara, at that time a Ford divisional vice-president (and later, of course,

Secretary of Defense), for a couple of months, and then
he moved to a staff job in company headquarters, stayed
there for about a year, and left to become a vice-president
of the Raytheon Company, of Waltham, Massachusetts, a
leading electronics firm. In April, 1960, he was made its
president. In the middle sixties he left to become a high-
priced management consultant on the West Coast. Doyle,
too, was offered a staff job with Ford, but after taking a
trip abroad to think it over he decided to retire. "It was a
question of my relationship to my dealers," he explains. "I
had assured them that the company was fully behind the
Edsel for keeps, and I didn't feel that I was the fellow to
tell them now that it wasn't." After his retirement, Doyle
remained about as busy as ever, keeping an eye on various
businesses in which he has set up various friends and relatives, and conducting a consulting business of his own in
Detroit. About a month before Edsel's consolidation with
Mercury and Lincoln, Warnock, the publicity man, left the
division to become director of news services for the International Telephone & Telegraph Corp., in New York—a
position he left in June, 1960, to become vice-president of
Communications Counselors, the public-relations arm of
McCann-Erickson. From there he went back to Ford, as
Eastern promotion chief for Lincoln-Mercury—a case of
a head that had not rolled but had instead been anointed.
Brown, the embattled stylist, stayed on in Detroit for a
while as chief stylist of Ford commercial vehicles and then
went with the Ford Motor Company, Ltd., of England,
where, again as chief stylist, he was assigned to direct the
design of Consuls, Anglias, trucks, and tractors. He insisted
that this post didn't represent the Ford version of Siberia.
"I have found it to be a most satisfying experience, and
one of the best steps I have ever taken in my . . . career,"
he stated firmly in a letter from England. "We are building a styling office and a styling team second to none in

Europe." Wallace, the semi-Brain Truster, was asked to continue semi-Brain Trusting for Ford, and, since he still didn't like living in Detroit, or near it, was permitted to move to New York and to spend only two days a week at headquarters. ("They didn't seem to care any more where I operated from," he says modestly.) At the end of 1958, he left Ford, and he has since finally achieved his heart's desire—to become a full-time scholar and teacher. He set about getting a doctorate in sociology at Columbia, writing his thesis on social change in Westport, Connecticut, which he investigated by busily quizzing its inhabitants; meanwhile, he taught a course on "The Dynamics of Social Behavior" at the New School for Social Research, in Greenwich Village. "I'm through with industry," he was heard to declare one day, with evident satisfaction, as he boarded a train for Westport, a bundle of questionnaires under his arm. Early in 1962, he became Dr. Wallace.

The subsequent euphoria of these former Edsel men did not stem entirely from the fact of their economic survival; they appear to have been enriched spiritually. They are inclined to speak of their Edsel experience—except for those still with Ford, who are inclined to speak of it as little as possible—with the verve and garrulity of old comrades-in-arms hashing over their most thrilling campaign. Doyle is perhaps the most passionate reminiscer in the group. "It was more fun than I've ever had before or since," he told a caller in 1960. "I suppose that's because I worked the hardest ever. We all did. It was a good crew. The people who came with Edsel knew they were taking a chance, and I like people who'll take chances. Yes, it was a wonderful experience, in spite of the unfortunate thing that happened. And we were on the right track, too! When I went to Europe just before retiring, I saw how it is there—nothing but compact cars, yet they've still got traffic jams over there, they've still got parking problems, they've still got accidents. Just try getting in and out of those low taxicabs without hitting your head, or try not to get clipped while you're walking around the Arc de Triomphe. This small-car thing won't last forever. I can't see American drivers being satisfied for long with manual gear-shifting and limited performance. The pendulum will swing back."

Warnock, like many a public-relations man before him, claims that his job gave him an ulcer—his second. "But I got over it," he says. "That great Edsel team—I'd just like to see what it could have done if it had had the right product at the right time. It could have made millions, that's what! The whole thing was two years out of my life that I'll never forget. It was history in the making. Doesn't it all tell you something about America in the fifties—high hopes, and less than complete fulfillment of them?"

Krafve, the boss of the great team *manqué*, is entirely prepared to testify that there is more to his former subordinates' talk than just the romantic vaporings of old soldiers. "It was a wonderful group to work with," he said not long ago. "They really put their hearts and guts into the job. I'm interested in a crew that's strongly motivated, and that one was. When things went bad, the Edsel boys could have cried about how they'd given up wonderful opportunities to come with us, but if anybody did, I never heard about it. I'm not surprised that they've mostly come out all right. In industry, you take a bump now and then, but you bounce back as long as you don't get defeated inside. I like to get together with somebody once in a while—Gayle Warnock or one of the others—and go over the humorous incidents, the tragic incidents. . . ."

Whether the nostalgia of the Edsel boys for the Edsel runs to the humorous or to the tragic, it is a thought-provoking phenomenon. Maybe it means merely that they miss the limelight they first basked in and later squirmed in, or maybe it means that a time has come when—as in Elizabethan drama but seldom before in American business—failure can have a certain grandeur that success never knows.

3

THE FEDERAL INCOME TAX

I

BEYOND A DOUBT, many prosperous and ostensibly intelligent Americans have in recent years done things that to a naïve observer might appear outlandish, if not actually lunatic. Men of inherited wealth, some of them given to the denunciation of government in all its forms and manifestations, have shown themselves to be passionately interested in the financing of state and municipal governments, and have contributed huge sums to this end. Weddings between persons with very high incomes and persons with not so high incomes have tended to take place most often near the end of December and least often during January. Some exceptionally successful people, especially in the arts, have been abruptly and urgently instructed by their financial advisers to do no more gainful work under any circumstances for the rest of the current calendar year, and have followed this advice, even though it sometimes came as early as May or June. Actors and other people with high incomes from personal services have again and again become the proprietors of sand-and-gravel businesses, bowling alleys, and telephone-answering services, doubtless adding a certain *élan* to the conduct of those humdrum establishments. Motion-picture people, as if fulfilling a clockwork schedule of renunciation and reconciliation, have repeatedly abjured their native soil in favor of foreign countries for periods of eighteen months—only to embrace it again in the nineteenth. Petroleum investors have peppered the earth of Texas with speculative oil wells, taking risks far beyond what would be dictated by normal business judgment. Businessmen travelling on planes, riding in taxis, or dining in restaurants have again and again been seen compulsively making entries in little notebooks that, if they were questioned, they would describe as "diaries;" however, far from being spiritual descendants of Samuel Pepys or Philip Hone, they were writing down only what everything cost. And owners and part owners of businesses have arranged to share their ownership with minor children, no matter how young; indeed, in at least one case of partnership agreement has been delayed pending the birth of one partner.

As hardly anyone needs to be told, all these odd actions are directly traceable to various provisions of the federal income-tax law. Since they deal with birth, marriage, work, and styles and places of living, they give some idea of the scope of the law's social effects, but since they are confined to the affairs of the well-to-do, they give no idea of the breadth of its economic impact. Inasmuch as almost sixty-three million individual returns were filed in a typical recent year—1964—it is not surprising that the income-tax law is often spoken of as the law of the land that most directly affects the most individuals, and inasmuch as income-tax collections account for almost three-quarters of our government's gross receipts, it is understandable that it is considered our most important single fiscal measure. (Out of a gross from all sources of a hundred and twelve billion dollars for the fiscal year that ended June 30th, 1964, roughly fifty-four and a half billion came from individual income taxes and twenty-three and a third billion from corporation income taxes.) "In the popular mind, it is THE TAX," the economics professors William J. Shultz and C. Lowell Harriss declare in their book "American Public Finance," and the writer David T. Bazelon has suggested that the economic effect of the tax has been so sweeping as to create two quite separate kinds of United States currency—before-tax money and after-tax money. At any rate, no corporation is ever formed, nor are any corporation's affairs conducted for as much as a single day, without the lavishing of earnest consideration upon the income tax, and hardly anyone in any income group can get by without thinking of it occasionally, while some people, of course, have had their fortunes or their reputations, or both, ruined as a result of their failure to comply with it. As far afield as Venice, an American visitor a few years ago was jolted to find on a brass plaque affixed to a coin box for contributions to the maintenance fund of the Basilica of San Marco the words "Deductible for U.S. Income-Tax Purposes."

A good deal of the attention given to the income tax is based on the proposition that the tax is neither logical nor equitable. Probably the broadest and most serious charge is that the law has close to its heart something very much like a lie; that is, it provides for taxing incomes at steeply progressive rates, and then goes on to supply an array of escape hatches so convenient that hardly anyone, no matter how rich, need pay the top rates or anything like them. For 1960, taxpayers with reportable incomes of between two hundred thousand and five hundred thousand dollars paid, on the average, about 44 per cent, and even those few who reported incomes of over a million dollars paid well under 50 per cent—which happened to be just about the percentage that a single taxpayer was supposed to pay, and often did pay, if his income was forty-two thousand dollars. Another frequently heard charge is that the income tax is a serpent in the American Garden of Eden, offering such tempting opportunities for petty evasion that it induces a national fall from grace every April. Still another school of critics contends that because of its labyrinthine quality (the basic statute, the Internal Revenue Code of 1954, runs to more than a thousand pages, and the court rulings and Internal Revenue Service regulations that elaborate it come to seventeen thousand) the income tax not only results in such idiocies as gravel-producing actors and unborn partners but is in fact that anomaly, a law that a citizen may be unable to comply with by himself. This situation, the critics declare, leads to an undemocratic state of affairs, for only the rich can afford the expensive professional advice necessary to minimize their taxes legally.

The income-tax law *in toto* has virtually no defenders, even though most fair-minded students of the subject agree that its effect over the half century that it has been in force has been to bring about a huge and healthy redistribution of wealth. When it comes to the income tax, we almost all want reform. As reformers, however, we are largely powerless, the chief reasons being the staggering complexity of the whole subject, which causes many people's minds to go blank at the very mention of it, and the specific, knowledgeable, and energetic advocacy by small groups of the particular provisions they benefit from. Like any tax law, ours had a kind of immunity to reform; the very riches that people accumulate through the use of tax-avoidance devices can be—and constantly are—applied to fighting the elimination of those devices. Such influences, combined with the fierce demands made on the Treasury by defense spending and other rising costs of government (even leaving aside hot wars like the one in Vietnam), have brought about two tendencies so marked that they have assumed the shape of a natural political law: In the United States it is comparatively easy to raise tax rates

and to introduce tax-avoidance devices, and it is comparatively hard to lower tax rates and to eliminate tax-avoidance
devices. Or so it seemed until 1964, when half of this natural law was spectacularly challenged by legislation, originally
proposed by President Kennedy and pushed forward by President Johnson, that reduced the basic rates on individuals in
two stages from a bottom of 20 per cent to a bottom of 14
per cent and from a top of 91 per cent to a top of 70 per cent,
and reduced the top tax on corporations from 52 per cent to
48 per cent—all in all, by far the largest tax cut in our history. Meanwhile, however, the other half of the natural law
remains immaculate. To be sure, the proposed tax changes
advanced by President Kennedy included a program of substantial reforms to eliminate tax-avoidance devices, but so
great was the outcry against the reforms that Kennedy himself
soon abandoned most of them, and virtually none of them
were enacted; on the contrary, the new law actually extended
or enlarged one or two of the devices.

"Let's face it, Clitus, we live in a tax era. Everything's
taxes," one lawyer says to another in Louis Auchincloss's
book of short stories called "Powers of Attorney," and the second lawyer, a traditionalist, can enter only a token demurrer.
Considering the omnipresence of the income tax in American
life, however, it is odd how rarely one encounters references
to it in American fiction. This omission probably reflects the
subject's lack of literary elegance, but it may also reflect a
national uneasiness about the income tax—a sense that we
have willed into existence, and cannot will out of existence,
a presence not wholly good or wholly bad but, rather, so
immense, outrageous, and morally ambiguous that it cannot
be encompassed by the imagination. How in the world, one
may ask, did it all happen?

An income tax can be truly effective only in an industrial
country where there are many wage and salary earners, and

thc annals of income taxation up to the present century are comparatively short and simple. The universal taxes of ancient times, like the one that brought Mary and Joseph to Bethlehem just before the birth of Jesus, were invariably head taxes, with one fixed sum to be paid by everybody, rather than income taxes. Before about 1800, only two important attempts were made to establish income taxes—one in Florence during the fifteenth century, and the other in France during the eighteenth. Generally speaking, both represented efforts by grasping rulers to mulct their subjccts. According to the foremost historian of the income tax, the late Edwin R. A. Seligman, the Florentine effort withered away as a result of corrupt and inefficient administration. The eighteenth-century French tax, in the words of the same authority, "soon became honeycombed with abuses" and degenerated into "a completely unequal and thoroughly arbitrary imposition upon the less well-to-do classes," and, as such, it undoubtedly played its part in whipping up the murderous fervor that went into the French Revolution. The rate of the *ancien-régime* tax, which was enacted by Louis XIV in 1710, was 10 per cent, a figure that was cut in half later, but not in time; the revolutionary regime eliminated the tax along with its perpetrators. In the face of this cautionary example, Britain enacted an income tax in 1798 to help finance her participation in the French revolutionary wars, and this was, in several respects, the first modern income tax; for one thing, it had graduated rates, progressing from zero, on annual incomes under sixty pounds, to 10 per cent, on incomes of two hundred pounds or more, and, for another, it was complicated, containing a hundred and twenty-four sections, which took up a hundred and fifty-two pages. Its unpopularity was general and instantaneous, and a spate of pamphlets denouncing it soon appeared; one pamphleteer, who purported to be looking back at ancient barbarities from the year 2000, spoke of the income-tax collectors of old as "merciless mercenaries" and "brutes . . . with all the rudeness that insolence and self-important ignorance could suggest." After yielding only about six million pounds a year for three years—in large part because of widespread evasion—it was repealed in 1802, after the Treaty of Amiens, but the following year, when the British treasury again found itself in straitened circumstances, Parliament enacted a new income-tax law. This one was extraordinarily far ahead of its time, in that it included a provision for the withholding of income at the source, and, perhaps for that reason, it was hated even more than the earlier tax had been, even though its top rate was only half as high. At a protest meeting held in the City of London in July, 1803, several speakers made what, for Britons, must surely have been the ultimate commitment of enmity toward the income tax. If such a measure were necessary to save the country, they said, then they would reluctantly have to choose to let the country go.

Yet gradually, despite repeated setbacks, and even extended periods of total oblivion, the British income tax began to flourish. This may have been, as much as anything else, a matter of simple habituation, for a common thread runs through the history of income taxes everywhere: Opposition is always at its most reckless and strident at the very outset; with every year that passes, the tax tends to become stronger and the voices of its enemies more muted. Britain's income tax was repealed the year after the victory at Waterloo, was revived in a halfhearted way in 1832, was sponsored with enthusiasm by Sir Robert Peel a decade later, and remained in effect thereafter. The basic rate during the second half of the nineteenth century varied between 5 per cent and less than 1 per cent, and it was only 2½ per cent, with a modest surtax on high incomes, as late as 1913. The American idea of very high rates on high incomes eventually caught on in Britain, though, and by the middle 1960's the top British bracket was over 90 per cent.

Elsewhere in the world—or at least in the economically

developed world—country after country took the cue from Britain and instituted an income tax at one time or another during the nineteenth century. Post-revolutionary France soon enacted an income tax, but then repealed it and managed to get along without one for a number of years in the second half of the century; eventually, though, the loss of revenue proved to be intolerable, and the tax returned, to become a fixture of the French economy. An income tax was one of the first, if not one of the sweetest, fruits of Italian unity, while several of the separate states that were to combine into the German nation had income taxes even before they were united. By 1911, income taxes also existed in Austria, Spain, Belgium, Sweden, Norway, Denmark, Switzerland, Holland, Greece, Luxembourg, Finland, Australia, New Zealand, Japan, and India.

As for the United States, the enormous size of whose income-tax collections and the apparent docility of whose taxpayers are now the envy of governments everywhere, it was a laggard in the matter of instituting an income tax and for years was an inveterate backslider in the matter of keeping one on its statute books. It is true that in Colonial times there were various revenue systems bearing some slight resemblance to income taxes—in Rhode Island at one point, for example, each citizen was supposed to guess the financial status of ten of his neighbors, in regard to both income and property, in order to provide a basis for tax assessments—but such schemes, being inefficient and subject to obvious opportunities for abuse, were short-lived. The first man to propose a federal income tax was President Madison's Secretary of the Treasury, Alexander J. Dallas; he did so in 1814, but a few months later the War of 1812 ended, the demand for government revenue eased, and the Secretary was hooted down so decisively that the subject was not revived until the time of the Civil War, when both the Union and the Confederacy enacted income-tax bills. Before 1900, very few new income taxes appear to have been enacted anywhere without the stimulus of a war. National income taxes were—and until quite recently largely remained—war and defense measures. In June of 1862, prodded by public concern over a public debt that was increasing at the rate of two million dollars a day, Congress reluctantly passed a law providing for an income tax at progressive rates up to a maximum of 10 per cent, and on July 1st President Lincoln signed it into law, along with a bill to punish the practice of polygamy. (The next day, stocks on the New York Exchange took a dive, which was probably not attributable to the polygamy bill.)

"I am taxed on my income! This is perfectly gorgeous! I never felt so important in my life before," Mark Twain wrote in the Virginia City, Nevada, *Territorial Enterprise* after he had paid his first income-tax bill, for the year 1864—$36.82, including a penalty of $3.12 for being late. Although few other taxpayers were so enthusiastic, the law remained in force until 1872. It was, however, subjected to a succession of rate reductions and amendments, one of them being the elimination, in 1865, of its progressive rates, on the arresting ground that collecting 10 per cent on high incomes and lower rates on lower incomes constituted undue discrimination against wealth. Annual revenue collections mounted from two million dollars in 1863 to seventy-three million in 1866, and then descended sharply. For two decades, beginning in the early eighteen-seventies, the very thought of an income tax did not enter the American mind, apart from rare occasions when some Populist or Socialist agitator would propose the establishment of such a tax designed specifically to soak the urban rich. Then, in 1893, when it had become clear that the country was relying on an obsolete revenue system that put too little burden on businessmen and members of the professions, President Cleveland proposed an income tax. The outcry that followed was shrill. Senator John Sherman, of Ohio, the father of the Sherman Antitrust Act, called the proposal "socialism, communism, and devilism," and another senator spoke darkly of "the professors with their books, the socialists with their schemes . . . [and] the anarchists with their bombs," while over in the House a congressman from Pennsylvania laid his cards on the table in the following terms:

> An income tax! A tax so odious that no administration ever dared to impose it except in time of war. . . . It is unutterably distasteful both in its moral and material aspects. It does not belong to a free country. It is class legislation. . . . Do you desire to offer a reward to dishonesty and to encourage perjury? The imposition of the tax will corrupt the people. It will bring in its train the spy and the informer. It will necessitate a swarm of officials with inquisitorial powers. . . . Mr. Chairman, pass this bill and the Democratic Party signs its death warrant.

The proposal that gave rise to these fulminations was for a tax at a uniform rate of 2 per cent on income in excess of four thousand dollars, and it was enacted into law in 1894. The Democratic Party survived, but the new law did not. Before it could be put into force, it was thrown out by the Supreme Court, on the ground that it violated the Constitutional provision forbidding "direct" taxes unless they were apportioned among the states according to population (curiously, this point had not been raised in connection with the Civil War income tax), and the income-tax issue was dead again, this time for a decade and a half. In 1909, by what a tax authority named Jerome Hellerstein has called "one of the most ironic twists of political events in American history," the Constitutional amendment (the sixteenth) that eventually gave Congress the power to levy taxes without apportionment among the states was put forward by the implacable opponents of the income tax, the Republicans, who took the step as a political move, confidently believing that the amendment would never be ratified by the states. To their dismay, it was ratified in 1913, and later that year Congress enacted a graduated tax on individuals at rates ranging from 1 per cent to 7 per cent, and also a flat tax of 1 per cent on the net profits of corporations. The income tax has been with us ever since.

By and large, its history since 1913 has been one of rising rates and of the seasonable appearance of special provisions to save people in the upper brackets from the inconvenience of having to pay those rates. The first sharp rise took place during the First World War, and by 1918 the bottom rate was 6 per cent and the top one, applicable to taxable income in excess of a million dollars, was 77 per cent, or far more than any government had previously ventured to exact on income of any amount. But the end of the war and the "return to normalcy" brought a reversal of the trend, and there followed an era of low taxes for rich and poor alike. Rates were reduced by degrees until 1925, when the standard rate scale ran from 1½ per cent to an absolute top of 25 per cent, and, furthermore, a great majority of the country's wage earners were relieved of paying any tax at all by being allowed personal exemptions of fifteen hundred dollars for a single person, thirty-five hundred dollars for a married couple, and four hundred dollars for each dependent. This was not the whole story, for it was during the twenties that special-interest provisions began to appear, stimulated into being by the complex of political forces that has accounted for their increase at intervals ever since. The first important one, adopted in 1922, established the principle of favored treatment for capital gains; this meant that money acquired through a rise in the value of investments was, for the first time, taxed at a lower rate than money earned in wages or for services—as, of course, it still is today. Then, in 1926, came the loophole that has undoubtedly caused more gnashing of teeth among those not in a position to profit by it than any other—the percentage depletion allowance on petroleum, which permits the owner of a producing oil well to deduct from his taxable income up to 27½ per cent of his gross annual income from the well and to keep deducting that much year after year, even though he has deducted the original cost of the well many times over. Whether or not the twenties were a golden age for the American people in general, they were assuredly a golden age for the American taxpayer.

The depression and the New Deal brought with them a trend toward higher tax rates and lower exemptions, which led up to a truly revolutionary era in federal income taxation—that of the Second World War. By 1936, largely because of greatly increased public spending, rates in the higher brackets were roughly double what they had been in the late twenties, and the very top bracket was 79 per cent, while, at the low end of the scale, personal exemptions had been reduced to the point where a single person was required to pay a small tax even if his income was only twelve hundred dollars. (As a matter of fact, at that time most industrial workers' incomes did not exceed twelve hundred dollars.) In 1944 and 1945, the rate scale for individuals reached its historic peak—23 per cent at the low end and 94 per cent at the high one—while income taxes on corporations, which had been creeping up gradually from the original 1913 rate of 1 per cent, reached the point where some companies were liable for 80 per cent. But the revolutionary thing about wartime taxation was not the very high rates on high incomes; indeed, in 1942, when this upward surge was approaching full flood, a new means of escape for high-bracket taxpayers appeared, or an old one widened, for the period during which stocks or other assets must be held in order to benefit from the capital-gains provision was reduced from eighteen months to six. What was revolutionary was the rise of industrial wages and the extension of substantial tax rates to the wage earner, making him, for the first time, an important contributor to government revenue. Abruptly, the income tax became a mass tax.

And so it has remained. Although taxes on big and middle-sized businesses settled down to a flat rate of 52 per cent, rates on individual income did not change significantly between 1945 and 1964. (That is to say, the basic rates did not change significantly; there were temporary remissions, amounting to anywhere from 5 per cent to 17 per cent of the sums due under the basic rates, during the years 1946 through 1950.) The range was from 20 per cent to 91 per cent until 1950; there was a small rise during the Korean War, but it went right back there in 1954. In 1950, another important escape route, the so-called "restricted stock option," opened up, enabling some corporate executives to be taxed on part of their compensation at low capital-gains rates. The significant change, invisible in the rate schedule, has been a continuation of the one begun in wartime; namely, the increase in the proportionate tax burden carried by the middle and lower income groups. Paradoxical as it may seem, the evolution of our income tax has been from a low-rate tax relying for revenue on the high income group to a high-rate tax relying on the middle and lower-middle income groups. The Civil War levy, which affected only one per cent of the population, was unmistakably a rich man's tax, and the same was true of the 1913 levy. Even in 1918, at the height of the budget squeeze produced by the First World War, less than four and a half million Americans, of a total population of more than a hundred million, had to file income-tax returns at all. In 1933, in the depths of the depression, only three and three-quarters million returns were filed, and in 1939 an élite consisting of seven hundred thousand taxpayers, of a population of a hundred and thirty million, accounted for nine-tenths of all income-tax collections, while in 1960 it took some thirty-two million taxpayers—something over one-sixth of the population—to account for nine-tenths of all collections, and a whopping big nine-tenths it was, totalling some thirty-five and a half billion dollars, compared to less than a billion in 1939.

The historian Seligman wrote in 1911 that the history of income taxation the world over consisted essentially of "evolution toward basing it on ability to pay." One wonders what qualifications he might add, on the basis of the American experience since then, if he were still alive. Of course, one reason people with middle incomes pay far more in taxes than they used to is that there are far more of them. Changes in the country's social and economic structure have been as big a factor in the shift as the structure of the income tax has. It remains probable, though, that, in actual practice, the aboriginal income tax of 1913 extracted money from citizens with stricter regard to their ability to pay than the present income tax does.

Whatever the faults of our income-tax law, it is beyond question the best-obeyed income-tax law in the world, and income taxes are now ubiquitous, from the Orient to the Occident and from pole to pole. (Practically all of the dozens of new nations that have come into being over the past few years have adopted income-tax measures. Walter H. Diamond, the editor of a publication called *Foreign Tax & Trade Briefs*, has noted that as recently as 1955 he could rattle off the names of two dozen countries, large and small, that did not tax the individual, but that in 1965 the only names he could rattle off were those of a couple of British colonies, Bermuda and the Bahamas; a couple of tiny republics, San Marino and Andorra; three oil-rich Middle Eastern countries, the Sultanate of Muscat and Oman, Kuwait, and Qatar; and two rather inhospitable countries, Monaco and Saudi Arabia, which taxed the incomes of resident foreigners but not those of nationals. Even Communist countries have income taxes, though they count on them for only a small percentage of their total revenue; Russia applies different rates to different occupations, shopkeepers and ecclesiastics being in the high tax bracket, artists and writers near the middle, and laborers and artisans at the bottom.) Evidence of the superior efficiency of tax collecting in the United States is plentiful; for instance, our costs for administration and enforcement come to only about forty-four cents for every hundred dollars collected, as against a rate more than twice as high in Canada, more than three times as high in England, France, and Belgium, and many times as high in other places. This kind of American efficiency is the despair of foreign tax collectors. Toward the end of his term in office Mortimer M. Caplin, who was commissioner of Internal Revenue from January, 1961, until July, 1964, held consultations with the leading tax administrators of six Western European countries, and the question heard again and again was "How do you do it? Do they *like* to pay taxes over there?" Of course, they do not, but, as Caplin said at the time, "we have a lot going for us that the Europeans haven't." One thing we have going for us is tradition. American income taxes originated and developed not as a result of the efforts of monarchs to fill their coffers at the expense of their subjects but as a result of the efforts of an elected government to serve the general interest. A widely travelled tax lawyer observed not long ago, "In most countries, it's impossible to engage in a serious discussion of income taxes, because they aren't taken seriously." They are taken seriously here, and part of the reason is the power and skill of our income-tax police force, the Internal Revenue Service.

Unquestionably, the "swarm of officials" feared by the Pennsylvania congressman in 1894 has come into being—and there are those who would add that the officials have the "inquisitorial powers" he also feared. As of the beginning of 1965, the Internal Revenue Service had approximately sixty thousand employees, including more than six thousand revenue officers and more than twelve thousand revenue agents, and these eighteen thousand men, possessing the right to inquire into every penny of everyone's income and into matters like exactly what was discussed at an expense-account meal, and armed with the threat of heavy punishments, have powers that might reasonably be called inquisitorial. But the I.R.S. engages in many activities besides actual tax collecting, and some of these suggest that it exercises its despotic powers in an equitable way, if not actually in a benevolent one. Notable among the additional activities is a taxpayer-education program on a scale that occasionally inspires an official to boast that the I.R.S. runs the largest university in the world. As part of this program, it puts out dozens of publications explicating various aspects of the law, and it is proud of the fact that the most general of these—a blue-covered pamphlet entitled "Your Federal Income Tax," which is issued annually and in 1965 could be bought for forty cents at any District Director's office—is so popular that it is often reprinted by private publishers, who sell it to the unwary for a dollar or more, pointing out, with triumphant accuracy, that it is an official government publication. (Since government publications are not copyrighted, this is perfectly legal.) The I.R.S. also conducts "institutes" on technical questions every December for the enlightenment of the vast corps of "tax practitioners"— accountants and lawyers—who will shortly be preparing the returns of individuals and corporations. It puts out elementary tax manuals designed specially for free distribution to any high schools that ask for them—and, according to one I.R.S. official, some eighty-five per cent of American high schools did ask for them in one recent year. (The question of whether schoolchildren ought to be spending their time boning up on the tax laws is one that the I.R.S. considers to be outside its scope.) Furthermore, just before the tax deadline each year, the I.R.S. customarily goes on television with spot advertisements offering tax pointers and reminders. It is proud to say that, of the various spots, a clear majority have been in the interests of protecting taxpayers from overpaying.

In the fall of 1963, the I.R.S. took a big step toward increasing the efficiency of its collections still further, and, by a feat worthy of the wolf in "Little Red Riding Hood," it managed to present the step to the public as a grandmotherly move to help everybody out. The step was the establishment of a so-called national-identity file, involving the assignment to every taxpayer of an account number (usually his Social Security number), and its intention was to practically eliminate the problem created by people who fail to declare their income from corporate dividends or from interest on bank accounts or bonds—a form of evasion that was thought to have been costing the Treasury hundreds of millions a year. But that is not all. When the number is entered in the proper place on a return, "this will make certain that you are given immediate credit for taxes reported and paid by you, and that any refund will be promptly recorded in your favor"—so Commissioner Caplin commented brightly on the front cover of the 1964 tax-return forms. The I.R.S. then began taking another giant step—the adoption of a system for automating a large part of the tax-checking process, in which seven regional computers would collect and collate data that would be fed into a master data-processing center at Martinsburg, West Virginia. This installation, designed to make a quarter of a million number comparisons per second, began to be called the Martinsburg Monster even before it was in full operation. In 1965, between four and five million returns a year were given a complete audit, and all returns were checked for mathematical errors. Some of this mathematical work was being done by computers and some by people, but by 1967, when the computer system was going full blast, *all* the mathematical work was done by machine, thus freeing many I.R.S. employees to subject even more returns to detailed audits. According to a publication authorized by the I.R.S. back in 1963, though, "the capacity and memory of the [computer] system will help taxpayers who forget prior year credits or who do not take full advantage of their rights under the laws." In short, it was going to be a *friendly* monster.

If the mask that the I.R.S. had presented to the country in recent years has worn a rather ghastly expression of benignity, part of the explanation is probably nothing more sinister than the fact that Caplin, the man who dominated it in those years, is a cheerful extrovert and a natural politician, and that his influence continued to be felt under the man who was appointed to succeed him as Commissioner in December 1964—a young Washington lawyer named Sheldon S. Cohen, who took over the job after a six-month interim during which an I.R.S. career man named Bertrand M. Harding served as Acting Commissioner. (When Caplin resigned as Commissioner, he stepped out of politics, at least temporarily, returning to his Washington law practice as a specialist in, among other things, the tax problems of businessmen.) Caplin is widely considered to have been one of the best Commissioners of Internal Revenue in history, and, at the very least, he was certainly an improvement on two fairly recent occupants of the post, one of whom, some time after leaving it, was convicted and sentenced to two years in prison for evading his own income taxes, and the other of whom subsequently ran for public office on a platform of opposition to any federal income tax—as a former umpire might stump the country against baseball. Among the accomplishments that Mortimer Caplin, a small, quick-spoken, dynamic man who grew up in New York City and used to be a University of Virginia law professor, is credited with as Commissioner is the abolition of the practice that had previously been alleged to exist of assigning collection quotas to I.R.S. agents. He gave the top echelons of I.R.S. an air of integrity beyond cavil, and, what was perhaps most striking, managed the strange feat of projecting to the nation a sort of enthusiasm for taxes, considered abstractly. Thus he managed to collect them with a certain style—a sort of subsidiary New Frontier, which he called the New Direction. The chief thrust of the New Direction was to put increased emphasis on education leading toward increased voluntary compliance with the tax law, instead of concentrating on the search for and prosecution of conscious offenders. In a manifesto that Caplin issued to his swarm of officials in the spring of 1961, he wrote, "We all should understand that the Service is not simply running a direct enforcement business aimed at making $2 billion in additional assessments, collecting another billion from delinquent accounts, and prosecuting a few hundred evaders. Rather, it is charged with administering an enormous self-assessment tax system which raises over $90 billion from what people themselves put down on their tax returns and voluntarily pay, with another $2 or $3 billion coming from direct enforcement activities. In short, we cannot forget that 97 per cent of our total revenue comes from self-assessment or voluntary compliance, with only three per cent coming directly from enforcement. *Our chief mission is to encourage and achieve more effective voluntary compliance.* . . . The New Direction is really a shift in emphasis. *But it is a very important shift.*" It may be, though, that the true spirit of the New Direction is better epitomized on the jacket of a book entitled "The American Way in Taxation," edited by Lillian Doris, which was published in 1963 with the blessing of Caplin, who wrote the foreword. "Here is the exciting story of the largest and most efficient tax collecting organization the world has ever known—the United States Internal Revenue Service!" the jacket announced, in part. "Here are the stirring events, the bitterly-fought legislative battles, the dedicated civil servants that have marched through the past century and left an indelible imprint on our nation. You'll thrill to the epic legal battle to kill the income tax . . . and you'll be astonished at the future plans of the I.R.S. You'll see how giant computers, now on the drawing boards, are going to affect the tax collection system and influence the lives of many American men and women in new and unusual ways!" It sounded a bit like a circus barker hawking a public execution.

It is debatable whether the New Direction watchword of "voluntary compliance" could properly be used to describe a system of tax collection under which some three-quarters of all collections from individuals are obtained through withholding at the source, under which the I.R.S. and its Martinsburg Monster lurk to catch the unwary evader, and under which the punishment for evasion runs up to five years in prison per offense in addition to extremely heavy financial penalties. Caplin, however, did not seem to feel a bit of concern over this point. With tireless good humor, he made the rounds of the nation's organizations of businessmen, accountants, and lawyers, giving luncheon talks in which he praised them for their voluntary compliance in the past, exhorted them to greater efforts in the future, and assured them that it was all in a good cause. "We're still striving for the human touch in our tax administration," declared the essay on the cover of the 1964 tax-return forms, which Caplin signed, and which he says he composed in collaboration with his wife. "I see a lot of humor in this job," he told a caller a few hours after remarking to a luncheon meeting of the Kiwanis Club of Washington at the Mayflower Hotel, "Last year was the fiftieth anniversary of the income-tax amendment to the Constitution, but the Internal Revenue Service somehow or other didn't seem to get any birthday cakes." This might perhaps be considered a form of gallows humor, except that the hangman is not supposed to be the one who makes the jokes.

Cohen, the Commissioner who succeeded Caplin and was still in office in mid-1968, is a born-and-bred Washingtonian who, in 1952, graduated from George Washington University Law School at the top of his class; served in a junior capacity with the I.R.S. for the next four years; practiced law in Washington for seven years after that, eventually becoming a partner in the celebrated firm of Arnold, Fortas & Porter; at the beginning of 1964 returned to the I.R.S., as its chief counsel; and a year later, at the age of thirty-seven, became the youngest Commissioner of Internal Revenue in history. A man with close-cropped brown hair, candid eyes, and a guileless manner that makes him seem even younger than he is, Cohen came from the chief counsel's office with the reputation of having uplifted it both practically and philosophically; he was responsible for an administrative reorganization that has been widely praised as making faster decisions possible, and for a demand that the I.R.S. be consistent in its legal stand in cases against taxpayers (that it refrain from taking one position on a fine point of Code interpretation in Philadelphia, say, and the opposite position on the same point in Omaha), which is considered a triumph of high principle over governmental greed. In general, Cohen said upon assuming office, he intended to continue Caplin's policies—to emphasize "voluntary compliance," to strive for agreeable, or at least not *dis*agreeable, relations with the taxpaying public, and so on. He is a less gregarious and a more reflective man than Caplin, however, and this difference has had its effect on the I.R.S. as a whole. He has stuck relatively close to his desk, leaving the luncheon-circuit pep talks to subordinates. "Mort was wonderful at that sort of thing," Cohen said in 1965. "Public opinion of the Service is high now as a result of his big push in that direction. We want to keep it high without more pushing on my part. Anyhow, I couldn't do it well—I'm not made that way."

A charge that has often been made, and continues to be made, is that the office of Commissioner carries with it far too much power. The Commissioner has no authority to propose changes in rates or initiate other new tax legislation—the authority to propose rate changes belongs to the Secretary of the Treasury, who may or may not seek the Commissioner's advice in the matter, and the enactment of new tax laws is, of course, the job of Congress and the President—but tax laws, since they must cover so many different situations, are necessarily written in rather general terms, and the Commissioner is solely responsible (subject to reversal in the courts) for writing the regulations that are supposed to explain the laws in detail. And sometimes the regulations are a bit cloudy themselves, and in such cases who is better qualified to explain *them* than their author, the Commissioner? Thus it comes about that almost every word that drops from the Commissioner's mouth, whether at his desk or at luncheon meetings, is immediately distributed by the various tax publishing services to tax accountants and lawyers all over the country and is gobbled up by them with an avidity not always accorded the remarks of an appointed official. Because of this, some people see the Commissioner as a virtual tyrant. Others, including both theoretical and practical tax experts, disagree. Jerome Hellerstein, who is a law professor at New York University Law School as well as a tax adviser, says, "The latitude of action given the Commissioner is great, and it's true that he can do things that may affect the economic development of the country as well as the fortunes of individuals and corporations. But if he had small freedom of action, it would result in rigidity and certainty of interpretation, and would make it much easier for tax practitioners like me to manipulate the law to their clients' advantage. The Commissioner's latitude gives him a healthy unpredictability."

Certainly Caplin did not knowingly abuse his power, nor has Cohen done so. Upon visiting first one man and then the other in the Commissioner's office, I found that both conveyed the impression of being men of high intelligence who were living—as Arthur M. Schlesinger, Jr., has said that Thoreau lived—at a high degree of moral tension. And the cause of the moral tension is not hard to find; it almost surely stemmed from the difficulty of presiding over compliance, voluntary or involuntary, with a law of which one does not very heartily approve. In 1958, when Caplin appeared—as a witness versed in tax matters, rather than as Commissioner of Internal Revenue—before the House Ways and Means Committee, he proposed an across-the-board program of reforms, including, among other things, either the total elimination or a drastic curbing of favored treatment for capital gains; the lowering of percentage depletion rates on petroleum and other minerals; the withholding of taxes on dividends and interest; and the eventual drafting of an entirely new income-tax law to replace the 1954 Code, which he declared had led to "hardships, complexities, and opportunities for tax avoidance." Shortly after Caplin left office, he explained in detail what his ideal tax law would be like. Compared to the present tax law, it would be heroically simple, with loopholes eliminated, and most personal deductions and exemptions eliminated, too, and with a rate scale ranging from 10 to 50 per cent.

In Caplin's case, the resolution of moral tension, insofar as he achieved it, was not entirely the result of rational analysis. "Some critics take a completely cynical view of the income tax," he mused one day during his stint as Commissioner. "They say, in effect, 'It's a mess, and nothing can be done about it.' I can't go along with that. True, many compromises are necessary, and will continue to be. But I refuse to accept a defeatist attitude. There's a mystic quality about our tax system. No matter how bad it may be from the technical standpoint, it has a vitality because of the very high level of compliance." He paused for quite a long time, perhaps finding a flaw in his own argument; in the past, after all, universal compliance with a law has not always been a sign that it was either intelligent or just. Then he went on, "Looking over the sweep of years, I think we'll come out well. Probably a point of crisis of some kind will make us begin to see beyond selfish interests. I'm optimistic that fifty years from now we'll have a pretty good tax."

As for Cohen, he was working in the legislation-drafting section of the I.R.S. at the time the present Code was written, and he had a hand in its composition. One might suppose that this fact would cause him to have a certain proprietary feeling toward it, but apparently that is not so. "Remember that we had a Republican administration then, and I'm a Democrat," he said one day in 1965. "When you are drafting a statute, you operate as a technician. Any pride you may feel afterward is pride in technical competence." So Cohen can reread his old prose, now enshrined as law, with neither elation nor remorse, and he has not the slightest hesitation about endorsing Caplin's opinion that the Code leads to "hardships, complexities, and opportunities for tax avoidance." He is more pessimistic than Caplin about finding the answer in simplification. "Perhaps we can move the rates down and get rid of some deductions," he says, "but then we may find we need new deductions, in the interests of fairness. I suspect that a complex society requires a complex tax law. If we put in a simpler code, it would probably be complex again in a few years."

II

"Every nation has the government it deserves," the French writer and diplomat Joseph de Maistre declared in 1811. Since the primary function of government is to make laws, the statement implies that every nation has the laws it deserves, and if the doctrine may be considered at best a half truth in the case of governments that exist by force, it does seem persuasive in the case of governments that exist by popular consent. If the single most important law now on the statute books of the United States is the income-tax law, it would follow that we must have the income-tax law we deserve. Much of the voluminous discussion of the income-tax law in recent years has centered on plain violations of it, among them the deliberate padding of tax-deductible business-expense accounts, the matter of taxable income that is left undeclared on tax returns, fraudulently or otherwise—a sum estimated at as high as twenty-five billion dollars a year—and the matter of corruption within the ranks of the Internal Revenue Service, which some authorities believe to be fairly common, at least in large cities. Such forms of outlawry, of course, reflect timeless and worldwide human frailties. The law itself, however, has certain characteristics that are more closely related to a particular time and place, and if de Maistre was right, these should reflect national characteristics; the income-tax law, that is, should be to some extent a national mirror. How does the reflection look?

To repeat, then, the basic law under which income taxes are now imposed is the Internal Revenue Code of 1954, as amplified by innumerable regulations issued by the Internal Revenue Service, interpreted by innumerable judicial decisions, and amended by several Acts of Congress, including the Revenue Act of 1964, which embodied the biggest tax cut in our history. The Code, a document longer than "War and Peace," is phrased—inevitably, perhaps—in the sort of jargon that stuns the mind and disheartens the spirit; a fairly typical sentence, dealing with the definition of the word "employment," starts near the bottom of page 564, includes more than a thousand words, nineteen semicolons, forty-two simple parentheses, three parentheses within parentheses, and even one unaccountable interstitial period, and comes to a gasping end, with a definitive period, near the top of page 567. Not until one has penetrated to the part of the Code dealing with export-import taxes (which fall within its province, along with estate taxes and various other federal imposts) does one come upon a comprehensible and diverting sentence like "Every person who shall export oleomargarine shall brand upon every tub, firkin, or other package containing such article the word 'Oleomargarine,' in plain Roman letters not less than one-half inch square." Yet a clause on page 2 of the Code, though it is not a sentence at all, is as clear and forthright as one could wish; it sets forth without ado the rates at which the incomes of single individuals are to be taxed: 20 per cent on taxable income of not over $2,000; 22 per cent on taxable income of over $2,000 but not over $4,000; and so on up to a top rate of 91 per cent on taxable income of over $200,000. (As we have seen, the rates were amended downward in 1964 to a top of 70 per cent.) Right at the start, then, the Code makes its declaration of principle, and, to judge by the rate table, it is implacably egalitarian, taxing the poor relatively lightly, the well-to-do moderately, and the very rich at levels that verge on the confiscatory.

But, to repeat a point that has become so well known that it scarcely needs repeating, the Code does not live up to its principles very well. For proof of this, one need look no further than some of the recent score sheets of the income tax—a set of volumes entitled *Statistics of Income*, which are published annually by the Internal Revenue Service. For 1960, individuals with gross incomes of between $4,000 and $5,000, after taking advantage of all their deductions and personal exemptions, and availing themselves of the provision that allows married couples and the heads of households to be taxed at rates generally lower than those for single persons, ended up paying an average tax bill of about one-tenth of their reportable receipts, while those in the $10,000–$15,000 range paid a bill of about one-seventh, those in the $25,000–$50,000 range paid a bill of not quite a quarter, and those in the $50,000–$100,000 range paid a bill of about a third. Up to this point, clearly, we find a progression according to ability to pay, much as the rate table prescribes. However, the progression stops abruptly when we reach the top income brackets—that is, at just the point where it is supposed to become most marked. For 1960, the $150,000–$200,000, $200,000–$500,000, $500,000 $1,000,000 and million-plus groups each paid, on the average, less than 50 per cent of their reportable incomes, and when one takes into consideration the fact that the richer a man is, the likelier it is that a huge proportion of his money need not even be reported as gross taxable income—all income from certain bonds, for example, and half of all income from long-term capital gains—it becomes evident that at the very top of the income scale the percentage rate of actual taxation turns downward. The evidence is confirmed by the *Statistics of Income* for 1961, which breaks down figures on payments according to bracket, and which shows that although 7,487 taxpayers declared gross incomes of $200,000 or more, fewer than five hundred of them had net income that was taxed at the rate of 91 per cent. Throughout its life, the rate of 91 per cent was a public tranquilizer, making everyone in the lower bracket feel fortunate not to be rich, and not hurting the rich very much. And then, to top off the joke, if that is what it is, there are the people with more income than anyone else who pay less tax than anyone else—that is, those with annual incomes of a million dollars or more who manage to find perfectly legal ways of paying no income tax at all. According to *Statistics of Income*, there were eleven of them in 1960, out of a national total of three hundred and six million-a-year men, and seventeen in 1961, out of a total of three hundred and ninety-eight. In plain fact, the income tax is hardly progressive at all.

The explanation of this disparity between appearance and reality, so huge that it lays the Code open to a broad accusation of hypocrisy, is to be found in the detailed exceptions to the standard rates which lurk in its dim depths—exceptions that are usually called special-interest provisions or, more bluntly, loopholes. ("Loophole," as all fair-minded users of the word are ready to admit, is a somewhat subjective designation, for one man's loophole may be another man's lifeline—or perhaps at some other time, the same man's lifeline.) Loopholes were noticeably absent from the original 1913 income-tax law. How they came to be law and why they remain law are questions involving politics and possibly metaphysics, but their actual workings are relatively simple, and are illuminating to watch. By far the simplest method of avoiding income taxes—at least for someone who has a large amount of capital at his disposal—is to invest in the bonds of states, municipalities, port authorities, and toll roads; the interest paid on all such bonds is unequivocally tax-exempt. Since the interest on high-grade tax-exempt bonds in recent years has run from three to five per cent, a man who invests ten million dollars in them can collect $300,000 to $500,000 a year tax-free without putting himself or his tax lawyer to the slightest trouble; if he had been foolish enough to sink the money in ordinary investments yielding, say, five per cent, he would have had a taxable income of $500,000, and at the 1964 rate, assuming that he was single, had no other income, and did not avail himself of any dodges, he would have to pay taxes of almost $367,000. The exemption on state and municipal bonds has been part of our income-tax law since its beginnings; it was based originally on Constitutional grounds and is now defended on the ground that the states and towns need the money. Most Secretaries of the Treasury have looked on the exemption with disfavor, but not one has been able to accomplish its repeal.

Probably the most important special-interest provision in the Code is the one that concerns capital gains. The staff of the Joint Economic Committee of Congress wrote in a report issued in 1961, "Capital gains treatment has become one of the most impressive loopholes in the federal revenue structure." What the provision says, in essence, is that a taxpayer who makes a capital investment (in real estate, a corporation, a block of stock, or whatever), holds on to it for at least six months, and then sells it at a profit is entitled to be taxed on the profit at a rate much lower than the rate on ordinary income; to be specific, the rate is half of that taxpayer's ordinary top tax rate or twenty-five per cent whichever is less. What this means to anyone whose income would normally put him in a very high tax bracket is obvious: he must find a way of getting as much as possible of that income in the form of capital gains. Consequently, the game of finding ways of converting ordinary income into capital gains has become very popular in the past decade or two. The game is often won without much of a struggle. On television one evening in the middle 1960s, David Susskind asked six assembled multimillionaires whether any of them considered tax rates a stumbling block on the highroad to wealth in America. There was a long silence, almost as if the notion were new to the multimillionaires, and then one of them, in the tone of some one explaining something to a child, mentioned the capital-gains provision and said that he didn't consider taxes much of a problem. There was no more discussion of high tax rates that night.

If the capital-gains provision resembles the exemption on certain bonds in that the advantages it affords are of benefit chiefly to the rich, it differs in other ways. It is by far the more accommodating of the two loopholes; indeed, it is a sort of mother loophole capable of spawning other loopholes. For example, one might think that a taxpayer would need to have capital before he could have a capital gain. Yet a way was discovered—and was passed into law in 1950—for him to get the gain before he has the capital. This is the stock-option provision. Under its terms, a corporation may give its executives the right to buy its shares at any time within a stipulated period—say, five years—at or near the open-market price at the time of the granting of the option; later on, if, as has happened so often, the market price of the stock goes sky-high, the executives may exercise their options to buy the stock at the old price, may sell it on the open market some time later at the new price, and may pay only capital-gains rates on the difference, provided that they go through these motions without unseemly haste. The beauty of it all from an executive's point of view is that once the stock has gone up substantially in value, his option itself becomes a valuable commodity, against which he can borrow the cash he needs in order to exercise it; then, having bought the stock and sold it again, he can pay off his debt and have a capital gain that has arisen from the investment of no capital. The beauty of it all from the corporations' point of view is that they can compensate their executives partly in money taxable at relatively low rates. Of course, the whole scheme comes to nothing if the company's stock goes down, which does happen occasionally, or if it simply doesn't go up, but even then the executive has had a free play on the roulette wheel of the stock market, with a chance of winning a great deal and practically no danger of losing anything—something that the tax law offers no other group.

By favoring capital gains over ordinary income, the Code seems to be putting forward two very dubious notions—that one form of unearned income is more deserving than any form of earned income, and that people with money to invest are more deserving than people without it. Hardly anyone contends that the favored treatment of capital gains can be justified on the ground of fairness; those who consider this aspect of the matter are apt to agree with Hellerstein, who has written, "From a sociological viewpoint, there is a good deal to be said for more severe taxation of profit from appreciation in the value of property than from personal-service income." The defense, then, is based on other grounds. For one, there is a respectable economic theory that supports a complete exemption of capital gains from income tax, the argument being that whereas wages and dividends or interest from investments are fruits of the capital tree, and are therefore taxable income, capital gains represent the growth of the tree itself, and are therefore not income at all. This distinction is actually embedded in the tax laws of some countries—most notably in the tax law of Britain, which in principle did not tax capital gains until 1964. Another argument—this one purely pragmatic—has it that the capital-gains provision is necessary to encourage people to take risks with their capital. (Similarly, the advocates of stock options say that corporations need them to attract and hold executive talent.) Finally, nearly all tax authorities are agreed that taxing capital gains on exactly the same basis as other income, which is what most reformers say ought to be done, would involve formidable technical difficulties.

Particular subcategories of the rich and the well-paid can avail themselves of various other avenues of escape, including corporate pension plans, which, like stock options, contribute to the solution of the tax problems of executives; tax-free foundations set up ostensibly for charitable and educational purposes, of which over fifteen thousand help to ease the tax burdens of their benefactors, though the charitable and educational activities of some of them are more or less invisible; and personal holding companies, which, subject to rather strict regulations, enable persons with very high incomes from personal services like writing and acting to reduce their taxes by what amounts to incorporating themselves. Of the whole array of loopholes in the Code, however, probably the most widely loathed is the percentage depletion allowance on oil. As the word "depletion" is used in the Code, it refers to the progressive exhaustion of irreplaceable natural resources, but as used on oilmen's tax returns, it proves to mean a miraculously glorified form of what is ordinarily called depreciation. Whereas a manufacturer may claim depreciation on a piece of machinery as a tax deduction only until he has deducted the original cost of the machine—until, that is, the machine is theoretically worthless from wear—an individual or corporate oil investor, for reasons that defy logical explanation, may go on claiming percentage depletion on a producing well indefinitely, even if this means that the original cost of the well has been recovered many times over. The oil-depletion allowance is 27.5 per cent a year up to a maximum of half of the oil investor's net income (there are smaller allowances on other natural resources, such as 23 per cent on uranium, 10 per cent on coal, and 5 per cent on oyster and clam shells), and the effect it has on the taxable income of an oil investor, especially when it is combined with the effects of other tax-avoidance devices, is truly astonishing; for instance, over a recent five-year period one oilman had a net income of fourteen and a third million dollars, on which he paid taxes of $80,000, or six-tenths of one per cent. Unsurprisingly, the percentage-depletion allowance is always under attack, but, also unsurprisingly, it is defended with tigerish zeal—so tigerish that even President Kennedy's 1961 and 1963 proposals for tax revision, which, taken together, are generally considered the broadest program of tax reform ever put forward by a chief executive, did not venture to suggest its repeal. The usual argument is that the percentage-depletion allowance is needed in order to compensate oilmen for the risks involved in speculative drilling, and thus insure an adequate supply of oil for national use, but many people feel that this argument amounts to saying, "The depletion allowance is a necessary and desirable federal subsidy to the oil industry," and thereby scuttles itself, since granting subsidies to individual industries is hardly the proper task of the income tax.

The 1964 Revenue Act does practically nothing to plug the loopholes, but it does make them somewhat less useful, in that the drastic reduction of the basic rates on high incomes has probably led some high-bracket taxpayers simply to quit bothering with the less convenient or effective of the dodges. Insofar as the new bill reduces the disparity between the Code's promises and its performance, that is, it represents a kind of adventitious reform. (One way to cure *all* income-tax evasion would be to repeal the income tax.) However, quite apart from the sophistry—since 1964 happily somewhat lessened—that the Code embodies, it has certain discernible and disturbing characteristics that have not been changed and may be particularly hard to change in the future. Some of them have to do with its methods of allowing and disallowing deductions for travel and entertainment expenses by persons who are in business for themselves, or by persons who are employed but are not reimbursed for their business expenses—deductions that were estimated fairly recently at between five and ten billion dollars a year, with a resulting reduction in federal revenue of between one and two billion. The travel-and-entertainment problem—or the T & E problem, as it is customarily called—has been around a long time, and has stubbornly resisted various attempts to solve it. One of the crucial points in T & E history occurred in 1930, when the courts ruled that the actor and songwriter George M. Cohan—and therefore anyone else—was entitled to deduct his business expenses on the basis of a reasonable estimate even if he could not produce any proof of having paid that sum or even produce a detailed accounting. The Cohan rule, as it came to be called, remained in effect for more than three decades, during which it was invoked every spring by thousands of businessmen as ritually as Moslems turn toward Mecca. Over those decades, estimated business deductions grew like kudzu vines as the estimators became bolder, with the result that the Cohan rule and other flexible parts of the T & E regulations were subjected to a series of attacks by would-be reformers. Bills that would have virtually or entirely eliminated the Cohan rule were introduced in Congress in 1951 and again in 1959, only to be defeated—in one case, after an outcry that T & E reform would mean the end of the Kentucky Derby—and in 1961 President Kennedy proposed legislation that not only would have swept aside the Cohan rule but, by reducing to between four and seven dollars a day the amount that a man could deduct for food and beverages, would have all but put an end to the era of deductibility in American life. No such fundamental social change took place. Loud and long wails of anguish instantly arose, from businessmen and also from hotels, restaurants, and night clubs, and many of the Kennedy proposals were soon abandoned. Nevertheless, through a series of amendments to the Code passed by Congress in 1962 and put into effect by a set of regulations issued by the Internal Revenue Service in 1963, they did lead to the abrogation of the Cohan rule, and the stipulation that, generally speaking, all business deductions, no matter how small, would thenceforward have to be substantiated by records, if not by actual receipts.

Yet even a cursory look at the law as it has stood since then shows that the new, reformed T & E rules fall somewhat short of the ideal—that, in fact, they are shot through with absurdities and underlaid by a kind of philistinism. For travel to be deductible, it must be undertaken primarily for business rather than for pleasure and it must be "away from home"—that is to say, not merely commuting. The "away-from-home" stipulation raises the question of where home is, and leads to the concept of a "tax home," the place one must be away from in order to qualify for travel deductions; a businessman's tax home, no matter how many country houses, hunting lodges, and branch offices he may have, is the general area—not just the particular building, that is—of his principal place of employment. As a result, marriage partners who commute to work in two different cities have separate tax homes, but, fortunately, the Code continues to recognize their union to the extent of allowing them the tax advantages available to other married people; although there have been tax marriages, the tax divorce still belongs to the future.

As for entertainment, now that the writers of I.R.S. regulations have been deprived of the far-reaching Cohan rule, they are forced to make distinctions of almost theological nicety, and the upshot of the distinctions is to put a direct premium on the habit—which some people have considered all too prevalent for many years anyhow—of talking business at all hours of the day and night, and in all kinds of company. For example, deductions are granted for the entertainment of business associates at night clubs, theatres, or concerts only if a "substantial and bona fide business discussion" takes place before, during, or after the entertainment. (One is reluctant to picture the results if businessmen take to carrying on business discussions in great numbers during plays or concerts.) On the other hand, a businessman who entertains another in a "quiet business setting," such as a restaurant with no floor show, may claim a deduction even if little or no business is actually discussed, as long as the meeting has a business purpose. Generally speaking, the noisier and more confusing or distracting the setting, the more business talk there must be; the regulations specifically include cocktail parties in the noisy-and-distracting category, and, accordingly, require conspicuous amounts of business discussion before, during, or after them, though a meal served to a business associate at the host's home may be deductible with no such discussion at all. In the latter case, however, as the J. K. Lasser Tax Institute cautions in its popular guide "Your Income Tax," you must "be ready to prove that your motive . . . was commercial rather than social." In other words, to be on the safe side, talk business anyhow. Hellerstein has written, "Henceforth, tax men will doubtless urge their clients to talk business at every turn, and will ask them to admonish their wives not to object to shop talk if they want to continue their accustomed style of living."

Entertainment on an elaborate scale is discouraged in the post-1963 rules, but, as the Lasser booklet notes, perhaps a little jubilantly, "Congress did not specifically put into law a provision barring lavish or extravagant entertainment." Instead, it decreed that a businessman may deduct depreciation and operating expenses on an "entertainment facility"—a yacht, a hunting lodge, a swimming pool, a bowling alley, or an airplane, for instance—provided he uses it more than half the time for business. In a booklet entitled "Expense Accounts 1963," which is one of many publications for the guidance of tax advisers that are issued periodically by Commerce Clearing House, Inc., the rule was explained by means of the following example:

> A yacht is maintained . . . for the entertainment of customers. It is used 25% of the time for relaxation. . . . Since the yacht is used 75% of the time for business purposes, it is used primarily for the furtherance of the taxpayer's business and 75% of the maintenance expenses . . . are deductible entertainment facility expenses. If the yacht had been used only 40% for business, no deduction would be allowed.

The method by which the yachtsman is to measure business time and pleasure time is not prescribed. Presumably, time when the yacht is in drydock or is in the water with only her crew aboard would count as neither, though it might be argued that the owner sometimes derives pleasure simply from watching her swing at anchor. The time to be apportioned, then, must be the time when he and some guests are aboard her, and perhaps his most efficient way of complying with the law would be to install two stopwatches, port and starboard, one to be kept running during business cruising and the other during pleasure cruising. Perhaps a favoring westerly might speed a social cruise home an hour early, or a September blow delay the last leg of a business cruise, and thus tip the season's business time above the crucial fiftypercent figure. Well might the skipper pray for such timely winds, since the deductibility of his yacht could easily double his after-tax income for the year. In short, the law is nonsense.

Some experts feel that the change in T & E regulations represents a gain for our society because quite a few taxpayers who may have been inclined to fudge a bit under general provisions like the Cohan rule do not have the stomach or the heart to put down specific fraudulent items. But what has been gained in the way of compliance may have been lost in a certain debasement of our national life. Scarcely ever has any part of the tax law tended so energetically to compel the commercialization of social intercourse, or penalized so particularly the amateur spirit, which, Richard Hofstadter declares in his book "Anti-Intellectualism in American Life," characterized the founders of the republic. Perhaps the greatest danger of all is that, by claiming deductions for activities that are technically business but actually social—that is, by complying with the letter of the law—a man may cheapen his life in his own eyes. One might argue that the founders, if they were alive today, would scornfully decline to mingle the social and the commercial, the amateur and the professional, and would disdain to claim any but the most unmistakable expenses. But, under the present tax laws, the question would be whether they could afford such a lordly overpayment of taxes, or should even be asked to make the choice.

It has been maintained that the Code discriminates against intellectual work, the principal evidence being that while depreciation may be claimed on all kinds of exhaustible physical property and depletion may be claimed on natural resources, no such deductions are allowed in the case of exhaustion of the mental or imaginative capacities of creative artists and inventors—even though the effects of brain fag are sometimes all too apparent in the later work and incomes of such persons. (It has also been argued that professional athletes are discriminated against, in that the Code does not allow for depreciation of their bodies.) Organizations like the Authors League of America have contended, further, that the

Code is unfair to authors and other creative people whose income, because of the nature of their work and the economics of its marketing, is apt to fluctuate wildly from year to year, so that they are taxed exorbitantly in good years and are left with too little to tide them over bad years. A provision of the 1964 bill intended to take care of this situation provided creative artists, inventors, and other receivers of sudden large income with a four-year averaging formula to ease the tax bite of a windfall year.

But if the Code *is* anti-intellectual, it is probably so only inadvertently—and is certainly so only inconsistently. By granting tax-exempt status to charitable foundations, it facilitates the award of millions of dollars a year—most of which would otherwise go into the government's coffers—to scholars for travel and living expenses while they carry out research projects of all kinds. And by making special provisions in respect to gifts of property that has appreciated in value, it has—whether advertently or inadvertently—tended not only to force up the prices that painters and sculptors receive for their work but to channel thousands of works out of private collections and into public museums. The mechanics of this process are by now so well known that they need be merely outlined: a collector who donates a work of art to a museum may deduct on his income-tax return the fair value of the work at the time of the donation, and need pay no capital-gains tax on any increase in its value since the time he bought it. If the increase in value has been great and the collector's tax bracket is very high, he may actually come out ahead on the deal. Besides burying some museums under such an avalanche of bounty that their staffs are kept busy digging themselves out, these provisions have tended to bring back into existence that lovable old figure from the pre-tax past, the rich dilettante. In recent years, some high-bracket people have fallen into the habit of making serial collections—Post-Impressionists for a few years, perhaps, followed by Chinese jade, and then by modern American painting. At the end of each period, the collector gives away his entire collection, and when the taxes he would otherwise have paid are calculated, the adventure is found to have cost him practically nothing.

The low cost of high-income people's charitable contributions, whether in the form of works of art or simply in the form of money and other property, is one of the oddest fruits of the Code. Of approximately five billion dollars claimed annually as deductible contributions on personal income-tax returns, by far the greater part is in the form of assets of one sort or another that have appreciated in value, and comes from persons with very high incomes. The reasons can be made clear by a simple example: A man with a top bracket of 20 per cent who gives away $1,000 in cash incurs a net cost of $800. A man with a top bracket of 60 per cent who gives away the same sum in cash incurs a net cost of $400. If, instead, this same high-bracket man gives $1,000 in the form of stock that he originally bought for $200, he incurs a net cost of only $200. It is the Code's enthusiastic encouragement of large-scale charity that has led to most of the cases of million-dollar-a-year men who pay no tax at all; under one of its most peculiar provisions, anyone whose income tax and contributions combined have amounted to nine-tenths or more of his taxable income for eight out of the ten preceding years is entitled by way of reward to disregard in the current year the usual restrictions on the amount of deductible contributions, and can escape the tax entirely.

Thus the Code's provisions often enable mere fiscal manipulation to masquerade as charity, substantiating a frequent charge that the Code is morally muddleheaded, or worse. The provisions also give rise to muddleheadedness in others. The appeal made by large fund-raising drives in recent years, for example, has been uneasily divided between a call to good works and an explanation of the tax advantages to the donor. An instructive example is a commendably thorough booklet entitled "Greater Tax Savings . . . A Constructive Approach," which was used by Princeton in a large capital-funds drive. (Similar, not to say nearly identical, booklets have been used by Harvard, Yale, and many other institutions.) "The responsibilities of leadership are great, particularly in an age when statesmen, scientists, and economists must make decisions which will almost certainly affect mankind for generations to come," the pamphlet's foreword starts out, loftily, and goes on to explain, "The chief purpose of this booklet is to urge all prospective donors to give more serious thought to the manner in which they make their gifts. . . . There are many different ways in which substantial gifts can be made at comparatively low cost to the donor. It is important that prospective donors acquaint themselves with these opportunities." The opportunities expounded in the subsequent pages include ways of saving on taxes through gifts of appreciated securities, industrial property, leases, royalties, jewelry, antiques, stock options, residences, life insurance, and inventory items, and through the use of trusts ("The trust approach has great versatility"). At one point, the suggestion is put forward that, instead of actually giving anything away, the owner of appreciated securities may wish to *sell* them to Princeton, for cash, at the price he originally paid for them; this might appear to the simple-minded to be a commercial transaction, but the booklet points out, accurately, that in the eyes of the Code the difference between the securities' current market value and the lower price at which they are sold to Princeton represents pure charity, and is fully deductible as such. "While we have laid heavy emphasis on the importance of careful tax planning," the final paragraph goes, "we hope no inference will be drawn that the thought and spirit of giving should in any way be subordinated to tax considerations." Indeed it should not, nor need it be; with the heavy substance of giving so deftly minimized, or actually removed, its spirit can surely fly unrestrained.

———

One of the most marked traits of the Code—to bring this ransacking of its character to a close—is its complexity, and this complexity is responsible for some of its most far-reaching social effects; it is a virtual necessity for many tax-payers to seek professional help if they want to minimize their taxes legally, and since first-rate advice is expensive and in short supply, the rich are thereby given still another advantage over the poor, and the Code becomes more undemocratic in its action than it is in its provisions. (And the fact that fees for tax advice are themselves deductible means that tax advice is one more item on the long list of things that cost less and less to those who have more and more.) All the free projects of taxpayer education and taxpayer assistance offered by the Internal Revenue Service—and they are extensive and well meant—cannot begin to compete with the paid services of a good independent tax expert, if only because the I.R.S., whose first duty is to collect revenue, is involved in an obvious conflict of interest when it sets about explaining to people how to avoid taxes. The fact that about half of all the revenue derived from individual returns for 1960 came from adjusted gross incomes of $9,000 or less is not attributable entirely to provisions of the Code; in part, it results from the fact that low-income taxpayers cannot afford to be shown how to pay less.

The huge army of people who give tax advice— "practitioners," they are called in the trade—is a strange and disturbing side effect of the Code's complexity. The exact size of this army is unknown, but there are a few guideposts. By a recent count some eighty thousand persons, most of them lawyers, accountants, and former I.R.S. employees, held cards, granted by the Treasury Department, that officially entitle them to practice the trade of tax adviser and to appear as such before the I.R.S.; in addition, there is an uncounted host of unlicensed, and often unqualified, persons who prepare tax returns for a fee—a service that anyone may legally perform. As for lawyers, the undisputed plutocrats, if not the undisputed aristocrats, of the tax-advice industry, there is scarcely a lawyer in the country who is not concerned with taxes at one time or another during a year's practice, and every year there are more lawyers who are concerned with nothing else. The American Bar Association's taxation section, composed mostly of nothing-but-tax lawyers, has some nine thousand members; in the typical large New York law firm one out of five lawyers devotes all of his time to tax matters; and the New York University Law School's tax department, an enormous brood hen for the hatching of tax lawyers, is larger than the whole of an average law school. The brains that go into tax avoidance, which are generally recognized as including some of the best legal brains extant, constitute a wasted national resource, it is widely contended—and this contention is cheerfully upheld by some leading tax lawyers, who seem only too glad to affirm, first, that their mental capacities are indeed exceptional, and, second, that these capacities are indeed being squandered on trivia. "The law has its cycles," one of them explained recently. "In the United States, the big thing until about 1890 was property law. Then came a period when it was corporation law, and now it's various specialties, of which the most important is taxes. I'm perfectly willing to admit that I'm engaged in work that has a limited social value. After all, what are we talking about when we talk about tax law? At best, only the question of what an individual or a corporation should fairly pay in support of the government. All right, why do I do tax work? In the first place, it's a fascinating intellectual game—along with litigation, probably the most intellectually challenging branch of the law as it is now practiced. In the second place, although it's specialized in one sense, in another sense it isn't. It cuts through every field of law. One day you may be working with a Hollywood producer, the next day with a big real-estate man, the next with a corporation executive. In the third place, it's a highly lucrative field."

Hypocritically egalitarian on the surface and systematically oligarchic underneath, unconscionably complicated, whimsically discriminatory, specious in its reasoning, pettifogging in its language, demoralizing to charity, an enemy of discourse, a promoter of shop talk, a squanderer of talent, a rock of support to the property owner but a weighty onus to the underpaid, an inconstant friend to the artist and scholar—if the national mirror-image is all these things, it has its good points as well. Certainly no conceivable income-tax law could please everybody, and probably no equitable one could entirely please anybody; Louis Eisenstein notes in his book "The Ideologies of Taxation," "Taxes are a changing product of the earnest effort to have others pay them." With the exception of its more flagrant special-interest provisions, the Code seems to be a sincerely written document—at worst misguided—that is aimed at collecting unprecedented amounts of money from an unprecedentedly complex society in the fairest possible way, at encouraging the national economy, and at promoting worthy undertakings. When it is intelligently and conscientiously administered, as it has been of late, our national income-tax law is quite possibly as equitable as any in the world.

But to enact an unsatisfactory law and then try to compensate for its shortcomings by good administration is, clearly, an absurd procedure. One solution that is more logical—to abolish the income tax—is proposed chiefly by some members of the radical right, who consider any income tax Socialistic or Communistic, and who would have the federal government simply stop spending money, though abolition is also advanced, as a theoretical ideal rather than as a practical possibility, by certain economists who are looking around for alternative ways of raising at least a significant fraction of the sums now produced by the income tax. One such alternative is a value-added tax, under which manufacturers, wholesalers, and retailers would be taxed on the difference between the value of the goods they bought and that of the goods they sold; among the advantages claimed for it are that it would spread the tax burden more evenly through the productive process than a business-income tax does, and that it would enable the government to get its money sooner. Several countries, including France and Germany, have value-added taxes, though as supplements rather than alternatives to income taxes, but no federal tax of the sort is more than remotely in prospect in this country. Other suggested means of lightening the burden of the income tax are to increase the number of items subject to excise taxes, and apply a uniform rate to them, so as to create what would amount to a federal sales tax; to increase user taxes, such as tolls on federally owned bridges and recreation facilities; and to enact a law permitting federal lotteries, like the lotteries that were permitted from colonial times up to 1895, which helped finance such projects as the building of Harvard, the fighting of the Revolutionary War, and the building of many schools, bridges, canals, and roads. One obvious disadvantage of all these schemes is that they would collect revenue with relatively little regard to ability to pay, and for this reason or others none of them stand a chance of being enacted in the foreseeable future.

A special favorite of theoreticians, but of hardly anyone else, is something called the expenditure tax—the taxing of individuals on the basis of their total annual expenditures rather than on their income. The proponents of this tax— diehard adherents of the economics of scarcity—argue that it would have the primary virtue of simplicity; that it would have the beneficial effect of encouraging savings; that it would be fairer than the income tax, because it would tax what people took out of the economy rather than what they put into it; and that it would give the government a particularly handy control instrument with which to keep the national economy on an even keel. Its opponents contend that it wouldn't really be simple at all, and would be ridiculously easy to evade; that it would cause the rich to become richer, and doubtless stingier as well; and, finally, that by putting a penalty on spending it would promote depression. In any event, both sides concede that its enactment in the United States is not now politically practicable. An expenditure tax was seriously proposed for the United States by Secretary of the Treasury Henry Morgenthau, Jr., in 1942, and for Britain by a Cambridge economist (later a special adviser to the National Treasury) named Nicholas Kaldor, in 1951, though neither proponent asked for repeal of the income tax. Both proposals were all but unanimously hooted down. "The expenditure tax is a beautiful thing to contemplate," one of its admirers said recently. "It would avoid almost all the pitfalls of the income tax. But it's a dream." And so it is, in the Western world; such a tax has been put in effect only in India and Ceylon.

With no feasible substitute in sight, then, the income tax seems to be here to stay, and any hope for better taxation seems to lie in its reform. Since one of the Code's chief flaws is its complexity, reform might well start with that. Efforts at simplification have been made with regularity since 1943, when Secretary Morgenthau set up a committee to study the subject, and there have been occasional small successes; simplified instructions, for example, and a shortened form for taxpayers who wish to itemize deductions but whose affairs are relatively uncomplicated were both introduced during the Kennedy administration. Obviously, though, these were mere guerrilla-skirmish victories. One obstacle to any victory more sweeping is the fact that many of the Code's complexities were introduced in no interest other than that of fairness to all, and apparently cannot be removed without sacrificing fairness. The evolution of the special family-support provisions provides a striking example of how the quest for equity sometimes leads straight to complexity. Up to 1948, the fact that some states had and some didn't have community-property laws resulted in an advantage to married couples in the community-property states; those couples, and those couples only, were allowed to be taxed as if their total income were divided equally between them, even though one spouse might actually have a high income and the other none at all. To correct this clear-cut inequity, the federal Code was modified to extend the income-dividing privilege to all married persons. Even apart from the resulting discrimination against single persons without dependents—which remains enshrined and unchallenged in the Code today—this correction of one inequity led to the creation of another, the correction of which led to still another; before the Chinese-box sequence was played out, account had been taken of the legitimate special problems of persons who had family responsibilities although they were not married, then of working wives with expenses for child care during business hours, and then of widows and widowers. And each change made the Code more complex.

The loopholes are another matter. In their case, complexity serves not equity but its opposite, and their persistent survival constitutes a puzzling paradox; in a system under which the majority presumably makes the laws, tax provisions that blatantly favor tiny minorities over everybody else would seem to represent the civil-rights principle run wild—a kind of anti-discrimination program for the protection of millionaires. The process by which new tax legislation comes into being—an original proposal from the Treasury Department or some other source, passage in turn by the House Ways and Means Committee, the whole House, the Senate Finance Committee, and the whole Senate, followed by the working out of a House-Senate compromise by a conference committee, followed by repassage by the House and the Senate and, finally, followed by signing by the President—is indeed a tortuous one, at any stage of which a bill may be killed or shelved. However, though the public has plenty of opportunity to protest special-interest provisions, what public pressure there is is apt to be greater in favor of them than against them. In the book on tax loopholes called "The Great Treasury Raid," Philip M. Stern points out several forces that seem to him to work against the enactment of tax-reform measures, among them the skill, power, and organization of the anti-reform lobbies; the diffuseness and political impotence of the pro-reform forces within the government; and the indifference of the general public, which expresses practically no enthusiasm for tax reform through letters to congressmen or by any other means, perhaps in large part because it is stunned into incomprehension and consequent silence by the mind-boggling technicality of the whole subject. In this sense, the Code's complexity is its impenetrable elephant hide. Thus the Treasury Department, which, as the agency charged with collecting federal revenues, has a natural interest in tax reform, is often left, along with a handful of reform-minded legislators, like Senators Paul H. Douglas of Illinois, Albert Gore of Tennessee, and Eugene J. McCarthy of Minnesota, on a lonely and indefensible salient.

Optimists believe that some "point of crisis" will eventually cause specially favored groups to look beyond their selfish interests, and the rest of the country to overcome its passivity, to such an extent that the income tax will come to give back a more flattering picture of the country than it does now. When this will happen, if ever, they do not specify. But the general shape of the picture hoped for by some of those who care most about it is known. The ideal income tax envisioned for the far future by many reformers would be characterized by a short and simple Code with comparatively low rates and with a minimum of exceptions to them. In its main structural features, this ideal tax would bear a marked resemblance to the 1913 income tax—the first ever to be put in effect in the United States in peacetime. So if the unattainable visions of today should eventually materialize, the income tax would be just about back where it started.

4

A REASONABLE AMOUNT OF TIME

PRIVATE INFORMATION, whether of distant public events, impending business developments, or even the health of political figures, has always been a valuable commodity to traders in securities—so valuable that some commentators have suggested that stock exchanges are markets for such information just as much as for stocks. The money value that a market puts on information is often precisely measurable in terms of the change in stock prices that it brings about, and the information is almost as readily convertible into money as any other commodity; indeed, to the extent that it is used for barter between traders, it *is* a kind of money. Moreover, until quite recently, the propriety of the use of inside dope for their own enrichment by those fortunate enough to possess it went largely unquestioned. Nathan Rothschild's judicious use of advance news of Wellington's victory at Waterloo was the chief basis of the Rothschild fortune in England, and no Royal commission or enraged public rose to protest; similarly, and almost simultaneously, on this side of the Atlantic John Jacob Astor made an unchallenged bundle on advance news of the

Ghent treaty ending the War of 1812. In the post-Civil War era in the United States the members of the investing public, such as it was, still docilely accepted the right of the insider to trade on his privileged knowledge, and were content to pick up any crumbs that he might drop along the way. (Daniel Drew, a vintage insider, cruelly denied them even this consolation by dropping poisoned crumbs in the form of misleading memoranda as to his investment plans, which he would elaborately strew in public places.) Most nineteenth-century American fortunes were enlarged by, if they were not actually founded on, the practice of insider trading, and just how different our present social and economic order would be if such trading had been effectively forbidden in those days provides a subject for fascinating, if bootless, speculation. Not until 1910 did anyone publicly question the morality of corporate officers, directors, and employees trading in the shares of their own companies, not until the nineteen twenties did it come to be widely thought of as outrageous that such persons should be permitted to play the market game with what amounts to a stacked deck, and not until 1934 did Congress pass legislation intended to restore equity. The legislation, the Securities Exchange Act, requires corporate insiders to forfeit to their corporations any profits they may realize on short-term trades in their own firms' stock, and provides further, in a section that was implemented in 1942 by a rule designated as 10B-5, that no stock trader may use any scheme to defraud or "make any untrue statement of a material fact or . . . omit to state a material fact."

Since omitting to state material facts is the essence of using inside information, the law—while it does not forbid insiders to buy their own stock, nor to keep the profits provided they hold onto the stock more than six months—would seem to outlaw the stacked deck. In practice, though, until very recently the 1942 rule was treated almost as if it didn't exist; it was invoked by the Securities and Exchange Commission, the federal enforcement body set up under the Securities Exchange Act, only rarely and in cases so flagrant as to be probably prosecutable even without it, under common law. And there were apparent reasons for this laxity. For one thing, it has been widely argued that the privilege of cashing in on their corporate secrets is a necessary incentive to business executives to goad them to their best efforts, and it is coolly contended by a few authorities that the uninhibited presence of insiders in the market, however offensive to the spirit of fair play, is essential to a smooth, orderly flow of trading. Moreover, it is contended that the majority of all stock traders, whether or not they are technically insiders, possess and conceal inside information of one sort or another, or at least hope and believe that they do, and that therefore an even-handed application of Rule 10B-5 would result in nothing less than chaos on Wall Street. So in letting the rule rest largely untroubled in the rulebook for twenty years, the S.E.C. seemed to be consciously refraining from hitting Wall Street in one of its most vulnerable spots. But then, after a couple of preliminary jabs, it went for the spot with a vengeance. The lawsuit in which it did so was a civil complaint against the Texas Gulf Sulphur Company and thirteen men who were directors or employees of that company; it was tried without a jury in the United States District Court in Foley Square on May 9th through June 21st, 1966, and as the presiding judge, Dudley J. Bonsal, remarked mildly at one point during the trial, "I guess we all agree that we are plowing new ground here to some extent." Plowing, and perhaps sowing too; Henry G. Manne, in a recent book entitled "Insider Trading and the Stock Market," says that the case presents in almost classic terms the whole problem of insider trading, and expresses the opinion that its resolution "may determine the law in this field for many years to come."

The events that led to the S.E.C.'s action began in March, 1959, when Texas Gulf, a New York City-based company that was the world's leading producer of sulphur, began conducting aerial geophysical surveys over the Canadian Shield, a vast, barren, forbidding area of eastern Canada that in the distant but not forgotten past had proved to be a fertile source of gold. What the Texas Gulf airmen were looking for was neither sulphur nor gold. Rather, it was sulphides—deposits of sulphur occurring in chemical combination with other useful minerals, such as zinc and copper. What they had in mind was discovering mineable veins of such minerals so that Texas Gulf could diversify its activities and be less dependent upon sulphur, the market price of which had been slipping. From time to time during the two years that the surveys went on intermittently, the geophysical instruments in the scanning planes would behave strangely, their needles jiggling in such a way as to indicate the presence of electrically conductive material in the earth. The areas where such things happened, called "anomalies" by geophysicists, were duly logged and mapped by the surveyors. All told, several thousand anomalies were found. It's a long way from an anomaly to a workable mine, as must be evident to anyone who knows that while most sulphides are electrically conductive, so are many other things, including graphite, the worthless pyrites called fool's gold, and even water; nevertheless, several hundred of the anomalies that the Texas Gulf men had found were considered to be worthy of ground investigation, and among the most promising-looking of all was one situated at a place designated on their maps as the Kidd-55 segment—one square mile of muskeg marsh, lightly wooded and almost devoid of outcropping rocks, about fifteen miles north of Timmins, Ontario, an old gold-mining town that is itself some three hundred and fifty miles northwest of Toronto. Since Kidd-55 was privately owned, the company's first problem was to get title to it, or to enough of it to make possible exploratory ground operations; for a large company to acquire land in an area where it is known to be engaged in mining exploration obviously involves delicacy in the extreme, and it was not until June, 1963, that Texas Gulf was able to get an option permitting it to drill on the northeast quarter section of Kidd-55. On October 29th and 30th of that year a Texas Gulf engineer, Richard H. Clayton, conducted a ground electromagnetic survey of the northeast quarter, and was satisfied with what he found. A drill rig was moved to the site, and on November 8th, the first test drill hole was begun.

There followed a thrilling, if uncomfortable, several days at Kidd-55. The man in charge of the drilling crew was a young Texas Gulf geologist named Kenneth Darke, a cigar smoker with a rakish gleam in his eye, who looked a good deal more like the traditional notion of a mining prospector than that of the organization man he was. For three days the drilling went on, bringing out of the earth a cylindrical core of material an inch and a quarter in diameter, which served as the first actual sample of what the rock under Kidd-55 contained. As the core came up, Darke studied it critically, inch by inch and foot by foot, using no instruments but only his eyes and his knowledge of what various mineral deposits look like in their natural state. On the evening of Sunday, November 10th, by which time the drill was down one hundred and fifty feet, Darke telephoned his immediate superior, Walter Holyk, Texas Gulf's chief geologist, at his home in Stamford, Conn. to report on his findings so far. (He made the call from Timmins, since there was no telephone at the Kidd-55 drill site.) Darke, Holyk has since said, was "excited." And so, apparently, was Holyk after he had heard what Darke had to say, because he immediately set in motion quite a corporate flap for a Sunday night. That same evening, Holyk called his superior, Richard D. Mollison, a Texas Gulf vice president who lived near Holyk in Greenwich, and—still the same evening—Mollison called *his* boss, Charles F. Fogarty, executive vice president and the company's No. 2 man, in nearby Rye, to pass Darke's report on up the line. Further reports were made the next day through the same labyrinth of command—Darke to Holyk to Mollison to Fogarty. As a result of them, Holyk, Mollison, and Fogarty all decided to go to Kidd-55 to see for themselves.

Holyk got there first; he arrived at Timmins on November 12th, checked in at the Bon Air Motel, and got out to Kidd-55 by jeep and muskeg tractor in time to see the completion of the drill hole and to help Darke visually estimate and log the core. By this time the weather, which had hitherto been passable for Timmins in mid-November, had turned nasty. In fact, it was "quite inclement," Holyk, a Canadian in his forties with a doctorate in geology from Massachusetts Institute of Technology, has since said. "It was cold, windy, threatening snow and rain, and . . . we were much more concerned with personal comfort than we were with the details of the core hole. Ken Darke was writing, and I was looking at the core, trying to make estimates of the mineral content." To add to the difficulty of working outdoors under such conditions, some of the core had come out of the ground covered with dirt and grease, and had to be washed with gasoline before its contents could even be guessed at. Despite all difficulties, Holyk succeeded in making an appraisal of the core that was, to say the least, startling. Over the six hundred or so feet of its final length, he estimated, there appeared to be an average copper content of 1.15% and an average zinc content of 8.64%. A Canadian stockbroker with special knowledge of the mining industry was to say later that a drill core of such length and such mineral content "is just beyond your wildest imagination."

Texas Gulf didn't have a surefire mine yet; there was always the possibility that the mineral vein was a long, thin one, too limited to be commercially exploitable, and that by a fantastic chance the drill had happened to go "down dip"—that is, straight into the vein like a sword into a sheath. What was needed was a pattern of several drill holes, beginning at different spots on the surface and entering the earth at different angles, to establish the shape and limits of the deposit. And such a pattern could not be made until Texas Gulf had title to the other three quarter-segments of Kidd-55. Getting title would take time if it were possible at all, but meanwhile, there were several steps that the company could and did take. The drill rig was moved away from the site of the test hole. Cut saplings were stuck in the ground around the hole, to restore the appearance of the place to a semblance of its natural state. A second test hole was drilled, as ostentatiously as possible, some distance away, at a place where a barren core was expected—and found. All of these camouflage measures, which were in conformity with long-established practice among miners who suspect that they have made a strike, were supplemented by an order from Texas Gulf's president, Claude O. Stephens, that no one outside the actual exploration group, even within the company, should be told what had been found. Late in November, the core was shipped off, in sections, to the Union Assay Office in Salt Lake City for scientific analysis of its contents. And meanwhile, of course, Texas Gulf began discreetly putting out feelers for the purchase of the rest of Kidd-55.

And meanwhile other measures, which may or may not have been related to the events north of Timmins, were being taken. On November 12th, Fogarty bought three hundred shares of Texas Gulf stock; on the 15th he added seven hundred more shares, on November 19th five hundred more, and on November 26th two hundred more. Clayton bought two hundred on the 15th, Mollison one hundred on the same day; and Mrs. Holyk bought fifty on the 29th and one hundred more on December 10th. But these purchases, as things turned out, were only the harbingers of a period of apparently intense affection for Texas Gulf stock among certain of its officers and employees, and even some of their friends. In mid-December, the report on the core came back from Salt Lake City, and it showed that Holyk's rough-and-ready estimate had been amazingly accurate; the copper and zinc contents were found to be almost exactly what he had said, and there were 3.94 ounces of silver per ton thrown in as a sort of bonus. Late in December, Darke made a trip to Washington, D.C. and vicinity, where he recommended Texas Gulf stock to a girl he knew there and her mother; these two, who came to be designated in the trial as the "tippees," subsequently passed along the recommendation to two other persons who, logically enough, thereby became the "sub-tippees." Between December 30th and the following February 17th, Darke's tippees and sub-tippees purchased all told 2,100 shares of Texas Gulf stock, and in addition they purchased what are known in the brokerage trade as "calls" on 1,500 additional shares. A call is an option to buy a stated amount of a certain stock at a fixed price—generally near the current market price—at any time during a stated period. Calls on most listed stocks are always on sale by dealers who specialize in them. The purchaser pays a generally rather moderate sum for his option; if the stock then goes up during the stated period, the rise can easily be converted into almost pure profit for him, while if the stock stays put or goes down, he simply tears up his call the way a horseplayer tears up a losing ticket, and loses nothing but the cost of the call. Therefore calls provide the cheapest possible way of gambling on the stock market, and the most convenient way of converting inside information into cash.

Back in Timmins, Darke, put temporarily out of business as a geologist by the winter freeze and the land-ownership problem at Kidd-55, seems to have managed to keep time from hanging heavy on his hands. In January, he entered into a private partnership with another Timmins man who wasn't a Texas Gulf employee to stake and claim Crown lands around Timmins for their own benefit. In February, he told Holyk of a barroom conversation that had occurred in Timmins one gelid winter evening, in which an acquaintance of his had let fall that he'd heard rumors of a Texas Gulf strike nearby and was therefore going to stake a few claims of his own. Horrified, Holyk, as he recalled later, told Darke to reverse the previous policy of avoiding Kidd-55 like the plague, and to "go right into the . . . area and stake all the claims we need;" also to "steer away this acquaintance. Give him a helicopter ride or anything, just get him out of the way." Darke presumably complied with this order. Moreover, during the first three months of 1964 he bought three hundred shares of Texas Gulf outright, bought calls on three thousand more shares, and added several more persons, one of them his brother, to his growing list of tippees. Holyk and Clayton were somewhat less financially active during the same period, but they did add substantially to their Texas Gulf holdings— in the case of Holyk and his wife, particularly through the use of calls, which they'd scarcely even heard of before, but which were getting to be quite the rage in Texas Gulf circles.

Signs of spring began to come at last, and with them came a triumphant conclusion to the company's land acquisition program. By March 27th, Texas Gulf had pretty much what it needed; that is, it had either clear title or mineral rights to the three remaining segments of Kidd-55, except for ten-per-cent profit concessions on two of the segments, the stubborn owner of the concession in one case being the Curtis Publishing Company. After a final burst of purchases by Darke, his tippees, and his sub-tippees on March 30th and 31st (among them all, six hundred shares and calls on 5,100 more shares for the two days), drilling was resumed in the still-frozen muskeg at Kidd-55, with Holyk and Darke both on the site this time. The new hole—the third in all, but only the second operational one, since one of the two drilled in November had been the dummy intended to create a diversion—was begun at a point some distance from the first and at an oblique angle to it, to advance the bracketing process. Observing and logging the core as it came out of the ground, Holyk found that he could scarcely hold a pencil because of the cold; but he must have been warmed inwardly by the fact that promising mineralization began to appear after the first hundred feet. He made his first progress report to Fogarty by telephone on April 1st. Now a gruelling daily routine was adopted at Timmins and Kidd-55. The actual drilling crew stayed at the site continuously, while the geologists, in order to keep their superiors in New York posted, had to make frequent trips to telephones in Timmins, and what with the seven-foot snowdrifts along the way the fifteen-mile trek between the town and the drilling camp customarily took three and a half to four hours. One after another, new drill holes, begun at different places around the anomaly and pitched at different angles to it, were plunged into the earth. At first, only one drill rig could be used at a time because of a shortage of water, which was necessary to the operation; the ground was frozen solid and covered by deep snow, and water had to be laboriously pumped from under the ice on a pond about a half mile from Kidd-55. The third hole was finished on April 7th, and a fourth immediately begun with the same rig; the following day, the water shortage having eased somewhat, a fifth hole was inaugurated with a second drill rig, and two days after that—on the 10th—a third rig was pressed into service to drill still another hole. All in all, during the first days of April the principals in the affair were kept busy; in fact, during that period their buying of calls on Texas Gulf seems to have come to a standstill.

Bit by bit the drilling revealed the lineaments of a huge ore deposit; the third hole established that the original one had not gone "down dip" as had been feared, the fourth established that the mineral vein was a satisfactorily deep one, and so on. At some point—the exact point was to become a matter of dispute—Texas Gulf came to know that it had a workable mine of considerable proportions, and as this point approached, the focus of attention shifted from drillers and geologists to staff men and financiers, who were to be the principal object of the S.E.C.'s disapproval later on. At Timmins, snow fell so heavily on April 8th and most of the 9th that not even the geologists could get from the town to Kidd-55, but toward evening on the 9th, when they finally made it after a hair-raising journey of seven and a half hours, with them was no lesser light than Vice President Mollison, who had turned up in Timmins the previous day. Mollison spent the night at the drill site and left at about noon the next day—in order, he explained later, to avoid the outdoorsmen's lunch they served at Kidd-55 which was too hearty for a deskbound man like him. But before going he issued instructions for the drilling of a mill test hole, which would produce a relatively large core that could be used to determine the amenability of the mineral material to routine mill processing. Normally, a mill test hole is not drilled until a workable mine is believed to exist. And so it may have been in this case; two S.E.C. mining experts were to insist later, against contrary opinions of experts for the defense, that by the time Mollison gave his order, Texas Gulf had information on the basis of which it could have calculated that the ore reserves at Kidd-55 had a gross assay value of at least two hundred million dollars.

The famous Canadian mining grapevine was humming by now, and in retrospect the wonder is that it had been relatively quiet for so long. (A Toronto broker was to remark during the trial, "I have seen drillers drop the goddam drill and beat it for a brokerage office as fast as they can . . . [or else] they pick up the telephone and call Toronto." After such a call, the broker went on, the status of every Bay Street penny-stock tout depends, for a time, on how close a personal acquaintance he can claim with the driller who made the strike, just as a racetrack tout's status depends sometimes on the degree of intimacy he can claim with a jockey or a horse.) "The moccasin telegraph has Texas Gulf's activity centered in Kidd Township. A battery of drills are reported to be at work," said *The Northern Miner*, a Toronto weekly of immense influence in the mining-stock set, on the 9th, and the same day the Toronto *Daily Star* declared that Timmins was "bug-eyed with excitement" and that "the magic word on every street corner and in every barber shop is Texas Gulf." The phones in Texas Gulf's New York headquarters were buzzing with frenzied queries, which the officers coldly turned aside. On the 10th, President Stephens was concerned enough about the rumors to seek counsel from one of his most trusted associates—Thomas S. Lamont, senior member of the Texas Gulf board of directors, former second-generation Morgan partner, holder of various lofty offices, past and present, in the Morgan Guaranty Trust Company, and bearer of a name that had long been one to conjure with in Wall Street. Stephens told Lamont what had been going on north of Timmins (it was the first Lamont had heard of it), made it clear that he himself did not yet feel that the evidence justified bug eyes, and asked what Lamont thought ought to be done about the exaggerated reports. As long as they stayed in the Canadian press, Lamont replied, "I think you might be able to live with them." However, he added, if they should get into the papers in the United States, it might be well to give the press an announcement that would set the record straight and avoid undue gyrations in the stock market.

The following day, Saturday the 11th, the reports reached the United States papers with a bang. The *Times* and *Herald Tribune* both ran accounts on the Texas Gulf discovery, and the latter, putting its story on the front page, spoke of "the biggest ore strike since gold was discovered more than sixty years ago in Canada." After reading these stories, perhaps with eyes bugging slightly, Stephens notified Fogarty that a press release should be issued in time for Monday's papers, and over the weekend Fogarty, with the help of several other company officials, worked one up. Meanwhile, things were not standing still at Kidd-55; on the contrary, later testimony held that on Saturday and Sunday, as more and more core came up from the drill holes full of copper and zinc ore, the calculable value of the mine was increasing almost hour by hour. However, Fogarty did not communicate with Timmins after Friday night, so the statement that he and his colleagues issued to the press on Sunday afternoon was not based on the most up-to-the-minute information. Whether because of that or for some other reason, the statement did not convey the idea that Texas Gulf thought it had a new Comstock Lode. Characterizing the published reports as exaggerated and unreliable, it admitted only that recent drilling on "one property near Timmins" had led to "preliminary indications that more drilling would be required for proper evaluation of the prospect;" went on to say that "the drilling done to date has not been conclusive;" and then, putting the same thought in what can hardly be called another way, added that "the work done to date has not been sufficient to reach definite conclusions."

The idea thus couched, or perhaps one should say bedded down, evidently came across to the public when it appeared in Monday morning's newspapers, because Texas Gulf stock was not nearly so buoyant early that week as it might have been expected to be if the enthusiastic *Times* and *Herald Tribune* stories had gone unchallenged. The stock, which had been selling at around 17 or 18 the previous November and had crept up over the intervening months to around 30, opened Monday on the New York Stock Exchange at 32—a rise of nearly two points over Friday's closing—only to reverse direction and sink to 30⅞ before the day's trading, was over, and to slip off still further on the following two days and at one point on Wednesday touch a low of 28⅞. Evidently, investors and traders had been considerably impressed by Texas Gulf's Sunday mood of deprecation. But on those same three days,

Texas Gulf people in both Canada and New York seem to have been in quite another mood. At Kidd-55 on Monday the 13th, the day the low-keyed press release was reported in newspapers, the mill test hole was completed, drills continued to grind away on three regular test holes, and a reporter for *The Northern Miner* was shown around and briefed on the findings by Mollison, Holyk, and Darke. The things they told the reporter make it clear, in retrospect, that whatever the drafters of the release may have believed on Sunday, the men at Kidd-55 knew on Monday that they had a mine and a big one. However, the world was not to know it, or at least not from that source, until Thursday morning, when the next issue of the *Miner* would appear in subscribers' mail and on newsstands.

Tuesday evening, Mollison and Holyk flew to Montreal, where they were planning to attend the annual convention of the Canadian Institute of Mining and Metallurgy, a gathering of several hundred leading mining and investment people. Upon arriving at the Queen Elizabeth Hotel where the convention was in progress, Mollison and Holyk were startled to find themselves greeted like film stars. The place had evidently been humming all day with rumors of a Texas Gulf discovery and everyone wanted to be the first to get the firsthand lowdown on it; in fact, a battery of television cameras had been set up for the express purpose of covering such remarks as the emissaries from Timmins might want to make. Not being authorized to make *any* remarks, Mollison and Holyk turned abruptly on their heels and fled the Queen Elizabeth, holing up for the night in a Montreal airport motel. The following day, Wednesday the 15th, they flew from Montreal to Toronto in the company, by prearrangement, of the Minister of Mines of the Province of Ontario and his deputy; en route they briefed the minister on the Kidd-55 situation, whereupon the minister declared that he wanted to clear the air by making a public announcement on the matter as soon as possible, and then, with Mollison's help, he drafted such an announcement. According to a copy that Mollison made and kept, the announcement stated, in part, that "the information now in hand . . . gives the company confidence to allow me to announce that Texas Gulf Sulphur has a mineable body of zinc, copper, and silver ore of substantial dimensions that will be developed and brought to production as soon as possible." Mollison and Holyk were given to believe that the minister would make his statement in Toronto at eleven o'clock that evening, over radio and television, and that thus Texas Gulf's good news would become public property a few hours before *The Northern Miner* appeared early the next day. But for reasons that have never been given, the minister didn't make the announcement that evening.

At Texas Gulf headquarters, at 200 Park Avenue, there was a similar air of mounting crisis. The company happened to have a regular monthly board-of-directors meeting scheduled for Thursday morning, and on Monday Francis G. Coates, a director who lived in Houston, Texas, and who hadn't heard of the Kidd-55 strike, telephoned Stephens to inquire whether he ought to bother to come. Stephens said he ought, but didn't explain why. Better and better news kept filtering in from the drill site, and some time on Wednesday, the Texas Gulf officers decided that it was time to write a new press release, to be issued at a press conference that would follow the Thursday-morning directors' meeting. Stephens, Fogarty, and David M. Crawford, the company's secretary, composed the release that afternoon. This time around, the release was based on the very latest information, and moreover, its language was happily devoid of both repetition and equivocation. It read, in part, "Texas Gulf Sulphur Company has made a major strike of zinc, copper, and silver in the Timmins area . . . Seven drill holes are now essentially complete and indicate an ore body of at least 800 feet in length, 300 feet in width, and having a vertical depth of more than 800 feet. This is a major discovery. The preliminary data indicate a reserve of more than 25 million tons of ore." As to the striking difference between this release and the one of three days earlier, the new one stated that "considerably more data has been accumulated" in the interim. And no one could deny this; a reserve of more than twenty-five million tons of ore meant that the value of the ore was not the two hundred million dollars that was alleged to have been calculable a week earlier, but many times that much.

In the course of the same hectic day in New York, the engineer Clayton and the company secretary Crawford found time to call their brokers and order themselves some Texas Gulf stock—two hundred shares in Clayton's case, three hundred in Crawford's. And Crawford soon decided that he hadn't plunged deeply enough; shortly after eight o'clock the next morning, after an apparently preoccupied night at the Park Lane Hotel, he awakened his broker with a second call and doubled his order.

On Thursday morning, the first hard news of the Timmins strike spread through the North American investment world, rapidly but erratically. Between seven and eight o'clock, mailmen and newsstands in Toronto began distributing copies of *The Northern-Miner* containing the piece by the reporter who had visited Kidd-55, in which he described the strike with a good deal of mining jargon but did not omit to call it, in language comprehensible enough for anyone, "a brilliant exploration success" and "a major new zinc-copper-silver mine." At about the same time, the *Miner* was on its way out to subscribers south of the border in Detroit and Buffalo, and a few hundred newsstand copies appear to have arrived in New York between nine and ten o'clock. The paper's physical appearance here, however, was preceded by telephone reports on its contents from Toronto, and by about 9:15 the news that Texas Gulf had hit it big for sure was the talk of

New York brokerage offices. A customer's man in the Sixtieth Street office of E. F. Hutton & Company complained later that his broker cronies had been so eager to natter on the telephone about Texas Gulf early that morning as to substantially prevent him from communicating with his customers; however, he did manage to squeeze in a call to two of them, a husband and wife for whom he was able to turn a rather quick profit in Texas Gulf—to be exact, a profit of $10,500 in less than an hour. ("It is clear that we are all in the wrong business," Judge Bonsal was to comment when he heard this. Or as the late Wieland Wagner once remarked in another context, "I shall be quite explicit. Valhalla is Wall Street.") At the Stock Exchange itself early that day, the traders in the Luncheon Club, which before the ten-o'clock opening serves as a breakfast club, were all munching on the Texas Gulf situation along with their toast and eggs.

At the directors' meeting at 200 Park, which began promptly at nine, the directors were shown the new statement that was shortly to be released to the press, and Stephens, Fogarty, Holyk, and Mollison, as representatives of the exploration group, commented in turn on the Timmins discovery. Stephens also stated that the Ontario Minister of Mines had announced it publicly in Toronto the previous evening (a misstatement, of course, although an unintentional one; actually, the minister was making his announcement to the Ontario Parliament press gallery in Toronto at almost the same moment Stephens was speaking). The directors' meeting ended at about ten o'clock, whereupon a clutch of reporters—twenty-two of them, representing many of the major United States newspapers and magazines, general and financial—trooped into the board room for the press conference, the Texas Gulf directors all remaining in their places. Stephens distributed copies of the press release to the reporters and then, in fulfillment of a curious ritual that governs such affairs, read it aloud. While he was engaged in this redundant recital various reporters began to drift away ("they began sort of leaking out of the room" was the way Lamont put it later) to telephone the sensational news to their publications; still more of them slipped away during the events that subsequently rounded out the press conference—the showing of some innocuous colored slides of the countryside around Timmins, and an exhibition and explanation by Holyk of some drill cores—and by the time it ended, at around 10:15, only a handful of reporters were left. This certainly didn't mean that the affair had been a flop. On the contrary, a press conference is perhaps the only kind of show whose success is in direct proportion to the number of people who leave before it is over.

The actions of two of the Texas Gulf directors, Coates and Lamont, during the next half hour or so were to give rise to the most controversial part of the S.E.C.'s complaint, and, since the controversy has now been inscribed in the law, those actions are likely to be studied for at least a generation by inside stock traders seeking guidance as to what they must do to be saved, or at least to avoid being damned. The essence of the controversy was timing, and in particular, the timing of Coates' and Lamont's maneuvers in relation to that of the dissemination of the Texas Gulf news by the Dow Jones News Service, the familiar spot-news facility for investors. Few investment offices in the United States are without the service, and its prestige is such that in some investment circles the moment a piece of news becomes public is considered to be determined by the moment it crosses the broad tape. As to the morning of April 16th, 1964, a Dow Jones reporter was not only among those at the Texas Gulf press conference but was among those who left early to telephone the news to his office. According to his recollection, the reporter made his call between 10:10 and 10:15, and normally an item of such importance as the one he sent would begin to be printed out by Dow Jones machines in offices from coast to coast within two or three minutes after being telephoned in. In fact, though, the Texas Gulf story did not begin to appear until 10:54, an entirely inexplicable forty-odd minutes later. The mystery of the broad tape message, like the mystery of the Minister of Mines' announcement, was left unraveled in the trial on grounds of irrelevance; an engaging aspect of the rules of evidence is their tendency to leave a few things to the imagination.

Coates, the Texan, was the first director to embark upon what he can hardly have thought of at the time as a historically significant course. Either before or immediately after the end of the press conference he went into an office adjoining the board room, where he borrowed a telephone and called his son-in-law, H. Fred Haemisegger, who is a stockbroker in Houston. Coates, as he related later, told Haemisegger of the Texas Gulf discovery and added that he had waited to call until "after the public announcement" because he was "too old to get into trouble with the S.E.C." He then placed an order for two thousand shares of Texas Gulf stock for four family trusts of which he was a trustee, though not personally a beneficiary. The stock, which had opened on the Stock Exchange some twenty minutes earlier at a fraction above 30 in very active but by no means decisively bullish trading, was now rapidly on its way up, but by acting quickly Haemisegger managed to buy the block for Coates at between 31 and 31⅝, getting his orders in to his firm's floor broker well before the unaccountably delayed news began to come out on the broad tape.

Lamont, in the Wall Street tradition of plungers rather than the Texas one, made his move with decision but with an elegant, almost languorous lack of hurry. Instead of leaving the board room at the conclusion of the press conference, he stayed there for some twenty minutes, not doing much of anything. "I milled around . . . and listened to some of them chatter and talk with each other, and slapped people on the back," he recounted later. Then, at 10:39 or 10:40, he went to a nearby office and telephoned a colleague and friend of his at the Morgan Guaranty Trust Company—Longstreet Hinton, the bank's executive vice president and the head of its trust department. Earlier in the week Hinton had asked Lamont if he, as a Texas Gulf director, could shed any light on the rumors of an ore discovery that were appearing in the press, and Lamont had replied that he couldn't. Now Lamont, as he recalled later, told Hinton "that there was news which had come out, or was shortly coming out, on the ticker, which would be of interest to him, regarding Texas Gulf Sulphur." "Is it good?" Hinton asked, and Lamont replied that it was "pretty good" or "very good." (Neither man is sure which he said, but it doesn't matter, since in New York bankerese "pretty good" *means* "very good.") In any case, Hinton did not follow the advice to look at the Dow Jones ticker, even though a machine was ticking twenty feet from his office; instead, he immediately called the bank's trading department and asked for a market quotation on Texas Gulf. After getting it, he placed an order to buy 3,000 shares for the account of the Nassau Hospital, of which he was treasurer. All this occupied no more than two minutes from the time Lamont had left the press conference. The order had been transmitted from the bank to the Stock Exchange and executed, and Nassau Hospital had its stock, before Hinton would have seen anything about Texas Gulf on the broad tape if he had been looking at it. But he was not looking at it; he was otherwise occupied. After placing the Nassau Hospital order, he went to the office of the Morgan Guaranty officer in charge of pension trusts and suggested that *he* buy some Texas Gulf for the trusts. In a matter of less than a half an hour, the bank had ordered 7,000 shares for its pension fund and profit-sharing account—two thousand of them before the announcement had begun to appear on the broad tape, and the rest either while it was appearing or within a few minutes afterward.

A bit more than an hour after that—at 12:33 p.m.—Lamont bought 3,000 shares for himself and members of his family, this time having to pay 34½ for them, since Texas Gulf by that time was on its way up for fair. As it was to continue to be for days, months, and years. It closed that afternoon at 36⅜, it reached a high of 58⅜ later that month, and by the end of 1966, when commercial production of ore was at last under way at Kidd-55 and the enormous new mine was expected to account for one-tenth of Canada's total annual production of copper and one-quarter of its total annual production of zinc, the stock was selling at over 100. Anyone who had bought Texas Gulf between November 12th, 1963 and the morning (or even the lunch hour) of April 16th, 1964 had therefore at least tripled his money.

Perhaps the most arresting aspect of the Texas Gulf trial—apart from the fact that a trial was taking place at all—was the vividness and variety of the defendants who came before Judge Bonsal, ranging as they did from a hot-eyed mining prospector like Clayton (a genuine Welchman with a degree in mining from the University of Cardiff) through vigorous and harried corporate nabobs like Fogarty and Stephens to a Texas wheeler-dealer like Coates and a polished Brahmin of finance like Lamont. (Darke, who had left Texas Gulf's employ soon after April, 1964 to become a private investor—which may or may not indicate that he had become a man of independent means—declined to appear at the trial on the ground that his Canadian nationality put him beyond the reach of subpoena by a United States court, and the S.E.C. grieved loudly over this refusal; defense counsel, however, scornfully insisted that the S.E.C. was really delighted to have Darke absent, thus allowing plaintiff to paint him as Mephistopheles hiding in the wings.) The S.E.C, after its counsel, Frank E. Kennamer Jr., had announced his intention to "drag to light and pillory the misconduct of these defendants," asked the court to issue a permanent injunction forbidding Fogarty, Mollison, Clayton, Holyk, Darke, Crawford, and several other corporate insiders who had bought stock or calls between November 8th, 1963 and April 15th, 1964, from ever again "engaging in any act . . . which operates or would operate as a fraud or deceit upon any person in connection with purchase or sale of securities"; further—and here it was breaking entirely new ground—it prayed that the Court order the defendants to make restitution to the persons they had allegedly defrauded by buying stock or calls from them on the basis of inside information. The S.E.C. also charged that the pessimistic April 12th press release was deliberately deceptive, and asked that because of it Texas Gulf be enjoined from "making any untrue statement of material fact or omitting to state a material fact." Apart from any question of loss of corporate face, the nub of the matter here lay in the fact that such a judgment, if granted, might well open the way for legal action against the company by *any* stockholder who had sold his Texas Gulf stock to *anybody* in the interim between the first press release and the second one, and since the shares that had changed hands during that period had run into the millions, it was a nub indeed.

Apart from legal technicalities, counsel based its defense of the early insider stock purchases chiefly on the argument that the information yielded by the first drill hole in November had made the prospect of a workable mine not a sure thing but only a sporting proposition, and to buttress this argument, it paraded before the judge a platoon of mining experts who testified as to the notorious fickleness of first drill holes, some of the witnesses going so far as to say that the hole might very well have turned out to be not an asset but a liability to Texas Gulf. The people who had bought stock or calls during the winter insisted that the drill hole had had little or nothing to do with their decision—they had been motivated simply by the feeling that Texas Gulf was a good investment at that juncture on general principles; and Clayton attributed

his abrupt appearance as a substantial investor to the fact that
he had just married a well-to-do wife. The S.E.C. countered
with its own parade of experts, maintaining that the nature of
the first core had been such as to make the existence of a rich
mine an overwhelming probability, and that therefore those
privy to the facts about it had possessed a material fact. As the
S.E.C. put it saltily in a post-trial brief, "the argument that the
defendants were free to purchase the stock until the existence
of a mine had been established beyond doubt is equivalent
to saying that there is no unfairness in betting on a horse
entered in a race, knowing that the animal has received an
illegal stimulant, because in the homestretch the horse might
drop dead." Defense counsel declined to be drawn into argument on the equine analogy. As to the pessimistic April 12th
release, the S.E.C. made much of the fact that Fogarty, its chief
drafter, had based it on information that was almost forty-
eight hours old when it was issued, despite the fact that communications between Kidd-55, Timmins, and New York were
relatively good at the time, and expressed the view that "the
most indulgent explanation for his strange conduct is that Dr.
Fogarty simply did not care whether he gave the shareholders
of Texas Gulf and the public a discouraging statement based
on stale information." Brushing aside the question of stale-
ness, the defense asserted that the release "accurately stated
the status of the drilling in the opinion of Stephens, Fogarty,
Mollison, Holyk, and Clayton," that "the problem presented
was obviously one of judgment," and that the company had
been in a particularly difficult and sensitive position in that
if it had, instead, issued an overly optimistic report that had
later proved to have been based on false hopes, it could just
as well have then been accused of fraud for that.

Weighing the crucial question of whether the information
obtained from the first drill hole had been "material," Judge
Bonsal concluded that the definition of materiality in such
instances must be a conservative one. There was, he pointed

out, a question of public policy involved: "It is important under our free-enterprise system that insiders, including directors, officers, and employees, be encouraged to own securities of their company. The incentive that comes with stock ownership benefits both the company and the stockholders." Keeping his definition conservative, he decided that up until the evening of April 9th, when three converging drill holes positively established the three-dimensionality of the ore deposit, material information had not been in hand, and the decisions of the insiders to buy Texas Gulf stock before that date, even if based on the drilling results, were no more than perfectly sporting, and legal, "educated guesses." (A newspaper columnist who disagreed with the judge's finding was to remark that the guesses had been so educated as to qualify for *summa cum laude*.) In the case of Darke, the judge found that the spate of stock purchases by his tippees and sub-tippees on the last days of March seemed highly likely to have been instigated by word from Darke that drilling at Kidd-55 was about to be resumed; but even here, according to Judge Bonsal's logic, material information did not yet exist and therefore could neither be acted upon nor passed along to others.

Case was therefore dismissed against all educated guessers who had bought stock or calls, or made recommendations to tippees, before the evening of April 9th. With Clayton and Crawford, who had been so injudicious as to buy or order stock on April 15th, it was another matter. The judge found no evidence that they had intended to deceive or defraud anyone, but they *had* made their purchases with the full knowledge that a great mine had been found and that it would be announced the next day—in short, with material private information in hand. Therefore they were found to have violated Rule 10B-5, and in due time would presumably be enjoined from doing such a thing again and made to offer restitution to the persons they bought their April 15th shares from—assuming, of course, that such persons can be found, the complexities of stock-exchange trading being such that it isn't always an easy matter to figure out exactly whom one has been dealing with on any particular transaction. The law in our time is, and probably ought to remain, almost unrealistically humanistic; in its eyes, corporations are people, stock exchanges are street-corner marketplaces where buyer and seller haggle face to face, and computers scarcely exist.

As for the April 12th press release, the judge found it in retrospect "gloomy" and "incomplete," but he acknowledged that its purpose had been the worthy one of correcting the exaggerated rumors that had been appearing and decided that the S.E.C. had failed to prove that it was false, misleading, or deceptive. Thus he dismissed the complaint that Texas Gulf had deliberately tried to confuse its stockholders and the public.

Up to this point, it was two wins against a whole string of losses for the S.E.C., and the right of a miner to drop his drill and run for a brokerage office appeared to have retained most of its sanctity, provided at least that his drill hole is the first of a series. But there remained to be settled the matter that, of all those contested in the case, was of the most consequence to stockholders, stock traders, and the national economy, as opposed to the members of corporate mining exploration groups. It was the matter of the April 16th activities of Coates and Lamont, and its importance lay in the fact that it turned on the question of precisely when, in the eyes of the law, a piece of information ceases to be inside and becomes public. The question had never before been subjected to anything like so exacting a test, so what came out of the Texas Gulf case would instantly become the legal authority on the subject until superseded by some even more refined case.

The basic position of the S.E.C. was that the stock purchases of Coates, and the circumspect tip given by Lamont to Hinton by telephone, were illegal use of inside information because they were accomplished before the announcement of the ore strike on the Dow Jones broad tape—an announcement that the S.E.C.'s lawyers kept referring to as the "official" one, although the Dow Jones service, much as it might like to, derives no such status from any authority other than custom. But the S.E.C. went further than that. Even if the two directors' telephone calls had been made after the "official" announcement, it contended, they would have been improper and illegal unless enough time had elapsed for the news to be thoroughly absorbed by members of the investing public not privileged to attend the press conference or even to be watching the broad tape at the right moment. Defense counsel saw things rather differently. In its view, far from being culpable regardless of whether or not they had acted before or after the broad tape announcement, its clients were innocent in either case. In the first place, the lawyers contended, Coates and Lamont had every reason to believe the news was out, since Stephens had said during the directors' meeting that it had been released by the Ontario Minister of Mines the previous evening, and therefore Coates and Lamont acted in good faith; in the second place, counsel went on, what with the buzzing in brokerage offices and the early-morning excitement at the Stock Exchange, to all intents and purposes the news really *was* out, via osmosis and *The Northern Miner*, considerably before it appeared on the ticker or before the mooted telephone calls were made. Lamont's lawyers argued that their client hadn't advised Hinton to buy Texas Gulf stock, anyhow; he'd merely advised him to look at the broad tape, an act as innocent to recommend as to perform, and what Hinton had done then had been entirely on his own hook. In sum, the lawyers for the two sides could agree on neither whether the rules had been violated nor what the rules actually were; indeed, it was one of the defense's contentions that the S.E.C. was asking the court to write new rules and then apply them retroactively, while the plaintiff insisted that he was merely asking that an old rule, 10B-5, be applied broadly, in the spirit of the Marquis of Queensberry. Near the end of the trial Lamont's lawyers, bearing down hard, created a courtroom sensation by introducing a surprise exhibit, a large, elaborate map of the United States dotted with colored flags, some blue, some red, some green, some gold, some silver—each flag, the lawyers announced, denoting a place where the Texas Gulf news had been disseminated before Lamont had acted or it had reached the broad tape. On questioning, it came out that all but eight of the flags represented offices of the brokerage firm of Merrill Lynch, Pierce, Fenner & Smith, on whose interoffice wire the news had been carried at 10:29; but while this revelation of the highly limited scope of the dissemination may have mitigated the legal force of the map, it apparently did not mitigate the esthetic impression on the judge. "Isn't that beautiful?" he exclaimed, while the S.E.C. men fumed in chagrin, and when one of the proud defense lawyers noticed a couple of locations on the map that had been overlooked and pointed out that there should really be even more flags, Judge Bonsal, still bemused, shook his head and said he was afraid that wouldn't work, since all known colors seemed to have been used already.

Lamont's fastidiousness in waiting until 12:33, almost two hours after his call to Hinton, before he bought stock for himself and his family left the S.E.C. unimpressed—and it was here that the Commission took its most avant-garde stand and asked the judge for a decision that would forge most fearlessly into the legal jungles of the future. As the stand was set forth in the S.E.C. briefs, "It is the Commission's position that even after corporate information has been published in the news media, insiders, are still under a duty to refrain from securities transactions until there had elapsed a reasonable amount of time in which the securities industry, the shareholders, and the investing public can evaluate the development and make informed investment decisions . . . Insiders must wait at least until the information is likely to have reached the average investor who follows the market and he has had some opportunity to consider it." In the Texas Gulf case, the S.E.C. argued, one hour and thirty-nine minutes after the start of the broad-tape transmission was not long enough for that evaluation, as evidenced by the fact that the enormous rise in the price of Texas Gulf stock had hardly more than started by that time, and therefore Lamont's 12:33 purchases had violated the Securities Exchange Act. What, then, did the S.E.C. think *would* be "a reasonable amount of time"? That would "vary from case to case," the S.E.C.'s counsel Kennamer said in his summation, according to the nature of the inside information; for example, word of a dividend cut would probably percolate through the dullest investor's brain in a very short time, while a piece of news as unusual and abstruse as Texas Gulf's might take days, or even longer. It would, Kennamer said, be "a nearly impossible task to formulate a rigid set of rules that would apply in all situations of this sort." Therefore, in the S.E.C.'s canon, the only way an insider could find out whether he had waited long enough before buying his company's stock was by being haled into court and seeing what the judge would decide.

Lamont's counsel, led by S. Hazard Gillespie, went after this stand with the same zeal, if not actually glee, that had marked its foray into cartography. First, Gillespie said, the S.E.C. had contended that Coates' call to Haemisegger and Lamont's to Hinton had been wrong because they had been made before the broadtape announcement; then it had said that Lamont's later stock purchase had been wrong because it had been made *after* the announcement, but not long enough after. If these apparently opposite courses of action were both fraud, what was right conduct? The S.E.C. seemed to want to have the rules made up as it went along—or, rather, to have the courts make them up. As Gillespie put the matter more formally, the S.E.C. was "asking the court to write . . . a rule judicially and to apply it retroactively to adjudicate Mr.

Lamont guilty of fraud because of conduct which he reasonably believed to be entirely proper."

It wouldn't stand up, Judge Bonsal agreed—and for that matter, neither would the S.E.C.'s contention that the time of the broad-tape transmission had been the time when the news had become public. He took the narrower view that, based on legal precedent, the controlling moment had been the one when the press release had been read and handed to the reporters, even though hardly any outsider—that is, hardly anybody at all—had known of it for some time afterward. Clearly troubled by the implications of this finding, Judge Bonsal added that "it may be, as the Commission contends, that a more effective rule should be established to preclude insiders from acting on information after it has been announced but before it has been absorbed by the public." But he didn't think it was up to him to write such a rule. Nor did he think it was up to him to determine whether or not Lamont had waited long enough before placing his 12:33 order. If it were left to judges to make such determinations, he said, "this could only lead to uncertainty. A decision in one case would not control another case with different facts. No insider would know whether he had waited long enough . . . If a waiting period is to be fixed, this could be most appropriately done by the Commission." No one would bell the cat, and the complaints against Coates and Lamont were dismissed.

The S.E.C. appealed all the dismissals, and Clayton and Crawford, the only two defendants found to have violated the Securities Exchange Act, appealed the judgments against them. In its appeal brief the Commission painstakingly reviewed the evidence and suggested to the Circuit Court that Judge Bonsal had erred in his interpretation of it, while the defense brief for Clayton and Crawford concentrated on the possibly detrimental effects of the doctrine implied in the finding against them. Might not the doctrine mean, for example, that every security analyst who does his best to ferret out little-known facts about a particular company, and then recommends that company's stock to his customers as he is paid to do, could be adjudged an insider improperly distributing tips precisely because of his diligence? Might it not tend to "stifle investment by corporate personnel and impede the flow of corporate information to investors"?

Perhaps so. At all events, in August, 1968, the U.S. Court of Appeals for the Second Circuit handed down a decision which flatly reversed Judge Bonsal's findings on just about every score except the findings against Crawford and Clayton, which were affirmed. The Appeals Court found that the original November drill hole *had* provided material evidence of a valuable ore deposit, and that therefore Fogarty, Mollison, Darke, Holyk, and all other insiders who had bought Texas Gulf stock or calls on it during the winter were guilty of violations of the law; that the gloomy April 12th press release had been ambiguous and perhaps misleading; and that Coates had improperly and illegally jumped the gun in placing his orders right after the April 16th press conference. Only Lamont—the charges against whom had been dropped following his death shortly after the lower court decision—and a Texas Gulf office manager, John Murray, remained exonerated.

The decision was a famous victory for the S.E.C., and the first reaction of Wall Street was to cry out that it would make for utter confusion. Pending further appeals to the Supreme Court, it would, at least, result in an interesting experiment. For the first time in the history of the world, the effort would have to be made, in Wall Street, to conduct a stock market without the use of a stacked deck.

5

XEROX XEROX XEROX XEROX

WHEN THE ORIGINAL MIMEOGRAPH MACHINE—the first mechanical duplicator of written pages that was practical for office use— was put on the market by the A. B. Dick Company, of Chicago, in 1887, it did not take the country by storm. On the contrary, Mr. Dick—a former lumberman who had become bored with copying his price lists by hand, had tried to invent a duplicating machine himself, and had finally obtained rights to produce the mimeograph from its inventor, Thomas Alva Edison—found himself faced with a formidable marketing problem. "People didn't *want* to make lots of copies of office documents," says his grandson C. Matthews Dick, Jr., currently a vice-president of the A. B. Dick Company, which now manufactures a whole line of office copiers and duplicators, including mimeograph machines. "By and large, the first users of the thing were non-business organizations like churches, schools, and Boy Scout troops. To attract companies and professional men, Grandfather and his associates had to undertake an enormous missionary effort. Office duplicating by machine was a new and unsettling idea that upset long-established office patterns. In 1887, after all, the typewriter had been on the market only a little over a decade and wasn't yet in widespread use, and neither was carbon paper. If a businessman or a lawyer wanted five copies of a document, he'd have a clerk make five copies—by hand. People would say to Grandfather, 'Why should I want to have a lot of copies of this and that lying around? Nothing but clutter in the office, a temptation to prying eyes, and a waste of good paper.'"

On another level, the troubles that the elder Mr. Dick encountered were perhaps connected with the generally bad repute that the notion of making copies of graphic material had been held in for a number of centuries—a bad repute reflected in the various overtones of the English noun and verb "copy." The Oxford English Dictionary makes it clear that during those centuries there was an aura of deceit associated with the word; indeed, from the late sixteenth century until Victorian times "copy" and "counterfeit" were nearly synonymous. (By the middle of the seventeenth century, the medieval use of the noun "copy" in the robust sense of "plenty" or "abundance" had faded out, leaving behind nothing but its adjective form, "copious.") "The only good copies are those which exhibit the defects of bad originals," La Rochefoucauld wrote in his "Maxims" in 1665. "Never buy a copy of a picture," Ruskin pronounced dogmatically in 1857, warning not against chicanery but against debasement. And the copying of written documents was often suspect, too. "Though the attested Copy of a Record be good proof, yet the Copy of a Copy never so well attested . . . will not be admitted as proof in Judicature," John Locke wrote in 1690. At about the same time, the printing trade contributed to the language the suggestive expression "foul copy," and it was a favorite Victorian habit to call one object, or person, a pale copy of another.

Practical necessity arising out of increasing industrialization was doubtless chiefly responsible for a twentieth-century reversal of these attitudes. In any case, office reproduction began to grow very rapidly. (It may seem paradoxical that this growth coincided with the rise of the telephone, but perhaps it isn't. All the evidence suggests that communication between people by whatever means, far from simply accomplishing its purpose, invariably breeds the need for more.) The typewriter and carbon paper came into common use after 1890, and mimeographing became a standard office procedure soon after 1900. "No office is complete without an Edison Mimeograph," the Dick Company felt able to boast in 1903. By that time, there were already about a hundred and fifty thousand of the devices in use; by 1910 there were probably over two hundred thousand, and by 1940 almost half a million. The offset printing press—a mettlesome competitor capable of producing work much handsomer than mimeographed output—was successfully adapted for office use in the nineteen-thirties and forties, and is now standard equipment in most large offices. As with the mimeograph machine, though, a special master page must be prepared before reproduction can start—a relatively expensive and time-consuming process—so the offset press is economically useful only when a substantial number of copies are wanted. In office-equipment jargon, the offset press and the mimeograph are "duplicators" rather than "copiers," the dividing line between duplicating and copying being generally drawn somewhere between ten and twenty copies. Where technology lagged longest was in the development of efficient and economical copiers. Various photographic devices that did not require the making of master pages—of which the most famous was (and still is) the Photostat—began appearing around 1910, but because of their high cost, slowness, and difficulty of operation, their usefulness was largely limited to the copying of architectural and engineering drawings and legal documents. Until after 1950, the only practical machine for making a copy of a business letter or a page of typescript was a typewriter with carbon paper in its platen.

The nineteen-fifties were the raw, pioneering years of mechanized office copying. Within a short time, there suddenly appeared on the market a whole batch of devices capable of reproducing most office papers without the use of a master page, at a cost of only a few cents per copy, and within a time span of a minute or less per copy. Their technology varied—Minnesota Mining & Manufacturing's Thermo-Fax, introduced in 1950, used heat-sensitive copying paper; American Photocopy's Dial-A-Matic Autostat (1952) was based on a refinement of ordinary photography; Eastman Kodak's Verifax (1953) used a method called dye transfer; and so on—but almost all of them, unlike Mr. Dick's mimeograph, immediately found a ready market, partly because they filled a genuine need and partly, it now seems clear, because they and their function exercised a powerful psychological fascination on their users. In a society that sociologists are forever characterizing as "mass," the notion of making one-of-a-kind things into many-of-a-kind things showed signs of becoming a real compulsion. However, all these pioneer copying machines had serious and frustrating inherent defects; for example, Autostat and Verifax were hard to operate and turned out damp copies that had to be dried, while Thermo-Fax copies tended to darken when exposed to too much heat, and all three could make copies only on special treated paper supplied by the manufacturer. What was needed for the compulsion to flower into a mania was a technological breakthrough, and the breakthrough came at the turn of the decade with the advent of a machine that worked on a new principle, known as xerography, and was able to make dry, good-quality, permanent copies on ordinary paper with a minimum of trouble. The effect was immediate. Largely as a result of xerography, the estimated number of copies (as opposed to duplicates) made annually in the United States sprang from some twenty million in the mid-fifties to nine and a half *billion* in 1964, and to fourteen billion in 1966—not to mention billions more in Europe, Asia, and Latin America. More than that, the attitude of educators toward printed textbooks and of business people toward written communication underwent a discernible change; avant-garde philosophers took to hailing xerography as a revolution comparable in importance to the invention of the wheel; and coin-operated copying machines began turning up in candy stores and beauty parlors. The mania—not as immediately disrupting as the tulip mania in seventeenth-century Holland but probably destined to be considerably farther-reaching—was in full swing.

The company responsible for the great breakthrough and the one on whose machines the majority of these billions of copies were made was, of course, the Xerox Corporation, of Rochester, New York. As a result, it became the most spectacular big-business success of the nineteen-sixties. In 1959, the year the company—then called Haloid Xerox, Inc.—introduced its first automatic xerographic office copier, its sales were thirty-three million dollars. In 1961, they were sixty-six million, in 1963 a hundred and seventy-six million, and in 1966 over half a billion. As Joseph C. Wilson, the chief executive of the firm, pointed out, this growth rate was such that if maintained for a couple of decades (which, perhaps fortunately for everyone, couldn't possibly happen), Xerox sales would be larger than the gross national product of the United States. Unplaced in *Fortune's* ranking of the five hundred largest American industrial companies in 1961, Xerox by 1964 had attained two-hundred-and-twenty-seventh place, and by 1967 it had climbed to hundred-and-twenty-sixth. *Fortune's* ranking is based on annual sales; according to certain other criteria, Xerox placed much higher than hundred-and-seventy-first. For example, early in 1966 it ranked about sixty-third in the country in net profits, probably ninth in ratio of profit to sales, and about fifteenth in terms of the market value of its stock—and in this last respect the young upstart was ahead of such long-established industrial giants as U.S. Steel, Chrysler, Procter & Gamble, and R.C.A. Indeed, the enthusiasm the investing public showed for Xerox made its shares the stock market Golconda of the sixties. Anyone who bought its stock toward the end of 1959 and held on to it until early 1967 would have found his holding worth about sixty-six times its original price, and anyone who was really fore-sighted and bought Haloid in 1955 would have seen his original investment grow—one might almost say miraculously—a hundred and eighty times. Not surprisingly, a covey of "Xerox millionaires" sprang up—several hundred of them all told, most of whom either lived in the Rochester area or had come from there.

The Haloid Company, started in Rochester in 1906, was the grandfather of Xerox, just as one of its founders—Joseph C. Wilson, a sometime pawnbroker and sometime mayor of Rochester—was the grandfather of his namesake, the 1946–1968 boss of Xerox. Haloid manufactured photographic papers, and, like all photographic companies—and especially those in Rochester—it lived in the giant shadow of its neighbor, Eastman Kodak. Even in this subdued light, though, it was effective enough to weather the Depression in modestly good shape. In the years immediately after the Second World War, however, both competition and labor costs increased, sending Haloid on a search for new products. One of the possibilities its scientists hit upon was a copying process that was being worked on at the Battelle Memorial Institute, a large non-profit industrial-research organization in Columbus, Ohio. At this point, the story flashes back to 1938 and a second-floor kitchen above a bar in Astoria, Queens, which was being used as a makeshift laboratory by an obscure thirty-two-year-old inventor named Chester F. Carlson. The son of a barber of Swedish extraction, and a graduate in physics of the California Institute of Technology, Carlson was employed in New York in the patent department of P. R. Mallory & Co., an Indianap-olis manufacturer of electrical and electronic components; in quest of fame, fortune, and independence, he was devoting his spare time to trying to invent an office copying machine, and to help him in this endeavor he had hired Otto Kornei, a German refugee physicist. The fruit of the two men's experiments was a process by which, on October 22, 1938, after using a good deal of clumsy equipment and producing considerable smoke and stench, they were able to transfer from one piece of paper to another the unheroic message "10–22–38 Astoria." The process, which Carlson called electrophotography, had—and has—five basic steps: sensitizing a photoconductive surface to light by giving it an electrostatic charge (for example, by rubbing it with fur); exposing this surface to a written page to form an electrostatic image; developing the latent image by dusting the surface with a powder that will adhere only to the charged areas; transferring the image to some sort of paper; and fixing the image by the application of heat. The steps, each of them in itself familiar enough in connection with other technologies, were utterly new in combination—so new, in fact, that the kings and captains of commerce were markedly slow to recognize the potentialities of the process. Applying the knowledge he had picked up in his job downtown, Carlson immediately wove a complicated net of patents around the invention (Kornei shortly left to take a job elsewhere, and thus vanished permanently from the electrophotographic scene) and set about trying to peddle it. Over the next five years, while continuing to work for Mallory, he pursued his moonlighting in a new form, offering rights to the process to every important office-equipment company in the country, only to be turned down every time. Finally, in 1944, Carlson persuaded Battelle Memorial Institute to undertake further development work on his process in exchange for three-quarters of any royalties that might accrue from its sale or license.

Here the flashback ends and xerography, as such, comes into being. By 1946, Battelle's work on the Carlson process had come to the attention of various people at Haloid, among them the younger Joseph C. Wilson, who was about to assume the presidency of the company. Wilson communicated his interest to a new friend of his—Sol M. Linowitz, a bright and vigorously public-spirited young lawyer, recently back from service in the Navy, who was then busy organizing a new Rochester radio station that would air liberal views as a counterbalance to the conservative views of the Gannett newspapers. Although Haloid had its own lawyers, Wilson, impressed with Linowitz, asked him to look into the Battelle thing as a "one-shot" job for the company. "We went to Columbus to see a piece of metal rubbed with cat's fur," Linowitz has since said. Out of that trip and others came an agreement giving Haloid rights to the Carlson process in exchange for royalties to Carlson and Battelle, and committing it to share with Battelle in the work and the costs of development. Everything else, it seemed, flowed from that agreement. In 1948, in search of a new name for the Carlson process, a Battelle man got together with a professor of classical languages at Ohio State University, and by combining two words from classical Greek they came up with "xerography," or "dry writing." Meanwhile, small teams of scientists at Battelle and Haloid, struggling to develop the process, were encountering baffling and unexpected technical problems one after another; at one point, indeed, the Haloid people became so discouraged that they considered selling most of their xerography rights to International Business Machines. But the deal was finally called off, and as the research went on and the bills for it mounted, Haloid's commitment to the process gradually became a do-or-die affair. In 1955, a new agreement was drawn up, under which Haloid took over full title to the Carlson patents and the full cost of the development project, in payment for which it issued huge bundles of Haloid shares to Battelle, which, in turn, issued a bundle or two to Carlson. The cost was staggering. Between 1947 and 1960,

Haloid spent about seventy-five million dollars on research in xerography, or about twice what it earned from its regular operations during that period; the balance was raised through borrowing and through the wholesale issuance of common stock to anyone who was kind, reckless, or prescient enough to take it. The University of Rochester, partly out of interest in a struggling local industry, bought an enormous quantity for its endowment fund at a price that subsequently, because of stock splits, amounted to fifty cents a share. "Please don't be mad at us if we find we have to sell our Haloid stock in a couple of years to cut our losses on it," a university official nervously warned Wilson. Wilson promised not to be mad. Meanwhile, he and other executives of the company took most of their pay in the form of stock, and some of them went as far as to put up their savings and the mortgages on their houses to help the cause along. (Prominent among the executives by this time was Linowitz, whose association with Haloid had turned out to be anything but a one-shot thing; instead, he became Wilson's right-hand man, taking charge of the company's crucial patent arrangements, organizing and guiding its international affiliations, and eventually serving for a time as chairman of its board of directors.) In 1958, after prayerful consideration, the company's name was changed to Haloid Xerox, even though no xerographic product of major importance was yet on the market. The trademark "XeroX" had been adopted by Haloid several years earlier—a shameless imitation of Eastman's "Kodak," as Wilson has admitted. The terminal "X" soon had to be downgraded to lower case, because it was found that nobody would bother to capitalize it, but the near-palindrome, at least as irresistible as Eastman's, remained. XeroX or Xerox, the trademark, Wilson has said, was adopted and retained against the vehement advice of many of the firm's consultants, who feared that the public would find it unpronounceable, or would think it denoted an anti-freeze, or would be put in mind of a word highly discouraging to financial ears—"zero."

Then, in 1960, the explosion came, and suddenly everything was reversed. Instead of worrying about whether its trade name would be successful, the company was worrying about its becoming *too* successful, for the new verb "to xerox" began to appear so frequently in conversation and in print that the company's proprietary rights in the name were threatened, and it had to embark on an elaborate campaign against such usage. (In 1961, the company went the whole hog and changed its name to plain Xerox Corporation.) And instead of worrying about the future of themselves and their families, the Xerox executives were worrying about their reputation with the friends and relatives whom they had prudently advised *not* to invest in the stock at twenty cents a share. In a word, everybody who held Xerox stock in quantity had got rich or richer—the executives who had scrimped and sacrificed, the University of Rochester, Battelle Memorial Institute, and even, of all people, Chester F. Carlson, who had come out of the various agreements with Xerox stock that at 1968 prices was worth many million dollars, putting him (according to *Fortune*) among the sixty-six richest people in the country.

Thus baldly outlined, the story of Xerox has an old-fashioned, even a nineteenth-century, ring—the lonely inventor in his crude laboratory, the small, family-oriented company, the initial setbacks, the reliance on the patent system, the resort to classical Greek for a trade name, the eventual triumph gloriously vindicating the free-enterprise system. But there is another dimension to Xerox. In the matter of demonstrating a sense of responsibility to society as a whole, rather than just to its stockholders, employees, and customers, it has shown itself to be the reverse of most nineteenth-century companies—to be, indeed, in the advance guard of twentieth-century companies. "To set high goals, to have almost unattainable aspirations, to imbue people with the belief that they can be achieved—these are as important as the balance sheet, perhaps more so," Wilson said once, and other Xerox executives have often gone out of their way to emphasize that "the Xerox spirit" is not so much a means to an end as a matter of emphasizing "human values" for their own sake. Such platform rhetoric is far from uncommon in big-business circles, of course, and when it comes from Xerox executives it is just as apt to arouse skepticism—or even, considering the company's huge profits, irritation. But there is evidence that Xerox means what it says. In 1965, the company donated $1,632,548 to educational and charitable institutions, and $2,246,000 in 1966; both years the biggest recipients were the University of Rochester and the Rochester Community Chest, and in each case the sum represented around one and a half per cent of the company's net income before taxes. This is markedly higher than the percentage that most large companies set aside for good works; to take a couple of examples from among those often cited for their liberality, R.C.A.'s contributions for 1965 amounted to about seven-tenths of one per cent of pre-tax income, and American Telephone & Telegraph's to considerably less than one per cent. That Xerox intended to persist in its high-minded ways was indicated by its commitment of itself in 1966 to the "one-per-cent program," often called the Cleveland Plan—a system inaugurated in that city under which local industries agree to give one per cent of pre-tax income annually to local educational institutions, apart from their other donations—so that if Xerox income continues to soar, the University of Rochester and its sister institutions in the area can face the future with a certain assurance.

In other matters, too, Xerox has taken risks for reasons that have nothing to do with profit. In a 1964 speech, Wilson said, "The corporation cannot refuse to take a stand on public issues of major concern"—a piece of business heresy if there ever was one, since taking a stand on a public issue is the obvious way of alienating customers and potential customers who take the opposite stand. The chief public stand that Xerox has taken is in favor of the United Nations—and, by implication, against its detractors. Early in 1964, the company decided to spend four million dollars—a year's advertising budget—on underwriting a series of network-television programs dealing with the U.N., the programs to be unaccompanied by commercials or any other identification of Xerox apart from a statement at the beginning and end of each that Xerox had paid for it. That July and August—some three months after the decision had been announced—Xerox suddenly received an avalanche of letters opposing the project and urging the company to abandon it. Numbering almost fifteen thousand, the letters ranged in tone from sweet reasonableness to strident and emotional denunciation. Many of them asserted that the U.N. was an instrument for depriving Americans of their Constitutional rights, that its charter had been written in part by American Communists, and that it was constantly being used to further Communist objectives, and a few letters, from company presidents, bluntly threatened to remove the Xerox machines from their offices unless the series was cancelled. Only a handful of the letter writers mentioned the John Birch Society, and none identified themselves as members of it, but circumstantial evidence suggested that the avalanche represented a carefully planned Birch campaign. For one thing, a recent Birch Society publication had urged that members write to Xerox to protest the U.N. series, pointing out that a flood of letters had succeeded in persuading a major airline to remove the U.N. insigne from its airplanes. Further evidence of a systematic campaign turned up when an analysis, made at Xerox's instigation, showed that the fifteen thousand letters had been written by only about four thousand persons. In any event, the Xerox offices and directors declined to be persuaded or intimidated; the U.N. series appeared on the American Broadcasting Company network in 1965, to plaudits all around. Wilson later maintained that the series—and the decision to ignore the protest against it—made Xerox many more friends than enemies. In all his public statements on the subject, he insisted on characterizing what many observers considered a rather rare stroke of business idealism, as simply sound business judgment.

In the fall of 1966, Xerox began encountering a measure of adversity for the first time since its introduction of xerography. By that time, there were more than forty companies in the office copier business, many of them producing xerographic devices under license from Xerox. (The only important part of its technology for which Xerox had refused to grant a license was a selenium drum that enables its own machines to make copies on ordinary paper. All competing products still required treated paper.) The great advantage that Xerox had been enjoying was the one that the first to enter a new field always enjoys—the advantage of charging high prices. Now, as *Barron's* pointed out in August, it appeared that "this once-fabulous invention may—as all technological advances inevitably must—soon evolve into an accepted commonplace." Cut-rate latecomers were swarming into copying; one company, in a letter sent to its stockholders in May, foresaw a time when a copier selling for ten or twenty dollars could be marketed "as a toy" (one was actually marketed for about thirty dollars in 1968) and there was even talk of the day when copiers would be given away to promote sales of paper, the way razors have long given away to promote razor blades. For some years, realizing that its cozy little monopoly would eventually pass into the public domain, Xerox had been widening its interests through mergers with companies in other fields, mainly publishing and education; for example, in 1962 it had bought University Microfilms, a library on microfilm of unpublished manuscripts, out-of-print books, doctoral dissertations, periodicals, and newspapers, and in 1965 it had tacked on two other companies—American Education Publications, the country's largest publisher of educational periodicals for primary- and secondary-school students, and Basic Systems, a manufacturer of teaching machines. But these moves failed to reassure that dogmatic critic the marketplace, and Xerox stock ran into a spell of heavy weather. Between late June, 1966, when it stood at 267¾, and early October, when it dipped to 131⅝, the market value of the company was more than cut in half. In the single business week of October 3rd through October 7th, Xerox dropped 42½ points, and on one particularly alarming day—October 6th—trading in Xerox on the New York Stock Exchange had to be suspended for five hours because there were about twenty-five million dollars' worth of shares on sale that no one wanted to buy.

I find that companies are inclined to be at their most interesting when they are undergoing a little misfortune, and therefore I chose the fall of 1966 as the time to have a look at Xerox and its people—something I'd had in mind to do for a year or so. I started out by getting acquainted with one of its products. The Xerox line of copiers and related items was by then a comprehensive one. There was, for instance, the 914, a desksize machine that makes black-and-white copies of almost any page—printed, handwritten, typed, or drawn, but not exceeding nine by fourteen inches in size—at a rate of about one copy every six seconds; the 813, a much smaller device, which can stand on top of a desk and is essentially a miniaturized version of the 914 (or, as Xerox technicians like to say, "a 914 with the air left out"); the 2400, a high-speed reproduction machine that looks like a modern kitchen stove and can cook up copies at a rate of forty a minute, or twenty-four hundred an hour; the Copyflo, which is capable of enlarging microfilmed pages into ordinary booksize pages and printing them; the LDX, by which documents can be transmitted over telephone wires, microwave radio, or coaxial cable; and the Telecopier, a non-xerographic device, designed and manufactured by Magnavox but sold by Xerox, which is a sort of junior version of the LDX and is especially interesting to a layman because it consists simply of a small box that, when attached to an ordinary telephone, permits the user to rapidly transmit a small picture (with a good deal of squeaking and clicking, to be sure) to anyone equipped with a telephone and a similar small box. Of all these, the 914, the first automatic xerographic product and the one that constituted the big breakthrough, was still much the most important both to Xerox and to its customers.

It has been suggested that the 914 is the most successful commercial product in history, but the statement cannot be authoritatively confirmed or denied, if only because Xerox does not publish precise revenue figures on its individual products; the company does say, though, that in 1965 the 914 accounted for about sixty-two per cent of its total operating revenues, which works out to something over $243,000,000. In 1966 it could be bought for $27,500, or it could be rented for twenty-five dollars monthly, plus at least forty-nine dollars' worth of copies at four cents each. These charges were deliberately set up to make renting more attractive than buying, because Xerox ultimately makes more money that way. The 914, which is painted beige and weighs six hundred and fifty pounds, looks a good deal like a modern L-shaped metal desk; the thing to be copied—a flat page, two pages of an open book, or even a small three-dimensional object like a watch or a medal—is placed face down on a glass window in the flat top surface, a button is pushed, and nine seconds later the copy pops into a tray where an "out" basket might be if the 914 actually were a desk. Technologically, the 914 is so complex (more complex, some Xerox salesmen insist, than an automobile) that it has an annoying tendency to go wrong, and consequently Xerox maintains a field staff of thousands of repairmen who are presumably ready to answer a call on short notice. The most common malfunction is a jamming of the supply of copy paper, which is rather picturesquely called a "mispuff," because each sheet of paper is raised into position to be inscribed by an interior puff of air, and the malfunction occurs when the puff goes wrong. A bad mispuff can occasionally put a piece of the paper in contact with hot parts, igniting it and causing an alarming cloud of white smoke to issue from the machine; in such a case the operator is urged to do nothing, or, at most, to use a small fire extinguisher that is attached to it, since the fire burns itself out comparatively harmlessly if left alone, whereas a bucket of water thrown over a 914 may convey potentially lethal voltages to its metal surface. Apart from malfunctions, the machine requires a good deal of regular attention from its operator, who is almost invariably a woman. (The girls who operated the earliest typewriters were themselves called "typewriters," but fortunately nobody calls Xerox operators "xeroxes.") Its supply of copying paper and black electrostatic powder, called "toner," must be replenished regularly, while its most crucial part, the selenium drum, must be cleaned regularly with a special non-scratchy cotton, and waxed every so often. I spent a couple of afternoons with one 914 and its operator, and observed what seemed to be the closest relationship between a woman and a piece of office equipment that I had ever seen. A girl who uses a typewriter or switchboard has no interest in the equipment, because it holds no mystery, while one who operates a computer is bored with it, because it is utterly incomprehensible. But a 914 has distinct animal traits: it has to be fed and curried; it is intimidating but can be tamed; it is subject to unpredictable bursts of misbehavior; and, generally speaking, it responds in kind to its treatment. "I was frightened of it at first," the operator I watched told me. "The Xerox men say, 'If you're frightened of it, it won't work,' and that's pretty much right. It's a good scout; I'm fond of it now."

Xerox salesmen, I learned from talks with some of them, are forever trying to think of new uses for the company's copiers, but they have found again and again that the public is well ahead of them. One rather odd use of xerography insures that brides get the wedding presents they want. The prospective bride submits her list of preferred presents to a department store; the store sends the list to its bridal-registry counter, which is equipped with a Xerox copier; each friend of the bride, having been tactfully briefed in advance, comes to this counter and is issued a copy of the list, whereupon he does his shopping and then returns the copy with the purchased items checked off, so that the master list may be revised and thus ready for the next donor. ("Hymen, iö Hymen, Hymen!") Again, police departments in New Orleans and various other places, instead of laboriously typing up a receipt for the property removed from people who spend the night in the lockup, now place the property itself—wallet, watch, keys, and such—on the scanning glass of a 914, and in a few seconds have a sort of pictographic receipt. Hospitals use xerography to copy electrocardiograms and laboratory reports, and brokerage firms to get hot tips to customers more quickly. In fact, anybody with any sort of idea that might be advanced by copying can go to one of the many cigar or stationery stores that have a coin-operated copier and indulge himself. (It is interesting to note that Xerox took to producing coin-operated 914s in two configurations—one that works for a dime and one that works for a quarter; the buyer or leaser of the machine could decide which he wanted to charge.)

Copying has its abuses, too, and they are clearly serious. The most obvious one is overcopying. A tendency formerly identified with bureaucrats has been spreading—the urge to make two or more copies when one would do, and to make one when none would do; the phrase "in triplicate," once used to denote bureaucratic waste, has become a gross understatement. The button waiting to be pushed, the whir of action, the neat reproduction dropping into the tray—all this adds up to a heady experience, and the neophyte operator of a copier feels an impulse to copy all the papers in his pockets. And once one has used a copier, one tends to be hooked. Perhaps the chief danger of this addiction is not so much the cluttering up of files and loss of important material through submersion as it is the insidious growth of a negative attitude toward originals—a feeling that nothing can be of importance *unless* it is copied, or is a copy itself.

A more immediate problem of xerography is the overwhelming temptation it offers to violate the copyright laws. Almost all large public and college libraries—and many high-school libraries as well—are now equipped with copying machines, and teachers and students in need of a few copies of a group of poems from a published book, a certain short story from an anthology, or a certain article from a scholarly journal have developed the habit of simply plucking it from the library's shelves, taking it to the library's reproduction department, and having the required number of Xerox copies made. The effect, of course, is to deprive the author and the publisher of income. There are no legal records of such infringements of copyright, since publishers and authors almost never sue educators, if only because they don't know that the infringements have occurred; furthermore, the educators themselves often have no idea that they have done anything illegal. The likelihood that many copyrights have already been infringed unknowingly through xerography became indirectly apparent a few years ago when a committee of educators sent a circular to teachers from coast to coast informing them explicitly what rights to reproduce copyrighted material they did and did not have, and the almost instant sequel was a marked rise in the number of requests from educators to publishers for permissions. And there was more concrete evidence of the way things were going; for example, in 1965 a staff member of the library school of the University of New Mexico publicly advocated that libraries spend ninety per cent of their budgets on staff, telephones, copying, telefacsimiles, and the like, and only ten per cent—a sort of tithe—on books and journals.

To a certain extent, libraries attempt to police copying on their own. The photographic service of the New York Public Library's main branch, which fills some fifteen hundred requests a week for copies of library matter, informs patrons that "copyrighted material will not be reproduced beyond 'fair use'"—that is, the amount and kind of reproduction, generally confined to brief excerpts, that have been established by legal precedent as not constituting infringement. The library goes on, "The applicant assumes all responsibility for any question that may arise in the making of the copy and in the use made thereof." In the first part of its statement the library seems to assume the responsibility and in the second part to renounce it, and this ambivalence may reflect an uneasiness widely felt among users of library copiers. Outside library walls, there often does not seem to be even this degree of scruple. Business people who are otherwise meticulous in their observance of the law seem to regard copyright infringement about as seriously as they regard jaywalking. A writer I've heard about was invited to a seminar of high-level and high-minded industrial leaders and was startled to find that a chapter from his most recent book had been copied and distributed to the participants, to serve as a basis for discussion. When the writer protested, the businessmen were taken aback, and even injured; they had thought the writer would be pleased by their attention to his work, but the flattery, after all, was of the sort shown by a thief who commends a lady's jewelry by making off with it.

In the opinion of some commentators, what has happened so far is only the first phase of a kind of revolution in graphics. "Xerography is bringing a reign of terror into the world of publishing, because it means that every reader can become both author and publisher," the Canadian sage Marshall McLuhan wrote in the spring, 1966, issue of the *American Scholar*. "Authorship and readership alike can become production-oriented under xerography. . . . Xerography is electricity invading the world of typography, and it means a total revolution in this old sphere." Even allowing for McLuhan's erratic ebullience ("I change my opinions daily," he once confessed), he seems to have got his teeth into something here. Various magazine articles have predicted nothing less than the disappearance of the book as it now exists, and pictured the library of the future as a sort of monster computer capable of storing and retrieving the contents of books electronically and xerographically. The "books" in such a library would be tiny chips of computer film—"editions of one." Everyone agrees that such a library is still some time away. (But not so far away as to preclude a wary reaction from forehanded publishers. Beginning late in 1966, the long-familiar "all rights reserved" rigmarole on the copyright page of all books published by Harcourt, Brace & World was altered to read, a bit spookily, "All rights reserved. No part of this publication may be reproduced or transmitted in any form or by any means, electronic or mechanical, including photocopy, recording, or any information storage and retrieval system . . ." Other publishers quickly followed the example.) One of the nearest approaches to it in the late sixties was the Xerox subsidiary University Microfilms, which could, and did, enlarge its microfilms of out-of-print books and print them as attractive and highly legible paperback volumes, at a cost to the customer of four cents a page; in cases where the book was covered by copyright, the firm paid a royalty to the author on each copy produced. But the time when almost anyone can make his own copy of a published book at lower than the market price is not some years away; it is now. All that the amateur publisher needs is access to a Xerox machine and a small offset printing press. One of the lesser but still important attributes of xerography is its ability to make master copies for use on offset presses, and make them much more cheaply and quickly than was previously possible. According to Irwin Karp, counsel to the Authors League of America, an edition of fifty copies of any printed book could in 1967 be handsomely "published" (minus the binding) by this combination of technologies in a matter of minutes at a cost of about eight-tenths of a cent per page, and less than that if the edition was larger. A teacher wishing to distribute to a class of fifty students the contents of a sixty-four-page book of poetry selling for three dollars and seventy-five cents could do so, if he were disposed to ignore the copyright laws, at a cost of slightly over fifty cents per copy.

The danger in the new technology, authors and publishers have contended, is that in doing away with the book it may do away with them, and thus with writing itself. Herbert S. Bailey, Jr., director of Princeton University Press, wrote in the *Saturday Review* of a scholar friend of his who has cancelled all his subscriptions to scholarly journals; instead, he now scans their tables of contents at his public library and makes copies of the articles that interest him. Bailey commented, "If all scholars followed [this] practice, there would be no scholarly journals." Beginning in the middle sixties, Congress has been considering a revision of the copyright laws—the first since 1909. At the hearings, a committee representing the National Education Association and a clutch of other education groups argued firmly and persuasively that if education is to keep up with our national growth, the present copyright law and the fair-use doctrine should be liberalized for scholastic purposes. The authors and publishers, not surprisingly, opposed such liberalization, insisting that any extension of existing rights would tend to deprive them of their livelihoods to some degree now, and to a far greater degree in the uncharted xerographic future. A bill that was approved in 1967 by the House Judiciary Committee seemed to represent a victory for them, since it explicitly set forth the fair-use doctrine and contained no educational-copying exemption. But the final outcome of the struggle was still uncertain late in 1968. McLuhan, for one, was convinced that all efforts to preserve the old forms of author protection represent backward thinking and are doomed to failure (or, anyway, he was convinced the day he wrote his *American Scholar* article). "There is no possible protection from technology except by technology," he wrote. "When you create a new environment with one phase of technology, you have to create an anti-environment with the next." But authors are seldom good at technology, and probably do not flourish in anti-environments.

In dealing with this Pandora's box that Xerox products have opened, the company seems to have measured up tolerably well to its lofty ideals as set forth by Wilson. Although it has a commercial interest in encouraging—or, at least, not *dis*couraging—more and more copying of just about anything that can be read, it makes more than a token effort to inform the users of its machines of their legal responsibilities; for example, each new machine that is shipped out is accompanied by a cardboard poster giving a long list of things that may not be copied, among them paper money, government bonds, postage stamps, passports, and "copyrighted material of any manner or kind without permission of the copyright owner." (How many of these posters end up in wastebaskets is another matter.) Moreover, caught in the middle between the contending factions in the fight over revision of copyright law, it resisted the temptation to stand piously aside while raking in the profits, and showed an exemplary sense of social responsibility—at least from the point of view of the authors and publishers. The copying industry in general, by contrast, tended either to remain neutral or to lean to the educators' side. At a 1963 symposium on copyright revision, an industry spokesman went as far as to argue that machine copying by a scholar is merely a convenient extension of hand

copying, which has traditionally been accepted as legitimate. But not Xerox. Instead, in September, 1965, Wilson
wrote to the House Judiciary Committee flatly opposing
any kind of special copying exemption in any new law.
Of course, in evaluating this seemingly quixotic stand one
ought to remember that Xerox is a publishing firm as well
as a copying-machine firm; indeed, what with American
Education Publications and University Microfilms, it is one
of the largest publishing firms in the country. Conventional
publishers, I gathered from my researches, sometimes find
it a bit bewildering to be confronted by this futuristic giant
not merely as an alien threat to their familiar world but as
an energetic colleague and competitor within it.

Having had a look at some Xerox products and devoted some
thought to the social implications of their use, I went to Rochester to scrape up a first-hand acquaintance with the company
and to get an idea how its people were reacting to their problems, material and moral. At the time I went, the material
problems certainly seemed to be to the fore, since the week of
the forty-two-and-a-half-point stock drop was not long past.
On the plane en route, I had before me a copy of Xerox's
most recent proxy statement, which listed the number of
Xerox shares held by each director as of February, 1966, and
I amused myself by calculating some of the directors' paper
losses in that one bad October week, assuming that they had
held on to their stock. Chairman Wilson, for example, had
held 154,026 common shares in February, so his loss would
have been $6,546,105. Linowitz's holding was 35,166 shares,
for a loss of $1,494,555. Dr. John H. Dessauer, executive
vice-president in charge of research, had held 73,845 shares
and was therefore presumably out $3,138,412.50. Such sums
could hardly be considered trivial even by Xerox executives.
Would I, then, find their premises pervaded by gloom, or at
least by signs of shock?

The Xerox executive offices were on the upper floors of Rochester's Midtown Tower, the ground level of which is occupied by Midtown Plaza, an indoor shopping mall. (Later that year, the company moved its headquarters across the street to Xerox Square, a complex that includes a thirty-story office building, an auditorium for civic as well as company use, and a sunken ice rink.) Before going up to the Xerox offices, I took a turn or two around the mall, and found it to be equipped with all kinds of shops, a café, kiosks, pools, trees, and benches that—in spite of an oppressively bland and affluent atmosphere, created mainly, I suspect, by bland piped-in music—were occupied in part by bums, just like the benches in outdoor malls. The trees had a tendency to languish for lack of light and air, but the bums looked O.K. Having ascended by elevator, I met a Xerox public-relations man with whom I had an appointment, and immediately asked him how the company had reacted to the stock drop. "Oh, nobody takes it too seriously," he replied. "You hear a lot of lighthearted talk about it at the golf clubs. One fellow will say to another, 'You buy the drinks—I dropped another eighty thousand dollars on Xerox yesterday.' Joe Wilson *did* find it a bit traumatic that day they had to suspend trading on the Stock Exchange, but otherwise he took it in stride. In fact, at a party the other day when the stock was way down and a lot of people were clustering around him asking him what it all meant, I heard him say, 'Well, you know, it's very rarely that opportunity knocks twice.' As for the office, you scarcely hear the subject mentioned at all." As a matter of fact, I scarcely did hear it mentioned again while I was at Xerox, and this sang-froid turned out to be justified, because within a little more than a month the stock had made up its entire loss, and within a few more months it had moved up to an all-time high.

I spent the rest of that morning calling on three scientific and technical Xerox men and listening to nostalgic tales of the early years of xerographic development. The first of these men was Dr. Dessauer, the previous week's three-million-dollar loser, whom I nevertheless found looking tranquil—as I guess I should have expected, in view of the fact that his Xerox stock was still presumably worth more than nine and a half million dollars. (A few months later it was presumably worth not quite *twenty* million.) Dr. Dessauer, a German-born veteran of the company who had been in charge of its research and engineering ever since 1938 and was then also vice-chairman of its board, was the man who first brought Carlson's invention to the attention of Joseph Wilson, after he had read an article about it in a technical journal in 1945. Stuck up on his office wall, I noticed, was a greeting card from members of his office staff in which he was hailed as the "Wizard," and I found him to be a smiling, youthful-looking man with just enough of an accent to pass muster for wizardry.

"You want to hear about the old days, eh?" Dr. Dessauer said. "Well, it was exciting. It was wonderful. It was also terrible. Sometimes I was going out of my mind, more or less literally. Money was the main problem. The company was fortunate in being modestly in the black, but not far enough. The members of our team were all gambling on the project. I even mortgaged my house—all I had left was my life insurance. My neck was way out. My feeling was that if it didn't work Wilson and I would be business failures but as far as I was concerned I'd also be a technical failure. Nobody would ever give me a job again. I'd have to give up science and sell insurance or something." Dr. Dessauer threw a retrospectively distracted glance at the ceiling and went on, "Hardly anybody was very optimistic in the early years. Various members of our own group would come in and tell me that the damn thing would never work. The biggest risk was that electrostatics would prove to be not feasible in high humidity. Almost all the experts assumed that—they'd say, 'You'll never make copies in New Orleans.' And even if it did work, the market-ing people thought we were dealing with a potential market of no more than a few thousand machines. Some advisers told us that we were absolutely crazy to go ahead with the project. Well, as you know, everything worked out all right—the 914 worked, even in New Orleans, and there was a big market for it. Then came the desk-top version, the 813. I stuck my neck way out again on that, holding out for a design that some experts considered too fragile."

I asked Dr. Dessauer whether his neck was now out on anything in the way of new research, and, if so, whether it is as exciting as xerography was. He replied, "Yes to both ques-tions, but beyond that the subject is privileged knowledge."

Dr. Harold E. Clark, the next man I saw, had been in direct charge of the xerography-development program under Dr. Dessauer's supervision, and he gave me more details on how the Carlson invention had been coaxed and nursed into a commercial product. "Chet Carlson was morphological," began Dr. Clark, a short man with a professorial manner who was, in fact, a professor of physics before he came to Haloid in 1949. I probably looked blank, because Dr. Clark gave a little laugh and went on, "I don't really know whether 'morphological' means anything. I *think* it means putting one thing together with another thing to get a new thing. Any-way, that's what Chet was. Xerography had practically no foundation in previous scientific work. Chet put together a rather odd lot of phenomena, each of which was obscure in itself and none of which had previously been related in any-one's thinking. The result was the biggest thing in imaging since the coming of photography itself. Furthermore, he did it entirely without the help of a favorable scientific climate. As you know, there are dozens of instances of simultaneous discovery down through scientific history, but no one came anywhere near being simultaneous with Chet. I'm as amazed by his discovery now as I was when I first heard of it. As an invention, it was magnificent. The only trouble was that as a product it wasn't any good."

Dr. Clark gave another little laugh and went on to explain that the turning point was reached at the Battelle Memorial Institute, and in a manner fully consonant with the tradition of scientific advances' occurring more or less by mistake. The main trouble was that Carlson's photoconductive surface, which was coated with sulphur, lost its qualities after it had made a few copies and became useless. Acting on a hunch unsupported by scientific theory, the Battelle researchers tried adding to the sulphur a small quantity of selenium, a non-metallic element previously used chiefly in electrical resistors and as a coloring material to redden glass. The selenium-and-sulphur surface worked a little better than the all-sulphur one, so the Battelle men tried adding a little more selenium. More improvement. They gradually kept increasing the percentage until they had a surface consisting entirely of selenium—no sulphur. That one worked best of all, and thus it was found, backhandedly, that selenium and selenium alone could make xerography practical.

"Think of it," Dr. Clark said, looking thoughtful himself. "A simple thing like selenium—one of the earth's elements, of which there are hardly more than a hundred altogether, and a common one at that. It turned out to be the key. Once its effectiveness was discovered, we were around the corner, although we didn't know it at the time. We still hold patents covering the use of selenium in xerography—almost a patent on one of the elements. Not bad, eh? Nor do we understand exactly *how* selenium works, even now. We're mystified, for example, by the fact that it has no memory effects—no traces of previous copies are left on the selenium-coated drum—and that it seems to be theoretically capable of lasting indefinitely. In the lab, a selenium-coated drum will last through a million processes, and we don't understand why it wears out even then. So, you see, the development of xerography was largely empirical. We were trained scientists, not Yankee tinkers, but we struck a balance between Yankee tinkering and scientific inquiry."

Next, I talked with Horace W. Becker, the Xerox engineer who was principally responsible for bringing the 914 from the working-model stage to the production line. A Brooklynite with a talent, appropriate to his assignment, for eloquent anguish, he told me of the hair-raising obstacles and hazards that surrounded this progress. When he joined Haloid Xerox in 1958, his laboratory was a loft above a Rochester garden-seed–packaging establishment; something was wrong with the roof, and on hot days drops of molten tar would ooze through it and spatter the engineers and the machines. The 914 finally came of age in another lab, on Orchard Street, early in 1960. "It was a beat-up old loft building, too, with a creaky elevator and a view of a railroad siding where cars full of pigs kept going by," Becker told me, "but we had the space we needed, and it didn't drip tar. It was at Orchard Street that we finally caught fire. Don't ask me how it happened. We decided it was time to set up an assembly line, and we did. Everybody was keyed up. The union people temporarily forgot their grievances, and the bosses forgot their performance ratings. You couldn't tell an engineer from an assembler in that place. No one could stay away—you'd sneak in on a Sunday, when the assembly line was shut down, and there would be somebody adjusting something or just puttering around and admiring our work. In other words, the 914 was on its way at last."

But once the machine was on its way out of the shop and on to showrooms and customers, Becker related, his troubles had only begun, because he was now held responsible for malfunctions and design deficiencies, and when it came to having a spectacular collapse just at the moment when the public spotlight was full on it, the 914 turned out to be a veritable Edsel. Intricate relays declined to work, springs broke, power supplies failed, inexperienced users dropped staples and paper clips into it and fouled the works (necessitating the installation in every machine of a staple-catcher), and the expected difficulties in humid climates developed, along with unanticipated ones at high altitudes. "All in all," Becker said, "at that time the machines had a bad habit, when you pressed the button, of doing nothing." Or if the machines did do something, it was something wrong. At the 914's first big showing in London, for instance, Wilson himself was on hand to put a ceremonial forefinger to its button; he did so, and not only was no copy made but a giant generator serving the line was blown out. Thus was xerography introduced in Great Britain, and, considering the nature of its début, the fact that Britain later become far and away the biggest overseas user of the 914 appears to be a tribute to both Xerox resilience and British patience.

That afternoon, a Xerox guide drove me out to Webster, a farm town near the edge of Lake Ontario, a few miles from Rochester, to see the incongruous successor to Becker's leaky and drafty lofts—a huge complex of modern industrial buildings, including one of roughly a million square feet where all Xerox copiers are assembled (except those made by the company's affiliates in Britain and Japan), and another, somewhat smaller but more svelte, where research and development are carried out. As we walked down one of the humming production lines in the manufacturing building, my guide explained that the line operates sixteen hours a day on two shifts, that it and the other lines have been lagging behind demand continuously for several years, that there are now almost two thousand employees working in the building, and that their union is a local of the Amalgamated Clothing Workers of America, this anomaly being due chiefly to the fact that Rochester used to be a center of the clothing business and the Clothing Workers has long been the strongest union in the area.

After my guide had delivered me back to Rochester, I set out on my own to collect some opinions on the community's attitude toward Xerox and its success. I found them to be ambivalent. "Xerox has been a good thing for Rochester," said a local businessman. "Eastman Kodak, of course, was the city's Great White Father for years, and it is still far and away the biggest local business, although Xerox is now second and coming up fast. Facing that kind of challenge doesn't do Kodak any harm in fact, it does it a lot of good. Besides, a successful new local company means new money and new jobs. On the other hand, some people around here resent Xerox. Most of the local industries go back to the nineteenth century, and their people aren't always noted for receptiveness to newcomers. When Xerox was going through its meteoric rise, some thought the bubble would burst—no, they *hoped* it would burst. On top of that, there's been a certain amount of feeling against the way Joe Wilson and Sol Linowitz are always talking about human values while making money hand over fist. But, you know—the price of success."

I went out to the University of Rochester, high on the banks of the Genesee River, and had a talk with its president, W. Allen Wallis. A tall man with red hair, trained as a statistician, Wallis served on the boards of several Rochester companies, including Eastman Kodak, which had always been the university's Santa Claus and remained its biggest annual benefactor. As for Xerox, the university had several sound reasons for feeling kindly toward it. In the first place, the university was a prize example of a Xerox *multi*millionaire, since its clear capital gain on the investment amounted to around a hundred million dollars and it had taken out more than ten million in profits. In the second place, Xerox annually comes through with annual cash gifts second only to Kodak's, and had recently pledged nearly six million dollars to the university's capital-funds drive. In the third place, Wilson, a University of Rochester graduate himself, had been on the university's board of trustees since 1949 and its chairman since 1959. "Before I came here, in 1962, I'd never even heard of corporations' giving universities such sums as Kodak and Xerox give us now," President Wallis said. "And all they want in return is for us to provide top-quality education—not do their research for them, or anything like that. Oh, there's a good deal of informal technical consulting between our scientific people and the Xerox people—same thing with Kodak, Bausch & Lomb, and others—but that's not why they're supporting the university. They want to make Rochester a place that will be attractive to the people they want here. The university has never invented anything for Xerox, and I guess it never will."

The next morning, in the Xerox executive offices, I met the three nontechnical Xerox men of the highest magnitude, ending with Wilson himself. The first of these was Linowitz, the lawyer whom Wilson took on "temporarily" in 1946 and kept on permanently as his least dispensable aide. (Since Xerox became famous, the general public tended to think of Linowitz as more than that—as, in fact, the company's chief executive. Xerox officials were aware of this popular misconception, and were mystified by it, since Wilson, whether he was called president, as he was until May of 1966, or chairman of the board, as he was after that, had been the boss right along.) I caught Linowitz almost literally on the run, since he had just been appointed United States Ambassador to the Organization of American States and was about to leave Rochester and Xerox for Washington and his new duties. A vigorous man in his fifties, he fairly exuded drive, intensity, and sincerity. After apologizing for the fact that he had only a few minutes to spend with me, he said, rapidly, that in his opinion the success of Xerox was proof that the old ideals of free enterprise still held true, and that the qualities that had made for the company's success were idealism, tenacity, the courage to take risks, and enthusiasm. With that, he waved goodbye and was off. I was left feeling a little like a whistle-stop voter who has just been briefly addressed by a candidate from the rear platform of a campaign train, but, like many such voters, I was impressed. Linowitz had used those banal words not merely as if he meant them but as if he had invented them, and I had the feeling that Wilson and Xerox were going to miss him.

I found C. Peter McColough, who had been president of the company since Wilson had moved up to chairman, and who was apparently destined eventually to succeed him as boss (as he did in 1968), pacing his office like a caged animal, pausing from time to time at a standup desk, where he would scribble something or bark a few words into a dictating machine. A liberal Democratic lawyer, like Linowitz, but a Canadian by birth, he is a cheerful extrovert who, being in his early forties, was spoken of as representing a new Xerox generation, charged with determining the course that the company would take next. "I face the problems of growth," he told me after he had abandoned his pacing for a restless perch on the edge of a chair. Future growth on a large scale simply isn't possible in xerography, he went on—there isn't room enough left—and the direction that Xerox is taking is toward educational techniques. He mentioned computers and teaching machines, and when he said he could "dream of a system whereby you'd write stuff in Connecticut and within hours reprint it in classrooms all over the country," I got the feeling that some of Xerox's educational dreams could easily become nightmares. But then he added, "The danger in ingenious hardware is that it distracts attention from education. What good is a wonderful machine if you don't know what to put on it?"

McColough said that since he came to Haloid, in 1954, he felt he'd been part of three entirely different companies—until 1959 a small one engaged in a dangerous and exciting gamble; from 1959 to 1964 a growing one enjoying the fruits of victory; and now a huge one branching out in new directions. I asked him which one he liked best, and he thought a long time. "I don't know," he said finally. "I used to feel greater freedom, and I used to feel that everyone in the company shared attitudes on specific matters like labor relations. I don't feel that way so much now. The pressures are greater, and the company is more impersonal. I wouldn't say that life has become easier, or that it is likely to get easier in the future."

Of all the surprising things about Joseph C. Wilson, not the least, I thought when I was ushered into his presence, was the fact that his office walls were decorated with old-fashioned flowered wallpaper. A sentimental streak in the man at the head of Xerox seemed the most unlikely of anomalies. But he had a homey, unthreatening bearing to go with the wallpaper; a smallish man in his late fifties, he looked serious— almost grave—during most of my visit, and spoke in a slow, rather hesitant way. I asked him how he had happened to go into his family's business, and he replied that as a matter of fact he nearly hadn't. English literature had been his second major at the university, and he had considered either taking up teaching or going into the financial and administrative end of university work. But after graduating he had gone on to the Harvard Business School, where he had been a top student, and somehow or other . . . In any case, he had joined Haloid the year he left Harvard, and there, he told me with a sudden smile, he was.

The subjects that Wilson seemed to be most keen on discussing were Xerox's non-profit activities and his theories of corporate responsibility. "There are certain feelings of resentment toward us on this," he said. "I don't mean just from stockholders complaining that we're giving their money away—that point of view is losing ground. I mean in the community. You don't actually hear it, but you sometimes get a kind of intuitive feeling that people are saying, 'Who do these young upstarts think they are, anyhow?'"

I asked whether the letter-writing campaign against the U.N. television series had caused any misgivings or downright faintheartedness within the company, and he said, "As an organization, we never wavered. Almost without exception, the people here felt that the attacks only served to call attention to the very point we were trying to make—that world coöperation is our business, because without it there might be no world and therefore no business. We believe we followed sound business policy in going ahead with the series. At the same time, I won't maintain that it was *only* sound business policy. I doubt whether we would have done it if, let's say, we had all been Birchers ourselves."

Wilson went on slowly, "The whole matter of committing the company to taking stands on major public issues raises questions that make us examine ourselves all the time. It's a matter of balance. You can't just be bland, or you throw away your influence. But you can't take a stand on every major issue, either. We don't think it's a corporation's job to take stands on national elections, for example—fortunately, perhaps, since Sol Linowitz is a Democrat and I'm a Republican. Issues like university education, civil rights, and Negro employment clearly *are* our business. I'd hope that we would have the courage to stand up for a point of view that was unpopular if we thought it was appropriate to do so. So far, we haven't faced that situation—we haven't found a conflict between what we consider our civic responsibility and good business. But the time may come. We may have to stand on the firing line yet. For example, we've tried, without much fanfare, to equip some Negro youths to take jobs beyond sweeping the floor and so on. The program required complete coöperation from our union, and we got it. But I've learned that, in subtle ways, the honeymoon is over. There's an undercurrent of opposition. Here's something started, then, that if it grows could confront us with a real business problem. If it becomes a few hundred objectors instead of a few dozen, things might even come to a strike, and in such a case I hope we and the union leadership would stand up and fight. But I don't really know. You can't honestly predict what you'd do in a case like that. I *think* I know what we'd do."

Getting up and walking to a window, Wilson said that, as he saw it, one of the company's major efforts now, and even more in the future, must be to keep the personal and human quality for which it has come to be known. "Already we see signs of losing it," he said. "We're trying to indoctrinate new people, but twenty thousand employees around the Western Hemisphere isn't like a thousand in Rochester."

I joined Wilson at the window, preparatory to leaving. It was a dank, dark morning, such as I'm told the city is famous for much of the year, and I asked him whether, on a gloomy day like this, he was ever assailed by doubts that the old quality *could* be preserved. He nodded briefly and said, "It's an everlasting battle, which we may or may not win."

6

MAKING THE CUSTOMERS WHOLE

ON THE MORNING OF TUESDAY, November 19th, 1963, a well-dressed but haggard-looking man in his middle thirties presented himself at the executive offices of the New York Stock Exchange, at 11 Wall Street, with the announcement that he was Morton Kamerman, managing partner of the brokerage firm of Ira Haupt & Co., a member of the Stock Exchange, and that he wanted to see Frank J. Coyle, head of the Exchange's member-firms department. After checking, a receptionist explained politely that Mr. Coyle was tied up in a meeting, whereupon the visitor said that his mission was an urgent one and asked to see Robert M. Bishop, the department's second-in-command. Bishop, the receptionist found, was unavailable, too; he was tied up with an important phone call. At length, Kamerman, who seemed to be growing more and more distracted, was ushered into the presence of a less exalted Exchange official named George H. Newman. He then duly delivered his message—that, to the best of his belief, the capital reserve of the Haupt firm had fallen below the Exchange's requirements for member firms, and that he was formally reporting the fact, in accordance with regulations. While this startling announcement was being made, Bishop, in a nearby office, was continuing his important telephone conversation, the second party to which was a knowledge- able Wall Streeter whom Bishop has since declined to iden- tify. The caller was telling Bishop he had reason to believe that two Stock Exchange member firms—J. R. Williston & Beane, Inc., and Ira Haupt & Co.—were in financial trouble serious enough to warrant the Exchange's attention. After hanging up, Bishop made an interoffice call to Newman to tell him what he had just heard. To Bishop's surprise, New- man already had the news, or part of it. "As a matter of fact, Kamerman is right here with me now," he said.

In this humdrum setting of office confusion there began one of the most trying—and in some ways one of the most serious—crises in the Stock Exchange's long history. Before it was over, this crisis had been exacerbated by the greater crisis resulting from the assassination of President Kennedy, and out of it the Stock Exchange—which has not always been noted for acting in the public interest, and, indeed, had been accused only a few months before by the Securities and Exchange Commission of an anti-social tendency to conduct itself like a private club—emerged temporarily poorer by almost ten mil- lion dollars but incalculably richer in the esteem of at least some of its countrymen. The event that had brought Haupt and Williston & Beane into straitened circumstances is his- tory—or, rather, future history. It was the sudden souring of a huge speculation that these two firms (along with various brokers not members of the Stock Exchange) had become involved in on behalf of a single customer—the Allied Crude Vegetable Oil & Refining Co., of Bayonne, New Jersey. The speculation was in contracts to buy vast quantities of cotton- seed oil and soybean oil for future delivery. Such contracts are known as commodity futures, and the element of speculation in them lies in the possibility that by delivery date the commodity will be worth more (or less) than the contract price. Vegetable-oil futures are traded daily at the New York Produce Exchange, at 2 Broadway, and at the Board of Trade, in Chicago, and they are bought and sold on behalf of customers by about eighty of the four hundred-odd firms that belong to the Stock Exchange and conduct a public business. On the day that Kamerman came to the Exchange, the Haupt firm was holding for Allied—on credit—so many cottonseed-oil and soybean-oil contracts that the change of a single penny per pound in the prices of the commodities meant a twelve-million-dollar change in the value of the Allied account with Haupt. On the two previous business days—Friday the fifteenth and Monday the eighteenth—the prices had dropped an average of a little less than a cent and a half per pound, and as a result Haupt had demanded that Allied put up about fifteen million dollars in cash to keep the account seaworthy. Allied had declined to do this, so Haupt—like any broker when a customer operating on credit has defaulted—was faced with the necessity of selling out the Allied contracts to get back what it could of its advances. The suicidal extent of the risk that Haupt had undertaken is further indicated by the fact that while the firm's capital in early November had amounted to only about eight million dollars, it had borrowed enough money to supply a single customer—Allied—with some thirty-seven million dollars to finance the oil speculations. Worse still, as things turned out it had accepted as collateral for some of these advances enormous amounts of actual cottonseed oil and soybean oil from Allied's inventory, the presence of which in tanks at Bayonne was attested to by warehouse receipts stating the precise amount and kind of oil on hand. Haupt had borrowed the money it supplied Allied with from various banks, passing along most of the warehouse receipts to the banks as collateral. All this would have been well and good if it had not developed later that many of the warehouse receipts were forged, that much of the oil they attested to was not, and probably never had been, in Bayonne, and that Allied's president, Anthony De Angelis (who was later sent to jail on a whole parcel of charges), had apparently pulled off the biggest commercial fraud since that of Ivar Kreuger, the match king.

Where was the missing oil? How could Allied's direct and indirect creditors, including some of the most powerful and worldly-wise banks of the United States and Great Britain, have been so thoroughly gulled? Would aggregate losses on the whole debacle finally total a hundred and fifty million dollars, as some authorities had estimated, or would the bill be even bigger? How could a leading Stock Exchange firm like Haupt have been so foolish as to take on such an inconceivably risky commitment for a single customer? These questions had not even been raised, let alone answered, on November 19th; some of them have not been answered yet, and some of them may not be answered for years. What began to emerge on November 19th, and what became clear in the harrowing days that followed, was that in the case of Haupt, which had about twenty thousand individual stock-market customers on its books, and in the case of Williston & Beane, which had about nine thousand, the impending disaster directly involved the personal savings of many totally innocent persons who had never heard of Allied and had only the vaguest notion of what commodity trading is.

Kamerman's report to the Stock Exchange did not mean that Haupt had gone broke, and at the time he made it Kamerman himself surely did not think that his firm *had* gone broke; there is a great difference between insolvency and a mere failure to meet the Exchange's rather stringent capital requirements, which are intended to provide a margin of safety. Indeed, various Stock Exchange officials have said that on that Tuesday morning they did not consider the Haupt situation to be especially serious, while the Williston & Beane situation, it was clear from the first, was even less so. One of the first reactions in the member-firms department was chagrin that Kamerman had come to the Exchange with his problem before the Exchange, through its elaborate system of audits and examinations, had discovered the problem for itself. This, the Exchange insists stubbornly, if a bit lamely, was a matter of bad luck rather than bad management. As a matter of routine, the Exchange required each of its member firms to fill out detailed questionnaires on its financial condition several times a year, and as an additional check an expert accountant from the Exchange staff descended unexpectedly on each member firm at least once a year to subject its books to a surprise inspection. Ira Haupt & Co. had filled out its most recent questionnaire early in October, and since the huge buildup in Allied's commodities position with Haupt took place after that, the questionnaire showed nothing amiss. As for the surprise inspection, the Exchange's man was in the Haupt offices conducting it at the very time the trouble broke. The auditor had been there for a week, his nose buried in Haupt's account books, but the task of conducting such an inspection is a tedious one, and by November 19th the auditor hadn't got around to examining the Haupt commodities department. "They had set our man up with a desk in a department where nothing unusual was going on," an Exchange official has since said. "It's easy to say now that he should have *smelled* trouble, but he didn't."

At midmorning on Tuesday the nineteenth, Coyle and Bishop sat down with Kamerman to see what needed to be done about Haupt's problem, and what could be done. Bishop remembers that the atmosphere of the meeting was by no means grim; according to Kamerman's figures, the amount of capital that Haupt needed to bring it up to snuff was about a hundred and eighty thousand dollars—an almost paltry sum for a firm of Haupt's size. Haupt could make up the deficiency either by obtaining new money from outside or by converting securities it owned into cash. Bishop urged the latter course as the quicker and surer, whereupon Kamerman telephoned his firm and instructed his partners to begin selling some of their securities at once. The difficulty apparently was going to be solved as simply as that.

But during the rest of the day, after Kamerman had left 11 Wall, the crisis showed a tendency to go through the process that in political circles had come to be called escalation. In the late afternoon, an ominous piece of news arrived. Allied had just filed a voluntary-bankruptcy petition in Newark. Theoretically, the bankruptcy did not affect the financial position of its former brokers, since they held security for the money they had supplied Allied with; nevertheless, the news was alarming in that it provided a hint of worse news to follow. Such news, indeed, was not long in coming; the same evening, word reached the Stock Exchange that the managers of the New York Produce Exchange, in an effort to forestall chaos in their market, had voted to suspend all trading in cotton-seed-oil futures until further notice, and to require immediate settlement of all outstanding contracts at a price dictated by them. Since the dictated price would have to be a low one, this meant that any remaining chance that Haupt or Williston & Beane had of getting out from under the Allied speculations on favorable terms was gone.

In the member-firms department that evening, Bishop was frantically trying to get in touch with G. Keith Funston, the president of the Stock Exchange, who was first at a midtown dinner and then on a train bound for Washington, where he was scheduled to testify the next day before a congressional committee. What with one thing and another, Bishop was busy in his office all evening; toward midnight, he found himself the last man in the member-firms department, and, having decided it was too late to go home to Fanwood, New Jersey, for the night, he collapsed on a leather couch in Coyle's office. He had a restless night there; the cleaning women were considerately quiet, he said afterward, but the phones kept ringing all night long.

Promptly at nine-thirty on Wednesday morning, the Stock Exchange's board of governors met in the sixth-floor Governors' Room—which, with its regal red carpet, fierce old portraits, and fluted gilt columns, carries rather uncomfortable connotations of Wall Street's checkered past—and, in accordance with Exchange regulations, voted to suspend Haupt and Williston & Beane because of their capital difficulties. The suspension was made public a few minutes after trading opened, at ten o'clock, by Henry M. Watts, Jr., chairman of the board of governors, who ascended a rostrum that overlooks the trading floor, rang the bell that normally signals the beginning or ending of a day's trading, and read an announcement of it. From the point of view of the public, the immediate effect of the action was that the accounts of the almost thirty thousand customers of the two suspended firms were now frozen—that is, the owners of the accounts could neither sell their stocks nor get their money out. Touched by the plight of these unfortunates, the Stock Exchange brass now set about trying to help the beleaguered firms raise enough capital to lift the suspensions and free the accounts. In the case of Williston & Beane, its efforts were triumphantly successful. It developed that this firm needed about half a million dollars to get back into business, and so many fellow-brokers came forward to help out with loans that the firm actually had to fight off unwanted offers. The half million was finally accepted partly from Walston & Co. and partly from Merrill Lynch, Pierce, Fenner & Smith. (Cozily, the Beane of Williston & Beane was the very man who had been the caboose when the firm's name was Merrill Lynch, Pierce, Fenner & Beane.) Restored to financial health by this timely injection of capital, Williston & Beane was relieved of its suspension—and its nine thousand customers were relieved of their anxiety—just after noon on Friday, or slightly more than two days after the suspension had been imposed.

But in the case of Haupt things went differently. It was clear by Wednesday that the capital-shortage figure of a hundred and eighty thousand dollars had been the rosiest of dreams. Even so, it appeared that the firm might still be solvent despite its losses on the forced sale of the oil contracts—on one condition. The condition was that the oil in Bayonne tanks that Allied had pledged to Haupt as collateral—and that now, through Allied's default, belonged to Haupt—could be sold to other oil processors at a fair price. Richard M. Crooks, an Exchange governor who, unlike nearly all his colleagues, was an expert on commodities trading, figured that if the Bayonne oil were thus unloaded, Haupt might still end up slightly in the black. He therefore telephoned a couple of the country's leading vegetable-oil processors and urged them to bid on the oil. The replies he received were unanimous and startling. The leading processors declined to make any bid at all, and they left Crooks with the feeling that they were suspicious of the Bayonne warehouse receipts held by Haupt—that they suspected some or all of them to be forgeries. If these suspicions were well founded, it would follow that some or all of the oil attested to by the receipts was not in Bayonne. "The situation was very simple," Crooks has said. "Warehouse receipts are accepted in the commodities business as practically as good as currency, and now the possibility had been raised that millions of dollars of Haupt's assets consisted of counterfeit money."

Still, all that Crooks knew definitely on Wednesday morning was that the processors would not bid on Allied oil, and throughout the rest of Wednesday and all day Thursday the Exchange furiously went on trying to help Haupt get back on its feet along with Williston & Beane. Needless to say, the fifteen partners of Haupt were busy at the same endeavor, and in aid of it Kamerman told the *Times* buoyantly on Wednesday evening, "Ira Haupt & Co. is solvent and is in an excellent financial position." Also on Wednesday evening, Crooks had dinner in New York with a veteran commodities broker from Chicago. "Although I'm an optimist by temperament, my experience tells me that these things always turn out to be much worse than they look at first," Crooks said recently. "I mentioned this to my broker friend, and he agreed. The next morning at about eleven-thirty, he called me and said, 'Dick, this thing is a hundred per cent worse than even *you* think.'" A bit later, at midday on Thursday, the Exchange's member-firms department learned that many of Allied's warehouse receipts were indeed fake.

As nearly as can be determined, the Haupt partners were making the same unhappy discovery at about the same time. At any rate, a number of them did not go home Thursday evening but spent the night at their offices at 111 Broadway, trying to figure out what their position was. Bishop got home to Fanwood that night, but he found that he could sleep hardly any better there than on Coyle's couch. Accordingly, he rose before dawn, took the Jersey Central's five-eight to the city, and on a hunch went to the Haupt offices. There, in the partners' area—recently redecorated with modern contour chairs, marble-topped filing cabinets, and refrigerators disguised as desks—he found several of the partners, unshaven and unkempt, drowsing in their chairs. "They were pretty shot by then," Bishop said later. And no wonder. After being awakened, they told him that they had been up all night calculating, and that at about three o'clock they had come to the conclusion that their position was hopeless; in view of the worthlessness of the warehouse receipts, the Haupt firm was insolvent. Bishop took this disastrous intelligence with him to the Stock Exchange, where he waited for the sun to come up and for everyone else to come to work.

———

At one-forty on Friday afternoon, when the stock market was already badly rattled by the rumors of Haupt's impending failure, the first reports of the President's assassination reached the Exchange floor, in garbled form. Crooks, who was there, says that the first thing he heard was that the President had been shot, the second was that the President's brother, the Attorney General, had also been shot, and the third was that the Vice-President had had a heart attack. "The rumors came like machine-gun bullets," Crooks says. And they struck with comparable impact. In the next twenty-seven minutes, during which no hard news arrived to relieve the atmosphere of apocalypse, the prices of stocks declined at a rate unparalleled in the Exchange's history. In less than half an hour, the values of listed stocks decreased by thirteen billion dollars, and they would no doubt have dropped further if the board of governors had not closed the market for the day at seven minutes past two. The panic's immediate effect on the Haupt situation was to make the status of the twenty thousand frozen accounts far worse, because now, in the event of Haupt's bankruptcy and the consequent liquidation of many of the accounts, the cashing in would have to be done at panic prices, with heavy losses to the accounts' owners. A larger and less calculable effect of the events in Dallas was paralyzing despair. However, Wall Street—or, rather, some Wall Streeters—had a psychological advantage over the rest of the country in that there was work at hand to be done. This convergence of disasters confronted them with a definable task.

Having testified in Washington on Wednesday afternoon, Funston had returned to New York that evening and had spent most of Thursday as well as Friday morning working on getting Williston & Beane back in business. Sometime during that period, as it was gradually made clear that Haupt was not merely short of capital but actually insolvent, Funston became convinced the Exchange and its member firms must consider doing something virtually unprecedented—that is, reimburse the innocent victims of Haupt's imprudence with their own money. (The nearest thing to a precedent for such action was the case of DuPont, Homsey & Co., a small Stock Exchange firm that went bankrupt in 1960 as a result of fraud by one of its partners; the Exchange then repaid the firm's customers the money they had been divested of—about eight hundred thousand dollars.) Now, having hurried back to his office from a lunch date shortly before the emergency closing of the market, Funston set about putting his plan into action, calling about thirty leading brokers whose offices happened to be nearby and asking them to trot over to the Exchange immediately as an unofficial delegation representing its membership. Shortly after three o'clock, the brokers were assembled in the South Committee Room—a somewhat smaller version of the Governors' Room—and Funston set before them the facts of the Haupt case as he then knew them, along with an outline of his plan for a solution. The facts were these: Haupt owed about thirty-six million dollars to a group of United States and British banks; since over twenty million of its assets were represented by warehouse receipts that now appeared to be worthless, there was no hope that Haupt could pay its debts. In the normal course of events, therefore, Haupt would be sued by the creditor banks when the courts reopened next week, the cash and many of the securities held by Haupt for its customers would be tied up by the creditors, and, according to Funston's liberal estimate, some of the customers might end up getting back—after an extended period caused by legal delays—no more than sixty-five cents on the dollar. And there was another side to the case. If Haupt were to go into bankruptcy, the psychological effect of this, combined with the palpable effect of Haupt's considerable assets' being thrown on the market, might well lead to further depression of a stock market already in wild retreat at a time of grave national crisis. Not only the welfare of the Haupt customers was at stake, then, but perhaps the national welfare, too. Funston's plan, simple enough in outline, was that the Stock Exchange or its members put up enough money to enable all the Haupt customers to get back their cash and securities—to be once again "whole," in the banking expression. (The banking expression is etymologically sound; "whole" derives from the Anglo-Saxon *"hal,"* which meant uninjured or recovered from injury, and from which "hale" is also derived.) Funston further proposed that Haupt's creditors, the banks, be persuaded to defer any efforts to collect their money until the customers had been taken care of. Funston estimated that the amount needed to do the job might run to seven million dollars, or even more.

Almost to a man, the assembled brokers agreed to support this public-spirited, if not downright eleemosynary, plan. But before the meeting was over a difficulty arose. Now that the Stock Exchange and the member firms had decided on a deed of self-sacrifice, the problem confronting each side—to a certain extent, anyway—was how to arrange to have the other side do the sacrificing. Funston urged the member firms to take over the entire matter. The firms declined this suggestion with thanks and countered by urging the Stock Exchange to handle it. "If we do," Funston said, "you'll have to repay us the amount we pay out." Out of this not very dignified dialogue emerged an agreement that initially the funds would come out of the Exchange's treasury, with repayment to be apportioned among the member firms later. A three-man committee, headed by Funston, was empowered to conduct negotiations to bring the deal off.

The chief parties that needed negotiating with were Haupt's creditor banks. Their unanimous consent to the plan was essential, because if even one of them insisted on immediate liquidation of its loans "the pot would fall in," as the Exchange's chairman, Henry Watts—a fatherly-looking graduate of Harvard and of Omaha Beach, 1944—pungently put it. Prominent among the creditors were four local banks of towering prestige—Chase Manhattan, Morgan Guaranty Trust, First National City, and Manufacturers Hanover Trust—which among them had lent Haupt about eighteen and a half million dollars. (Three of the banks have remained notably reticent about the exact amount of their ill-fated loans to Haupt, but blaming them for their silence would be like blaming a poker player who is less than garrulous about a losing night. The Chase, however, has said that Haupt owed it $5,700,000.) Earlier in the week, George Champion, chairman of the Chase, had telephoned Funston; not only did the Stock Exchange have a friend at Chase, Champion assured him, but the bank stood ready to give any help it could in the Haupt matter. Funston now called Champion and said he was ready to take him up on his offer. He and Bishop then began to try to assemble representatives of the Chase and the three other banks for an immediate conference. Bishop remembers that he felt highly bearish about the chances of rounding up a group of bankers at five o'clock on a Friday—even such an exceptional Friday as this one—but to his surprise he found practically all of them at their battle stations and willing to come straight to the Exchange.

Funston and his fellow-negotiators for the Exchange—Chairman Watts and Vice-Chairman Walter N. Frank—conferred with the bankers from shortly after five until well into the dinner hour. The meeting was constructive, if tense. "First, we all agreed that it was a devil of a situation all around," Funston subsequently recalled. "Then we got down to business. The bankers, of course, were hoping that the Exchange would pick up the whole thing, but we quickly disabused them of that notion. Instead, I made them an offer. We would put up a certain sum in cash solely for the benefit of the Haupt customers; in exchange for every dollar that we put up, the banks would defer collection—that is, would temporarily refrain from foreclosing—on two dollars. If, as we then estimated, twenty-two and a half million was needed to make Haupt solvent, we would put up seven and a half, and the banks would defer collection of fifteen. They weren't so sure about our figures—they thought we were too low— and they insisted that the Exchange's claim to get back any of its contribution out of Haupt assets would have to come after the banks' claims for their loans. We agreed to that. We all fought and negotiated, and when we finally went home there was general agreement on the broad outline of the thing. Of course, everyone recognized that this meeting was only pre- liminary—to begin with, by no means all the creditor banks were represented at it—and that both the detail work and much of the hard bargaining would have to be done over the weekend."

Just how much detail work and hard bargaining lay ahead became manifest on Saturday. The Exchange's board met at eleven, and more than two-thirds of its thirty-three members were present; because of the Haupt crisis, some governors had cancelled weekend plans, and others had flown in from their regular stands in such outposts as Georgia and Florida. The board's first action—a decision to keep the Exchange closed on Monday, the day of the President's funeral—was accomplished with deep relief, because the holiday would give the negotiators an additional twenty-four hours in which to hammer out a deal before the deadline represented by the reopening of the courts and the markets. Funston brought the governors up to date on what was known about Haupt's financial position and on the status of the negotiations that had been begun with the banks; he also gave them a new esti- mate of the sum that might be required to make the Haupt customers whole—nine million dollars. After a fractional moment of silence, several governors rose to say, in essence, that they felt that more than money was at stake; it was a question of the relation of the Stock Exchange to the country's many million investors. The meeting was then temporarily adjourned, and, with the authority of the governors' lofty sentiments to back it up, the Exchange's three-man committee got down to negotiations with the bankers.

Thus, the pattern for Saturday and Sunday was set. While the rest of the nation sat stupefied in front of its television sets, and while the downtown Manhattan streets were as deserted as they must have been during the yellow-fever epidemics of the early nineteenth century, the sixth floor of 11 Wall Street was a nexus of utterly absorbed activity. The Exchange's committee would remain closeted with the bankers until a point was reached at which Funston and his colleagues needed further authorization; then the board of governors would go into session again and either grant the new authority or decline to do so. Between sessions, the governors congregated in the hallways or smoked and brooded in empty offices. An ordinarily obscure corner of the Exchange bureaucracy called the Conduct and Complaints Department was having a busy weekend, too; a staff of half a dozen there was continuously on the phone dealing with anxious inquiries from Haupt customers, who were feeling anything but hale. And, of course, there were lawyers everywhere—"I never saw so many lawyers in my life," one veteran Stock Exchange man has said. Coyle estimates that there were more than a hundred people at 11 Wall Street during most of the weekend, and since practically all local restaurants as well as the Exchange's own eating facilities were closed, the food problem was acute. On Saturday, the entire output of a downtown lunch counter that had shrewdly stayed open was bought up and consumed, after which a taxi was dispatched to Greenwich Village for more supplies; on Sunday, one of the Exchange secretaries thoughtfully brought in an electric coffee-maker and a huge bag of groceries and set up shop in the Chairman's Dining Room.

The bankers' negotiating committee now included men from two Haupt creditors that had not been represented on

Friday—the National State Bank of Newark and the Continental Illinois National Bank & Trust Co., of Chicago. (Still unrepresented were the four British creditors—Henry Ansbacher & Co.; William Brandt's Sons & Co., Ltd.; S. Japhet & Co., Ltd.; and Kleinwort, Benson, Ltd. Moreover, with the weekend half gone, they seemed to be temporarily unrepresentable. It was decided to continue negotiating without the British banks and then, on Monday morning, present any agreement to them for approval.) A crucial point at issue, it now developed, was the amount of cash that would be needed from the Stock Exchange to fulfill its part of the bargain. The bankers accepted Funston's formula under which they would defer collection of two dollars for every dollar that the Exchange contributed to the cause, and they did not doubt that Haupt was stuck with about twenty-two and a half million dollars' worth of useless warehouse receipts; however, they were unwilling to take that figure as the maximum amount that might be necessary to liquidate Haupt. To be on the safe side, they argued, the amount ought to be based on Haupt's over-all indebtedness to them—thirty-six million—and this meant that the Exchange's cash contribution would have to be not seven and a half million but twelve. Another point at issue was the question of to whom the Exchange would pay whatever sum was agreed upon. Some of the bankers thought the money ought to go straight into the coffers of Ira Haupt & Co., to be dispensed by the firm itself to its customers; the trouble with this suggestion, as the Exchange's representatives were not slow to point out, was that it would put the Exchange's contribution entirely beyond its control. As a final complication, one bank—the Continental Illinois—was distinctly reluctant to enter into the deal at all. "The Continental's people were thinking in terms of their bank's exposure," an Exchange man has explained sympathetically. "They thought our arrangement might ultimately be more damaging to them than a formal Haupt bankruptcy and receivership.

They needed time to consider, to make sure they were taking the proper action, but I must say they were coöperative." Indeed, since it was primarily the Stock Exchange's good name that was at the center of the planned deal, it would appear that all the banks were marvels of coöperation. After all, a banker is legally and morally charged with doing the best he can for his depositors and stockholders, and is therefore hardly in a position to indulge in grand gestures for the public good; if his eyes are flinty, they may mask a kind, but stifled, heart. As for the Continental, it had reason to be particularly slow to act, because its "exposure" amounted to well over ten million dollars, or much more than that of any other bank. No one concerned has been willing to say exactly what the points were on which the Continental held out, but it seems safe to assume that no bank or person who had lent Haupt less than ten million dollars can know exactly how the Continental felt.

By the time the negotiations were recessed, at about six o'clock Saturday evening, a compromise had been reached on the main issues—on the amount-of-cash controversy by an agreement that the Exchange would put up an initial seven and a half million with a pledge to go up to twelve million if it became necessary, and on the controversy about how the money would be paid to the Haupt customers by agreement that the Exchange's chief examiner would be appointed liquidator of Haupt. But the Continental was still recalcitrant, and, of course, the British banks had not yet even been approached. In any event, everybody shut up shop for the night, with pledges to return early the next afternoon, even though it was Sunday. Funston, who was coming down with a bad cold, went home to Greenwich. The bankers went home to places like Glen Cove and Basking Ridge. Watts, a diehard commuter from Philadelphia, went home to that tranquil city. Even Bishop went home to Fanwood.

At two o'clock Sunday afternoon, the Exchange gover-

nors, their ranks now augmented by arrivals from Los Angeles, Minneapolis, Pittsburgh, and Richmond, met in joint
session with the thirty representatives of member firms, who
were anxious to learn what they were being committed to.
After the current status of the emerging agreement had been
explained to them, they voted unanimously in favor of going
ahead with it. As the afternoon progressed, even Continental
Illinois softened its opposition, and at about six o'clock, after
a series of frantic long-distance telephone calls and attempts
to track down Continental officers on trains and in airports,
the Chicago bank agreed to go along, explaining that it was
doing so in the public interest rather than in pursuance of its
officers' best business judgment. At about the same time, the
Times' financial editor, Thomas E. Mullaney—who, like the
rest of the press, had been rigidly excluded from the sixth
floor throughout the negotiations—called Funston to say he
had heard rumors of a plan on Haupt in the offing. Because
the British banks would have reason to be miffed, at the very
least, if they should read in the next morning's air editions
of a scheme to dispose of their credits without their agreement, or even their knowledge, Funston had to give a reply
that could only depress still further the spirits of the waiting
twenty thousand customers. "There is no plan," he said.

The question of who would undertake the delicate task of
cajoling the British banks had come up early Sunday afternoon. Funston, despite his cold, was anxious to make the trip
(for one thing, he has since admitted, the drama of it appealed
to him), and had gone as far as getting his secretary to reserve
space on a plane, but as the afternoon progressed and the local
problems continued to appear intractable, it was decided that
he couldn't be spared. Several other governors quickly volun-
teered to go, and one of them, Gustave L. Levy, was eventually selected, on the ground that his firm, Goldman, Sachs &
Co., had had a long and close association with Kleinwort,

Benson, one of the British banks, and that Levy himself was on excellent terms with some of the Kleinwort, Benson partners. (Levy would later succeed Watts as chairman.) Accordingly, Levy, accompanied by an executive and a lawyer of the Chase—who were presumably included in the hope that they would set the British banks an inspiring example of coöperation—left 11 Wall Street shortly after five o'clock and caught a London-bound jet at seven. The trio sat up on the plane most of the night, carefully planning the approach they would make to the bankers in the morning. They were well advised to do so, because the British banks certainly had no cause to feel coöperative; *their* Stock Exchange wasn't in trouble. And there was more to it than that. According to unimpeachable sources, the four British banks had lent Haupt a total of five and a half million dollars, and these loans, like many short-term loans made by foreign banks to American brokers, had not been secured by any collateral. Sources only fractionally more impeachable maintain that some of the loans had been extended very recently—that is, a week or less before the debacle. The money lent is known to have consisted of Eurodollars, a phantom but nonetheless serviceable currency consisting of dollar deposits in European banks; some four billion Eurodollars were actively traded among European financial institutions at that time, and the banks that lent the five and a half million to Haupt had first borrowed them from somebody else. According to a local expert in international banking, Eurodollars are customarily traded in huge blocks at a relatively tiny profit; for instance, a bank might borrow a block at four and a quarter per cent and lend it at four and a half per cent, at a net advantage of one fourth of one per cent per annum. Obviously, such transactions are looked upon as practically without risk. One-fourth of one per cent of five and a half million dollars over a period of one week amounts to $264.42, which gives some indication of the size of the profit on the Haupt deal that the four British banks would have been able to divide among themselves, less expenses, if everything had gone as planned. Instead, they now stood to lose the whole bundle.

Levy and the Chase men arrived red-eyed in London shortly after daybreak on a depressingly drizzly morning. They went to the Savoy to change their clothes and have breakfast and then headed straight for the City, London's financial district. Their first meeting was at the Fenchurch Street establishment of William Brandt's Sons, which had put up over half of the five and a half million. The Brandt partners courteously offered condolences on the death of the President, and the Americans agreed that it was a terrible thing, where-upon both sides came to the point. The Brandt men knew of Haupt's impending failure but not of the plan now afoot to rescue the Haupt customers by avoiding a formal bankruptcy; Levy explained this, and an hour's discussion followed, in the course of which the Britons showed a certain reluctance to go along—as well they might. Having just been taken in by one group of Yankees, they were not anxious to be immedi-ately taken in by another. "They were very unhappy," Levy says. "They raised hell with me as a representative of the New York Stock Exchange, one of whose members had got them into this jam. They wanted to make a trade with us—to get a priority in the collection of their claims in exchange for com-ing along with us and agreeing to defer collection. But their trading position wasn't really good; in a bankruptcy proceed-ing, their claims, based on unsecured loans, would have been considered *after* the claims of creditors who held collateral, and in my opinion they would have never collected a nickel. On the other hand, under the terms of our offer they would be treated equally with all the other Haupt creditors except the customers. We had to explain to them that we weren't trading."

The Brandt men replied that before deciding they wanted to think the matter over, and also to hear what the other British banks said. The American delegates then repaired to the London office of the Chase, on Lombard Street, where, by prearrangement, they met with representatives of the three other British banks and Levy had a chance for a reunion with his Kleinwort, Benson friends. The circumstances of the reunion were obviously less than happy, but Levy says that his friends took a realistic view of their situation and, with heroic objectivity, actually helped their fellow-Britons to see the American side of the question. Nevertheless, this meeting, like the earlier one, broke up without commitment by anyone. Levy and his colleagues stayed at the Chase for lunch and then walked over to the Bank of England, which was interested in the Haupt loans to the extent that their default would affect Britain's balance of payments. The Bank of England, through one of its deputies, assured the visitors of its distress over both America's national tragedy and Wall Street's parochial one, and advised them that while it lacked the power to tell the London banks what to do, in its judgment they would be wise to go along with the American scheme. Then, at about two o'clock, the trio returned to Lombard Street to wait nervously for word from the banks. As it happened, a parallel vigil was then beginning on Wall Street, where it was nine o'clock on Monday morning, and where Funston, just arrived in his office and very much aware that only one day remained in which to get the deal wrapped up, was pacing his rug as he waited for a call that would tell him whether London was going to cause the pot to fall in.

Kleinwort, Benson and S. Japhet & Co. were the first to agree to go along, Levy recalls. Then—after a silence of perhaps half an hour, during which Levy and his colleagues began to have an agonizing sense of the minutes ticking away in New York—an affirmative answer came from Brandt. That was the big one; with the chief creditor and two of the three others in line, it was all but certain that Ansbacher would join up. At around 4 P.M. London time, Ansbacher did, and

Levy was finally able to place the call that Funston had been waiting for. Their mission accomplished, the Americans went straight to the London airport, and within three hours were on a plane headed home.

On getting the good news, Funston felt that the whole agreement was pretty well in the bag at last, since all that was needed to seal the bag was the signatures of the fifteen Haupt general partners, who seemed to have nothing to lose and everything to gain from the plan. Still, the task of getting those signatures was a vital one. Short of a bankruptcy suit, which everyone was trying to avoid, no liquidator could distribute the Haupt assets—not even the marble-topped cabinets and the refrigerators—without the partners' permission. Accordingly, late on Monday afternoon the Haupt partners, each accompanied by his lawyer, trooped into Chairman Watts's office at the Stock Exchange to learn exactly what fate the Wall Street powers had been arranging for them.

The Haupt partners could hardly have found the projected agreement pleasant reading, inasmuch as it prescribed, among other things, that they were to execute powers of attorney giving a liquidator full control over Haupt's affairs. However, one of their own lawyers gave them a short, pungent talk pointing out that they were personally liable for the firm's debts whether or not they signed the agreement, so they might as well be public-spirited and sign it. More briefly, they were over a barrel. (Many of them later filed personal bankruptcy papers.) One startling event broke the even tenor of this gloomy meeting. Shortly after the Haupt lawyer had wound up his disquisition on the facts of life, someone noticed an unfamiliar and strikingly youthful face in the crowd and asked its owner to identify himself. The unhesitating reply was "I'm Russell Watson, a reporter for the *Wall Street Journal*." There was a short, stunned silence, in recognition of the fact that an untimely leak might still disturb the delicate balance of money and emotion that made up the agreement. Watson himself, who was twenty-four and had been on the *Journal* for a year, has since explained how he got into the meeting, and under what circumstances he left it. "I was new on the Stock Exchange beat then," he said afterward. "Earlier in the day, there had been word that Funston would probably hold a press conference sometime that evening, so I went over to the Exchange. At the main entrance, I asked a guard where Mr. Funston's conference was. The guard said it was on the sixth floor, and ushered me into an elevator. I suppose he thought I was a banker, a Haupt partner, or a lawyer. On the sixth floor, people were milling around everywhere. I just walked off the elevator and into the office where the meeting was—nobody stopped me. I didn't understand much of what was going on. I got the feeling that whatever was at stake, there was general agreement but still a lot of haggling over details to be done. I didn't recognize anybody there but Funston. I stood around quietly for about five minutes before anybody noticed me, and then everybody said, pretty much at once, 'Good God, get out of here!' They didn't exactly *kick* me out, but I saw it was time to go."

During the haggling phase that followed—a painfully protracted one, it developed—the Haupt partners and their lawyers made a command post of Watts's office, while the bank representatives and *their* lawyers camped in the North Committee Room, just down the hall. Funston, who was determined that news of a settlement should be in the hands of investors before the opening of the market next morning, was going wild with irritation and frustration, and in an effort to speed things up he constituted himself a sort of combination messenger boy and envoy. "All Monday evening, I kept running back and forth saying, 'Look, they won't give in on this point, so you've got to,'" he recalls. "Or I'd say, 'Look what time it is—only twelve hours until tomorrow's market opening! Initial here.'"

At fifteen minutes past midnight, nine and three-quarters

hours before the market's reopening, the agreement was signed in the South Committee Room by the twenty-eight parties at interest, in an atmosphere that a participant has described as one of exhaustion and general relief. As soon as the banks opened on Tuesday morning, the Stock Exchange deposited seven and a half million dollars, a sum amounting to roughly one-third of its available reserve, in an account on which the Haupt liquidator could draw; the same morning, the liquidator himself—James P. Mahony, a veteran member of the Exchange's staff—moved into the Haupt offices to take charge. The stock market, encouraged by confidence in the new President or by news of the Haupt settlement, or by a combination of the two, had its greatest one-day rise in history, more than eliminating Friday's losses. A week later, on December 2nd, Mahony announced that $1,750,000, had already been paid out of the Stock Exchange account to bail out Haupt customers; by December 12th, the figure was up to $5,400,000, and by Christmas to $6,700,000. Finally, on March 11, 1964, the Exchange was able to report that it had dispensed nine and a half million dollars, and that the Haupt customers, with the exception of a handful who couldn't be found, were whole again.

The agreement, in which some people saw an unmistakable implication that Wall Street's Establishment now felt accountable for public harm caused by the misdeeds, or even the misfortunes, of any of its members, gave rise to a variety of reactions. The rescued Haupt customers were predictably grateful, of course. The *Times* said that the agreement was evidence of "a sense of responsibility that served to inspire investor confidence" and "may have helped to avoid a potential panic." In Washington, President Johnson interrupted his first business day in office to telephone Funston and congratulate him. The chairman of the S.E.C., William L. Cary, who was not ordinarily given to throwing bouquets at the Stock Exchange, said in December that it had furnished "a dramatic, impressive demonstration of its strength and concern for the public interest." Other stock exchanges around the world were silent on the matter, but if one may judge by the unsentimental way that most of them do business, some of their officials must have been indulging in a certain amount of headshaking over the strange doings in New York. The Stock Exchange's member firms, who were assessed for the nine and a half million dollars over a period of three years, appeared to be generally satisfied, although a few of them were heard to grumble that fine old firms with justified reputations for skill and probity should not be asked to pay the losses of greedy upstarts who overstep and get caught out. Oddly, almost no one seems to have expressed gratitude to the British and American banks, which recouped something like half of their losses. It may be that people simply don't thank banks, except in television commercials.

The Stock Exchange itself, meanwhile, was torn between blushingly accepting congratulations and prudently, if perhaps gracelessly, insisting that what it had done wasn't to be regarded as a precedent—that it wouldn't necessarily do the same thing again. Nor were the Exchange's officials at all sure that the same thing would have been done if the Haupt case had occurred earlier—even a very little earlier. Crooks, who was chairman of the Exchange in the early 1950s, felt that the chances of such action during his term would have been about fifty-fifty. Funston, who assumed his office in 1951, felt that the matter would have been "questionable" during the early years of his incumbency. "One's idea of public responsibility is evolutionary," he said. He was particularly annoyed by the idea, which he had heard repeatedly, that the Exchange had acted out of a sense of guilt. Psychoanalytic interpretations of the event, he felt, were gratuitous, not to say churlish.

As for those older governors who glared, quite possibly balefully, at the negotiations from their gilt frames in the Governors' Room and the North and South Committee Rooms, their reaction to the whole proceeding may be imagined but cannot be known.

7

THE IMPACTED PHILOSOPHERS

AMONG THE GREATEST PROBLEMS facing American industry today, one may learn by talking with any of a large number of industrialists who are not known to be especially given to pontificating, is "the problem of communication." This preoccupation with the difficulty of getting a thought out of one head and into another is something the industrialists share with a substantial number of intellectuals and creative writers, more and more of whom seem inclined to regard communication, or the lack of it, as one of the greatest problems not just of industry but of humanity. (A group of avant-garde writers and artists have given the importance of communication a backhanded boost by flatly and unequivocally proclaiming themselves to be *against* it.) As far as the industrialists are concerned, I admit that in the course of hearing them invoke the word "communication"—often in an almost mystical way—over a period of years I have had a lot of trouble figuring out exactly what they meant. The general thesis is clear enough; namely, that everything would be all right, first, if they could get through to each other within their own organizations, and, second, if they, or their organizations, could get through to everybody else. What has puzzled me is how and why, in this day when the foundations sponsor one study of communication after another, individuals and organizations fail so consistently to express themselves understandably, or how and why their listeners fail to grasp what they hear.

A few years ago, I acquired a two-volume publication of the United States Government Printing Office entitled Hearings Before the Subcommittee on Antitrust and Monopoly of the Committee on the Judiciary, United States Senate, Eighty-seventh Congress, First Session, Pursuant to S. Res. 52, and after a fairly diligent perusal of its 1,459 pages I thought I could begin to see what the industrialists are talking about. The hearings, conducted in April, May, and June, 1961, under the chairmanship of Senator Estes Kefauver, of Tennessee, had to do with the now famous price-fixing and bid-rigging conspiracies in the electrical-manufacturing industry, which had already resulted, the previous February, in the imposition by a federal judge in Philadelphia of fines totaling $1,924,500 on twenty-nine firms and forty-five of their employees, and also of thirty-day prison sentences on seven of the employees. Since there had been no public presentation of evidence, all the defendants having pleaded either guilty or no defense, and since the records of the grand juries that indicted them were secret, the public had had little opportunity to hear about the details of the violations, and Senator Kefauver felt that the whole matter needed a good airing. The transcript shows that it got one, and what the airing revealed—at least within the biggest company involved—was a breakdown in intramural communication so drastic as to make the building of the Tower of Babel seem a triumph of organizational rapport.

In a series of indictments brought by the government in the United States District Court in Philadelphia between February and October, 1960, the twenty-nine companies and their executives were charged with having repeatedly violated

Section 1 of the Sherman Act of 1890, which declares illegal "every contract, combination in the form of trust or otherwise, or conspiracy, in restraint of trade or commerce among the several States, or with foreign nations." (The Sherman Act was the instrument used in the celebrated trust-busting activities of Theodore Roosevelt, and along with the Clayton Act of 1914 it has served as the government's weapon against cartels and monopolies ever since.) The violations, the government alleged, were committed in connection with the sale of large and expensive pieces of apparatus of a variety that is required chiefly by public and private electric-utility companies (power transformers, switchgear assemblies, and turbine-generator units, among many others), and were the outcome of a series of meetings attended by executives of the supposedly competing companies—beginning at least as early as 1956 and continuing into 1959—at which noncompetitive price levels were agreed upon, nominally sealed bids on individual contracts were rigged in advance, and each company was allocated a certain percentage of the available business. The government further alleged that, in an effort to preserve the secrecy of these meetings, the executives had resorted to such devices as referring to their companies by code numbers in their correspondence, making telephone calls from public booths or from their homes rather than from their offices, and doctoring the expense accounts covering their get-togethers to conceal the fact that they had all been in a certain city on a certain day. But their stratagems did not prevail. The federals, forcefully led by Robert A. Bicks, then head of the Antitrust Division of the Department of Justice, succeeded in exposing them, with considerable help from some of the conspirators themselves, who, after an employee of a small conspirator company saw fit to spill the story in the early fall of 1959, flocked to turn state's evidence.

The economic and social significance of the whole affair may be demonstrated clearly enough by citing just a few figures. In an average year at the time of the conspiracies, a total of more than one and three-quarters billion dollars was spent to purchase machines of the sort in question, nearly a fourth of it by federal, state, and local governments (which, of course, means the taxpayers), and most of the rest by private utility companies (which are inclined to pass along any rise in the cost of their equipment to the public in the form of rate increases). To take a specific example of the kind of money involved in an individual transaction, the list price of a 500,000-kilowatt turbine-generator—a monstrous device for producing electric power from steam power—was often something like sixteen million dollars. Actually, manufacturers sometimes cut their prices by as much as 25 percent in order to make a sale, and therefore, if everything was above board, it might have been possible to buy the machine at a saving of four million dollars; if representatives of the companies making such generators held a single meeting and agreed to fix prices, they could, in effect, increase the cost to the customer by the four million. And in the end, the customer was almost sure to be the public.

In presenting the indictments in Philadelphia, Bicks stated that, considered collectively, they revealed "a pattern of violations which can fairly be said to range among the most serious, the most flagrant, the most pervasive that have ever marked any basic American industry." Just before imposing the sentences, Judge J. Cullen Ganey went even further; in his view, the violations constituted "a shocking indictment of a vast section of our economy, for what is really at stake here is the survival of . . . the free-enterprise system." The prison sentences showed that he meant it; although there had been many successful prosecutions for violation of the Sherman Act during the seven decades since its passage, it was rare indeed for executives to be jailed. Not surprisingly, therefore, the case kicked up quite a ruckus in the press. The

New Republic, to be sure, complained that the newspapers and magazines were intentionally playing down "the biggest business scandal in decades," but the charge did not seem to have much foundation. Considering such things as the public's apathy toward switchgear, the woeful bloodlessness of criminal cases involving antitrust laws, and the relatively few details of the conspiracies that had emerged, the press in general gave the story a good deal of space, and even the *Wall Street Journal* and *Fortune* ran uncompromising and highly informative accounts of the debacle; here and there, in fact, one could detect signs of a revival of the spirit of old-time antibusiness journalism as it existed back in the thirties. After all, what could be more exhilarating than to see several dignified, impeccably tailored, and highly paid executives of a few of the nation's most respected corporations being trooped off to jail like common pickpockets? It was certainly the biggest moment for business-baiters since 1938, when Richard Whitney, the former president of the New York Stock Exchange, was put behind bars for speculating with his customers' money. Some called it the biggest since Teapot Dome.

To top it all off, there was a prevalent suspicion of hypocrisy in the very highest places. Neither the chairman of the board nor the president of General Electric, the largest of the corporate defendants, had been caught in the government's dragnet, and the same was true of Westinghouse Electric, the second-largest; these four ultimate bosses let it be known that they had been entirely ignorant of what had been going on within their commands right up to the time the first testimony on the subject was given to the Justice Department. Many people, however, were not satisfied by these disclaimers, and, instead, took the position that the defendant executives were men in the middle, who had broken the law only in response either to actual orders or to a corporate climate favoring price-fixing, and who were now being allowed to suffer for the sins of their superiors. Among the unsatisfied was Judge

Ganey himself, who said at the time of the sentencing, "One would be most naïve indeed to believe that these violations of the law, so long persisted in, affecting so large a segment of the industry, and, finally, involving so many millions upon millions of dollars, were facts unknown to those responsible for the conduct of the corporation. . . . I am convinced that in the great number of these defendants' cases, they were torn between conscience and approved corporate policy, with the rewarding objectives of promotion, comfortable security, and large salaries."

The public naturally wanted a ringleader, an archconspirator, and it appeared to find what it wanted in General Electric, which—to the acute consternation of the men endeavoring to guide its destinies from company headquarters, at 570 Lexington Avenue, New York City—got the lion's share of attention both in the press and in the Subcommittee hearings. With some 300,000 employees, and sales averaging some four billion dollars a year over the past ten years, it was not only far and away the biggest of the twenty-nine accused companies but, judged on the basis of sales in 1959, the fifth-biggest company in the country. It also drew a higher total of fines ($437,500) than any other company, and saw more of its executives sent to jail (three, with eight others receiving suspended sentences). Furthermore, as if to intensify in this hour of crisis the horror and shock of true believers—and the glee of scoffers—its highest-ranking executives had for years tried to represent it to the public as a paragon of successful virtue by issuing encomiums to the free competitive system, the very system that the price-fixing meetings were set up to mock. In 1959, shortly after the government's investigation of the violations had been brought to the attention of G.E.'s policymakers, the company demoted and cut the pay of those of its executives who admitted that they had been involved; one vice-president, for example, was informed that instead of the $127,000 a year he had been getting he would now get $40,000. (He had scarcely adjusted himself to that blow when Judge Ganey fined him four thousand dollars and sent him to prison for thirty days, and shortly after he regained his freedom, General Electric eased him out entirely.) The G.E. policy of imposing penalties of its own on these employees, regardless of what punishment the court might prescribe, was not adopted by Westinghouse, which waited until the judge had disposed of the case and then decided that the fines and prison sentences he had handed out to its stable of offenders were chastisement enough, and did not itself penalize them at all. Some people saw this attitude as evidence that Westinghouse was condoning the conspiracies, but others regarded it as a commendable, if tacit, admission that management at the highest level in the conniving companies was responsible—morally, at least—for the whole mess and was therefore in no position to discipline its erring employees. In the view of these people, G.E.'s haste to penalize the acknowledged culprits on its payroll strongly suggested that the firm was trying to save its own skin by throwing a few luckless employees to the wolves, or—as Senator Philip A. Hart, of Michigan, put it, more pungently, during the hearings—"to do a Pontius Pilate operation."

Embattled days at 570 Lexington Avenue! After years of cloaking the company in the mantle of a wise and benevolent corporate institution, the public-relations people at G.E. headquarters were faced with the ugly choice of representing its role in the price-fixing affair as that of either a fool or a knave. They tended strongly toward "fool." Judge Ganey, by his statement that he assumed the conspiracies to have been not only condoned but approved by the top brass and the company as a whole, clearly chose "knave." But his analysis may or may not have been the right one, and after reading the Kefauver Subcommittee testimony I have come to the melancholy conclusion that the truth will very likely never be known. For, as the testimony shows, the clear waters of moral responsibility at G.E. became hopelessly muddied by a struggle to communicate—a struggle so confused that in some cases, it would appear, if one of the big bosses at G.E. *had* ordered a subordinate to break the law, the message would somehow have been garbled in its reception, and if the subordinate *had* informed the boss that he was holding conspiratorial meetings with competitors, the boss might well have been under the impression that the subordinate was gossiping idly about lawn parties or pinochle sessions. Specifically, it would appear that a subordinate who received a direct oral order from his boss had to figure out whether it meant what it seemed to or the exact opposite, while the boss, in conversing with a subordinate, had to figure out whether he should take what the man told *him* at face value or should attempt to translate it out of a secret code to which he was by no means sure he had the key. That was the problem in a nutshell, and I state it here thus baldly as a suggestion for any potential beneficiary of a foundation who may be casting about for a suitable project on which to draw up a prospectus.

For the past eight years or so, G.E. had had a company rule called Directive Policy 20.5, which read, in part, "No employee shall enter into any understanding, agreement, plan or scheme, expressed or implied, formal or informal, with any competitor, in regard to prices, terms or conditions of sale, production, distribution, territories, or customers; nor exchange or discuss with a competitor prices, terms or conditions of sale, or any other competitive information." In effect, this rule was simply an injunction to G.E.'s personnel to obey the federal antitrust laws, except that it was somewhat more concrete and comprehensive in the matter of price than they are. It was almost impossible for executives with jurisdiction over pricing policies at G.E. to be unaware of 20.5, or even hazy about it, because to make sure that new executives were acquainted with it and to refresh the memories of old ones, the company formally reissued and distributed it at intervals, and all such executives were asked to sign their names to it as an earnest that they were currently complying with it and intended to keep on doing so. The trouble—at least during the period covered by the court action, and apparently for a long time before that as well—was that some people at G.E., including some of those who regularly signed 20.5, simply did not believe that it was to be taken seriously. They assumed that 20.5 was mere window dressing: that it was on the books solely to provide legal protection for the company and for the higher-ups; that meeting illegally with competitors was recognized and accepted as standard practice within the company; and that often when a ranking executive ordered a subordinate executive to comply with 20.5, he was actually ordering him to violate it. Illogical as it might seem, this last assumption becomes comprehensible in the light of the fact that, for a time, when some executives orally conveyed, or reconveyed, the order, they were apparently in the habit of accompanying it with an unmistakable wink. In May of 1948, for example, there was a meeting of G.E. sales managers during which the custom of winking was openly discussed. Robert Paxton, an upper-level G.E. executive who later became the company's president, addressed the meeting and delivered the usual admonition about antitrust violations, whereupon William S. Ginn, then a sales executive in the transformer division, under Paxton's authority, startled him by saying, "I didn't see you wink." Paxton replied firmly, "There was no wink. We mean it, and these are the orders." Asked by Senator Kefauver how long he had been aware that orders issued at G.E. were sometimes accompanied by winks, Paxton replied that he had first observed the practice way back in 1935, when his boss had given him an instruction along with a wink or its equivalent, and that when, some time later, the significance of the gesture dawned on him, he had become so incensed that he had with difficulty restrained himself from jeopardizing his career by punching the boss in the nose. Paxton went on to say that his objections to the practice of winking had been so strong as to earn him a reputation in the company for being an antiwink man, and that he, for his part, had never winked.

Although Paxton would seem to have left little doubt as to how he intended his winkless order of 1948 to be interpreted, its meaning failed to get through to Ginn, for not long after it was issued, he went out and fixed prices to a fare-thee-well. (Obviously, it takes more than one company to make a price-fixing agreement, but all the testimony tends to indicate that it was G.E. that generally set the pattern for the rest of the industry in such matters.) Thirteen years later, Ginn—fresh from a few weeks in jail, and fresh out of a $135,000-a-year job—appeared before the Subcommittee to account for, among other things, his strange response to the winkless order. He had disregarded it, he said, because he had received a contrary order from two of his other superiors in the G.E. chain of command, Henry V. B. Erben and Francis Fairman, and in explaining why he had heeded their order rather than Paxton's he introduced the fascinating concept of degrees of communication—another theme for a foundation grantee to get his teeth into. Erben and Fairman, Ginn said, had been more articulate, persuasive, and forceful in issuing their order than Paxton had been in issuing his; Fairman, especially, Ginn stressed, had proved to be "a great communicator, a great philosopher, and, frankly, a great believer in stability of prices." Both Erben and Fairman had dismissed Paxton as naïve, Ginn testified, and, in further summary of how he had been led astray, he said that "the people who were advocating the Devil were able to sell me better than the philosophers that were selling the Lord."

It would be helpful to have at hand a report from Erben and Fairman themselves on the communication technique that enabled them to prevail over Paxton, but unfortunately neither of these philosophers could testify before the Subcommittee, because by the time of the hearings both of them were dead. Paxton, who was available, was described in Ginn's testimony as having been at all times one of the philosopher-salesmen on the side of the Lord. "I can clarify Mr. Paxton by saying Mr. Paxton came closer to being an Adam Smith advocate than any businessman I have met in America," Ginn declared. Still, in 1950, when Ginn admitted to Paxton in casual conversation that he had "compromised himself" in respect to antitrust matters, Paxton merely told him that he was a damned fool, and did not report the confession to anyone else in the company. Testifying as to why he did not, Paxton said that when the conversation occurred he was no longer Ginn's boss, and that, in the light of his personal ethics, repeating such an admission by a man not under his authority would be "gossip" and "talebearing."

Meanwhile, Ginn, no longer answerable to Paxton, was meeting with competitors at frequent intervals and moving steadily up the corporate ladder. In November, 1954, he was made general manager of the transformer division, whose headquarters were in Pittsfield, Massachusetts—a job that put him in line for a vice-presidency. At the time of Ginn's shift, Ralph J. Cordiner, who has been chairman of the board of General Electric since 1949, called him down to New York for the express purpose of enjoining him to comply strictly and undeviatingly with Directive Policy 20.5. Cordiner communicated this idea so successfully that it was clear enough to Ginn at the moment, but it remained so only as long as it took him, after leaving the chairman, to walk to Erben's office. There his comprehension of what he had just heard became clouded. Erben, who was head of G.E.'s distribution group, ranked directly below Cordiner and directly above Ginn, and, according to Ginn's testimony, no sooner were they alone in his office than he countermanded Cordiner's injunction, saying, "Now, keep on doing the way that you have been doing, but just be sensible about it and use your head on the subject."

Erben's extraordinary communicative prowess again carried the day, and Ginn continued to meet with competitors. "I knew Mr. Cordiner could fire me," he told Senator Kefauver, "but also I knew I was working for Mr. Erben."

At the end of 1954, Paxton took over Erben's job and thereby became Ginn's boss again. Ginn went right on meeting with competitors, but, since he was aware that Paxton disapproved of the practice, didn't tell him about it. Moreover, he testified, within a month or two he had become convinced that he could not afford to discontinue attending the meetings under any circumstances, for in January, 1955, the entire electrical-equipment industry became embroiled in a drastic price war—known as the "white sale," because of its timing and the bargains it afforded to buyers—in which the erstwhile amiable competitors began fiercely undercutting one another. Such a manifestation of free enterprise was, of course, exactly what the intercompany conspiracies were intended to prevent, but just at that time the supply of electrical apparatus so greatly exceeded the demand that first a few of the conspirators and then more and more began breaking the agreements they themselves had made. In dealing with the situation as best he could, Ginn said, he "used the philosophies that had been taught me previously"—by which he meant that he continued to conduct price-fixing meetings, in the hope that at least *some* of the agreements made at them would be honored. As for Paxton, in Ginn's opinion that philosopher was not only ignorant of the meetings but so constant in his devotion to the concept of free and aggressive competition that he actually enjoyed the price war, disastrous though it was to everybody's profits. (In his own testimony, Paxton vigorously denied that he had enjoyed it.)

Within a year or so, the electrical-equipment industry took an upturn, and in January, 1957, Ginn, having ridden out the storm relatively well, got his vice-presidency. At the same time, he was transferred to Schenectady, to become general manager of G.E.'s turbine-generator division, and Cordiner again called him into headquarters and gave him a lecture on 20.5. Such lectures were getting to be a routine with Cordiner; every time a new employee was assigned to a strategic managerial post, or an old employee was promoted to such a post, the lucky fellow could be reasonably certain that he would be summoned to the chairman's office to hear a rendition of the austere creed. In his book *The Heart of Japan*, Alexander Campbell reports that a large Japanese electrical concern has drawn up a list of seven company commandments (for example, "Be courteous and sincere!"), and that each morning, in each of its thirty factories, the workers are required to stand at attention and recite these in unison, and then to sing the company song ("For ever-increasing production / Love your work, give your all!"). Cordiner did not require his subordinates to recite or sing 20.5—as far as is known, he never even had it set to music—but from the number of times men like Ginn had it read to them or otherwise recalled to their attention, they must have come to know it well enough to chant it, improvising a tune as they went along.

This time, Cordiner's message not only made an impression on Ginn's mind but stuck there in unadulterated form. Ginn, according to his testimony, became a reformed executive and dropped his price-fixing habits overnight. However, it appears that his sudden conversion cannot be attributed wholly to Cordiner's powers of communication, or even to the drip-drip-drip effect of repetition, for it was to a considerable extent pragmatic in character, like the conversion of Henry VIII to Protestantism. He reformed, Ginn explained to the Subcommittee, because his "air cover was gone."

"Your what was gone?" Senator Kefauver asked.

"My air cover was gone," replied Ginn. "I mean I had lost my air cover. Mr. Erben wasn't around any more, and all of my colleagues had gone, and I was now working directly for Mr. Paxton, knowing his feelings on the matter. . . . Any philosophy that I had grown up with before in the past was now out the window."

If Erben, who had not been Ginn's boss since late in 1954, had been the source of his air cover, Ginn must have been without its protection for over two years, but, presumably, in the excitement of the price war he had failed to notice its absence. However that may have been, here he now was, a man suddenly shorn not only of his air cover but of his philosophy. Swiftly filling the latter void with a whole new set of principles, he circulated copies of 20.5 among his department managers in the turbine-generator division and topped this off by energetically adopting what he called a "leprosy policy"; that is, he advised his subordinates to avoid even casual social contacts with their counterparts in competing companies, because "once the relationships are established, I have come to the conclusion after many years of hard experience that the relationships tend to spread and the hanky-panky begins to get going." But now fate played a cruel trick on Ginn, and, all unknowing, he landed in the very position that Paxton and Cordiner had been in for years—that of a philosopher vainly endeavoring to sell the Lord to a flock that declined to buy his message and was, in fact, systematically engaging in the hanky-panky its leader had warned it against. Specifically, during the whole of 1957 and 1958 and the first part of 1959 two of Ginn's subordinates were piously signing 20.5 with one hand and, with the other, briskly drawing up price-fixing agreements at a whole series of meetings—in New York; Philadelphia; Chicago; Hot Springs, Virginia; and Skytop, Pennsylvania, to name a few of their gathering places.

It appears that Ginn had not been able to impart much of his shining new philosophy to others, and that at the root of his difficulty lay that old jinx, the problem of communicating. Asked at the hearings how his subordinates could possibly have gone so far astray, he replied, "I have got to admit that I made a communication error. I didn't sell this thing to the boys well enough. . . . The price is so important in the complete running of a business that, philosophically, we have got to sell people not only just the fact that it is against the law, but . . . that it shouldn't be done for many, many reasons. But it has got to be a philosophical approach and a communication approach. . . . Even though . . . I had told my associates not to do this, some of the boys did get off the reservation. . . . I have to admit to myself here an area of a failure in communications . . . which I am perfectly willing to accept my part of the responsibility for."

In earnestly striving to analyze the cause of the failure, Ginn said, he had reached the conclusion that merely issuing directives, no matter how frequently, was not enough; what was needed was "a complete philosophy, a complete understanding, a complete breakdown of barriers between people, if we are going to get some understanding and really live and manage these companies within the philosophies that they should be managed in."

Senator Hart permitted himself to comment, "You can communicate until you are dead and gone, but if the point you are communicating about, even though it be a law of the land, strikes your audience as something that is just a folklore . . . you will never sell the package."

Ginn ruefully conceded that that was true.

The concept of degrees of communication was further developed, by implication, in the testimony of another defendant, Frank E. Stehlik, who had been general manager of the G.E. low-voltage-switchgear department from May, 1956, to February, 1960. (As all but a tiny minority of the users of electricity are contentedly unaware, switchgear serves to control and protect apparatus used in the generation, conversion, transmission, and distribution of electrical energy, and more than $100 million worth of it is sold annually in the United States.) Stehlik received some of his business guidance in the conventional form of orders, oral and written, and some—perhaps just as much, to judge by his testimony—through a less intellectual, more visceral medium of communication that he called "impacts." Apparently, when something happened within the company that made an impression on him, he would consult a sort of internal metaphysical voltmeter to ascertain the force of the jolt that he had received, and, from the reading he got, would attempt to gauge the true drift of company policy. For example, he testified that during 1956, 1957, and most of 1958 he believed that G.E. was frankly and fully in favor of complying with 20.5. But then, in the autumn of 1958, George E. Burens, Stehlik's immediate superior, told him that he, Burens, had been directed by Paxton, who by then was president of G.E., to have lunch with Max Scott, president of the I-T-E Circuit Breaker Company, an important competitor in the switchgear market. Paxton said in his own testimony that while he had indeed asked Burens to have lunch with Scott, he had instructed him categorically not to talk about prices, but apparently Burens did not mention this caveat to Stehlik; in any event, the disclosure that the high command had told Burens to lunch with an archrival, Stehlik testified, "had a heavy impact on me." Asked to amplify this, he said, "There are a great many impacts that influence me in my thinking as to the true attitude of the company, and that was one of them." As the impacts, great and small, piled up, their cumulative effect finally communicated to Stehlik that he had been wrong in supposing the company had any real respect for 20.5. Accordingly, when, late in 1958, Stehlik was ordered by Burens to begin holding price meetings with the competitors, he was not in the least surprised.

Stehlik's compliance with Burens' order ultimately brought on a whole new series of impacts, of a much more crudely communicative sort. In February, 1960, General Electric cut his annual pay from $70,000 to $26,000 for violating 20.5; a year later Judge Ganey gave him a three-thousand-dollar fine and a suspended thirty-day jail sentence for violating the Sherman Act; and about a month after *that* G.E. asked for, and got, his resignation. Indeed, during his last years with the firm Stehlik seems to have received almost as many lacerating impacts as a Raymond Chandler hero. But testimony given at the hearings by L. B. Gezon, manager of the marketing section of the low-voltage-switchgear department, indicated that Stehlik, again like a Chandler hero, was capable of dishing out blunt impacts as well as taking them. Gezon, who was directly under Stehlik in the line of command, told the Subcommittee that although he had taken part in price-fixing meetings prior to April, 1956, when Stehlik became his boss, he did not subsequently engage in any antitrust violations until late 1958, and that he did so then only as the result of an impact that bore none of the subtlety noted by Stehlik in his early experience with this phenomenon. The impact came directly from Stehlik, who, it seems, left nothing to chance in communicating with his subordinates. In Gezon's words, Stehlik told him "to resume the meetings; that the company policy was unchanged; the risk was just as great as it ever had been; and that if our activities were discovered, I personally would be dismissed or disciplined [by the company], as well as punished by the government." So Gezon was left with three choices: to quit, to disobey the direct order of his superior (in which case, he thought, "they might have found somebody else to do my job"), or to obey the order, and thereby violate the antitrust laws, with no immunity against the possible consequences. In short, his alternatives were comparable to those faced by an international spy.

Although Gezon did resume the meetings, he was not indicted, possibly because he had been a relatively minor price-fixer. General Electric, for its part, demoted him but did not require him to resign. Yet it would be a mistake to assume that Gezon was relatively untouched by his experience. Asked by Senator Kefauver if he did not think that Stehlik's order had placed him in an intolerable position, he replied that it had not struck him that way at the time. Asked whether he thought it unjust that he had suffered demotion for carrying out the order of a superior, he replied, "I personally don't consider it so." To judge by his answers, the impact on Gezon's heart and mind would seem to have been heavy indeed.

The other side of the communication problem—the difficulty that a superior is likely to encounter in understanding what a subordinate tells him—is graphically illustrated by the testimony of Raymond W. Smith, who was general manager of G.E.'s transformer division from the beginning of 1957 until late in 1959, and of Arthur F. Vinson, who in October, 1957, was appointed vice-president in charge of G.E.'s apparatus group, and also a member of the company's executive committee. Smith's job was the one Ginn had held for the previous two years, and when Vinson got *his* job, he became Smith's immediate boss. Smith's highest pay during the period in question was roughly $100,000 a year, while Vinson reached a basic salary of $110,000 and also got a variable bonus, ranging from $45,000 to $100,000. Smith testified that on January 1, 1957, the very day he took charge of the transformer division—and a holiday, at that—he met with Chairman Cordiner and Executive Vice-President Paxton, and Cordiner gave him the familiar admonition about living up to 20.5. However, later that year, the competitive going got so rough that transformers were selling at discounts of as much as 35 percent, and Smith decided on his own hook that the time had come to begin negotiating with rival firms in the hope of stabilizing the market. He felt that he was justified in doing this, he said, because he was convinced that both in company circles and in the whole industry negotiations of this kind were "the order of the day."

By the time Vinson became his superior, in October, Smith

was regularly attending price-fixing meetings, and he felt that he ought to let his new boss know what he was doing. Accordingly, he told the Subcommittee, on two or three occasions when the two men found themselves alone together in the normal course of business, he said to Vinson, "I had a meeting with the clan this morning." Counsel for the Subcommittee asked Smith whether he had ever put the matter more bluntly—whether, for example, he had ever said anything like "We're meeting with competitors to fix prices. We're going to have a little conspiracy here and I don't want it to get out." Smith replied that he had never said anything remotely like that—had done nothing more than make remarks on the order of "I had a meeting with the clan this morning." He did not elaborate on why he did not speak with greater directness, but two logical possibilities present themselves. Perhaps he hoped that he could keep Vinson informed about the situation and at the same time protect him from the risk of becoming an accomplice. Or perhaps he had no such intention, and was simply expressing himself in the oblique, colloquial way that characterized much of his speaking. (Paxton, a close friend of Smith's, had once complained to Smith that he was "given to being somewhat cryptic" in his remarks.) Anyhow, Vinson, according to his own testimony, had flatly misunderstood what Smith meant; indeed, he could not recall ever hearing Smith use the expression "meeting of the clan," although he did recall his saying things like "Well, I am going to take this new plan on transformers and show it to the boys." Vinson testified that he had thought the "boys" meant the G.E. district sales people and the company's customers, and that the "new plan" was a new marketing plan; he said that it had come as a rude shock to him to learn—a couple of years later, after the case had broken—that in speaking of the "boys" and the "new plan," Smith had been referring to competitors and a price-fixing scheme. "I think Mr. Smith is a sincere man," Vinson testified. "I am sure Mr. Smith . . . thought he was telling me that he was going to one of these meetings. This meant nothing to me."

Smith, on the other hand, was confident that his meaning had got through to Vinson. "I never got the impression that he misunderstood me," he insisted to the Subcommittee. Questioning Vinson later, Kefauver asked whether an executive in his position, with thirty-odd years' experience in the electrical industry, could possibly be so naive as to misunderstand a subordinate on such a substantive matter as grasping who the "boys" were. "I don't think it is too naive," replied Vinson. "We have a lot of boys. . . . I may be naïve, but I am certainly telling the truth, and in this kind of thing I am sure I am naïve."

SENATOR KEFAUVER: Mr. Vinson, you wouldn't be a vice-president at $200,000 a year if you were naïve.

MR. VINSON: I think I could well get there by being naïve in this area. It might help.

Here, in a different field altogether, the communication problem again comes to the fore. Was Vinson really saying to Kefauver what he seemed to be saying—that naïveté about antitrust violations might be a help to a man in getting and holding a $200,000-a-year job at General Electric? It seems unlikely. And yet what else could he have meant? Whatever the answer, neither the federal antitrust men nor the Senate investigators were able to prove that Smith succeeded in his attempts to communicate to Vinson the fact that he was engaging in price-fixing. And, lacking such proof, they were unable to establish what they gave every appearance of going all out to establish if they could: namely, that at least some one man at the pinnacle of G.E.'s management—some member of the sacred executive committee itself—was implicated. Actually, when the story of the conspiracies first became known, Vinson not only concurred in a company decision to punish Smith by drastically demoting him but personally informed him of the decision—two acts that, if he had grasped Smith's meaning back in 1957, would have denoted a remarkable degree of cynicism and hypocrisy. (Smith, by the way, rather than accept the demotion, quit General Electric and, after being fined three thousand dollars and given a suspended thirty-day prison sentence by Judge Ganey, found a job elsewhere, at ten thousand dollars a year.)

This was not Vinson's only brush with the case. He was also among those named in one of the grand jury indictments that precipitated the court action, this time in connection not with his comprehension of Smith's jargon but with the conspiracy in the switchgear department. On this aspect of the case, four switchgear executives—Burens, Stehlik, Clarence E. Burke, and H. Frank Hentschel—testified before the grand jury (and later before the Subcommittee) that at some time in July, August, or September of 1958 (none of them could establish the precise date) Vinson had had lunch with them in Dining Room B of G.E.'s switchgear works in Philadelphia, and that during the meal he had instructed them to hold price meetings with competitors. As a result of this order, they said, a meeting attended by representatives of G.E., Westinghouse, the Allis-Chalmers Manufacturing Company, the Federal Pacific Electric Company, and the I-T-E Circuit Breaker Company was held at the Hotel Traymore in Atlantic City on November 9, 1958, at which sales of switchgear to federal, state, and municipal agencies were divvied up, with General Electric to get 39 percent of the business, Westinghouse 35 percent, I-T-E 11 percent, Allis-Chalmers 8 percent, and Federal Pacific Electric 7 percent. At subsequent meetings, agreement was reached on allocating sales of switchgear to private buyers as well, and an elaborate formula was worked out whereby the privilege of submitting the lowest bid to prospective customers was rotated among the conspiring companies at two-week intervals. Because of its periodic nature, this was called the phase-of-the-moon formula—a designation that in due time led to the following lyrical exchange between the Subcommittee and L. W. Long, an executive of Allis-Chalmers:

> SENATOR KEFAUVER: Who were the phasers-of-the-mooners—phase-of-the-mooners?

> MR. LONG: As it developed, this so-called phase-of-the-moon operation was carried out at a level below me, I think referred to as a working group. . . .

> MR. FERRALL [counsel for the Subcommittee]: Did they ever report to you about it?

> MR. LONG: Phase of the moon? No.

Vinson told the Justice Department prosecutors, and repeated to the Subcommittee, that he had not known about the Traymore meeting, the phase-of-the-mooners, or the existence of the conspiracy itself until the case broke; as for the lunch in Dining Room B, he insisted that it had never taken place. On this point, Burens, Stehlik, Burke, and Hentschel submitted to lie-detector tests, administered by the F.B.I., and passed them. Vinson refused to take a lie-detector test, at first explaining that he was acting on advice of counsel and against his personal inclination, and later, after hearing how the four other men had fared, arguing that if the machine had not pronounced them liars, it couldn't be any good. It was established that on only eight business days during July, August, and September had Burens, Burke, Stehlik, and Hentschel all been together in the Philadelphia plant at the lunch hour, and Vinson produced some of his expense accounts, which, he pointed out to the Justice Department, showed that he had been elsewhere on each of those days. Confronted with this evidence, the Justice Department dropped its case against Vinson, and he stayed on as a vice-president of General Electric. Nothing that the Subcommittee elicited from him cast any substantive doubt on the defense that had impressed the government prosecutors.

Thus, the uppermost echelon at G.E. came through unscathed; the record showed that participation in the conspiracy went fairly far down in the organization but not all the way to the top. Gezon, everybody agreed, had followed orders from Stehlik, and Stehlik had followed orders from Burens, but that was the end of the trail, because although Burens said he had followed orders from Vinson, Vinson denied it and made the denial stick. The government, at the end of its investigation, stated in court that it could not prove, and did not claim, that either Chairman Cordiner or President Paxton had authorized, or even known about, the conspiracies, and thereby officially ruled out the possibility that they had resorted to at least a figurative wink. Later, Paxton and Cordiner showed up in Washington to testify before the Subcommittee, and its interrogators were similarly unable to establish that they had ever indulged in any variety of winking.

After being described by Ginn as General Electric's stubbornest and most dedicated advocate of free competition, Paxton explained to the Subcommittee that his thinking on the subject had been influenced not directly by Adam Smith but, rather, by way of a former G.E. boss he had worked under—the late Gerard Swope. Swope, Paxton testified, had always believed firmly that the ultimate goal of business was to produce more goods for more people at lower cost. "I bought that then, I buy it now," said Paxton. "I think it is the most marvelous statement of economic philosophy that any industrialist has ever expressed." In the course of his testimony, Paxton had an explanation, philosophical or otherwise, of each of the several situations related to price-fixing in which his name had earlier been mentioned. For instance, it had been brought out that in 1956 or 1957 a young man named Jerry Page, a minor employee in G.E.'s switchgear division, had written directly to Cordiner alleging that the switchgear divisions of G.E. and of several competitor companies were involved in a conspiracy in which information about prices was exchanged by means of a secret code based on different colors of letter paper. Cordiner had turned the matter over to Paxton with orders that he get to the bottom of it, and Paxton had thereupon conducted an investigation that led him to conclude that the color-code conspiracy was "wholly a hallucination on the part of this boy." In arriving at that conclusion, Paxton had apparently been right, although it later came out that there had been a conspiracy in the switchgear division during 1956 and 1957; this, however, was a rather conventional one, based simply on price-fixing meetings, rather than on anything so gaudy as a color code. Page could not be called to testify because of ill health.

Paxton conceded that there had been some occasions when he "must have been pretty damn dumb." (Dumb or not, for his services as the company's president he was, of course, remunerated on a considerably grander scale than Vinson—receiving a basic annual salary of $125,000, plus annual incentive compensation of about $175,000, plus stock options designed to enable him to collect much more at low tax rates.) As for Paxton's attitude toward company communications, he emerges as a pessimist on this score. Upon being asked at the hearings to comment on the Smith-Vinson conversations of 1957, he said that, knowing Smith, he just could not "cast the man in the role of a liar," and went on:

When I was younger, I used to play a good deal of bridge. We played about fifty rubbers of bridge, four of us, every winter, and I think we probably played some rather good bridge. If you gentlemen are bridge players, you know that there is a code of signals that is exchanged between partners as the game progresses. It is a stylized form of playing. . . . Now, as I think about this—and I was particularly impressed when I read Smith's testimony when he talked about a "meeting of the clan" or "meeting of the boys"—I begin to think that there must have been a stylized method of communication between these people who were dealing with competition. Now, Smith could say, "I told Vinson what I was doing," and Vinson wouldn't have the foggiest idea what was being told to him, and both men could testify under oath, one saying yes and the other man saying no, and both be telling the truth. . . . [They] wouldn't be on the same wavelength. [They] wouldn't have the same meanings. I think, I believe now that these men did think that they were telling the truth, but they weren't communicating between each other with understanding.

Here, certainly, is the gloomiest possible analysis of the communications problem.

Chairman Cordiner's status, it appears from his testimony, was approximately that of the Boston Cabots in the celebrated jingle. His services to the company, for which he was recompensed in truly handsome style (with, for 1960, a salary of just over $280,000, plus contingent deferred income of about $120,000, plus stock options potentially worth hundreds of thousands more), were indubitably many and valuable, but they were performed on such an exalted level that, at least in antitrust matters, he does not seem to have been able to have any earthly communication at all. When he emphatically told the Subcommittee that at no time had he had so much as an inkling of the network of conspiracies, it could be deduced that his was a case not of faulty communication but of no communication. He did not speak to the Subcommittee of philosophy or philosophers, as Ginn and Paxton had done, but from his past record of ordering reissues of 20.5 and of peppering his speeches and public statements with praise of free enterprise, it seems clear that he was *un philosophe sans le savoir*—and one on the side of selling the Lord, since no evidence was adduced to suggest that he was given to winking in any form. Kefauver ran through a long list of antitrust violations of which General Electric had been accused over the past half-century, asking Cordiner, who joined the company in 1922, how much he knew about each of them; usually, he replied that he had known about them only after the fact. In commenting on Ginn's testimony that Erben had countermanded Cordiner's direct order in 1954, Cordiner said that he had read it with "great alarm" and "great wonderment," since Erben had always indicated to him "an intense competitive spirit," rather than any disposition to be friendly with rival companies.

Throughout his testimony, Cordiner used the curious expression "be responsive to." If, for instance, Kefauver inadvertently asked the same question twice, Cordiner would say, "I was responsive to that a moment ago," or if Kefauver interrupted him, as he often did, Cordiner would ask politely, "May I be responsive?" This, too, offers a small lead for a foundation grantee, who might want to look into the distinction between being responsive (a passive state) and answering (an act), and their relative effectiveness in the process of communication.

Summing up his position on the case as a whole, in reply to a question of Kefauver's about whether he thought that G.E. had incurred "corporate disgrace," Cordiner said, "No, I am not going to be responsive and say that General Electric had corporate disgrace. I am going to say that we are deeply grieved and concerned. . . . I am not proud of it."

Chairman Cordiner, then, had been able to fairly deafen his subordinate officers with lectures on compliance with the rules of the company and the laws of the country, but he had not been able to get all those officers to comply with either, and President Paxton could muse thoughtfully on how it was that two of his subordinates who had given radically different accounts of a conversation between them could be not liars but merely poor communicators. Philosophy seems to have reached a high point at G.E., and communication a low one. If executives could just learn to understand one another, most of the witnesses said or implied, the problem of antitrust violations would be solved. But perhaps the problem is cultural as well as technical, and has something to do with a loss of personal identity that comes from working in a huge organization. The cartoonist Jules Feiffer, contemplating the communication problem in a nonindustrial context, has said, "Actually, the breakdown is between the person and himself. If you're not able to communicate successfully between yourself and yourself, how are you supposed to make it with the strangers outside?" Suppose, purely as a hypothesis, that the owner of a company who orders his subordinates to obey the antitrust laws has such poor communication with himself that he does not really know whether he wants the order to be complied with or not. If his order is disobeyed, the resulting price-fixing may benefit his company's coffers; if it is obeyed, then he has done the right thing. In the first instance, he is not personally implicated in any wrongdoing, while in the second he is positively involved in *right* doing. What, after all, can he lose? It is perhaps reasonable to suppose that such an executive might communicate his uncertainty more forcefully than his order. Possibly yet another foundation grantee should have a look at the reverse of communication failure, where he might discover that messages the sender does not even realize he is sending sometimes turn out to have got across only too effectively.

Meanwhile, in the first years after the Subcommittee concluded its investigation, the defendant companies were by no means allowed to forget their transgressions. The law permits customers who can prove that they have paid artificially high prices as a result of antitrust violations to sue for damages—in most cases, triple damages—and suits running into many millions of dollars piled up so high that Chief Justice Warren had to set up a special panel of federal judges to plan how they should all be handled. Needless to say, Cordiner was not allowed to forget about the matter, either; indeed, it would be surprising if he was allowed a chance to think about much else, for, in addition to the suits, he had to contend with active efforts—unsuccessful, as it turned out—by a minority group of stockholders to unseat him. Paxton retired as president in April, 1961, because of ill health dating back at least to the previous January, when he underwent a major operation. As for the executives who pleaded guilty and were fined or imprisoned, most of those who had been employed by companies other than G.E. remained with them, either in their old jobs or in similar ones. Of those who had been employed by G.E., none remained there. Some retired permanently from business, others settled for comparatively small jobs, and a few landed big ones—most spectacularly Ginn, who in June, 1961, became president of Baldwin-Lima-Hamilton, manufacturers of heavy machinery. And as for the future of price-fixing in the electrical industry, it seems safe to say that what with the Justice Department, Judge Ganey, Senator Kefauver, and the triple-damage suits, the impact on the philosophers who guide corporate policy was such that they, and even their subordinates, were likely to try to hew scrupulously to the line for quite some time. Quite a different question, however, is whether they had made any headway in their ability to communicate.

8

THE LAST GREAT CORNER

BETWEEN SPRING AND MIDSUMMER, 1958, the common stock of
the E. L. Bruce Company, the nation's leading maker of hardwood floors, moved from a low of just under $17 a share to
a high of $190 a share. This startling, even alarming, rise was
made in an ascending scale that was climaxed by a frantic
crescendo in which the price went up a hundred dollars a
share in a single day. Nothing of the sort had happened for
a generation. Furthermore—and even more alarming—the
rise did not seem to have the slightest bit of relation to any
sudden hunger on the part of the American public for new
hardwood floors. To the consternation of almost everyone
concerned, conceivably including even some of the holders of
Bruce stock, it seemed to be entirely the result of a technical
stock-market situation called a corner. With the exception of
a general panic such as occurred in 1929, a corner is the most
drastic and spectacular of all developments that can occur in
the stock market, and more than once in the nineteenth and
early twentieth centuries, corners had threatened to wreck the
national economy.

The Bruce situation never threatened to do that. For one thing, the Bruce Company was so small in relation to the economy as a whole that even the wildest gyrations in its stock could hardly have much national effect. For another, the Bruce "corner" was accidental—the by-product of a fight for corporate control—rather than the result of calculated manipulations, as most of the historic corners had been. Finally, this one eventually turned out to be not a true corner at all, but only a near thing; in September, Bruce stock quieted down and settled at a reasonable level. But the incident served to stir up memories, some of them perhaps tinged with nostalgia, among those flinty old Wall Streeters who had been around to see the classic corners—or at least the last of them.

In June of 1922, the New York Stock Exchange began listing the shares of a corporation called Piggly Wiggly Stores— a chain of retail self-service markets situated mostly in the South and West, with headquarters in Memphis—and the stage was set for one of the most dramatic financial battles of that gaudy decade when Wall Street, only negligently watched over by the federal government, was frequently sent reeling by the machinations of operators seeking to enrich themselves and destroy their enemies. Among the theatrical aspects of this particular battle—a battle so celebrated in its time that headline writers referred to it simply as the "Piggly Crisis"— was the personality of the hero (or, as some people saw it, the villain), who was a newcomer to Wall Street, a country boy setting out defiantly, amid the cheers of a good part of rural America, to lay the slick manipulators of New York by the heels. He was Clarence Saunders, of Memphis, a plump, neat, handsome man of forty-one who was already something of a legend in his home town, chiefly because of a house he was putting up there for himself. Called the Pink Palace, it was an enormous structure faced with pink Georgia marble and built around an awe-inspiring white-marble Roman atrium, and, according to Saunders, it would stand for a thousand years.

Unfinished though it was, the Pink Palace was like nothing Memphis had ever seen before. Its grounds were to include a private golf course, since Saunders liked to do his golfing in seclusion. Even the makeshift estate where he and his wife and four children were camping out pending completion of the Palace had its own golf course. (Some people said that his preference for privacy was induced by the attitude of the local country club governors, who complained that he had corrupted their entire supply of caddies by the grandeur of his tips.) Saunders, who had founded the Piggly Wiggly Stores in 1919, had most of the standard traits of the flamboyant American promoters—suspect generosity, a knack for attracting publicity, love of ostentation, and so on—but he also had some much less common traits, notably a remarkably vivid style, both in speech and writing, and a gift, of which he may or may not have been aware, for comedy. But like so many great men before him, he had a weakness, a tragic flaw. It was that he insisted on thinking of himself as a hick, a boob, and a sucker, and, in doing so, he sometimes became all three.

This unlikely fellow was the man who engineered the last real corner in a nationally traded stock.

The game of Corner—for in its heyday it was a game, a high-stakes gambling game, pure and simple, embodying a good many of the characteristics of poker—was one phase of the endless Wall Street contest between bulls, who want the price of a stock to go up, and bears, who want it to go down. When a game of Corner was under way, the bulls' basic method of operation was, of course, to buy stock, and the bears' was to sell it. Since the average bear didn't own any of the stock issue in contest, he would resort to the common practice of selling short. When a short sale is made, the transaction is consummated with stock that the seller has borrowed (at a suitable rate of interest) from a broker. Since brokers are merely agents, and not outright owners, they, in turn, must borrow the stock themselves. This they do by tapping the "floating supply" of stock that is in constant circulation among investment houses—stock that private investors have left with one house or another for trading purposes, stock that is owned by estates and trusts and has been released for action under certain prescribed conditions, and so on. In essence, the floating supply consists of all the stock in a particular corporation that is available for trading and is not immured in a safe-deposit box or encased in a mattress. Though the supply floats, it is scrupulously kept track of; the short seller, borrowing, say, a thousand shares from his broker, knows that he has incurred an immutable debt. What he hopes—the hope that keeps him alive—is that the market price of the stock will go down, enabling him to buy the thousand shares he owes at a bargain rate, pay off his debt, and pocket the difference. What he risks is that the lender, for one reason or another, may demand that he deliver up his thousand borrowed shares at a moment when their market price is at a high. Then the grinding truth of the old Wall Street jingle is borne in upon him: "He who sells what isn't his'n must buy it back or go to prison." And in the days when corners were possible, the short seller's sleep was further disturbed by the fact that he was operating behind blank walls; dealing only with agents, he never knew either the identity of the purchaser of his stock (a prospective cornerer?) or the identity of the owner of the stock he had borrowed (the same prospective cornerer, attacking from the rear?).

Although it is sometimes condemned as being the tool of the speculator, short selling is still sanctioned, in a severely restricted form, on all of the nation's exchanges. In its unfettered state, it was the standard gambit in the game of Corner. The situation would be set up when a group of bears would go on a well-organized spree of short selling, and would often help their cause along by spreading rumors that the company back of the stock in question was on its last legs. This operation was called a bear raid. The bulls' most formidable—but, of course, riskiest—counter-move was to try for a corner. Only a stock that many traders were selling short could be cornered; a stock that was in the throes of a real bear raid was ideal. In the latter situation, the would-be cornerer would attempt to buy up the investment houses' floating supply of the stock and enough of the privately held shares to freeze out the bears; if the attempt succeeded, when he called for the short sellers to make good the stock they had borrowed, they could buy it from no one but him. And they would have to buy it at any price he chose to ask, their only alternatives—at least theoretically—being to go into bankruptcy or to jail for failure to meet their obligations.

In the old days of titanic financial death struggles, when Adam Smith's ghost still smiled on Wall Street, corners were fairly common and were often extremely sanguinary, with hundreds of innocent bystanders, as well as the embattled principals, getting their financial heads lopped off. The most famous cornerer in history was that celebrated old pirate, Commodore Cornelius Vanderbilt, who engineered no less than three successful corners during the eighteen-sixties. Probably his classic job was in the stock of the Harlem Railway. By dint of secretly buying up all its available shares while simultaneously circulating a series of untruthful rumors of imminent bankruptcy to lure the short sellers in, he achieved an airtight trap. Finally, with the air of a man doing them a favor by saving them from jail, he offered the cornered shorts at $179 a share the stock he had bought up at a small fraction of that figure. The most generally disastrous corner was that of 1901 in the stock of Northern Pacific; to raise the huge quantities of cash they needed to cover themselves, the Northern Pacific shorts sold so many other stocks as to cause a national panic with world-wide repercussions. The next-to-last great corner occurred in 1920, when Allan A. Ryan, a son of the legendary Thomas Fortune Ryan, in order to harass his enemies in the New York Stock Exchange, sought to corner the stock of the Stutz Motor Company, makers of the renowned Stutz Bearcat. Ryan achieved his corner and the Stock Exchange short sellers were duly squeezed. But Ryan, it turned out, had a bearcat by the tail. The Stock Exchange suspended Stutz dealings, lengthy litigation followed, and Ryan came out of the affair financially ruined.

Then, as at other times, the game of Corner suffered from a difficulty that plagues other games—post-mortem disputes about the rules. The reform legislation of the nineteen-thirties, by outlawing any short selling that is specifically intended to demoralize a stock, as well as other manipulations leading toward corners, virtually ruled the game out of existence. Wall Streeters who speak of the Corner these days are referring to the intersection of Broad and Wall. In U.S. stock markets, only an accidental corner (or near-corner, like the Bruce one) is now possible; Clarence Saunders was the last intentional player of the game.

Saunders has been variously characterized by people who knew him well as "a man of limitless imagination and energy," "arrogant and conceited as all getout," "essentially a four-year-old child, playing at things," and "one of the most remarkable men of his generation." But there is no doubt that even many of the people who lost money on his promotional schemes believed that he was the soul of honesty. He was born in 1881 to a poor family in Amherst County, Virginia, and in his teens was employed by the local grocer at the pittance that is orthodox for future tycoons taking on their first jobs—in his case, four dollars a week. Moving ahead fast, he went on to a wholesale grocery company in Clarksville, Tennessee, and then to one in Memphis, and, while still in his twenties, organized a small retail food chain called United Stores. He sold that after a few years, did a stint as a wholesale grocer on his own, and then, in 1919, began to build a chain of retail self-service markets, to which he gave the engaging name of Piggly Wiggly Stores. (When a Memphis business associate once asked him why he had chosen that name, he replied, "So people would ask me what you just did.") The stores flourished so exuberantly that by the autumn of 1922 there were over twelve hundred of them. Of these, some six hundred and fifty were owned outright by Saunders' Piggly Wiggly Stores, Inc.; the rest were independently owned, but their owners paid royalties to the parent company for the right to adopt its patented method of operations. In 1923, an era when a grocery store meant clerks in white aprons and often a thumb on the scale, this method was described by the *New York Times* with astonishment: "The customer in a Piggly Wiggly Store rambles down aisle after aisle, on both sides of which are shelves. The customer collects his purchases and pays as he goes out." Although Saunders did not know it, he had invented the supermarket.

A natural concomitant of the rapid rise of Piggly Wiggly Stores, Inc., was the acceptance of its shares for listing on the New York Stock Exchange, and within six months of that event Piggly Wiggly stock had become known as a dependable, if unsensational, dividend-payer—the kind of widows'-and-orphans' stock that speculators regard with the respectful indifference that crap-shooters feel about bridge. This reputation, however, was shortlived. In November, 1922, several small companies that had been operating grocery stores in New York, New Jersey, and Connecticut under the name Piggly Wiggly failed and went into receivership. These companies had scarcely any connection with Saunders' concern; he had merely sold them the right to use his firm's catchy trade name, leased them some patented equipment, and washed his hands of them. But when these independent Piggly Wigglys failed, a group of stock-market operators (whose identities never were revealed, because they dealt through tight-lipped brokers) saw in the situation a heaven-sent opportunity for a bear raid.

If individual Piggly Wiggly stores were failing, they reasoned, then rumors could be spread that would lead the uninformed public to believe that the parent firm was failing, too. To further this belief, they began briskly selling Piggly Wiggly short, in order to force the price down. The stock yielded readily to their pressure, and within a few weeks its price, which earlier in the year had hovered around fifty dollars a share, dropped to below forty.

At this point, Saunders announced to the press that he was about to "beat the Wall Street professionals at their own game" with a buying campaign. He was by no means a professional himself; in fact, prior to the listing of Piggly Wiggly he had never owned a single share of any stock quoted on the New York Stock Exchange. There is little reason to believe that at the beginning of his buying campaign he had any intention of trying for a corner; it seems more likely that his announced motive—the unassailable one of supporting the price of the stock in order to protect his own investment and that of other Piggly Wiggly stockholders—was all he had in mind. In any case, he took on the bears with characteristic zest, supplementing his own funds with a loan of about ten million dollars from a group of bankers in Memphis, Nashville, New Orleans, Chattanooga, and St. Louis. Legend has it that he stuffed his ten million-plus, in bills of large denomination, into a suitcase, boarded a train for New York, and, his pockets bulging with currency that wouldn't fit in the suitcase, marched on Wall Street, ready to do battle. He emphatically denied this in later years, insisting that he had remained in Memphis and masterminded his campaign by means of telegrams and long-distance telephone calls to various Wall Street brokers. Wherever he was at the time, he did round up a corps of some twenty brokers, among them Jesse L. Livermore, who served as his chief of staff. Livermore, one of the most celebrated American speculators of this century, was then forty-five years old but was still occasionally, and derisively, referred to by the nickname he had earned a couple of decades earlier—the Boy Plunger of Wall Street. Since Saunders regarded Wall Streeters in general and speculators in particular as parasitic scoundrels intent only on battering down his stock, it seemed likely that his decision to make an ally of Livermore was a reluctant one, arrived at simply with the idea of getting the enemy chieftain into his own camp.

On the first day of his duel with the bears, Saunders, operating behind his mask of brokers, bought 33,000 shares of Piggly Wiggly, mostly from the short sellers; within a week he had brought the total to 105,000—more than half of the 200,000 shares outstanding. Meanwhile, ventilating his emotions at the cost of tipping his hand, he began running a series of advertisements in which he vigorously and pungently told the readers of Southern and Western newspapers what he thought of Wall Street. "Shall the gambler rule?" he demanded in one of these effusions. "On a white horse he rides. Bluff is his coat of mail and thus shielded is a yellow heart. His helmet is deceit, his spurs clink with treachery, and the hoofbeats of his horse thunder destruction. Shall good business flee? Shall it tremble with fear? Shall it be the loot of the speculator?" On Wall Street, Livermore went on buying Piggly Wiggly.

The effectiveness of Saunders' buying campaign was readily apparent; by late January of 1923 it had driven the price of the stock up over 60, or higher than ever before. Then, to intensify the bear raiders' jitters, reports came in from Chicago, where the stock was also traded, that Piggly Wiggly was cornered—that the short sellers could not replace the stock they had borrowed without coming to Saunders for supplies. The reports were immediately denied by the New York Stock Exchange, which announced that the floating supply of Piggly Wiggly was ample, but they may have put an idea into Saunders' head, and this, in turn, may have prompted a curious and—at first glance—mystifying move he made in mid-

February, when, in another widely disseminated newspaper advertisement, he offered to *sell* fifty thousand shares of Piggly Wiggly stock to the public at fifty-five dollars a share. The ad pointed out, persuasively enough, that the stock was paying a dividend of a dollar four times a year—a return of more than 7 percent. "This is to be a quick proposition, subject to withdrawal without prior notice," the ad went on, calmly but urgently. "To get in on the ground floor of any big proposition is the opportunity that comes to few, and then only once in a lifetime."

Anyone who is even slightly familiar with modern economic life can scarcely help wondering what the Securities and Exchange Commission, which is charged with seeing to it that all financial advertising is kept factual, impersonal, and unemotional, would have had to say about the hard sell in those last two sentences. But if Saunders' first stock-offering ad would have caused an S.E.C. examiner to turn pale, his second, published four days later, might well have induced an apoplectic seizure. A full-page affair, it cried out, in huge black type:

OPPORTUNITY! OPPORTUNITY!
It Knocks! It Knocks! It Knocks!
Do you hear? Do you listen? Do you understand?
Do you wait? Do you act now?...
Has a new Daniel appeared and the lions eat him not?
Has a new Joseph come that riddles may be made plain?
Has a new Moses been born to a new Promised Land?
Why, then, asks the skeptical, can CLARENCE SAUNDERS ... be so generous to the public?

After finally making it clear that he was selling common stock and not snake oil, Saunders repeated his offer to sell at fifty-five dollars a share, and went on to explain that he was being so generous because, as a farsighted businessman, he was anxious to have Piggly Wiggly owned by its customers and other small investors, rather than by Wall Street sharks. To many people, though, it appeared that Saunders was being generous to the point of folly. The price of Piggly Wiggly on the New York Stock Exchange was just then pushing 70; it looked as if Saunders were handing anyone who had fifty-five dollars in his pocket a chance to make fifteen dollars with no risk. The arrival of a new Daniel, Joseph, or Moses might be debatable, but opportunity certainly did seem to be knocking, all right.

Actually, as the skeptical must have suspected, there was a catch. In making what sounded like such a costly and unbusinesslike offer, Saunders, a rank novice at Corner, had devised one of the craftiest dodges ever used in the game. One of the great hazards in Corner was always that even though a player might defeat his opponents, he would discover that he had won a Pyrrhic victory. Once the short sellers had been squeezed dry, that is, the cornerer might find that the reams of stock he had accumulated in the process were a dead weight around his neck; by pushing it all back into the market in one shove, he would drive its price down close to zero. And if, like Saunders, he had had to borrow heavily to get into the game in the first place, his creditors could be expected to close in on him and perhaps not only divest him of his gains but drive him into bankruptcy. Saunders apparently anticipated this hazard almost as soon as a corner was in sight, and accordingly made plans to unload some of his stock before winning instead of afterward. His problem was to keep the stock he sold from going right back into the floating supply, thus breaking his corner; and his solution was to sell his fifty-five-dollar shares on the installment plan. In his February advertisements, he stipulated that the public could buy shares only by paying twenty-five dollars down and the balance in three ten-dollar installments, due June 1st, September 1st, and December 1st. In addition—and vastly more important—he said he would not turn over the stock certificates to the buyers until the final installment had been paid. Since the buyers obviously couldn't sell the certificates until they had them, the stock could not be used to replenish the floating supply. Thus Saunders had until December 1st to squeeze the short sellers dry.

Easy as it may be to see through Saunders' plan by hindsight, his maneuver was then so unorthodox that for a while neither the governors of the Stock Exchange nor Livermore himself could be quite sure what the man in Memphis was up to. The Stock Exchange began making formal inquiries, and Livermore began getting skittish, but he went on buying for Saunders' account, and succeeded in pushing Piggly Wiggly's price up well above 70. In Memphis, Saunders sat back comfortably; he temporarily ceased singing the praises of Piggly Wiggly stock in his ads, and devoted them to eulogizing apples, grapefruit, onions, hams, and Lady Baltimore cakes. Early in March, though, he ran another financial ad, repeating his stock offer and inviting any readers who wanted to discuss it with him to drop in at his Memphis office. He also emphasized that quick action was necessary; time was running out.

By now, it was apparent that Saunders was trying for a corner, and on Wall Street it was not only the Piggly Wiggly bears who were becoming apprehensive. Finally, Livermore, possibly reflecting that in 1908 he had lost almost a million dollars trying to get a corner in cotton, could stand it no longer. He demanded that Saunders come to New York and talk things over. Saunders arrived on the morning of March 12th. As he later described the meeting to reporters, there was a difference of opinion; Livermore, he said—and his tone was that of a man rather set up over having made a piker out of the Boy Plunger—"gave me the impression that he was a little afraid of my financial situation and that he did not care to be involved in any market crash." The upshot of the conference was that Livermore bowed out of the Piggly Wiggly operation, leaving Saunders to run it by himself. Saunders then boarded a train for Chicago to attend to some business there. At Albany, he was handed a telegram from a member of the Stock Exchange who was the nearest thing he had to a friend in the white-charger-and-coat-of-mail set. The telegram informed him that his antics had provoked a great deal of head-shaking in the councils of the Exchange, and urged him to stop creating a second market by advertising stock for sale at a price so far below the quotation on the Exchange. At the next station, Saunders telegraphed back a rather unresponsive reply. If it was a possible corner the Exchange was fretting about, he said, he could assure the governors that they could put their fears aside, since he himself was maintaining the floating supply by daily offering stock for loan in any amount desired. But he didn't say how long he would continue to do so.

A week later, on Monday, March 19th, Saunders ran a newspaper ad stating that his stock offer was about to be withdrawn; this was the last call. At the time, or so he claimed afterward, he had acquired all but 1,128 of Piggly Wiggly's 200,000 outstanding shares, for a total of 198,872, some of which he owned and the rest of which he "controlled"—a reference to the installment-plan shares whose certificates he still held. Actually, this figure was open to considerable argument (there was one private investor in Providence, for instance, who alone held eleven hundred shares), but there is no denying that Saunders had in his hands practically every single share of Piggly Wiggly then available for trading—and that he therefore had his corner. On that same Monday, it is believed, Saunders telephoned Livermore and asked if he would relent long enough to see the Piggly Wiggly project through by calling for delivery of all the shares that were owed Saunders; in other words, would Livermore please spring the trap? Nothing doing, Livermore is supposed to have replied, evidently considering himself well out of the whole affair. So the following morning, Tuesday, March 20th, Saunders sprang the trap himself.

It turned out to be one of Wall Street's wilder days. Piggly Wiggly opened at 75½, up 5½ from the previous days' closing price. An hour after the opening, word arrived that Saunders had called for delivery of all his Piggly Wiggly stock. According to the rules of the Exchange, stock called for under such circumstances had to be produced by two-fifteen the following afternoon. But Piggly Wiggly, as Saunders well knew, simply wasn't to be had—except, of course, from him. To be sure, there were a few shares around that were still held by private investors, and frantic short sellers trying to shake them loose bid their price up and up. But by and large there wasn't much actual trading in Piggly Wiggly, because there was so little Piggly Wiggly to be traded. The Stock Exchange post where it was bought and sold became the center of a mob scene as two-thirds of the brokers on the floor clustered around it, a few of them to bid but most of them just to push, whoop, and otherwise get in on the excitement. Desperate short sellers bought Piggly Wiggly at 90, then at 100, then at 110. Reports of sensational profits made the rounds. The Providence investor, who had picked up his eleven hundred shares at 39 in the previous autumn, while the bear raid was in full cry, came to town to be in on the kill, unloaded his holdings at an average price of 105, and then caught an afternoon train back home, taking with him a profit of over seventy thousand dollars. As it happened, he could have done even better if he had bided his time; by noon, or a little after, the price of Piggly Wiggly had risen to 124, and it seemed destined to zoom straight through the lofty roof above the traders' heads. But 124 was as high as it went, for that figure had barely been recorded when a rumor reached the floor that the governors of the Exchange were meeting to consider the suspension of further trading in the stock and the postponement of the short sellers' deadline for delivery. The effect of such action would be to give the bears time to beat the bushes for stock, and thus to weaken, if not break, Saunders' corner. On the basis of the rumor alone, Piggly Wiggly fell to 82 by the time the Exchange's closing bell ended the chaotic session.

The rumor proved to be true. After the close of business, the Governing Committee of the Exchange announced both the suspension of trading in Piggly Wiggly and the extension of the short sellers' delivery deadline "until further action by this committee." There was no immediate official reason given for this decision, but some members of the committee unofficially let it be known that they had been afraid of a repetition of the Northern Pacific panic if the corner were not broken. On the other hand, irreverent side-liners were inclined to wonder whether the Governing Committee had not been moved by the pitiful plight of the cornered short sellers, many of whom—as in the Stutz Motor case two years earlier—were believed to be members of the Exchange.

Despite all this, Saunders, in Memphis, was in a jubilant, expansive mood that Tuesday evening. After all, his paper profits at that moment ran to several million dollars. The hitch, of course, was that he could not realize them, but he seems to have been slow to grasp that fact or to understand the extent to which his position had been undermined. The indications are that he went to bed convinced that, besides having personally brought about a first-class mess on the hated Stock Exchange, he had made himself a bundle and had demonstrated how a poor Southern boy could teach the city slickers a lesson. It all must have added up to a heady sensation. But, like most such sensations, it didn't last long. By Wednesday evening, when Saunders issued his first public utterance on the Piggly Crisis, his mood had changed to an odd mixture of puzzlement, defiance, and a somewhat muted echo of the crowing triumph of the night before. "A razor to my throat, figuratively speaking, is why I suddenly and without warning kicked the pegs from under Wall Street and its gang of gamblers and market manipulators," he declared in a press interview. "It was strictly a question of whether I should survive, and likewise my business and the fortunes of my friends, or whether I should be 'licked' and pointed to as a boob from Tennessee. And the consequence was that the boastful and supposedly invulnerable Wall Street powers found their methods controverted by well-laid plans and quick action." Saunders wound up his statement by laying down his terms: the Stock Exchange's deadline extension notwithstanding, he would expect settlement in full on all short stock by 3 P.M. the next day—Thursday—at $150 a share; thereafter his price would be $250.

On Thursday, to Saunders' surprise, very few short sellers came forward to settle; presumably those who did couldn't stand the uncertainty. But then the Governing Committee kicked the pegs from under Saunders by announcing that the stock of Piggly Wiggly was permanently stricken from its trading list and that the short sellers would be given a full five days from the original deadline—that is, until two-fifteen the following Monday—to meet their obligations. In Memphis, Saunders, far removed from the scene though he was, could not miss the import of these moves—he was now on the losing end of things. Nor could he any longer fail to see that the postponement of the short sellers' deadline was the vital issue. "As I understand it," he said in another statement, handed to reporters that evening, "the failure of a broker to meet his clearings through the Stock Exchange at the appointed time is the same as a bank that would be unable to meet its clearings, and all of us know what would happen to that kind of a bank. . . . The bank examiner would have a sign stuck up on the door with the word 'Closed.' It is unbelievable to me that the august and all-powerful New York Stock Exchange is a welcher. Therefore I continue to believe that the . . . shares of stock still due me on contracts . . . will be settled on the proper basis." An editorial in the Memphis *Commercial Appeal* backed up Saunders' cry of treachery, declaring, "This looks like what gamblers call welching. We hope the home boy beats them to a frazzle."

That same Thursday, by a coincidence, the annual financial report of Piggly Wiggly Stores, Inc., was made public. It was a highly favorable one—sales, profits, current assets, and all other significant figures were up sharply over the year before—but nobody paid any attention to it. For the moment, the real worth of the company was irrelevant; the point was the game.

On Friday morning, the Piggly Wiggly bubble burst. It burst because Saunders, who had said his price would rise to $250 a share after 3 P.M. Thursday, made the startling announcement that he would settle for a hundred. E. W. Bradford, Saunders' New York lawyer, was asked why Saunders had suddenly granted this striking concession. Saunders had done it out of the generosity of his heart, Bradford replied gamely, but the truth was soon obvious: Saunders had made the concession because he'd had to. The postponement granted by the Stock Exchange had given the short sellers and their brokers a chance to scan lists of Piggly Wiggly stockholders, and from these they had been able to smoke out small blocks of shares that Saunders had not cornered. Widows and orphans in Albuquerque and Sioux City, who knew nothing about short sellers and corners, were only too happy, when pressed, to dig into their mattresses or safe-deposit boxes and sell—in the so-called over-the-counter market, since the stock could no longer be traded on the Exchange—their ten or twenty shares of Piggly Wiggly for at least double what they had paid for them. Consequently, instead of having to buy stock from Saunders at his price of $250 and then hand it back to him in settlement of their loans, many of the short sellers were able to buy it in over-the-counter trading at around a hundred dollars, and thus, with bitter pleasure, pay off their Memphis adversary not in cash but in shares of Piggly Wiggly—the very last thing he wanted just then. By nightfall Friday, virtually all the short sellers were in the clear, having redeemed their indebtedness either by these over-the-counter purchases or by paying Saunders cash at his own suddenly deflated rate of a hundred dollars a share.

That evening, Saunders released still another statement, and this one, while still defiant, was unmistakably a howl of anguish. "Wall Street got licked and then called for 'mamma,'" it read. "Of all the institutions in America, the New York Stock Exchange is the worst menace of all in its power to ruin all who dare to oppose it. A law unto itself . . . an association of men who claim the right that no king or autocrat ever dared to take: to make a rule that applies one day on contracts and abrogate it the next day to let out a bunch of welchers. . . . My whole life from this day on will be aimed toward the end of having the public protected from a like occurrence. . . . I am not afraid. Let Wall Street get me if they can." But it appeared that Wall Street had got him; his corner was broken, leaving him deeply in debt to the syndicate of Southern bankers and encumbered with a mountain of stock whose immediate future was, to say the least, precarious.

Saundees' fulminations did not go unheeded on Wall Street, and as a result the Exchange felt compelled to justify itself. On Monday, March 26th, shortly after the Piggly Wiggly short sellers' deadline had passed and Saunders' corner was, for all practical purposes, a dead issue, the Exchange offered its apologia, in the form of a lengthy review of the crisis from beginning to end. In presenting its case, the Exchange emphasized the public harm that might have been done if the corner had gone unbroken, explaining, "The enforcement simultaneously of all contracts for the return of the stock would have forced the stock to any price that might be fixed by Mr. Saunders, and competitive bidding for the insufficient supply might have brought about conditions illustrated by other corners, notably the Northern Pacific corner in 1901." Then, its syntax yielding to its sincerity, the Exchange went on to say that "the demoralizing effects of such a situation are not limited to those directly affected by the contracts but extends to the whole market." Getting down to the two specific actions it had taken—the suspension of trading in Piggly Wiggly and the extension of the short sellers' deadline—the Exchange argued that both of them were within the bounds of its own constitution and rules, and therefore irreproachable. Arrogant as this may sound now, the Exchange had a point; in those days its rules were just about the only controls over stock trading.

The question of whether, even by their own rules, the slickers really played fair with the boob is still debated among fiscal antiquarians. There is strong presumptive evidence that the slickers themselves later came to have their doubts. Regarding the right of the Exchange to suspend trading in a stock there can be no argument, since the right was, as the Exchange claimed at the time, specifically granted in its constitution. But the right to postpone the deadline for short sellers to honor their contracts, though also claimed at the time, is another matter. In June, 1925, two years after Saunders' corner, the Exchange felt constrained to amend its constitution with an article stating that "whenever in the opinion of the Governing Committee a corner has been created in a security listed on the Exchange . . . the Governing Committee may postpone the time for deliveries on Exchange contracts therein." By adopting a statute authorizing it to do what it had done long before, the Exchange would seem, at the very least, to have exposed a guilty conscience.

The immediate aftermath of the Piggly Crisis was a wave of sympathy for Saunders. Throughout the hinterland, the public image of him became that of a gallant champion of the underdog who had been ruthlessly crushed. Even in New York, the very lair of the Stock Exchange, the *Times* conceded in an editorial that in the minds of many people Saunders represented St. George and the Stock Exchange the dragon. That the dragon triumphed in the end, said the *Times*, was "bad news for a nation at least 66⅔ per cent 'sucker,' which had its moment of triumph when it read that a sucker had trimmed the interests and had his foot on Wall Street's neck while the vicious manipulators gasped their lives away."

Not a man to ignore such a host of friendly fellow suckers, Saunders went to work to turn them to account. And he needed them, for his position was perilous indeed. His biggest problem was what to do about the ten million dollars that he owed his banker backers—and didn't have. The basic plan behind his corner—if he had had any plan at all—must have been to make such a killing that he could pay back a big slice of his debt out of the profits, pay back the rest out of the proceeds from his public stock sale, and then walk off with a still huge block of Piggly Wiggly stock free and clear. Even though the cut-rate hundred-dollar settlement had netted him a killing by most men's standards (just how much of a killing is not known, but it has been reliably estimated at half a million or so), it was not a fraction of what he might have reasonably expected it to be, and because it wasn't his whole structure became an arch without a keystone.

Having paid his bankers what he had received from the short sellers and from his public stock sale, Saunders found that he still owed them about five million dollars, half of it due September 1, 1923, and the balance on January 1, 1924. His best hope of raising the money lay in selling more of the vast bundle of Piggly Wiggly shares he still had on hand. Since he could no longer sell them on the Exchange, he resorted to his favorite form of self-expression—newspaper advertising, this time supplemented with a mail-order pitch offering Piggly Wiggly again at fifty-five dollars. It soon became evident, though, that public sympathy was one thing and public willingness to translate sympathy into cash was quite another. Everyone, whether in New York, Memphis, or Texarkana, knew about the recent speculative shenanigans in Piggly Wiggly and about the dubious state of the president's finances. Not even Saunders' fellow suckers would have any part of his deal now, and the campaign was a bleak failure.

Sadly accepting this fact, Saunders next appealed to the local and regional pride of his Memphis neighbors by turning his remarkable powers of persuasion to the job of convincing them that his financial dilemma was a civic issue. If he should go broke, he argued, it would reflect not only on the character and business acumen of Memphis but on Southern honor in general. "I do not ask for charity," he wrote in one of the large ads he always seemed able to find the cash for, "and I do not request any flowers for my financial funeral, but I do ask . . . everybody in Memphis to recognize and know that this is a serious statement made for the purpose of acquainting those who wish to assist in this matter, that they may work with me, and with other friends and believers in my business, in a Memphis campaign to have every man and woman who possibly can in this city become one of the partners of the Piggly Wiggly business, because it is a good investment first, and, second, because it is the right thing to do." Raising his sights in a second ad, he declared, "For Piggly Wiggly to be ruined would shame the whole South."

Just which argument proved the clincher in persuading Memphis that it should try to pull Saunders' chestnuts out of the fire is hard to say, but some part of his line of reasoning clicked, and soon the Memphis *Commercial Appeal* was urging the town to get behind the embattled local boy. The response of the city's business leaders was truly inspiring to Saunders. A whirlwind three-day campaign was planned, with the object of selling fifty thousand shares of his stock to the citizens of Memphis at the old magic figure of fifty-five dollars a share; in order to give buyers some degree of assurance that they would not later find themselves alone out on a limb, it was stipulated that unless the whole block was sold within the three days, all sales would be called off. The Chamber of Commerce sponsored the drive; the American Legion, the Civitan Club, and the Exchange Club fell into line; and even the Bowers Stores and the Arrow Stores, both competitors of Piggly Wiggly in Memphis, agreed to plug the worthy cause. Hundreds of civic-minded volunteers signed up to ring doorbells. On May 3rd, five days before the scheduled start of the campaign, 250 Memphis businessmen assembled at the Gayoso Hotel for a kickoff dinner. There were cheers when Saunders, accompanied by his wife, entered the dining room; one of the many after-dinner speakers described him as "the man who has done more for Memphis than any in the last thousand years"—a rousing tribute that put God knew how many Chickasaw chiefs in their place. "Business rivalries and personal differences were swept away like mists before the sun," a *Commercial Appeal* reporter wrote of the dinner.

The drive got off to a splendid start. On the opening day—May 8th—society women and Boy Scouts paraded the streets of Memphis wearing badges that read, "We're One Hundred Per Cent for Clarence Saunders and Piggly Wiggly." Merchants adorned their windows with placards bearing the slogan "A Share of Piggly Wiggly Stock in Every Home." Telephones and doorbells rang incessantly. In short order, 23,698 of the 50,000 shares had been subscribed for. Yet at the very moment when most of Memphis had become miraculously convinced that the peddling of Piggly Wiggly stock was an activity fully as uplifting as soliciting for the Red Cross or the Community Chest, ugly doubts were brewing, and some vipers in the home nest suddenly demanded that Saunders consent to an immediate spot audit of his company's books. Saunders, for whatever reasons, refused, but offered to placate the skeptics by stepping down as president of Piggly Wiggly if such a move "would facilitate the stock-selling campaign." He was not asked to give up the presidency, but on May 9th, the second day of the campaign, a watchdog committee of four—three bankers and a businessman—was appointed by the Piggly Wiggly directors to help him run the company for an interim period, while the dust settled. That same day, Saunders was confronted with another embarrassing situation: why, the campaign leaders wanted to know, was he continuing to build his million-dollar Pink Palace at a time when the whole town was working for him for nothing? He replied hastily that he would have the place boarded up the very next day and that there would be no further construction until his financial future looked bright again.

The confusion attendant on these two issues brought the drive to a standstill. At the end of the third day, the total number of shares subscribed for was still under 25,000, and the sales that had been made were canceled. Saunders had to admit that the drive had been a failure. "Memphis has fizzled," he reportedly added—although he was at great pains to deny this a few years later, when he needed more of Memphis' money for a new venture. It would not be surprising, though, if he had made some such imprudent remark, for he was understandably suffering from a case of frazzled nerves, and was showing the strain. Just before the announcement of the campaign's unhappy end, he went into a closed conference with several Memphis business leaders and came out of it with a bruised cheekbone and a torn collar. None of the other men at the meeting showed any marks of violence. It just wasn't Saunders' day.

Although it was never established that Saunders had had his hand improperly in the Piggly Wiggly corporate till during his cornering operation, his first business move after the collapse of his attempt to unload stock suggested that he had at least had good reason to refuse a spot audit of the company's books. In spite of futile grunts of protest from the watchdog committee, he began selling not Piggly Wiggly stock but Piggly Wiggly stores—partly liquidating the company, that is—and no one knew where he would stop. The Chicago stores went first, and those in Denver and Kansas City soon followed. His announced intention was to build up the company's treasury so that *it* could buy the stock that the public had spurned, but there was some suspicion that the treasury desperately needed a transfusion just then—and not of Piggly Wiggly stock, either. "I've got Wall Street and the whole gang licked," Saunders reported cheerfully in June. But in mid-August, with the September 1st deadline for repayment of two and a half million dollars on his loan staring him in the face and with nothing like that amount of cash either on hand or in prospect, he resigned as president of Piggly Wiggly Stores, Inc., and turned over his assets—his stock in the company, his Pink Palace, and all the rest of his property—to his creditors.

It remained only for the formal stamp of failure to be put on Saunders personally and on Piggly Wiggly under his management. On August 22nd, the New York auction firm of Adrian H. Muller & Son, which dealt in so many next-to-worthless stocks that its salesroom was often called "the securities graveyard," knocked down fifteen hundred shares of Piggly Wiggly at a dollar a share—the traditional price for securities that have been run into the ground—and the following spring Saunders went through formal bankruptcy proceedings. But these were anticlimaxes. The real low point of Saunders' career was probably the day he was forced out of his company's presidency, and it was then that, in the opinion of many of his admirers, he achieved his rhetorical peak. When he emerged, harassed but still defiant, from a directors' conference and announced his resignation to reporters, a hush fell. Then Saunders added hoarsely, "They have the body of Piggly Wiggly, but they cannot have the soul."

If by the soul of Piggly Wiggly Saunders meant himself, then it did remain free—free to go marching on in its own erratic way. He never ventured to play another game of Corner, but his spirit was far from broken. Although officially bankrupt, he managed to find people of truly rocklike faith who were still willing to finance him, and they enabled him to live on a scale only slightly less grand than in the past; reduced to playing golf at the Memphis Country Club rather than on his own private course, he handed out caddy tips that the club governors considered as corrupting as ever. To be sure, he no longer owned the Pink Palace, but this was about the only evidence that served to remind his fellow townsmen of his misfortunes. Eventually, the unfinished pleasure dome came into the hands of the city of Memphis, which appropriated $150,000 to finish it and turn it into a museum of natural history and industrial arts. As such, it continues to sustain the Saunders legend in Memphis.

After his downfall, Saunders spent the better part of three years in seeking redress of the wrongs that he felt he had suffered in the Piggly Wiggly fight, and in foiling the efforts of his enemies and creditors to make things still more unpleasant for him. For a while, he kept threatening to sue the Stock Exchange for conspiracy and breach of contract, but a test suit, brought by some small Piggly Wiggly stockholders, failed, and he dropped the idea. Then, in January, 1926, he learned that a federal indictment was about to be brought against him for using the mails to defraud in his mail-order campaign to sell his Piggly Wiggly stock. He believed, incorrectly, that the government had been egged on to bring the indictment by an old associate of his—John C. Burch, of Memphis, who had become secretary-treasurer of Piggly Wiggly after the shakeup. His patience once more exhausted, Saunders went around to

Piggly Wiggly headquarters and confronted Burch. This conference proved far more satisfactory to Saunders than his board-room scuffle on the day the Memphis civic stock-selling drive failed. Burch, according to Saunders, "undertook in a stammering way to deny" the accusation, whereupon Saunders delivered a right to the jaw, knocking off Burch's glasses but not doing much other damage. Burch afterward belittled the blow as "glancing," and added an alibi that sounded like that of any outpointed pugilist: "The assault upon me was made so suddenly that I did not have time or opportunity to strike Mr. Saunders." Burch refused to press charges.

About a month later, the mail-fraud indictment was brought against Saunders, but by that time, satisfied that Burch was innocent of any dirty work, he was his amiable old self again. "I have only one thing to regret in this new affair," he announced pleasantly, "and that is my fistic encounter with John C. Burch." The new affair didn't last long; in April the indictment was quashed by the Memphis District Court, and Saunders and Piggly Wiggly were finally quits. By then, the company was well on its way back up, and, with a greatly changed corporate structure, it flourished on into the nineteen sixties; housewives continued to ramble down the aisles of hundreds of Piggly Wiggly stores, now operated under a franchise agreement with the Piggly Wiggly Corporation, of Jacksonville, Florida.

Saunders, too, was well on his way back up. In 1928, he started a new grocery chain, which he—but hardly anyone else—called the Clarence Saunders, Sole Owner of My Name, Stores, Inc. Its outlets soon came to be known as Sole Owner stores, which was precisely what they weren't, for without Saunders' faithful backers they would have existed only in his mind. Saunders' choice of a corporate title, however, was not designed to mislead the public; rather, it was his ironic way of reminding the world that, after the skinning Wall Street had given him, his name was about the only thing he still had a clear title to. How many Sole Owner customers—or governors of the Stock Exchange, for that matter—got the point is questionable. In any case, the new stores caught on so rapidly and did so well that Saunders leaped back up from bankruptcy to riches, and bought a million-dollar estate just outside Memphis. He also organized and underwrote a professional football team called the Sole Owner Tigers—an investment that paid off handsomely on the fall afternoons when he could hear cries of "Rah! Rah! Rah! Sole Owner! Sole Owner! Sole Owner!" ringing through the Memphis Stadium.

For the second time, Saunders' glory was fleeting. The very first wave of the depression hit Sole Owner Stores such a crushing blow that in 1930 they went bankrupt, and he was broke again. But again he pulled himself together and survived the debacle. Finding backers, he planned a new chain of grocery stores, and thought up a name for it that was more outlandish, if possible, than either of its predecessors—Keedoozle. He never made another killing, however, or bought another million-dollar estate, though it was always clear that he expected to. His hopes were pinned on the Keedoozle, an electrically operated grocery store, and he spent the better part of the last twenty years of his life trying to perfect it. In a Keedoozle store, the merchandise was displayed behind glass panels, each with a slot beside it, like the food in an Automat. There the similarity ended, for, instead of inserting coins in the slot to open a panel and lift out a purchase, Keedoozle customers inserted a key that they were given on entering the store. Moreover, Saunders' thinking had advanced far beyond the elementary stage of having the key open the panel; each time a Keedoozle key was inserted in a slot, the identity of the item selected was inscribed in code on a segment of recording tape embedded in the key itself, and simultaneously the item was automatically transferred to a conveyor belt that carried it to an exit gate at the front of the store. When a customer had finished his shopping, he would present his key to an attendant at the gate, who would decipher the tape and add up the bill. As soon as this was paid, the purchases would be catapulted into the customer's arms, all bagged and wrapped, by a device at the end of the conveyor belt.

A couple of pilot Keedoozle stores were tried out—one in Memphis and the other in Chicago—but it was found that the machinery was too complex and expensive to compete with supermarket pushcarts. Undeterred, Saunders set to work on an even more intricate mechanism—the Foodelectric, which would do everything the Keedoozle could do and add up the bill as well. It will never corner the retail-store-equipment market, though, because it was still unfinished when Saunders died, in October, 1953, five years too soon for him to see the Bruce "corner", which, in any case, he would have been fully entitled to scoff at as a mere squabble among ribbon clerks.

9

A SECOND SORT OF LIFE

DURING FRANKLIN D. ROOSEVELT'S PRESIDENCY, when Wall Street and Washington tended to be on cat-and-dog terms, perhaps no New Dealer other than That Man himself better typified the New Deal in the eyes of Wall Street than David Eli Lilienthal. The explanation of this estimate of him in southern Manhattan lay not in any specific anti-Wall Street acts of Lilienthal's—indeed, the scattering of financiers, among them Wendell L. Willkie, who had personal dealings with him generally found him to be a reasonable sort of fellow—but in what he had come to symbolize through his association with the Tennessee Valley Authority, which, as a government-owned electric-power concern far larger than any private power corporation in the country, embodied Wall Street's notion of galloping Socialism. Because Lilienthal was a conspicuous and vigorous member of the T.V.A.'s three-man board of directors from 1933 until 1941, and was its chairman from 1941 until 1946, the business community of that period, in his phrase, thought he "wore horns." In 1946, he became the first chairman of the United States Atomic Energy Commission, and when he gave up that position, in February, 1950, at the age of fifty, the *Times* said in a news story that he had been "perhaps the most controversial figure in Washington since the end of the war."

What has Lilienthal been up to in the years since he left the government? As a matter of public record, he has been up to a number of things, all of them, surprisingly, centered on Wall Street or on private business, or both. For one thing, Lilienthal is listed in any number of business compendiums as the co-founder and the chairman of the board of the Development & Resources Corporation. Several years ago, I phoned D. & R.'s offices, then at 50 Broadway, New York City, and discovered it to be a private firm—Wall Street-backed as well as, give or take a block, Wall Street-based—that provides managerial, technical, business, and planning services toward the development of natural resources abroad. That is to say, D. & R.—whose other co-founder, the late Gordon R. Clapp, was Lilienthal's successor as T.V.A. chairman—is in the business of helping governments set up programs more or less similar to the T.V.A. Since its formation, in 1955, I learned, D. & R. had, at moderate but gratifying profit to itself, planned and managed the beginnings of a vast scheme for the reclamation of Khuzistan, an arid and poverty-stricken, though oil-rich, region of western Iran; advised the government of Italy on the development of its backward southern provinces; helped the Republic of Colombia set up a T.V.A.-like authority for its potentially fertile but flood-plagued Cauca Valley; and offered advice to Ghana on water supply, to the Ivory Coast on mineral development, and to Puerto Rico on electric power and atomic energy.

For another thing—and when I found out about this, it struck me as considerably more astonishing, on form, than D. & R.—Lilienthal has made an authentic fortune as a corporate officer and entrepreneur. In a proxy statement of the Minerals & Chemicals Corporation of America, dated June

24, 1960, that fell into my hands, I found Lilienthal listed as a director of the firm and the holder of 41,366 shares of its common stock. These shares at the time of my investigation were being traded on the New York Stock Exchange at something over twenty-five dollars each, and simple multiplication revealed that they represented a thumping sum by most men's standards, certainly including those of a man who had spent most of his life on government wages, without the help of private resources.

And, for still another thing, in 1953 Harper & Brothers brought out Lilienthal's third book, "Big Business: A New Era." (His previous books were "T.V.A.: Democracy on the March" and "This I Do Believe," which appeared in 1944 and 1949, respectively.) In "Big Business," Lilienthal argues that not only the productive and distributive superiority of the United States but also its national security depends on industrial bigness; that we now have adequate public safeguards against abuses of big business, or know well enough how to fashion them as required; that big business does not tend to destroy small business, as is often supposed, but, rather, tends to promote it; and, finally, that a big-business society does not suppress individualism, as most intellectuals believe, but actually tends to encourage it by reducing poverty, disease, and physical insecurity and increasing the opportunities for leisure and travel. Fighting words, in short, from an old New Dealer.

Lilienthal is a man whose government career I, as a newspaper reader, had followed fairly closely. My interest in him as a government official had reached its peak in February, 1947, when, in answer to a fierce attack on him by his old enemy Senator Kenneth D. McKellar, of Tennessee, during Congressional hearings on his fitness for the A.E.C. job, he uttered a spontaneous statement of personal democratic faith that for many people still ranks as one of the most stirring attacks on what later came to be known as McCarthyism. ("One of the tenets of democracy that grow out of this central core of a belief that the individual comes first, that all men are the children of God and their personalities are therefore sacred," Lilienthal said, among other things, "is a deep belief in civil liberties and their protection; and a repugnance to anyone who would steal from a human being that which is most precious to him, his good name, by imputing things to him, by innuendo, or by insinuation.") The fragments of information I picked up about his new, private career left me confused. Wondering how Wall Street and business life had affected Lilienthal, and vice versa, in their belated *rapprochement*, I got in touch with him, and a day or so later, at his invitation, drove out to New Jersey to spend the afternoon with him.

Lilienthal and his wife, Helen Lamb Lilienthal, lived on Battle Road, in Princeton, where they had settled in 1957, after six years in New York City, at first in a house on Beekman Place and later in an apartment on Sutton Place. The Princeton house, which stands in a plot of less than an acre, is of Georgian brick with green shutters. Surrounded by other houses of its kind, the place is capacious yet anything but pretentious. Lilienthal, wearing gray slacks and a plaid sports shirt, met me at the front door. At just past sixty, he was a tall, trim man with a receding hairline, a slightly hawklike profile, and candid, piercing eyes. He led me into the living room, where he introduced Mrs. Lilienthal and then pointed out a couple of household treasures—a large Oriental rug in front of the fireplace, which he said was a gift from the Shah of Iran, and, hanging on the wall opposite the fireplace, a Chinese scroll of the late nineteenth century showing four rather roguish men, who, he told me, have a special meaning for him, since they are upper-middle-rank civil servants. Pointing to a particularly enigmatic-looking fellow, he added, with a smile, that he always thought of that one as his Oriental counterpart.

Mrs. Lilienthal went to get coffee, and while she was gone,

I asked Lilienthal to tell me something of his post-government life, starting at the beginning. "All right," he said. "The beginning: I left the A.E.C. for a number of reasons. In that kind of work, I feel, a fellow is highly expendable. If you stayed too long, you might find yourself placating industry or the military, or both—building up what would amount to an atomic pork barrel. Another thing—I wanted to be allowed to speak my mind more freely than I could as a government official. I felt I'd served my term. So I turned in my resignation in November, 1949, and it went into effect three months later. As for the timing, I resigned then because, for once, I wasn't under fire. Originally, I'd planned to do it earlier in 1949, but then came the last Congressional attack on me—the time Hickenlooper, of Iowa, accused me of 'incredible mismanagement.'" I noticed that Lilienthal did not smile in referring to the Hickenlooper affair. "I entered private life with both trepidation and relief," he went on. "The trepidation was about my ability to make a living, and it was very real. Oh, I'd been a practicing lawyer as a young man, in Chicago, before going into government work, and made quite a lot of money at it, too. But now I didn't *want* to practice law. And I was worried about what else I could do. I was so obsessed with the subject that I harped on it all the time, and my wife and my friends began to kid me. That Christmas of 1949, my wife gave me a beggar's tin cup, and one of my friends gave me a guitar to go with it. The feeling of relief—well, that was a matter of personal privacy and freedom. As a private citizen, I wouldn't have to be trailed around by hordes of security officers as I had been at the A.E.C. I wouldn't have to answer the charges of Congressional committees. And, above all, I'd be able to talk freely to my wife again."

Mrs. Lilienthal had returned with the coffee as her husband was talking, and now she sat down with us. She comes, I knew, from a family of pioneers who, over several generations, moved westward from New England to Ohio to Indiana to Oklahoma, where she was born. She seemed to me to look the part—that of a woman of dignity, patience, practicality, and gentle strength. "I can tell you that my husband's resignation was a relief to *me*," she said. "Before he went with the A.E.C., we'd always talked over all aspects of his work. When he took that job, we agreed between us that although we'd indulge in the discussion of personalities as freely as we pleased, he would never tell me anything about the work of the A.E.C. that I couldn't read in the newspapers. It was a terrible constraint to be under."

Lilienthal nodded. "I'd come home at night with some frightful experience in me," he said. "No one who so much as touches the atom is ever quite the same again. Perhaps I'd have been in a series of conferences and listened to the kind of talk that many military and scientific men go in for—cities full of human beings referred to as 'targets,' and that sort of thing. I never got used to that impersonal jargon. I'd come home sick at heart. But I couldn't talk about it to Helen. I wasn't allowed to get it off my chest."

"And now there wouldn't be any more hearings," Mrs. Lilienthal said. "Those terrible hearings! I'll never forget one Washington cocktail party we went to, for our sins. My husband had been going through one of the endless series of Congressional hearings. A woman in a funny hat came gushing up to him and said something like 'Oh, Mr. Lilienthal, I was *so* anxious to come to your hearings, but I just couldn't make it. I'm so sorry. I just *love* hearings, don't you?'"

Husband and wife looked at each other, and this time Lilienthal managed a grin.

Lilienthal seemed glad to get on to what happened next. At about the time his resignation became effective, he told me, he was approached by various men from Harvard representing the fields of history, public administration, and law, who asked him to accept an appointment to the faculty. But he decided he didn't want to become a professor any more than he wanted to practice law. Within the next few weeks came offers from numerous law firms in New York and Washington, and from some industrial companies. Reassured by these that he was not going to need the tin cup and guitar after all, Lilienthal, after mulling over the offers, finally turned them all down and settled, in May, 1950, for a part-time job as a consultant to the celebrated banking firm of Lazard Frères & Co., whose senior partner, André Meyer, he had met through Albert Lasker, a mutual friend. Lazard gave him an office in its headquarters at 44 Wall, but before he could do much consulting, he was off on a lecture tour across the United States, followed by a trip to Europe that summer, with his wife, on behalf of the late *Collier's* magazine. The trip did not result in any articles, though, and on returning home in the fall he found it necessary to get back on a full-time income-producing basis; this he did by becoming a consultant to various other companies, among them the Carrier Corporation and the Radio Corporation of America. To Carrier he offered advice on managerial problems. For R.C.A., he worked on the question of color television, ultimately advising his client to concentrate on technical research rather than on law-court squabbles over patents; he also helped persuade the company to press its computer program and to stay out of the construction of atomic reactors. Early in 1951, he took another trip abroad for *Collier's*—to India, Pakistan, Thailand, and Japan. This trip produced an article—published in *Collier's* that August— in which he proposed a solution to the dispute between India and Pakistan over Kashmir and the headwaters of the Indus River. Lilienthal's idea was that the tension between the two countries could best be lessened by a coöperative program to improve living conditions in the whole disputed area through economic development of the Indus Basin. Nine years later, largely through the financial backing and moral support of Eugene R. Black and the World Bank, the Lilienthal plan was essentially adopted, and an Indus treaty signed between India and Pakistan. But the immediate reaction to his article was general indifference, and Lilienthal, temporarily stymied and considerably disillusioned, once more settled down to the humbler problems of private business.

At this point in Lilienthal's narrative, the doorbell rang. Mrs. Lilienthal went to answer it, and I could hear her talking to someone—a gardener, evidently—about the pruning of some roses. After listening restlessly for a minute or two, Lilienthal called to his wife, "Helen, please tell Domenic to prune those roses farther back than he did last year!" Mrs. Lilienthal went outside with Domenic, and Lilienthal remarked, "Domenic always prunes too gently, to my way of thinking. It's a case of our backgrounds—Italy versus the Middle West." Then, resuming where he had left off, he said that his association with Lazard Frères, and more particularly with Meyer, had led him into an association, first as a consultant and later as an executive, with a small company called the Minerals Separation North American Corporation, in which Lazard Frères had a large interest. It was in this undertaking that, unexpectedly, he made his fortune. The company was in trouble, and Meyer's notion was that Lilienthal might be the man to do something about it. Subsequently, in the course of a series of mergers, acquisitions, and other maneuvers, the company's name was changed to, successively, the Attapulgus Minerals & Chemicals Corporation, the Minerals & Chemicals Corporation of America, and, in 1960, the Minerals & Chemicals Philipp Corporation; meanwhile, its annual receipts rose from about seven hundred and fifty thousand dollars, for 1952, to something over two hundred and seventy-four million, for 1960. For Lilienthal, the acceptance of Meyer's commission to look into the company's affairs was the beginning of a four-year immersion in the day-to-day problems of managing a business; the experience, he said decisively, turned out to be one of his life's richest, and by no means only in the literal sense of that word.

I have reconstructed the corporate facts behind Lilienthal's experience partly from what he told me in Princeton, partly from a subsequent study of some of the company's published documents, and partly from talks with other persons interested in the firm. Minerals Separation North American, which was founded in 1916 as an offshoot of a British firm, was a patent company, deriving its chief income from royalties on patents for processes used in refining copper ore and the ores of other nonferrous minerals. Its activities were twofold—attempting to develop new patents in its research laboratory, and offering technical services to the mining and manufacturing companies that leased its old ones. By 1950, although it was still netting a nice annual profit, it was in a bad way. Under the direction of its long-time president, Dr. Seth Gregory—who was then over ninety but still ruled the company with an iron hand, commuting daily between his midtown apartment hotel and his office, at 11 Broadway, in a regally purple Rolls-Royce—it had cut down its research activities to almost nothing and was living on half a dozen old patents, all of which were scheduled to go into the public domain in from five to eight years. In effect, it was a still healthy company living under a death sentence. Lazard Frères, as a large stockholder, was understandably concerned. Dr. Gregory was persuaded to retire on a handsome pension, and in February, 1952, after working with Minerals Separation for some time as a consultant, Lilienthal was installed as the company's president and a member of its board of directors. His first task was to find a new source of income to replace the fast-expiring patents, and he and the other directors agreed that the way to accomplish this was through a merger; it fell to Lilienthal to participate in arranging one between Minerals

Separation and another company in which Lazard Frères—along with the Wall Street firm of F. Eberstadt & Co.—had large holdings: the Attapulgus Clay Company, of Attapulgus, Georgia, which produced a very rare kind of clay that is useful in purifying petroleum products, and which manufactured various household products, among them a floor cleaner called Speedi-Dri.

As a marriage broker between Minerals Separation and Attapulgus, Lilienthal had the touchy job of persuading the executives of the Southern company that they were not being used as pawns by a bunch of rapacious Wall Street bankers. Being an agent of the bankers was an unaccustomed role for Lilienthal, but he evidently carried it off with aplomb, despite the fact that his presence complicated the emotional problems still further by introducing into the situation a whiff of galloping Socialism. "Dave was very effective in building up the Attapulgus people's morale and confidence," another Wall Streeter has told me. "He reconciled them to the merger, and showed them its advantages for them." Lilienthal himself told me, "I felt at home in the administrative and technical parts of the job, but the financial part had to be done by the people from Lazard and Eberstadt. Every time they began talking about spinoffs and exchanges of shares, I was lost. I didn't even know what a spinoff *was*." (As Lilienthal knows now, it is, not to get too technical about it, a division of a company into two or more companies—the opposite of a merger.) The merger took place in December, 1952, and neither the Attapulgus people nor the Minerals Separation people had any reason to regret it, because both the profits and the stock price of the newly formed company—the Attapulgus Minerals & Chemicals Corporation—soon began to rise. At the time of the merger, Lilienthal was made chairman of the board of directors, at an annual salary of eighteen thousand dollars. Over the next three years, while serving first in this position and later as chairman of the executive committee, he had a large part not only in the conduct of the company's routine affairs but also in its further growth through a series of new mergers—one in 1954, with Edgar Brothers, a leading producer of kaolin for paper coating, and two in 1955, with a pair of limestone concerns in Ohio and Virginia. The mergers and the increased efficiency that went with them were not long in paying off; between 1952 and 1955 the company's net profit per share more than quintupled.

The mechanics of Lilienthal's own rise from the comparative rags of a public servant to the riches of a successful entrepreneur are baldly outlined in the company's proxy statements for its annual and special stockholders' meetings. (There are few public documents more indiscreet than proxy statements, in which the precise private stockholdings of directors must be listed.) In November, 1952, Minerals Separation North American granted Lilienthal, as a supplement to his annual salary, a stock option.* His option entitled him to buy as many as fifty thousand shares of the firm's stock from its treasury at $4.87½ per share, then the going rate, any time before the end of 1955, and in exchange he signed a contract agreeing to serve the company as an active executive throughout 1953, 1954, and 1955. The potential financial advantage to him, of course, as to all other recipients of stock options, lay in the fact that if the price of the stock rose substantially, he could buy shares at the option price and thus have a holding that would immediately be worth much more than he paid for it. Furthermore, and more important, if he should later decide to sell his shares, the proceeds would be a capital gain, taxable at a maximum rate of 25%. Of course, if the stock failed to go up, the option would be worthless. But, like so many stocks of the mid-fifties, Lilienthal's did go up, fantastically. By the end of 1954, according to the proxy statements, Lilienthal had exercised his option to the extent of buying twelve thousand seven hundred and fifty shares,

---

* For a detailed discussion of stock options, see p. 101.

which were then worth not $4.87½ each but about $20. In February, 1955, he sold off four thousand shares at $22.75 each, bringing in ninety-one thousand dollars. This sum, less capital-gains tax, was then applied against further purchases under the option, and in August, 1955, the proxy statements show, Lilienthal raised his holdings to almost forty thousand shares, or close to the number he held at the time of my visit to him. By that time, the stock, which had at first been sold over the counter, not only had achieved a listing on the New York Stock Exchange but had become one of the Exchange's highflying speculative favorites; its price had skyrocketed to about forty dollars a share, and Lilienthal, obviously, was solidly in the millionaire class. Moreover, the company was now on a sound long-term basis, paying an annual cash dividend of fifty cents a share, and the Lilienthal family's financial worries were permanently over.

Fiscally speaking, Lilienthal told me, his symbolic moment of triumph was the day, in June of 1955, when the shares of Minerals & Chemicals graduated to a listing on the New York Stock Exchange. In accordance with custom, Lilienthal, as a top officer, was invited onto the floor to shake hands with the president of the Exchange and be shown around generally. "I went through it in a daze," Lilienthal told me. "Until then, I'd never been inside any stock exchange in my life. It was all mysterious and fascinating. No zoo could have seemed more strange to me." How the Stock Exchange felt at this stage about having the former wearer of horns on its floor is not recorded.

In telling me about his experience with the company, Lilienthal had spoken with zest and had made the whole thing sound mysterious and fascinating. I asked him what, apart from the obvious financial inducement, had led him to devote himself to the affairs of a small firm, and how it had felt for the former boss of T.V.A. and A.E.C. to be, in effect, peddling Attapulgite, kaolin, limestone, and Speedi-Dri. Lilienthal leaned back in his chair and stared at the ceiling. "I wanted an entrepreneurial experience," he said. "I found a great appeal in the idea of taking a small and quite crippled company and trying to make something of it. Building. That kind of building, I thought, is the central thing in American free enterprise, and something I'd missed in all my government work. I wanted to try my hand at it. Now, about how it felt. Well, it felt plenty exciting. It was full of intellectual stimulation, and a lot of my old ideas changed. I conceived a great new respect for financiers—men like André Meyer. There's a correctness about them, a certain high sense of honor, that I'd never had any conception of. I found that business life is full of creative, original minds—along with the usual number of second-guessers, of course. Furthermore, I found it seductive. In fact, I was in danger of becoming a slave. Business has its man-eating side, and part of the man-eating side is that it's so absorbing. I found that the things you read—for instance, that acquiring money for its own sake can become an addiction if you're not careful—are literally true. Certain good friends helped keep me on the track—men like Ferdinand Eberstadt, who became my fellow-director after the Attapulgus merger, and Nathan Greene, special counsel to Lazard Frères, who was on the board for a while. Greene was a kind of business father confessor to me. I remember his saying, 'You think you'll make your pile and then be independent. My friend, in Wall Street you don't just win your independence at one stroke. To paraphrase Thomas Jefferson, you have to win your independence over again every day.' I found that he was right about that. Oh, I had my problems. I questioned myself at every step. It was exhausting. You see, for so long I'd been associated with two pretty far-reaching things—institutions. I had a feeling of identity with them; in that kind of work you are able to lose your sense of self. Now, with myself to worry about—my personal standards as well as my financial future—I found myself wondering all the time whether I was making the right move. But that part's all in my journal, and you can read it there, if you like." *

I said I certainly would like to read it, and Lilienthal led me to his study, in the basement. It proved to be a good-sized room whose windows opened on window wells into which strands of ivy were trailing; light came in from outside, and even a little slanting sunshine, but the tops of the window wells were too high to permit a view of the garden or the neighborhood. Lilienthal remarked, "My neighbor Robert Oppenheimer complained about the enclosed feeling when he first saw this room. I told him that was just the feeling I wanted!" Then he showed me a filing cabinet, standing in a corner; it contained the journal, in rows and rows of loose-leaf notebooks, the earliest of them dating back to its author's high-school days. Having invited me to make myself at home, Lilienthal left me alone in his study and went back upstairs.

Taking him at his word, I went for a turn or two around the room, looking at the pictures on the walls and finding about what might have been expected: inscribed photographs from Franklin D. Roosevelt, Harry S. Truman, Senator George Norris, Louis Brandeis; pictures of Lilienthal with Roosevelt, with Willkie, with Fiorello LaGuardia, with Nelson Rockefeller, with Nehru in India; a night view of the Fontana Dam, in the Tennessee Valley, being built under a blaze of electricity supplied by T.V.A. power plants. A man's study reflects himself as he wishes to be seen publicly, but his journal, if he is honest, reflects something else. I had not browsed long in Lilienthal's journal before I realized that it was an extraordinary document—not merely a historical source of unusual interest but a searching record of a public man's thoughts and emotions. I leafed through the years of his association with Minerals & Chemicals, and, scattered amid much about family, Democratic politics, friends, trips abroad, reflections on national policies, and hopes and fears for the republic, I came

* This part of Lilienthal's journal was eventually published, in 1966.

upon the following entries having to do with business and life in New York:

May 24, 1951: Looks as if I am in the minerals business. In a small way, that could become a big way. [He goes on to explain that he has just had his first interview with Dr. Gregory, and is apparently acceptable to the old man as the new president of the company.]

May 31, 1951: [Starting in business] is like learning to walk after a long illness. . . . At first you have to think: move the right foot, move the left foot, etc. Then you are walking without thinking, and then walking is something one does with unconsciousness and utter confidence. This latter state, as to business, has yet to come, but I had the first touch of it today.

July 22, 1951: I recall Wendell Willkie saying to me years ago, "Living in New York is a great experience. I wouldn't live anywhere else. It is the most exciting, stimulating, satisfying spot in the world," etc. I think this was apropos of some remark I had made on a business visit to New York—that I was certainly glad I didn't have to live in that madhouse of noise and dirt. [Last] Thursday was a day in which I shared some of Willkie's feeling. . . . There was a grandeur about the place, and adventure, a sense of being in the center of a great achievement, New York City in the fifties.

October 28, 1951: What I am reaching for, perhaps, is to have my cake and eat it, too, but in a way this is not wholly senseless nor futile. That is, I can have enough actual contact with the affairs of business to keep a sense of reality, or develop one. How otherwise can I explain the pleasure

I get in visiting a copper mine or talking to operators of an electric furnace, or a coal-research project, or watching how André Meyer works. . . . But along with that I want to be free enough to think about what these things mean, free enough to read outside the immediate field of interest. This requires keeping out of status (the absence of which I know makes me vaguely unhappy).

December 8, 1952: What is it that investment bankers do for their money? Well, I have certainly had my eyes opened, as to the amount of toil, sweat, frustrations, problems—yes, and tears—that has to be gone through. . . . If everyone who has something to sell in the market had to be as meticulous and detailed in his statements about what he is selling as those who offer stock in the market are now, under the Truth in Securities law, darn little would be sold, in time to be useful, at least.

December 20, 1952: My purpose in this Attapulgus venture is to make a good deal of money in a short time, in a way (i.e., old man capital gains) that enables me to keep three-fourths of it, instead of paying 80% or more in income taxes. . . . But there is another purpose: to have had the experience of business. . . . The real reason, or the chief reason, is a feeling that my life wouldn't be complete, living in a business period—that is, a time dominated by the business of business—unless I had been active in that area. What I wanted was to be an observer of this fascinating activity that so colors and affects the world's life, not . . . an observer from without (as a writer, teacher) but from the arena itself. I still have this feeling, and when I get low and glad to chuck the whole thing (as I have from time to time), the sustaining part is that even the bumps and sore spots are experiences, actual experiences within the business world. . . .

Then, too, [I wanted to be able to make] a comparison of the managers of business, the spirit, the tensions, the motivations, etc., with those of government (something I keep doing anyway)—and that needs doing to understand either government or business. This requires actual valid experience in the business world somewhat comparable to my long hiring out in government matters.

I don't kid myself that I will ever be accepted as a businessman, not after those long years when I wore horns, for all of them outside the Tennessee Valley at least. And I feel less defensive—usually shown by a belligerence—on this score than I did when I rarely saw a tycoon or a Wall Streeter, whereas now I live with them. . . .

January 18, 1953: I am now definitely committed [to Minerals & Chemicals] for not less than three more years . . . and morally committed to see the thing through. While I can't conceive that this business will ever seem enough, an end of itself, to make up a satisfactory life, yet the busy-ness, the activity, the crises, the gambles, the management problems I must face, the judgment about people, all combine to make something far from dull. Add to this the good chance of making a good deal of money. . . . My decision to try business—that seemed to so many people a bit of romantic moonshine—makes more sense today than it did a year ago.

But there is something missing. . . .

December 2, 1953: Crawford Greenewalt [president of du Pont] . . . introduced me in a speech (in Philadelphia). . . . He noted that I had entered the chemical business; bearing in mind that I had previously headed the biggest things in America, bigger than [any] private corporations, he was naturally a little nervous about seeing me become a potential competitor. It was kidding, but it was good kidding. And it certainly gave little ole Attapulgus quite a notice.

June 30, 1954: I have found a new kind of satisfaction, and in a sense, fulfillment, in a business career. I really never felt that the "consultant" thing was being a businessman, or engaging in the realities of a life of business. Too remote from the actual thinking process, the exercise of judgment and decision. . . . In this company, as we are evolving it, there are so many of the elements of fun. . . . The starting with almost nothing . . . the company depending on patents alone . . . acquisition, mergers, stock issues, proxy statements, the methods of financing internally and by bank loans . . . also the way stock prices are made, the silly and almost childlike basis upon which grown men decide that a stock should be bought, and at what price . . . the merger with Edgar, the great [subsequent] rise in the price of their stock . . . the review of the price structure. The beginning of better costs. The catalyst idea. The drive and energy and imagination: the nights and days (in the lab until 2 A.M. night after night) and finally the beginning of a new business. . . . It is quite a story.

(Later I got a rather different perspective on Lilienthal's reactions to the transition from government to business by talking to the man he had described as his "business father confessor," Nathan Greene. "What happens to a man who leaves top-level government work and comes to Wall Street as a consultant?" Greene asked me rhetorically. "Well, usually it's a big letdown. In the government, Dave was used to a sense of great authority and power—tremendous national and international responsibility. People wanted to be seen with him. Foreign dignitaries sought him out. He had all sorts of facilities—rows of buttons on his desk. He pushed them, and lawyers, technicians, accountants appeared to do his bidding. All right, now he comes to Wall Street. There's a big welcoming reception, he meets all the partners of his new firm and their wives, he's given a nice office with a carpet. But there's nothing on his desk—only one button, and all it summons is a secretary. He doesn't have perquisites like limousines. Furthermore, he really has no responsibility. He says to himself, 'I'm an idea man, I've got to have some ideas.' He has some, but they're not given much attention by the partners. So the outward form of his new work is a letdown. The same with its content. In Washington, it had been development of natural resources, atomic energy, or the like—world-shaking things. Now it turns out to be some little business to make money. It all seems a bit petty.

"Then, there's the matter of money itself. In the government, our hypothetical man didn't need it so badly. He had all these services and the basic comforts supplied him at no personal cost, and besides he had a great sense of moral superiority. He was able to sneer at people who were out making money. He could think of somebody in his law-school class who was making a pile in the Street, and say, 'He's sold out.' Then our man leaves government and goes to the Wall Street fleshpots himself, and he says, 'Boy, am I going to make these guys pay for my services!' They do pay, too. He gets big fees for consulting. Then he finds out about big income taxes, how he has to pay most of his income to the government now instead of getting his livelihood from it. The shoe is on the other foot. He may—sometimes he does—begin to scream 'Confiscation!,' just like any old Wall Streeter.

"How did Dave handle these problems? Well, he had his troubles—after all, he was starting a second sort of life—but he handled them just about as well as they can be handled. He was never bored, and he never screamed 'Confiscation!' He has a great capacity for sinking himself in something. The subject matter isn't so important to him. It's almost as if he were able to think that what he's doing is important, whether it is or not, simply *because* he's doing it. His ability was invaluable to Minerals & Chemicals, and not just as an administrator. Dave is a lawyer, after all; he knows more about corporate finances than he likes to admit. He enjoys playing the barefoot boy, but he's hardly that. Dave is an almost perfect example of somebody who kept his independence while getting rich on Wall Street.")

One way and another, then—reading through these ambivalent protestations in the journal, and later hearing Greene—I seemed to detect under the exuberance and the absorption a nagging sense of dissatisfaction, almost of compromise. For Lilienthal, the obviously genuine thrill of having a new kind of experience, and an almost unimaginably profitable one, had been, I sensed, a rose with a worm in it. I went back up to the living room. There I found Lilienthal fiat on his back on the Shah's rug underneath a pile of pre-school-age children. At least, it looked at first glance like a pile; on closer inspection I found that it consisted of just two boys. Mrs. Lilienthal, who had returned from the garden, introduced them as Allen and Daniel Bromberger, sons of the Lilienthals' daughter, Nancy, and Sylvain Bromberger, adding that the Brombergers were living nearby, since Sylvain was teaching philosophy at the university. (A few weeks later, Bromberger moved on to the University of Chicago.) The Lilienthals' only other offspring, David, Jr., lived in Edgartown, Massachusetts, where he had settled down to become a writer, as he subsequently did. In response to the urging of the senior Lilienthals, the grandchildren climbed off their grandfather and disappeared from the room. When things were normal again, I told Lilienthal my reaction to the entries I had read in the journal, and he hesitated for a while before speaking. "Yes," he said, finally. "Well, one thing—it wasn't making all that money that worried me. That didn't make me feel either good or bad, by itself. In the government years, we'd always paid our bills, and by scrimping we'd been able to save enough to send the kids to college.

We'd never thought much about money. And then making a lot of it, making a million—I was surprised, of course. I'd never especially aimed at that or thought it might happen to me. It's like when you're a boy and you try to jump six feet. Then you find you can jump six feet, and you say, 'Well, so what?' It's sort of irrelevant. Over the past few years, a lot of people have said to me, 'How does it feel to be rich?' At first, I was kind of offended—there seemed to be an implied criticism in the question—but I'm over that. I tell them it doesn't feel any special way. The way I feel is—But this is going to sound stuffy."

"No, I don't think it's stuffy," said Mrs. Lilienthal, anticipating what was coming.

"Yes, it is, but I'm going to say it anyway," said Lilienthal. "I don't think money makes much difference, as long as you have enough."

"I don't quite agree," said Mrs. Lilienthal. "It doesn't make much difference when you're young. You don't mind then, as long as you can struggle along. But as you get older, it *is* helpful."

Lilienthal nodded in deference to that. Then he said that he thought the undertone of dissatisfaction I had noticed in the journal probably stemmed, at least in part, from the fact that his career in private business, absorbing though it was, did not bring with it the gratifications of public-service work. True, he had not been deprived of them entirely, because it was at the height of his Minerals & Chemicals operations, in 1954, that he first went to Colombia, at the request of that country's government, and, serving as a peso-a-year consultant, started the Cauca Valley project that was later continued by the Development & Resources Corporation. But for the most part being a top officer of Minerals & Chemicals had kept him pretty well tied down, and he'd had to regard the Colombia work as a sideline, if not merely a hobby. I found it impossible to avoid seeing symbolic significance in the fact

303

that the principal material with which Lilienthal the business-man had been engaged was—clay.

I thought of something else in Lilienthal's life at that time that might have taken some of the kick out of the process of becoming a successful businessman. His "Big Business" book had come out when he was in the thick of the Minerals & Chemicals work. I wondered whether, since it is such an uncritical paean to free enterprise, it had been construed by some people as a rationalization of his new career, and I asked about this.

"Well, the ideas in the book were rather a shock to some of my husband's New Deal friends, all right," Mrs. Lilienthal said, a bit dryly.

"They needed shocking, damn it!" Lilienthal burst out. He spoke with some heat, and I thought of the phrase in his journal—used there in an entirely different context but still in reference to himself—about defensiveness shown by belligerence. After a moment, he went on, in a normal tone, "My wife and daughter thought I didn't spend enough time working on the book, and they were right. I wrote it in too much of a hurry. My conclusions aren't supported by enough argument. For one thing, I should have spelled out in more detail my opposition to the way the antitrust laws are administered. But the anti-trust part wasn't the real trouble. The thing that really shook up some of my old friends was what I said about big industry in relation to individualism, and about the machine in relation to aesthetics. Morris Cooke, who used to be administrator of the Rural Electrification Administration—he was one who was shaken up. He took me apart over the book, and I took him apart back. The anti-bigness dogmatists stopped having anything to do with me. They simply wrote me off. I wasn't hurt or disappointed. Those people are living on nostalgia; they look backward, and I try to look forward. Then, of course, there were the trust busters. They *really* went after me. But isn't trust busting, in the sense of breaking up big companies simply because they're big, pretty much a relic of a past era? Yes, I still think I was right in the main things I said—perhaps ahead of my time, but right."

"The trouble was the timing," Mrs. Lilienthal said. "The book came so close to coinciding with my husband's leaving public service and going into private business. Some people thought it represented a change in point of view induced by expediency. Which it didn't!"

"No," Lilienthal said. "The book was written mostly in 1952, but all the ideas in it were hatched while I was still in public service. For example, my idea that bigness is essential for national security came in large part out of my experiences in the A.E.C. The company that had the research and manufacturing facilities to make the atomic bomb an operational weapon, so engineered that it wouldn't require Ph.D.s to use it in the field—Bell Telephone, to be specific—was a big company. Because it was so big, the Anti-Trust Division of the Department of Justice was seeking to break the Bell System into several parts—unsuccessfully, as it turned out—at the very time we in the A.E.C. were calling on it to do a vital defense job that required unity. That seemed wrong. More generally, the whole point of view I expressed in the book goes way back to my quarrel with Arthur Morgan, the first T.V.A. chairman, in the early thirties. He had great faith in a handicraft economy, I was for large-scale industry. T.V.A., after all, was, and is, the biggest power system in the free world. In T.V.A. I always believed in bigness—along with decentralization. But, you know, the chapter I hoped would produce the most discussion was the one on bigness as a promoter of individualism. It *did* produce discussion, of a sort. I remember people—academic people, mostly—coming up to me with incredulous expressions and saying something that started with 'Do you *really* believe . . .' Well, my answer would start with 'Yes, I really do believe . . .'"

One other touchy matter that Lilienthal may have questioned himself about in the process of making his Wall Street fortune was the fact that in making it he had not really *needed* to scream "Confiscation," since he had made it through a tax loophole, the stock option. Possibly there have been liberal, reformist businessmen who have refused to accept stock options on principle, although I have never heard of one doing so, and I am not convinced that such a renunciation would be a sensible or useful form of protest. In any event, I didn't ask Lilienthal about the matter; in the absence of any accepted code of journalism every journalist writes his own, and in mine, such a question would have come close to invasion of moral privacy. In retrospect, though, I almost wish I had violated my code that one time. Lilienthal, being Lilienthal, might have objected to the question strenuously, but I think he would have answered it equally strenuously, and without hedging. As things were, after discoursing on the critical reactions to his book, "Big Business," he got up and walked to a window. "I see Domenic has been pretty cautious about his rose-pruning," he said to his wife. "Maybe I'll go out later and cut them back some more." His jaw was set in a way that made me feel pretty sure I knew how the rose-pruning controversy was going to be resolved.

The triumphant solution to Lilienthal's problem—the way that he eventually found to have his cake and eat it—was the Development & Resources Corporation. The corporation arose out of a series of conversations between Lilienthal and Meyer during the spring of 1955, in the course of which Lilienthal pointed out that he was well acquainted with dozens of foreign dignitaries and technical personnel who had come to visit the T.V.A., and said that their intense interest in that project seemed to indicate that at least some of their countries would be receptive to the idea of starting similar programs. "Our aim in forming D. & R. was not to try to remold the world, or any large part of it, but only to try to help accomplish some rather specific things, and, incidentally, make a profit," Lilienthal told me. "André was not so sure about the profit—we both knew there would be a deficit at first—but he liked the idea of doing constructive things, and Lazard Frères decided to back us, in return for a half interest in the corporation." Clapp, who was serving at the time as deputy New York City administrator, came in as co-founder of the venture, and the subsequent executive appointments made D. & R. virtually a T.V.A. alumni association: John Oliver, who became executive vice-president, had been with T.V.A. from 1942 to 1954, ending up as its general manager; W. L. Voorduin, who became director of engineering, had been with T.V.A. for a decade and had planned its whole system of dams; Walton Seymour, who became vice-president for industrial development, had been a T.V.A. consultant on electric-power marketing for thirteen years; and a dozen other former T.V.A. men were scattered on down through the ranks.

In July, 1955, D. & R. set up shop at 44 Wall, and set to work finding clients. What was to prove its most important one came to light during a World Bank meeting in Istanbul that Lilienthal and his wife attended in September of that year. At the meeting, Lilienthal fell in with Abolhassan Ebtehaj, then head of a seven-year development plan in Iran; as it happened, Iran was just about the ideal D. & R. client, since, for one thing, the royalties on its nationalized oil industry gave it considerable capital with which to pay for the development of its resources, and, for another, what it desperately needed was technical and professional guidance. The encounter with Ebtehaj led to an invitation to Lilienthal and Clapp to visit Iran as the guests of the Shah, and see what they thought could be done about Khuzistan. Lilienthal's employment contract with Minerals & Chemicals ended that December; although he stayed on as a director, he was now free to devote all his time, or nearly all of it, to D. & R. In February, 1956, he and Clapp went to Iran. "Before then, I blush to say, I had never heard of Khuzistan," Lilienthal told me. "I've learned a lot about it since then. It was the heart of the Old Testament Elamite kingdom and later of the Persian Empire. The ruins of Persepolis are not far away, and those of Susa, where King Darius had his winter palace, are in the very center of Khuzistan. In ancient times, the whole region had an extensive water-conservation system—you can still find the remains of canals that were probably built by Darius twenty-five hundred years ago—but after the decline of the Persian Empire the water system was ruined by invasion and neglect. Lord Curzon described what the Khuzistan uplands looked like a century ago—'a desert over which the eye may roam unarrested for miles.' It was that way when we got there. Nowadays, Khuzistan is one of the world's richest oil fields—the famous Abadan refinery is at its southern tip—but the inhabitants, two and a half million of them, haven't benefited from that. The rivers have flowed unused, the fabulously rich soil has lain fallow, and all but a tiny fraction of the people have continued to live in desperate poverty. When Clapp and I first saw the place, we were appalled. Still, for two old T.V.A. hands like us, it was a dream; it was simply crying out for development. We looked for sites for dams, likely spots to hunt for minerals and make soil-fertility studies, and so on. We saw flares of natural gas rising from oil fields. That was waste, and it suggested petrochemical plants, to use the gas for making fertilizer and plastics. In eight days we'd roughed out a plan, and in about two weeks D. & R. had signed a five-year contract with the Iranian government.

"That was only the beginning. Bill Voorduin, our chief engineer, flew out there and spotted a wonderful dam site at a place just a few miles from the ruins of Susa—a narrow canyon with walls that rise almost vertically from the bed of the Dez River. We found we were going to have to manage the project as well as advise on it, and so our next job was lining up our managerial group. To give you some idea of the size of the project, right now there are about seven hundred people working on it at the professional level—a hundred Americans, three hundred Iranians, and three hundred others, mostly Europeans, who work directly for firms under subcontracts. Besides that, there are about forty-seven hundred Iranian laborers. Over five thousand people, all told. The entire plan includes fourteen dams, on five different rivers, and will take many years to finish. D. & R. has just completed its first contract, for five years, and signed a new one, for a year and a half, with option to renew for another five years. Quite a bit has been accomplished already. Take the first dam—the Dez one. It's to be six hundred and twenty feet high, or more than half again as high as the Aswan, in Egypt, and it will eventually irrigate three hundred and sixty thousand acres and generate five hundred and twenty thousand kilowatts of electricity. It should be finished early in 1963. Meanwhile, a sugar plantation—the first in Khuzistan in twenty-five centuries—has been started, with irrigation by pumped water; it should yield its first crop this summer, and a sugar refinery will be ready by the time the sugar is. Another thing: eventually the region will supply its own electric power from the dams, but for the interim period a high-tension line, the first anywhere in Iran, has been put in over the seventy-two miles from Abadan to Ahwaz—a city of a hundred and twenty thousand that previously had no power source except half a dozen little diesels, which seldom worked."

While the Iranian project was proceeding, D. & R. was also busy lining up and carrying out its programs for Italy, Colombia, Ghana, the Ivory Coast, and Puerto Rico, as well as programs for private business groups in Chile and the Philippines. A job that D. & R. had just taken on for the United States Army Corps of Engineers excited Lilienthal enormously—an investigation of the economic impact of power from a proposed dam on the Alaskan sector of the Yukon, which he described as "the river with the greatest hydroelectric potential remaining on this continent." Meanwhile, Lazard Frères retained its financial interest in the firm and now very happily collected its share of a substantial annual profit, and Lilienthal happily took to teasing Meyer about his former skepticism as to D. & R. financial prospects.

Lilienthal's new career had meant a highly peripatetic life both for him and for Mrs. Lilienthal. He showed me his foreign-travel log for 1960, which he said was a fairly typical year, and it read as follows:

> January 23-March 26: Honolulu, Tokyo, Manila; Iligan, Mindanao; Manila, Bangkok, Siemreap, Bangkok; Tehran, Ahwaz, Andimeshk, Ahwaz, Tehran; Geneva, Brussels, Madrid; home. October 11–17: Buenos Aires; Patagonia; home. November 18–December 5: London, Tehran, Rome, Milan, Paris, home.

Then he went and got the volume of his journal that relates to those trips. Turning to the pages on his stay in Iran early last spring, I was particularly struck by a few excerpts:

> Ahwaz, March 5: The cry of the Arab women as the Shah's big black Chrysler passed them, a solid row along the road from the airport, made me think of the rebel yell; then I recognized it: it was the Indian yelp, the kind we used to make as kids, moving our hand over our mouths to give that undulating wail. Ahwaz, March 11: Our experience in the villagers' huts on Wednesday threw me into a deep pit. I hovered between despair—which is an emotion I consider a sin—and anger, which doesn't do much good, I suppose. Andimeshk, March 9: . . . We have travelled many miles, through dust, mudholes where we got stuck fast, and some of the roughest "roads" I have ever known—and we also travelled back to the ninth century, and earlier, visit-

ing villages and going into mud "homes" quite unbelievable—and unforgettable forever and ever. As the Biblical
oath has it: Let my right hand wither if I ever forget how
some of the most attractive of my fellow human beings
live—are living tonight, only a few kilometres from here,
where we visited them this afternoon. . . .

And yet I am as sure as I am writing these notes that
the Ghebli area, of only 45,000 acres, swallowed in the
vastness of the Khuzistan, will become as well known as,
say, the community of Tupelo . . . became, or New Har-
mony or Salt Lake City when it was founded by a handful
of dedicated men in a pass of the great Rockies.

The afternoon shadows were getting long on Battle Road,
and it was time for me to be going. Lilienthal walked out to
my car with me, and on the way I asked him whether he ever
missed the rough-and-tumble, and the limelight, of being perhaps the most controversial man in Washington. He grinned,
and said, "Sure." When we reached the car, he went on, "I
never intended to be especially combative, in Washington or
in the Tennessee Valley. It was just that people kept disagree-
ing with me. But, all right, I wouldn't have put myself in controversial situations so much if I hadn't wanted to. I guess I
was combative. When I was a kid, I was interested in boxing. At high school—in Michigan City, Indiana—I boxed a lot
with a cousin of mine, and while I was in college, at DePauw,
in central Indiana, I took to boxing during the summers with
a man who had been a professional light-heavyweight. The
Tacoma Tiger, he'd been called. Working out with him was a
challenge. If I made a mistake, I'd be on the floor. I wanted
just once to land on him *good*. It was my ambition. I never
did, of course, but I got to be a fairly good boxer. I became
boxing coach at DePauw while I was an undergraduate. Later
on, at Harvard Law, I didn't have time to keep it up, and I
never boxed seriously again. But I don't think that for me

boxing was an expression of combativeness for its own sake. I think I considered competence at defending yourself a means of preserving your personal independence. I learned that from my father. 'Be your own man,' he used to say. He'd come from Austria-Hungary, the part that's now eastern Czechoslovakia, in the eighteen-eighties, when he was about twenty, and he spent his adult life as a storekeeper in various Middle Western towns: Morton, Illinois, where I was born; Valparaiso, Indiana; Springfield, Missouri; Michigan City and, later, Winamac, Indiana. He had very pale-blue eyes that reflected the insides of him. You could tell by looking at him that he wouldn't trade independence for security. He didn't know how to dissemble, and wouldn't have wanted to if he had known how. Well, to get back to my being controversial, or combative, or whatever you call it, in Washington—yes, there's something missing when you don't have a McKellar laying it on the line any more. The moral equivalent of that for me now is taking on challenges, different kinds of McKellars or Tacoma Tigers, maybe—the Minerals & Chemicals thing, the D. & R. thing— and trying to meet them."

I revisited Lilienthal in early summer, 1968, this time at D. & R.'s third home office, a suite with a splendid harbor view at I Whitehall Street. Both D. & R. and he had moved along in the interim. In Khuzistan, the Dez Dam had been completed on schedule; water impounding had begun in November, 1962, the first power had been delivered in May, 1963, and the region was now not only supplying its own power but producing enough surplus to attract foreign industry. Meanwhile, agriculture in the once-barren region was flourishing as a result of irrigation made possible by the dam, and, as Lilienthal—sixty-eight now, and as combative as ever—put it, "The gloomy economists have to be gloomy about some other underdeveloped country." D. & R. had just signed a new five-year contract with Iran to carry on the work. Otherwise, the firm had expanded its clientele to include fourteen countries; its most controversial undertaking was in Vietnam, where, under contract with the United States government, it was cooperating with a similar group of South Vietnamese in working up plans for the postwar development of the Mekong Valley. (This assignment had led to criticism of Lilienthal by those who took it to imply that he supported the war; in fact, he told me, he regarded the war as the disastrous outcome of a series of "horrible miscalculations," and the planning of postwar resources development as a separate matter. It was clear enough, nevertheless, that the criticism hurt. At the same time, D. & R. was widening its horizons by beginning to move, unexpectedly, into domestic urban development, having been engaged by private foundation-sponsored groups in Queens County, New York and Oakland County, Michigan to see whether the T.V.A. approach might have some value in dealing with those modern deserts, the slums. "Just pretend this is Zambia and tell us what you would do," these groups had said, in effect, to D. & R.—a wildly imaginative idea, surely, the usefulness of which remained to be proved.

As for D. & R. itself and its place in American business, Lilienthal recounted that since I had seen him it had expanded to the extent of opening a second permanent office on the West Coast, had considerably increased its profits, and become essentially employee-owned, with Lazard retaining only a token interest. Most encouraging of all, at a time when old-line business was having serious recruitment problems because its obsession with profit was repelling high-minded youth, D. & R. found that its idealistic objectives made it a magnet for the most promising new graduates. And as a result of all these things, Lillienthal could at last say what he had not been able to say on the earlier occasion—that private enterprise was now affording him more satisfaction than he had ever derived from public service.

Is D. & R., then, a prototype of the free enterprise of the

future, accountable half to its stockholders and half to the rest of humanity? If so, then the irony is complete, and Lilienthal, of all people, ends up as the prototypical businessman.

10

STOCKHOLDER SEASON

A FEW YEARS AGO, a European diplomat was quoted in the *Times* as saying, "The American economy has become so big that it is beyond the imagination to comprehend. But now on top of size you are getting rapid growth as well. It is a situation of fundamental power unequalled in the history of the world." At about the same time, A. A. Berle wrote, in a study of corporate power, that the five hundred or so corporations that dominate that economy "represent a concentration of power over economics which makes the medieval feudal system look like a Sunday-school party." As for the power within those corporations, it clearly rests, for all practical purposes, with their directors and their professional managers (often not substantial owners), who, Berle goes on to suggest in the same essay, sometimes constitute a self-perpetuating oligarchy. Most fair-minded observers these days seem to feel that the stewardship of the oligarchs, from a social point of view, isn't anything like as bad as it might be, and in many cases is pretty good, yet, however that may be, the ultimate power theoretically does not reside in them at all. According to the corporate form of organization, it resides in the stockholders, of whom, in United States business enterprises of all sizes and descriptions, there are more than twenty million. Even though the courts have repeatedly ruled that a director does not have to follow stockholder instructions, any more than a congressman has to follow the instructions of his constituents, stockholders nevertheless do elect directors, on the logical, if not exactly democratic, basis of one share, one vote. The stockholders are deprived of their real power by a number of factors, among which are their indifference to it in times of rising profits and dividends, their ignorance of corporate affairs, and their sheer numbers. One way or another, they vote the management slate, and the results of most director elections have a certain Russian ring—ninety-nine per cent or more of the votes cast in favor. The chief, and in many cases the only, occasion when stockholders make their presence felt by management is at the annual meeting. Company annual meetings are customarily held in the spring, and one spring—it was that of 1966—I made the rounds of a few of them to get a line on what the theoretical holders of all that feudal power had to say for themselves, and also on the state of their relations with their elected directors.

What particularly commended the 1966 season to me was that it promised to be a particularly lively one. Various reports of a new "hard-line approach" by company managements to stockholders had appeared in the press. (I was charmed by the notion of a candidate for office announcing his new hard-line approach to voters right before an election.) The new approach, it was reported, was the upshot of events at the previous year's meetings, where a new high in stockholder unruliness was reached. The chairman of the Communications Satellite Corporation was forced to call on guards to eject bodily two badgering stockholders at his company's meeting, in Washington. Harland C. Forbes, who was then the chairman of Consolidated Edison, ordered one heckler off the premises in New York, and, in Philadelphia, American Telephone & Telegraph Chairman Frederick R. Kappel was goaded into announcing abruptly, "This meeting is not being run by Robert's [Rules of Order]. It's being run by me." (The executive director of the American Society of Corporate Secretaries later explained that precise application of Robert's rules would have had the effect not of increasing the stockholders' freedom of speech but, rather, of restricting it. Mr. Kappel, the secretary implied, had merely been protecting stockholders from parliamentary tyranny.) In Schenectady, Gerald L. Phillippe, chairman of General Electric, after several hours of fencing with stockholders, summed up his new hard line by saying, "I should like it to be clear that next year, and in the years to come, the chair may well adopt a more rigorous attitude." According to *Business Week*, the General Electric management then assigned a special task force to the job of seeing what could be done about cracking down on hecklers by changing the annual-meeting pattern, and early in 1966 the bible of management, the *Harvard Business Review*, entered the lists with an article by O. Glenn Saxon, Jr., the head of a company specializing in investor services to management, in which he recommended crisply that the chairmen of annual meetings "recognize the authority inherent in the role of the chair, and resolve to use it appropriately." Apparently, the theoretical holders of fundamental power unequalled in the history of the world were about to be put in their place.

One thing I couldn't help noticing as I went over the schedule of the year's leading meetings was a trend away from holding them in or near New York. Invariably, the official reason given was that the move would accommodate stockholders from other areas who had seldom, if ever, been able to attend in the past; however, most of the noisiest dissident stockholders seem to be based in the New York area, and the moves were taking place in the year of the new hard line, so I found the likelihood of a relationship between these two facts by no means remote. United States Steel holders, for example, were to meet in Cleveland, making their second foray outside their company's nominal home state of New Jersey since its formation, in 1901. General Electric was going outside New York State for the third time in recent years—and going all the way to Georgia, a state in which management appeared to have suddenly discovered fifty-six hundred stockholders (or a bit more than one per cent of the firm's total roll) who were badly in need of a chance to attend an annual meeting. The biggest company of them all, American Telephone & Telegraph, had chosen Detroit, which was its third site outside New York City in its eighty-one-year history, the second having been Philadelphia, where the 1965 session was held.

To open my own meeting-going season, I tracked A.T.& T. to Detroit. Leafing through some papers on the plane going out there, I learned that the number of A.T. & T. stockholders had increased to an all-time record of almost three million, and I fell to wondering what would happen in the unlikely event that all of them, or even half of them, appeared in Detroit and demanded seats at the meeting. At any rate, each one of them had received by mail, a few weeks earlier, a notice of the meeting along with a formal invitation to attend, and it seemed to me almost certain that American industry had achieved another "first"—the first time almost three million individual invitations had ever been mailed out to any event of any kind anywhere. My fears on the first score were put to rest when I got to Cobo Hall, a huge riverfront auditorium, where the meeting was to take place. The hall was far from filled; the Yankees in their better days would have been disgusted with such a turnout on any weekday afternoon. (The papers next day said the attendance was four thousand and sixteen.) Looking around, I noticed in the crowd several families with small children, one woman in a wheelchair, one man with a beard, and just two Negro stockholders—the last observation suggesting that the trumpeters of "people's capitalism" might well do some coordinating with the civil-rights movement. The announced time of the meeting was one-thirty, and Chairman Kappel entered on the dot and marched to a reading stand on the platform; the eighteen other A.T. & T. directors trooped to a row of seats just behind him, and Mr. Kappel gavelled the meeting to order.

From my reading and from annual meetings that I'd attended in past years, I knew that the meetings of the biggest companies are usually marked by the presence of so-called professional stockholders—persons who make a full-time occupation of buying stock in companies or obtaining the proxies of other stockholders, then informing themselves more or less intimately about the corporations' affairs and attending annual meetings to raise questions or propose resolutions—and that the most celebrated members of this breed were Mrs. Wilma Soss, of New York, who heads an organization of women stockholders and votes the proxies of its members as well as her own shares, and Lewis D. Gilbert, also of New York, who represents his own holdings and those of his family—a considerable total. Something I did not know, and learned at the A.T. & T. meeting (and at others I attended subsequently), was that, apart from the prepared speeches of management, a good many big-company meetings really consist of a dialogue—in some cases it's more of a duel—between the chairman and the few professional stockholders. The contributions of non-professionals run strongly to ill-informed or tame questions and windy encomiums of management, and thus the task of making cogent criticisms or asking embarrassing questions falls to the professionals. Though largely self-appointed, they become, by default, the sole representatives of a huge constituency that may badly need representing. Some of them are not very good representatives, and a few are so bad that their conduct raises a problem in American manners; these few repeatedly say things at

annual meetings—boorish, silly, insulting, or abusive things—
that are apparently permissible by corporate rules but are certainly impermissible by drawing-room rules, and sometimes
succeed in giving the annual meetings of mighty companies
the general air of barnyard squabbles. Mrs. Soss, a former
public-relations woman who has been a tireless professional
stockholder since 1947, is usually a good many cuts above
this level. True, she is not beyond playing to the gallery by
wearing bizarre costumes to meetings; she tries, with occasional success, to taunt recalcitrant chairmen into throwing
her out; she is often scolding and occasionally abusive; and
nobody could accuse her of being unduly concise. I confess
that her customary tone and manner set my teeth on edge,
but I can't help recognizing that, because she does her home-
work, she usually has a point. Mr. Gilbert, who has been at it
since 1933 and is the dean of them all, almost invariably has
a point, and by comparison with his colleagues he is the soul
of brevity and punctilio as well as of dedication and diligence.
Despised as professional stockholders are by most company
managements, Mrs. Soss and Mr. Gilbert are widely enough
recognized to be listed in *Who's Who in America;* furthermore, for what satisfaction it may bring them, they are the
nameless Agamemnons and Ajaxes, invariably called "individuals," in some of the prose epics produced by the business
Establishment itself. ("The greater portion of the discussion
period was taken up by questions and statements of a few
individuals on matters that can scarcely be deemed relevant.
. . . Two individuals interrupted the opening statement of the
chairman. . . . The chairman advised the individuals who had
interrupted to choose between ceasing their interruption or
leaving the meeting. . . ." So reads, in part, the official report
of the 1965 A.T. & T. annual meeting.) And although Mr.
Saxon's piece in the *Harvard Business Review* was entirely
about professional stockholders and how to deal with them,
the author's corporate dignity did not permit him to mention

the name of even one of them. Avoiding this was quite a trick, but Mr. Saxon pulled it off.

Both Mrs. Soss and Mr. Gilbert were present at Cobo Hall. Indeed, the meeting had barely got under way before Mr. Gilbert was on his feet complaining that several resolutions he had asked the company to include in the proxy statement and the meeting agenda had been omitted from both. Mr. Kappel—a stern-looking man with steel-rimmed spectacles, who was unmistakably cast in the old-fashioned, aloof corporate mold, rather than the new, more permissive one—replied shortly that the Gilbert proposals had referred to matters that were not proper for stockholder consideration, and had been submitted too late, anyhow. Mr. Kappel then announced that he was about to report on company operations, whereupon the eighteen other directors filed off the platform. Evidently, they had been there only to be introduced, not to field questions from stockholders. Exactly where they went I don't know; they vanished from my field of vision, and I wasn't enlightened when, later on in the meeting, Mr. Kappel responded to a stockholder's question as to their whereabouts with the laconic statement "They're here." Going it alone, Mr. Kappel said in his report that "business is booming, earnings are good, and the prospect ahead is for more of the same," declared that A.T. & T. was eager for the Federal Communications Commission to get on with its investigation of telephone rates, since the company had "no skeletons in the closet," and then painted a picture of a bright telephonic future in which "picture phones" will be commonplace and light beams will carry messages.

When Mr. Kappel's address was over and the management-sponsored slate of directors for the coming year had been duly nominated, Mrs. Soss rose to make a nomination of her own—Dr. Frances Arkin, a psychoanalyst. In explanation, Mrs. Soss said that she felt A.T. & T. ought to have a woman on its board, and that, furthermore, she sometimes felt some of the company's executives would be benefited by occasional psychiatric examinations. (This remark seemed to me gratuitous, but the balance of manners between bosses and stockholders was subsequently redressed, at least to my mind, at another meeting, when the chairman suggested that some of his firm's stockholders ought to see a psychiatrist.) The nomination of Dr. Arkin was seconded by Mr. Gilbert, although not until Mrs. Soss, who was sitting a couple of seats from him, had reached over and nudged him vigorously in the ribs. Presently, a professional stockholder named Evelyn Y. Davis protested the venue of the meeting, complaining that she had been forced to come all the way from New York by bus. Mrs. Davis, a brunette, was the youngest and perhaps the best-looking of the professional stockholders but, on the basis of what I saw at the A.T. & T. meeting and others, not the best informed or the most temperate, serious-minded, or worldly-wise. On this occasion, she was greeted by thunderous boos, and when Mr. Kappel answered her by saying, "You're out of order. You're just talking to the wind," he was loudly cheered. It was only then that I understood the nature of the advantage that the company had gained by moving its meeting away from New York: it had not succeeded in shaking off the gad-flies, but it had succeeded in putting them in a climate where they were subject to the rigors of that great American emotion, regional pride. A lady in a flowered hat who said she was from Des Plaines, Illinois, emphasized the point by rising to say, "I wish some of the people here would behave like intelligent adults, rather than two-year-olds." (Prolonged applause.)

Even so, the sniping from the East went on, and by three-thirty, when the meeting had been in session for two hours, Mr. Kappel was clearly getting testy; he began pacing impatiently around the platform, and his answers got shorter and shorter. "O.K., O.K." was all he replied to one complaint that he was dictatorial. The climax came in a wrangle between him and Mrs. Soss about the fact that A.T. & T., although it had listed the business affiliations of its nominees for director in a pamphlet that was handed out at the meeting, had failed to list them in the material mailed out to the stockholders, the overwhelming majority of whom were not at the meeting and had done their voting by proxy. Most other big companies make such disclosures in their mailed proxy statements, so the stockholders were apparently entitled to a reasonable explanation of why A.T. & T. had failed to do so, but somewhere along the way reason was left behind. As the exchange progressed, Mrs. Soss adopted a scolding tone and Mr. Kappel an icy one; as for the crowd, it was having a fine time booing the Christian, if that is what Mrs. Soss represented, and cheering the lion, if that is what Mr. Kappel represented. "I can't hear you, sir," Mrs. Soss said at one point. "Well, if you'd just listen instead of talking—" Mr. Kappel returned. Then Mrs. Soss said something I didn't catch, and it must have been a telling bit of chairman-baiting, because Mr. Kappel's manner changed completely, from ice to fire; he began shaking his finger and saying he wouldn't stand for any more abuse, and the floor microphone that Mrs. Soss had been using was abruptly turned off. Followed at a distance of ten or fifteen feet by a uniformed security guard, and to the accompaniment of deafening booing and stamping, Mrs. Soss marched up the aisle and took a stand in front of the platform, facing Mr. Kappel, who informed her that he knew she wanted him to have her thrown out and that he declined to comply.

Eventually, Mrs. Soss went back to her seat and everybody calmed down. The rest of the meeting, given over largely to questions and comments from amateur stockholders, rather than professional ones, was certainly less lively than what had gone before, and not noticeably higher in intellectual content. Stockholders from Grand Rapids, Detroit, and Ann Arbor all expressed the view that it would be best to let the directors run the company, although the Grand Rapids man objected mildly that the "Bell Telephone Hour" couldn't be received on television in his locality anymore. A man from Pleasant Ridge, Michigan, spoke up for retired stockholders who would like A.T. & T. to plow less of its earnings back into expansion, so that it could pay higher dividends. A stockholder from rural Louisiana stated that when he picked up his telephone lately, the operator didn't answer for five or ten minutes. "Ah brang it to your attention," the Louisiana man said, and Mr. Kappel promised to have somebody look into the matter. Mrs. Davis raised a complaint about A.T. & T.'s contributions to charity, giving Mr. Kappel the opportunity to reply that he was glad the world contained people more charitable than she. (Tax-exempt applause.) A Detroit man said, "I hope you won't let the abuse you've been subjected to by a few malcontents keep you from bringing the meeting back to the great Midwest again." It was announced that Dr. Arkin had been defeated for a seat on the board, since she had received a vote of only 19,106 shares against some four hundred million, proxy votes included, for each candidate on the management slate. (By approving the management slate, a proxy voter can, in effect, oppose a floor nomination, even though he knows nothing about it.) And that was how the 1966 annual meeting of the world's largest company went—or how it went until five-thirty, when all but a few hundred stockholders had left, and when I headed for the airport to catch a plane back to New York.

The A.T. & T. meeting left me in a thoughtful mood. Annual meetings, I reflected, can be times to try the soul of an admirer of representative democratic government, especially when he finds himself guiltily sympathizing with the chairman who is being badgered from the floor. The professional stockholders, in their wilder moments, are management's secret weapon; a Mrs. Soss and a Mrs. Davis at their most strident could have made Commodore Vanderbilt and Pierpont Morgan seem like affable old gentlemen, and they can make a latter-day magnate like Mr. Kappel seem like a henpecked husband, if not actually a champion of stockholders' rights. At such moments, the professional stockholders become, from a practical standpoint, enemies of intelligent dissent. On the other hand, I thought, they deserve sympathy, too, whether or not one believes they have right on their side, because they are in the position of representing a constituency that doesn't want to be represented. It's hard to imagine anyone more reluctant to claim his democratic rights, or more suspicious of anyone who tries to claim them for him, than a dividend-fattened stockholder—and, of course, most stockholders are thoroughly dividend-fattened these days. Berle speaks of the estate of stockholding as being by its nature "passive-receptive," rather than "managing and creating;" most of the A.T. & T. stockholders in Detroit, it seemed to me, were so deeply devoted to the notion of the company as Santa Claus that they went beyond passive receptivity to active cupboard love. And the professional stockholders, I felt, had taken on an assignment almost as thankless as that of recruiting for the Young Communist League among the junior executives of the Chase Manhattan Bank.

In view of Chairman Phillippe's warning to General Electric stockholders at Schenectady in 1965, and of the report about the company's hard-line task force, it was with a sense of being engaged in hot pursuit that I boarded a southbound Pullman for the General Electric annual meeting. This one was held in Atlanta's Municipal Auditorium, a snappy hall, the rear of which was brightened by an interior garden complete with trees and a lawn, and in spite of the fact that it was held on a languorous, rainy Southern spring morning, more than a thousand G.E. stockholders turned out. As far as I could see, three of them were Negroes, and it was not long before I saw that another of them was Mrs. Soss.

However exasperated he may have become the previous year in Schenectady, Mr. Phillippe, who also conducted the

1966 meeting, was in perfect control of himself and of the situation this time around. Whether he was expatiating on the wonders of G.E.'s balance sheet and its laboratory discoveries or sparring with the professional stockholders, he spoke in the same singsong way, delicately treading the thin line between patient, careful exposition and irony. Mr. Saxon, in his *Harvard Business Review* article, had written, "Top executives are finding it necessary to learn how to lessen the adverse impact of the few disrupters on the majority of shareowners, while simultaneously enhancing the positive effects of the good things which do take place in the annual meeting," and, having learned sometime earlier that the same Mr. Saxon had been engaged by G.E. as an adviser on stockholder relations, I couldn't help suspecting that Mr. Philippe's performance was a demonstration of Saxonism in action. The professional stockholders, for their part, responded by adopting precisely the same ambiguous style, and the resulting dialogue had the general air of a conversation between two people who have quarrelled and then decided, not quite wholeheartedly, to make it up. (The professional stockholders might have demanded to know how much money G.E. had spent in the interest of keeping them under control, but they missed the chance.) One of the exchanges in this vein achieved a touch of wit. Mrs. Soss, speaking in her sweetest tone, called attention to the fact that one of the board-of-directors candidates— Frederick L. Hovde, President of Purdue University and former chairman of the Army Scientific Advisory Panel—owned only ten shares of G.E. stock, and said she felt that the board should be made up of more substantial holders, whereupon Mr. Philippe pointed out, just as sweetly, that the company had many thousands of holders of ten or fewer shares, Mrs. Soss among them, and suggested that perhaps these small holders were deserving of representation on the board by one of their number. Mrs. Soss had to concede a fine stroke of chairmanship, and she did. On another matter, although decorum was stringently maintained by both sides, outward accord was less complete. Several stockholders, Mrs. Soss among them, had formally proposed that the company adopt for its director elections the system called cumulative voting, under which a stockholder may concentrate all the votes he is entitled to on a single candidate rather than spread them over the whole slate, and which therefore gives a minority group of stockholders a much better chance of electing one representative to the board. Cumulative voting, though a subject of controversy in big-business circles, for obvious reasons, is nevertheless a perfectly respectable idea; indeed, it is mandatory for companies incorporated in more than twenty states, and it is used by some four hundred companies listed on the New York Stock Exchange. Nevertheless, Mr. Phillippe did not find it necessary to answer Mrs. Soss's argument for cumulative voting; he chose instead to stand on a brief company statement on this subject that had been previously mailed out to stockholders, the main point of which was that the presence on the G.E. board, as a result of cumulative voting, of representatives of special-interest groups might have a "divisive and disruptive effect." Of course, Mr. Phillippe did not say he knew, as he doubtless did know, that the company had in hand more than enough proxies to defeat the proposal.

Some companies, like some animals, have their private, highly specialized gadflies, who harass them and nobody else, and General Electric is one. In this instance, the gadfly was Louis A. Brusati, of Chicago, who at the company's meetings over the past thirteen years had advanced thirty-one proposals, all of which had been defeated by a vote of at least ninety-seven per cent to three per cent. In Atlanta, Mr. Brusati, a gray-haired man built like a football player, was at it again—not with proposals this time but with questions. For one thing, he wanted to know why Mr. Phillippe's personal holdings of G.E. stock, listed in the proxy statement, now were four hundred and twenty-three shares fewer than they had been a year ago. Mr. Phillippe replied that the difference represented shares that he had contributed to family trust funds, and added, mildly but with emphasis, "I could say it's none of your business. I believe I have a right to the privacy of my affairs." There was more reason for the mildness than for the emphasis, as Mr. Brusati did not fail to point out, in an impeccably unemotional monotone; many of Mr. Phillippe's shares had been acquired under options at preferential prices not available to others, and, moreover, the fact that Mr. Phillippe's precise holdings had been included in the proxy statement clearly showed that in the opinion of the Securities and Exchange Commission his holdings *were* Mr. Brusati's business. Going on to the matter of the fees paid directors, Mr. Brusati elicited from Mr. Phillippe the information that over the past seven years these had been raised from twenty-five hundred dollars per annum first to five thousand dollars and then to seventy-five hundred. The ensuing dialogue between the two men went like this:

"By the way, who establishes those fees?"

"Those fees are established by the board of directors."

"The board of directors establish their own fees?"

"Yes."

"Thank you."

"Thank *you*, Mr. Brusati."

Later on in the morning, there were several lengthy and eloquent orations by stockholders on the virtues of General Electric and of the South, but this rather elegantly elliptical exchange between Mr. Brusati and Mr. Phillippe stuck in my mind, for it seemed to sum up the spirit of the meeting. Only after adjournment—which came at twelve-thirty, following Mr. Phillippe's announcement that the unopposed slate of directors had been elected and that cumulative voting had lost by 97.51 per cent to 2.49 per cent—did I realize that not only had there been no stamping, booing, or shouting, as there had been in Detroit, but regional pride had not had to be invoked against the professional stockholders. It had been General Electric's hole card, I felt, but General Electric had won on the board, without needing to turn it up.

Each meeting I attended had its easily discernible characteristic tone, and that of Chas. Pfizer & Co., the diversified pharmaceutical and chemical firm, was amicability. Pfizer, which in previous years had customarily held its annual meeting at its headquarters in Brooklyn, reversed the trend by moving this year's meeting right into the lair of the most vocal dissenters, midtown Manhattan, but everything that I saw and heard convinced me that the motivation behind this move had been not a brash resolve on the company's part to beard the lions in their den but a highly unfashionable desire to get the maximum possible turnout. Pfizer seemed to feel self-confident enough to meet its stockholders with its guard down. For instance, in contrast with the other meetings I attended, no stockholder tickets were collected or credentials checked at the entrance to the Grand Ballroom of the Commodore Hotel, where the Pfizer meeting was held; Fidel Castro himself, whose oratorical style I have occasionally felt that the professional stockholders were using as a model, could presumably have walked in and said whatever he chose. Some seventeen hundred persons, or nearly enough to fill the ballroom, showed up, and all the members of the Pfizer board of directors sat on the platform from start to finish and answered any questions addressed to them individually.

Speaking, appropriately, with a faint trace of a Brooklyn accent, Chairman John E. McKeen welcomed the stockholders as "my dear and cherished friends" (I tried to imagine Mr. Kappel and Mr. Phillippe addressing their stockholders that way, and couldn't, but then their companies are bigger), and said that on the way out everyone present would be given a big free-sample kit of Pfizer consumer products, such as Barbasol, Desitin, and Imprévu. Wooed thus by endearments and the promise of gifts, and further softened up by the report of President John J. Powers, Jr., on current operations (records all around) and immediate prospects (more records expected), the most intransigent professional stockholder would have been hard put to it to mount much of a rebellion at this particular meeting, and, as it happened, the only professional present seemed to be John Gilbert, brother of Lewis. (I learned later that Lewis Gilbert and Mrs. Davis were in Cleveland that day, attending the U.S. Steel meeting.) John Gilbert is the sort of professional stockholder the Pfizer management deserves, or would like to think it does. With an easygoing manner and a habit of punctuating his words with self-deprecating little laughs, he is the most ingratiating gadfly imaginable (or was on this occasion; I'm told he isn't always), and as he ran through what seemed to be the standard Gilbert-family repertoire of questions—on the reliability of the firm's auditors, the salaries of its officers, the fees of its directors—he seemed almost apologetic that duty called on him to commit the indelicacy of asking such things. As for the amateur stockholders present, their questions and comments were about like those at the other meetings I'd attended, but this time their attitude toward the role of the professional stockholder was noticeably different. Instead of being overwhelmingly opposed, they appeared to be split; to judge from the volume of clapping and of discreet groaning, about half of those present considered Gilbert a nuisance and half considered him a help. Powers left no doubt about how *he* felt; before adjourning the meeting he said, without irony, that he had welcomed Gilbert's questions, and made a point of inviting him to come again next year. And, indeed, during the later stages of the Pfizer meeting, when Gilbert, in a conversational way, was praising the company for some things and criticizing it for others, and the various members of the board were replying to his comments just as informally, I got for the first time a fleeting sense of genuine communication between stockholders and managers.

The Radio Corporation of America, which had held its last two meetings far from its New York headquarters—in Los Angeles in 1964, in Chicago in 1965—reserved the current trend even more decisively than Pfizer by convening this time in Carnegie Hall. The entire orchestra and the two tiers of boxes were completely filled with stockholders—about twenty-three hundred of them, of whom a strikingly larger proportion than at any of my other meetings was male. Mrs. Soss and Mrs. Davis were on hand, though, along with Lewis Gilbert and some professional stockholders I hadn't seen before, and, as with Pfizer, the company's whole board of directors sat on the platform, where the chief centers of attraction in R.C.A.'s case were David Sarnoff, the company's seventy-five-year-old chairman, and his forty-eight-year-old son, Robert W. Sarnoff, who had been its president since the beginning of the year. For me, two aspects of the R.C.A. meeting stood out: the evident respect, amounting almost to veneration, of the stockholders for their celebrated chairman, and an unaccustomed disposition of the amateur stockholders to speak up for themselves. The elder Mr. Sarnoff, looking hale and ready for anything, conducted the meeting, and he and several other R.C.A. executives gave reports on company operations and prospects, in the course of which the words "record" and "growth" recurred so monotonously that I, not being an R.C.A. stockholder, began to nod. I was brought wide awake with a jolt on one occasion, though, when I heard Walter D. Scott, chairman of R.C.A.'s subsidiary the National Broadcasting Company, say in connection with his network's television programming that "creative resources are always running ahead of demand."

No one objected to that statement or to anything else in

the glowing reports, but when they were over the stockholders had their say on other matters. Mr. Gilbert raised some favorite questions of his about accounting procedures, and a representative of R.C.A.'s accountants, Arthur Young & Co., made replies that seemed to satisfy Mr. Gilbert. A Dickensian elderly lady, who identified herself as Mrs. Martha Brand and said she held "many thousands" of shares of R.C.A. stock, expressed the view that the accounting procedures of the company should not even be questioned. I have since learned that Mrs. Brand is a professional stockholder who is an anomaly within the profession, in that she leans strongly toward the management view of things. Mr. Gilbert then advanced a proposal for the adoption of cumulative voting, supporting it with about the same arguments that Mrs. Soss had used at the G.E. meeting. Mr. Sarnoff opposed the motion, and so did Mrs. Brand, who explained that she was sure the present directors always worked tirelessly for the welfare of the corporation, and added this time that she was the holder of "many, many thousands" of shares. Two or three other stockholders spoke up in favor of cumulative voting—the only occasion at any meeting on which I saw stockholders not easily identifiable as professionals speak in dissent on a matter of substance. (Cumulative voting was defeated, 95.3 per cent to 4.7 per cent.) Mrs. Soss, still in as mild a mood as in Atlanta, said she was delighted to see a woman, Mrs. Josephine Young Case, sitting on the stage as a member of the R.C.A. board, but deplored the fact that Mrs. Case's principal occupation was given on the proxy statement as "housewife." Couldn't a woman who was chairman of the board of Skidmore College at least be called a "home executive"? Another lady stockholder set off a round of applause by delivering a paean to Chairman Sarnoff, whom she called "the marvellous Cinderella man of the twentieth century."

Mrs. Davis—who had earlier objected to the site of the meeting on the ground, which I found dumfounding, that

Carnegie Hall was "too unsophisticated" for R.C.A.—advanced a resolution calling for company action "to insure that hereafter no person shall serve as a director after he shall have attained the age of seventy-two." Even though similar rulings are in effect in many companies, and even though the proposal, not being retroactive, would have no effect upon Mr. Sarnoff's status, it *seemed* to be aimed at him, and thus Mrs. Davis demonstrated again her uncanny knack of playing into management's hands. Nor did she appear to help her cause by putting on a Batman mask (the symbolism of which I didn't grasp) when she made it. At all events, the proposal gave rise to several impassioned defenses of Mr. Sarnoff, and one of the speakers went on to complain bitterly that Mrs. Davis was insulting the intelligence of everyone present. At this, the serious-minded Mr. Gilbert leaped up to say, "I quite agree about the silliness of her costume, but there is a valid principle in her proposal." In making this Voltairian distinction, Mr. Gilbert, to judge from his evident state of agitation, was achieving a triumph of reason over inclination that was costing him plenty. Mrs. Davis's resolution was defeated overwhelmingly; the margin against it served to end the meeting with what amounted to a rousing vote of confidence in the Cinderella man.

Classic farce, with elements of slapstick, was the dominant mood of the meeting of the Communications Satellite Corporation, with which I wound up my meeting-going season. Comsat is, of course, the glamorous space-age communications company that was set up by the government in 1963 and turned over to public ownership in a celebrated stock sale in 1964. Upon arriving at the meeting site—the Shoreham Hotel, in Washington—I was scarcely startled to discover Mrs. Davis, Mrs. Soss, and Lewis Gilbert among the thousand or so stockholders present. Mrs. Davis, decked out in stage makeup, an orange pith helmet, a short red skirt, white boots, and a black sweater bearing in white letters the legend "I Was Born to Raise Hell," had planted herself squarely in front of a battery of television cameras. Mrs. Soss, as I had learned by now was her custom, had taken a place at the opposite side of the room from Mrs. Davis, and this meant that she was now as far as possible from the television cameras. Considering that Mrs. Soss does not ordinarily seem to be averse to being photographed, I could write down this choice of seat only as a hard-won triumph of conscience akin to Mr. Gilbert's at Carnegie Hall. As for Mr. Gilbert, he took a place not far from Mrs. Soss, and thus, of course, a long way from Mrs. Davis.

Since the previous year, Leo D. Welch, the man who had conducted the 1965 Comsat meeting with such a firm hand, has been replaced as chairman of the company by James McCormack, a West Point graduate, former Rhodes Scholar, and retired Air Force general with an impeccably polished manner, who bears a certain resemblance to the Duke of Windsor, and Mr. McCormack was conducting this year's session. He warmed up with some preliminary remarks in the course of which he noted—-smoothly, but not without emphasis— that as for the subject of any intervention that a stockholder might choose to make, "the field of relevance is quite narrow." When Mr. McCormack had finished his warmup, Mrs. Soss made a brief speech that may or may not have come within the field of relevance; I missed most of it, because the floor microphone supplied to her wasn't working right. Mrs. Davis then claimed the floor, and *her* mike was working all too well; as the cameras ground, she launched into an ear-splitting tirade against the company and its directors because there had been a special door to the meeting room reserved for the entrance of "distinguished guests." Mrs. Davis, in a good many words, said she considered this procedure undemocratic. "We apologize, and when you go out, please go by any door you want," Mr. McCormack said, but Mrs. Davis, clearly unappeased, went on speaking. And now the mood of farce was heightened when it became clear that the Soss-Gilbert faction had decided to abandon all efforts to keep ranks closed with Mrs. Davis. Near the height of her oration, Mr. Gilbert, looking as outraged as a boy whose ball game is being spoiled by a player who doesn't know the rules or care about the game, got up and began shouting, "Point of order! Point of order!" But Mr. McCormack spurned this offer of parliamentary help; he ruled Mr. Gilbert's point of order out of order, and bade Mrs. Davis proceed. I had no trouble deducing why he did this. There were unmistakable signs that he, unlike any other corporate chairman I had seen in action, was enjoying every minute of the goings on. Through most of the meeting, and especially when the professional stockholders had the floor, Mr. McCormack wore the dreamy smile of a wholly bemused spectator.

Eventually, Mrs. Davis's speech built up to a peak of both volume and content at which she began making specific allegations against individual Comsat directors, and at this point three security guards—two beefy men and a determined-looking woman, all dressed in gaudy bottle-green uniforms that might have been costumes for "The Pirates of Penzance"—appeared at the rear, marched with brisk yet stately tread up the center aisle, and assumed the position of parade rest in the aisle within handy reach of Mrs. Davis, whereupon she abruptly concluded her speech and sat down. "All right," Mr. McCormack said, still grinning. "Everything's cool now."

The guards retired, and the meeting proceeded. Mr. McCormack and the Comsat president, Joseph V. Charyk, gave the sort of glowing report on the company that I had grown accustomed to, Mr. McCormack going so far as to say that Comsat might start showing its first profit the following year rather than in 1969, as originally forecast. (It did.) Mr. Gilbert asked what fee, apart from his regular salary, Mr.

McCormack received for attending directors' meetings. Mr. McCormack replied that he got no fee, and when Mr. Gilbert said, "I'm glad you get nothing, I approve of that," everybody laughed and Mr. McCormack grinned more broadly than ever. (Mr. Gilbert was clearly trying to make what he considered to be a serious point, but this didn't seem to be the day for that sort of thing.) Mrs. Soss took a dig at Mrs. Davis by saying pointedly that anyone who opposed Mr. McCormack as company chairman was "lacking in perspicacity;" she did note, however, that she couldn't quite bring herself to vote for Mr. Welch, the former chairman, who was now a candidate for the board, inasmuch as he had ordered her thrown out last year. A peppy old gentleman said that he thought the company was doing fine and everyone should have faith in it. Once, when Mr. Gilbert said something that Mrs. Davis didn't like and Mrs. Davis, without waiting to be recognized, began shouting her objection across the room, Mr. McCormack gave a short irrepressible giggle. That single falsetto syllable, magnificently amplified by the chairman's microphone, was the motif of the Comsat meeting.

On the plane returning from Washington, as I was musing on the meetings I had attended, it occurred to me that if there had been no professional stockholders at them I would probably have learned almost as much as I did about the companies' affairs but that I would have learned a good deal less about their chief executives' personalities. It had, after all, been the questions, interruptions, and speeches of the professional stockholders that brought the companies to life, in a sense, by forcing each chairman to shed his official portrait-by-Bachrach mask and engage in a human relationship. More often than not, this had been the hardly satisfactory human relationship of nagger and nagged, but anyone looking for humanity in high corporate affairs can't afford to pick and choose. Still, some doubts remained. Being thirty thousand feet up in the air is conducive to taking the broader view, and, doing so as we winged over Philadelphia, I concluded that, on the basis of what I had seen and heard, both company managements and stockholders might well consider a lesson King Lear learned—that when the role of dissenter is left to the Fool, there may be trouble ahead for everybody.

11

ONE FREE BITE

AMONG THE THOUSANDS OF YOUNG SCIENTISTS who were doing very well in the research-and-development programs of American companies in the fall of 1962 was one named Donald W. Wohlgemuth, who was working for the B. F. Goodrich Company, in Akron, Ohio. A 1954 graduate of the University of Michigan, where he had taken the degree of Bachelor of Science in chemical engineering, he had gone directly from the university to a job in the chemical laboratories of Goodrich, at a starting salary of three hundred and sixty-five dollars a month. Since then, except for two years spent in the Army, he had worked continuously for Goodrich, in various engineering and research capacities, and had received a total of fifteen salary increases over the six and a half years. In November, 1962, as he approached his thirty-first birthday, he was earning $10,644 a year. A tall, self-contained, serious-looking man of German ancestry, whose horn-rimmed glasses gave him an owlish expression, Wohlgemuth lived in a ranch house in Wadsworth, a suburb of Akron, with his wife and their fifteen-month-old daughter. All in all, he seemed to be the young American *homme moyen réussi* to the point of boredom. What was decidedly not routine about him, though, was the nature of his job; he was the manager of Goodrich's department of space-suit engineering, and over the past years, in the process of working his way up to that position, he had had a considerable part in the designing and construction of the suits worn by our Mercury astronauts on their orbital and suborbital flights.

Then, in the first week of November, Wohlgemuth got a phone call from an employment agent in New York, who informed him that the executives of a large company in Dover, Delaware, were most anxious to talk to him about the possibility of his taking a job with them. Despite the caller's reticence—a trait common among employment agents making first approaches to prospective employees—Wohlgemuth instantly knew the identity of the large company. The International Latex Corporation, which is best known to the public as a maker of girdles and brassiéres, but which Wohlgemuth knew to be also one of Goodrich's three major competitors in the space-suit field, is situated in Dover. He knew, further, that Latex had recently been awarded a subcontract, amounting to some three-quarters of a million dollars, to do research and development on space suits for the Apollo, or man-on-the-moon, project. As a matter of fact, Latex had won this contract in competition with Goodrich, among others, and was thus for the moment much the hottest company in the space-suit field. On top of that, Wohlgemuth was somewhat discontented with his situation at Goodrich; for one thing, his salary, however bountiful it might seem to many thirty-year-olds, was considerably below the average for Goodrich employees of his rank, and, for another, he had been turned down not long before by the company authorities when he asked for air-conditioning or filtering to keep dust out of the plant area allocated to space-suit work. Accordingly, after making arrangements by phone with the executives mentioned by the employment agent—and they did indeed prove to be Latex men—Wohlgemuth went to Dover the following Sunday.

He stayed there a day and a half, borrowing Monday from vacation time that was due him from Goodrich, and getting what he subsequently described as "a real red-carpet treatment." He was taken on a tour of the Latex space-suit–development facilities by Leonard Shepard, director of the company's Industrial Products Division. He was entertained at the home of Max Feller, a Latex vice-president. He was shown the Dover housing situation by another company executive. Finally, before lunch on Monday, he had a talk with all three of the Latex executives, following which—as Wohlgemuth later described the scene in court—the three "removed themselves to another room for approximately ten minutes." When they reappeared, one of them offered Wohlgemuth the position of manager of engineering for the Industrial Products Division, which included responsibility for space-suit development, at an annual salary of $13,700, effective at the beginning of December. After getting his wife's approval by telephone—and it was not hard to get, since she was originally from Baltimore and was delighted at the prospect of moving back to her own part of the world—Wohlgemuth accepted. He flew back to Akron that night. First thing Tuesday morning, Wohlgemuth confronted Carl Effler, his immediate boss at Goodrich, with the news that he was quitting at the end of the month to take another job.

"Are you kidding?" Effler asked.

"No, I am not," Wohlgemuth replied.

Following this crisp exchange, which Wohlgemuth later reported in court, Effler, in the time-honored tradition of bereaved bosses, grumbled a bit about the difficulty of finding a qualified replacement before the end of the month. Wohlgemuth spent the rest of the day putting his department's papers in order and clearing his desk of unfinished business, and the next morning he went to see Wayne Galloway, a Goodrich space-suit executive with whom he had worked closely and had been on the friendliest of terms for a long time; he said later that he felt he owed it to Galloway "to explain to him my side of the picture" in person, even though at the moment he was not under Galloway's supervision in the company chain of command. Wohlgemuth began this interview by rather melodramatically handing Galloway a lapel pin in the form of a Mercury capsule, which had been awarded to him for his work on the Mercury space suits; now, he said, he felt he was no longer entitled to wear it. Why, then, Galloway asked, was he leaving? Simple enough, Wohlgemuth said—he considered the Latex offer a step up both in salary and in responsibility. Galloway replied that in making the move Wohlgemuth would be taking to Latex certain things that did not belong to him—specifically, knowledge of the processes that Goodrich used in making space suits. In the course of the conversation, Wohlgemuth asked Galloway what he would do if he were to receive a similar offer. Galloway replied that he didn't know; for that matter, he added, he didn't know what he would do if he were approached by a group who had a foolproof plan for robbing a bank. Wohlgemuth had to base his decision on loyalty and ethics, Galloway said—a remark that Wohlgemuth took as an accusation of bad faith. He lost his temper, he later explained, and gave Galloway a rash answer. "Loyalty and ethics have their price, and International Latex has paid it," he said.

After that, the fat was in the fire. Later in the morning, Effler called Wohlgemuth into his office and told him it had been decided that he should leave the Goodrich premises as soon as possible, staying around only long enough to make a list of projects that were pending and to go through certain other formalities. In mid-afternoon, while Wohlgemuth was occupied with these tasks, Galloway called him and told him that the Goodrich legal department wanted to see him. In the legal department, he was asked whether he intended to use confidential information belonging to Goodrich on behalf of Latex. According to the subsequent affidavit of a Goodrich lawyer, he replied—again rashly—"How are you going to prove it?" He was then advised that he was not legally free to make the move to Latex. While he was not bound to Goodrich by the kind of contract, common in American industry, in which an employee agrees not to do similar work for any competing company for a stated period of time, he had, on his return from the Army, signed a routine paper agreeing "to keep confidential all information, records, and documents of the company of which I may have knowledge because of my employment"—something Wohlgemuth had entirely forgotten until the Goodrich lawyer reminded him. Even if he had not made that agreement, the lawyer told him now, he would be prevented from going to work on space suits for Latex by established principles of trade-secrets law. Moreover, if he persisted in his plan, Goodrich might sue him.

Wohlgemuth returned to his office and put in a call to Feller, the Latex vice-president he had met in Dover. While he was waiting for the call to be completed, he talked with Effler, who had come in to see him, and whose attitude toward his defection seemed to have stiffened considerably. Wohlgemuth complained that he felt at the mercy of Goodrich, which, it seemed to him, was unreasonably blocking his freedom of action, and Effler upset him further by saying that what had happened during the past forty-eight hours could not be forgotten and might well affect his future with Goodrich. Wohlgemuth, it appeared, might be sued if he left and scorned if he didn't leave. When the Dover call came through, Wohlgemuth told Feller that in view of the new situation he would be unable to go to work for Latex.

That evening, however, Wohlgemuth's prospects seemed to take a turn for the better. Home in Wadsworth, he called the family dentist, and the dentist recommended a local lawyer.

Wohlgemuth told his story to the lawyer, who thereupon consulted another lawyer by phone. The two counsellors agreed that Goodrich was probably bluffing and would not really sue Wohlgemuth if he went to Latex. The next morning—Thursday—officials of Latex called him back to assure him that their firm would bear his legal expenses in the event of a lawsuit, and, furthermore, would indemnify him against any salary losses. Thus emboldened, Wohlgemuth delivered two messages within the next couple of hours—one in person and one by phone. He told Effler what the two lawyers had told him, and he called the legal department to report that he had now changed his mind and was going to work at International Latex after all. Later that day, after completing the cleanup job in his office, he left the Goodrich premises for good, taking with him no documents.

The following day—Friday—R. G. Jeter, general counsel of Goodrich, telephoned Emerson P. Barrett, director of industrial relations for Latex, and spoke of Goodrich's concern for its trade secrets if Wohlgemuth went to work there. Barrett replied that although "the work for which Wohlgemuth was hired was design and construction of space suits," Latex was not interested in learning any Goodrich trade secrets but was "only interested in securing the general professional abilities of Mr. Wohlgemuth." That this answer did not satisfy Jeter, or Goodrich, became manifest the following Monday. That evening, while Wohlgemuth was in an Akron restaurant called the Brown Derby, attending a farewell dinner in his honor given by forty or fifty of his friends, a waitress told him that there was a man outside who wanted to see him. The man was a deputy sheriff of Summit County, of which Akron is the seat, and when Wohlgemuth came out, the man handed him two papers. One was a summons to appear in the Court of Common Pleas on a date a week or so off. The other was a copy of a petition that had been filed in the same court that day by Goodrich, praying that Wohlgemuth be permanently enjoined from, among other things, disclosing to any unauthorized person any trade secrets belonging to Goodrich, and "performing any work for any corporation . . . other than plaintiff, relating to the design, manufacture and/or sale of high-altitude pressure suits, space suits and/or similar protective garments."

The need for the protection of trade secrets was fully recognized in the Middle Ages, when they were so jealously guarded by the craft guilds that the guilds' employees were rigorously prevented from changing jobs. *Laissez-faire* industrial society, since it emphasizes the principle that the individual is entitled to rise in the world by taking the best opportunity he is offered, has been far more lenient about job-jumping, but the right of an organization to keep its secrets has survived. In American law, the basic commandment on the subject was laid down by Justice Oliver Wendell Holmes in connection with a 1905 Chicago case. Holmes wrote, "The plaintiff has the right to keep the work which it has done, or paid for doing, to itself. The fact that others might do similar work, if they wished, does not authorize them to steal plaintiff's." This admirably downright, if not highly sophisticated, ukase has been cited in almost every trade-secrets case that has come up since, but over the years, as both scientific research and industrial organization have become infinitely more complex, so have the questions of what, exactly, constitutes a trade secret, and what constitutes stealing it. The American Law Institute's "Restatement of the Law of Torts," an authoritative text issued in 1939, grapples manfully with the first question by stating, or restating, that "a trade secret may consist of any formula, pattern, device, or compilation of information which is used in one's business, and which gives him an opportunity to obtain an advantage over competitors who do not know or use it." But in a case heard in 1952 an Ohio court decided that the Arthur Murray method of teaching dancing, though

it was unique and was presumably helpful in luring customers away from competitors, was not a trade secret. "All of us
have 'our method' of doing a million things—our method of
combing our hair, shining our shoes, mowing our lawn," the
court mused, and concluded that a trade secret must not only
be unique and commercially helpful but also have inherent
value. As for what constitutes thievery of trade secrets, in a
proceeding heard in Michigan in 1939, in which the Dutch
Cookie Machine Company complained that one of its former
employees was threatening to use its highly classified methods
to make cookie machines on his own, the trial court decided
that there were no fewer than three secret processes by which
Dutch Cookie machines were made, and enjoined the former employee from using them in any manner; however, the
Michigan Supreme Court, on appeal, found that the defendant, although he knew the three secrets, did not plan to use
them in his own operations, and, accordingly, it reversed the
lower court's decision and vacated the injunction.

And so on. Outraged dancing teachers, cookie-machine
manufacturers, and others have made their way through
American courts, and the principles of law regarding the protection of trade secrets have become well established; any difficulty arises chiefly in the application of these principles to
individual cases. The number of such cases has been rising
sharply in recent years, as research and development by private industry have expanded, and a good index to the rate
of such expansion is the fact that eleven and a half billion
dollars was spent in this work in 1962, more than three times
the figure for 1953. No company wants to see the discoveries
produced by all that money go out of its doors in the atta-
ché cases, or even in the heads, of young scientists bound for
greener pastures. In nineteenth-century America, the builder
of a better mousetrap was supposed to have been a cyno-
sure—provided, of course, that the mousetrap was properly
patented. In those days of comparatively simple technology,

patents covered most proprietary rights in business, so trade-secrets cases were rare. The better mousetraps of today, however, like the processes involved in outfitting a man to go into orbit or to the moon, are often unpatentable.

Since thousands of scientists and billions of dollars might be affected by the results of the trial of Goodrich v. Wohlgemuth, it naturally attracted an unusual amount of public attention. In Akron, the court proceedings were much discussed both in the local paper, the *Beacon Journal,* and in conversation. Goodrich is an old-line company, with a strong streak of paternalism in its relations with its employees, and with strong feelings about what it regards as business ethics. "We were exceptionally upset by what Wohlgemuth did," a Goodrich executive of long standing said recently. "In my judgment, the episode caused more concern to the company than anything that has happened in years. In fact, in the ninety-three years that Goodrich has been in business, we had never before entered a suit to restrain a former employee from disclosing trade secrets. Of course, many employees in sensitive positions have left us. But in those cases the companies doing the hiring have recognized their responsibilities. On one occasion, a Goodrich chemist went to work for another company under circumstances that made it appear to us that he was going to use our methods. We talked to the man, and to his new employer, too. The upshot was that the competing company never brought out the product it had hired our man to work on. That was responsible conduct on the part of both employee and company. As for the Wohlgemuth case, the local community and our employees were a bit hostile toward us at first—a big company suing a little guy, and so on. But they gradually came around to our point of view."

Interest outside Akron, which was evidenced by a small flood of letters of inquiry about the case, addressed to the Goodrich legal department, made it clear that Goodrich v. Wohlgemuth was being watched as a bellwether. Some inquiries were from companies that had similar problems, or anticipated having them, and a surprising number were from relatives of young scientists, asking, "Does this mean my boy is stuck in his present job for the rest of his life?" In truth, an important issue was at stake, and pitfalls awaited the judge who heard the case, no matter which way he decided. On one side was the danger that discoveries made in the course of corporate research might become unprotectable—a situation that would eventually lead to the drying up of private research funds. On the other side was the danger that thousands of scientists might, through their very ability and ingenuity, find themselves permanently locked in a deplorable, and possibly unconstitutional, kind of intellectual servitude—they would be barred from changing jobs because they knew too much.

The trial—held in Akron, presided over by Judge Frank H. Harvey, and conducted, like all proceedings of its type, without a jury—began on November 26th and continued through December 12th, with a week's recess in the middle; Wohlgemuth, who was supposed to have started work at Latex on December 3rd, remained in Akron under a voluntary agreement with the court, and testified extensively in his own defense. Injunction, the form of relief that was sought by Goodrich and the chief form of relief that is available to anyone whose secrets have been stolen, is a remedy that originated in Roman law; it was anciently called "interdict," and is still so called in Scotland. What Goodrich was asking, in effect, was that the court issue a direct order to Wohlgemuth not only forbidding him to reveal Goodrich secrets but also forbidding him to take employment in any other company's space-suit department. Any violation of such an order would be contempt of court, punishable by a fine, or imprisonment, or both. Just how seriously Goodrich viewed the case became clear when its team of lawyers proved to be headed by Jeter himself, who, as vice-president, secretary, the company's ultimate authority on patent law, general law, employee relations, union relations, and workmen's compensation, and Lord High Practically Everything Else, had not found time to try a case in court himself for ten years. The chief defense counsel was Richard A. Chenoweth, of the Akron law firm of Buckingham, Doolittle & Burroughs, which Latex, though it was not a defendant in the action, had retained to handle the case, in fulfillment of its promise to Wohlgemuth.

From the outset, the two sides recognized that if Goodrich was to prevail, it had to prove, first, that it possessed trade secrets; second, that Wohlgemuth also possessed them, and that a substantial peril of disclosure existed; and, third, that it would suffer irreparable injury if injunctive relief was not granted. On the first point, Goodrich attorneys, through their questioning of Effler, Galloway, and one other company employee, set out to establish that Goodrich had a number of unassailable space-suit secrets, among them a way of making the hard shell of a space helmet, a way of making the visor seal, a way of making a sock ending, a way of making the inner liner of gloves, a way of fastening the helmet onto the rest of the suit, and a way of applying a wear-resistant material called neoprene to two-way-stretch fabric. Wohlgemuth, through his counsel's cross-examinations, sought to show that none of these processes were secrets at all; for example, in the case of the neoprene process, which Effler had described as "a very critical trade secret" of Goodrich, defense counsel brought out evidence that a Latex product that is neither secret nor intended to be worn in outer space— the Playtex Golden Girdle—was made of two-way-stretch fabric with neoprene applied to it, and, to emphasize the point, Chenoweth introduced a Playtex Golden Girdle for all to see. Nor did either side neglect to bring into court a space suit, in each instance inhabited. The Goodrich suit, a 1961 model, was intended to demonstrate what the company had achieved by means of research—research that it did not want to see compromised through the loss of its secrets. The Latex suit, also a 1961 model, was intended to show that Latex was already ahead of Goodrich in space-suit development and would therefore have no interest in stealing Goodrich secrets. The Latex suit was particularly bizarre-looking, and the Latex employee who wore it in court looked almost excruciatingly uncomfortable, as if he were unaccustomed to the air of earth, or of Akron. "His air tubes weren't hooked up, and he was hot," the *Beacon Journal* explained next day. At any rate, after he had sat suffering for ten or fifteen minutes while defense counsel questioned a witness about his costume, he suddenly pointed in an agonized way to his head, and the court record of what followed, probably unique in the annals of jurisprudence, reads like this:

> MAN IN THE SPACE SUIT: May I take this off? (Helmet)....
> THE COURT: All right.

The second element in Goodrich's burden of proof—that Wohlgemuth was privy to Goodrich secrets—was fairly quickly dealt with, because Wohlgemuth's lawyers conceded that hardly anything the company knew about space suits had been kept from him; they based their defense on, first, the unquestioned fact that he had taken no papers away with him and, second, the unlikelihood that he would be able to remember the details of complex scientific processes, even if he wanted to. On the third element—the matter of irreparable injury—Jeter pointed out that Goodrich, which had made the first full-pressure flying suit in history, for the late Wiley Post's high-altitude experiments in 1934, and which had since poured vast sums into space-suit research and development, was the unquestioned pioneer and had up to then been considered the leader in the field; he tried to paint Latex, which had been making full-pressure suits only since the mid-fifties, as a parvenu with the nefarious plan of cashing in on Goodrich's years of research by hiring Wohlgemuth.

Even if the intentions of Latex and Wohlgemuth were the best in the world, Jeter contended, Wohlgemuth would inevitably reveal Goodrich secrets in the course of working in Latex's space-suit department. In any event, Jeter was unwilling to assume good intentions. As evidence of bad ones, there was, on the part of Latex, the fact that the firm had deliberately sought out Wohlgemuth, and, on the part of Wohlgemuth, the statement he had made to Galloway about the price of loyalty and ethics. The defense disputed the contention that a disclosure of secrets would be inevitable, and, of course, denied evil intentions on anyone's part. It rounded out its case with a statement made in court under oath by Wohlgemuth: "I will not reveal [to International Latex] any items which in my own mind I would consider to be trade secrets of the B. F. Goodrich Company." This, of course, was cold comfort to Goodrich.

Having heard the evidence and the lawyers' summations, Judge Harvey reserved decision until a later date and issued an order temporarily forbidding Wohlgemuth to reveal the alleged secrets or to work in the Latex space-suit program; he could go on the Latex payroll, but he had to stay out of space suits until the court's decision was handed down. In mid-December, Wohlgemuth, leaving his family behind, went to Dover and began working for Latex on other products; early in January, by which time he had succeeded in selling his house in Wadsworth and buying one in Dover, his family joined him at his new stand.

In Akron, meanwhile, the lawyers had at each other in briefs intended to sway Judge Harvey. Various fine points of law were debated, learnedly but inconclusively; yet as the briefs wore on, it became increasingly clear that the essence of the case was quite simple. For all practical purposes, there was no controversy over the facts. What remained in controversy was the answers to two questions: First, should a man be formally restrained from revealing trade secrets when he has not yet committed any such act, and when it is not clear that he intends to? And, secondly, should a man be prevented from taking a job simply because the job presents him with unique temptations to break the law? Having scoured the lawbooks, counsel for the defense found exactly the text quotation they wanted in support of the argument that both questions should be answered in the negative. (Unlike the decisions of other courts, the general statements of the authors of law textbooks have no official standing in any court, but by using them judiciously an advocate can express his own opinions in someone else's words and buttress them with bibliographical references.) The quotation was from a text entitled "Trade Secrets," which was written by a lawyer named Ridsdale Ellis and published in 1953, and it read, in part, "Usually it is not until there is evidence that the employee [who has changed jobs] has not lived up to his contract, expressed or implied, to maintain secrecy, that the former employer can take action. In the law of torts there is the maxim: Every dog has one free bite. A dog cannot be presumed to be vicious until he has proved that he is by biting someone. As with a dog, the former employer may have to wait for a former employee to commit some overt act before he can act." To counter this doctrine—which, besides being picturesque, appeared to have a crushingly exact applicability to the case under dispute—Goodrich's lawyers came up with a quotation of their own from the very same book. ("Ellis on trade secrets," as the lawyers referred to it in their briefs, was repeatedly used by the two sides to belabor each other, for the good reason that it was the only text on the subject available in the Summit County law library, where both sides did the bulk of their research.) In support of *their* cause, Goodrich counsel found that Ellis had said, in connection with trade-secrets cases in which the defendant was a company accused of luring away another company's confidential employee: "Where the confidential employee left to enter defendant's employment, an inference can be drawn to supplement other circumstantial evidence that the latter employment was stimulated by a desire by the defendant to learn plaintiff's secrets."

In other words, Ellis apparently felt that when the circumstances look suspicious, one free bite is *not* permitted. Whether he contradicted himself or merely refined his position is a nice question; Ellis himself had died several years earlier, so it was not possible to consult him on the matter.

On February 20th, 1963, having studied the briefs and deliberated on them, Judge Harvey delivered his decision, in the form of a nine-page essay fraught with suspense. To begin with, the Judge wrote, he was convinced that Goodrich did have trade secrets relative to space suits, and that Wohlgemuth might be able to remember and therefore be able to disclose some of them to Latex, to the irreparable injury of Goodrich. He declared, further, that "there isn't any doubt that the Latex company was attempting to gain [Wohlgemuth's] valuable experience in this particular specialized field for the reason that they had this so-called 'Apollo' contract with the government, and there isn't any doubt that if he is permitted to work in the space-suit division of the Latex company . . . he would have an opportunity to disclose confidential information of the B. F. Goodrich Company." Still further, Judge Harvey was convinced by the attitude of Latex, as this was evidenced by the conduct of its representatives in court, that the company intended to try to get Wohlgemuth to give it "the benefit of every kind of information he had." At this point in the opinion, things certainly looked black for the defense. However—and the Judge was well down page 6 before he got to the "however"—what he had concluded after studying the one-free-bite controversy among the lawyers was that an injunction cannot be issued against disclosure of trade secrets before such disclosure has occurred unless there is clear and substantial evidence of evil intent on the part of the defendant. The defendant in this case, the Judge pointed out, was Wohlgemuth, and if any evil intent was involved, it appeared to be attributable to Latex rather than to him. For this reason, along with some technical ones, he wound up, "It is the view and the Order of this Court that Injunction be denied against the defendant."

Goodrich promptly appealed the decision, and the Summit County Court of Appeals, pending its own decision on the case, issued another restraining order, which differed from Judge Harvey's in that it permitted Wohlgemuth to do space-suit work for Latex, but still forbade him to disclose Goodrich's alleged trade secrets. Accordingly, Wohlgemuth, with an initial victory under his belt but with a new legal struggle on his behalf ahead, went to work in the Latex moon-suit shop.

Jeter and his colleagues, in their brief to the Court of Appeals, stated unequivocally that Judge Harvey had been wrong not only in some of the technical aspects of his decision but in his finding that there must be evidence of bad faith on the defendant's part before an injunction can be granted. "The question to be decided is not one of good or bad faith, but, rather, whether there is a threat or a likelihood that trade secrets will be disclosed," the Goodrich brief declared roundly—and a little inconsistently, in view of all the time and effort the company had expended on attempts to pin bad faith on both Latex and Wohlgemuth. Wohlgemuth's lawyers, of course, did not fail to point out the inconsistency. "It seems strange indeed that Goodrich should find fault with this finding of Judge Harvey," they remarked in their brief. Quite clearly, they had conceived for Judge Harvey feelings so tender as to border on the protective.

The decision of the Court of Appeals was handed down on May 22nd. Written by Judge Arthur W. Doyle, with his two colleagues of the court concurring, it was a partial reversal of Judge Harvey. Finding that "there exists a present real threat of disclosure, even without actual disclosure," and that "an injunction may . . . prevent a future wrong," the court granted an injunction that restrained Wohlgemuth from disclosing to Latex any of the processes and information claimed as trade secrets by Goodrich. On the other hand, Judge Doyle wrote, "We have no doubt that Wohlgemuth had the right to take employment in a competitive business, and to use his knowledge (other than trade secrets) and experience for the benefit of his new employer." Plainly put, Wohlgemuth was at last free to accept a permanent job doing space-suit work for Latex, provided only that he refrained from disclosing Goodrich secrets in the course of his work.

Neither side carried the case above the Summit County Court of Appeals—to the Ohio Supreme Court and, beyond that, to the United States Supreme Court—so with the decision of the Appeals Court the Wohlgemuth case was settled. Public interest in it subsided soon after the trial was over, but professional interest continued to mount, and, of course, it mounted still more after the Appeals Court decision in May. In March, the New York City Bar Association, in collaboration with the American Bar Association, had presented a symposium on trade secrets, with the Wohlgemuth case as its focus. In the later months of that year, employers worried about loss of trade secrets brought numerous suits against former employees, presumably relying on the Wohlgemuth decision as a precedent. A year later there were more than two dozen trade-secrets cases pending in the courts, the most publicized of them being the effort of E. I. du Pont de Nemours & Co. to prevent one of its former research engineers from taking part in the production of certain rare pigments for the American Potash & Chemical Corporation.

It would be logical to suppose that Jeter might be worried about enforcement of the Appeals Court's order—might be afraid that Wohlgemuth, working behind the locked door of the Latex laboratory, and perhaps nursing a grudge against Goodrich, would take his one free bite in spite of the order, on the assumption that he would not be caught. However, Jeter didn't look at things that way. "Until and unless we learn otherwise, we assume that Wohlgemuth and International Latex, both having knowledge of the court order, will comply with the law," Jeter said after the case was concluded. "No specific steps by Goodrich to police the enforcement of the order have been taken, or are contemplated. However, it if should be violated, there are various ways in which we would be likely to find out. Wohlgemuth, after all, is working with others, who come and go. Out of perhaps twenty-five employees in constant touch with him, it's likely that one or two will leave Latex within a couple of years. Furthermore, you can learn quite a lot from suppliers who deal with both Latex and Goodrich; and also from customers. However, I do not feel that the order will be violated. Wohlgemuth has been through a lawsuit. It was quite an experience for him. He now knows his responsibilities under the law, which he may not have known before."

Wohlgemuth himself said late in 1963 that since the conclusion of the case he had received a great many inquiries from other scientists working in industry, the gist of their questions being, "Does your case mean that I'm married to my job?" He told them that they would have to draw their own conclusions. Wohlgemuth also said that the court order had had no effect on his work in the Latex space-suit department. "Precisely what the Goodrich secrets are is not spelled out in the order, and therefore I have acted as if all the things they alleged to be secrets actually *are* secrets," he said. "Nevertheless, my efficiency is not impaired by my avoiding disclosure of those things. Take, for example, the use of polyurethane as an inner liner—a process that Goodrich claimed as a trade secret. That was something Latex had tried previously and found unsatisfactory. Therefore, it wasn't planning to investigate further along those lines, and it still isn't, I am just as effective for Latex as if there had never been an injunction. However, I will say this. If I were to get a better offer from some other company now, I'm sure I would evaluate the question very carefully—which is what I didn't do the last time." Wohlgemuth—the new, post-trial Wohlgemuth—spoke in a noticeably slow, tense way, with long pauses for thought, as if the wrong word might bring lightning down on his head. He was a young man with a strong sense of belonging to the future, and he looked forward to making, if he could, a material contribution to putting man on the moon. At the same time, Jeter may have been right; he was also a man who had recently spent almost six months in the toils of the law, and who worked, and would continue to work, in the knowledge that a slip of the tongue might mean a fine, imprisonment, and professional ruin.

12

IN DEFENSE OF STERLING

I

THE FEDERAL RESERVE BANK OF NEW YORK stands on the block bounded by Liberty, Nassau, and William Streets and Maiden Lane, on the slope of one of the few noticeable hillocks remaining in the bulldozed, skyscraper-flattened earth of downtown Manhattan. Its entrance faces Liberty, and its mien is dignified and grim. Its arched ground-floor windows, designed in imitation of those of the Pitti and Riccardi Palaces in Florence, are protected by iron grilles made of bars as thick as a boy's wrist, and above them are rows of small rectangular windows set in a blufflike fourteen-story wall of sandstone and limestone, the blocks of which once varied in color from brown through gray to blue, but which soot has reduced to a common gray; the façade's austerity is relieved only at the level of the twelfth floor, by a Florentine loggia. Two giant iron lanterns—near-replicas of lanterns that adorn the Strozzi Palace in Florence—flank the main entrance, but they seem to be there less to please or illuminate the entrant than to intimidate him. Nor is the building's interior much more cheery or hospitable; the ground floor features cavernous groin vaulting and high ironwork partitions in intricate geometric, floral, and animal designs, and it is guarded by hordes of bank security men, whose dark-blue uniforms make them look much like policemen.

Huge and dour as it is, the Federal Reserve Bank, as a building, arouses varied feelings in its beholders. To admirers of the debonair new Chase Manhattan Bank across Liberty Street, which is notable for huge windows, bright-colored tiled walls, and stylish Abstract Expressionist paintings, it is an epitome of nineteenth-century heavy-footedness in bank architecture, even though it was actually completed in 1924. To an awestruck writer for the magazine *Architecture* in 1927, it seemed "as inviolable as the Rock of Gibraltar and no less inspiring of one's reverent obeisance," and possessed of "a quality which, for lack of a better word, I can best describe as 'epic'" To the mothers of young girls who work in it as secretaries or pages, it looks like a particularly sinister sort of prison. Bank robbers are apparently equally respectful of its inviolability; there has never been the slightest hint of an attempt on it. To the Municipal Art Society of New York, which now rates it as a full-fledged landmark, it was until 1967 only a second-class landmark, being assigned to Category II, "Structures of Great Local or Regional Importance Which Should Be Preserved," rather than Category I, "Structures of National Importance Which Should Be Preserved at All Costs." On the other hand, it has one indisputable edge on the Pitti, Riccardi, and Strozzi Palaces: It is bigger than any of them. In fact, it is a bigger Florentine palace than has ever stood in Florence.

The Federal Reserve Bank of New York is set apart from the other banks of Wall Street in purpose and function as well as in appearance. As by far the largest and most important of the twelve regional Federal Reserve Banks—which, together with the Federal Reserve Board in Washington and the sixty-two hundred commercial banks that are members, make up the Federal Reserve System—it is the chief operating arm of the United States' central-banking institution. Most other countries have only one central bank—the Bank of England, the Bank of France, and so on—rather than a network of such banks, but the central banks of all countries have the same dual purpose: to keep the national currency in a healthy state by regulating its supply, partly through the degree of ease or difficulty with which it may be borrowed, and, when necessary, to defend its value in relation to that of other national currencies. To accomplish the first objective, the New York bank coöperates with its parent board and its eleven brother banks in periodically adjusting a number of monetary throttles, of which the most visible (although not necessarily the most important) is the rate of interest at which it lends money to other banks. As to the second objective, by virtue of tradition and of its situation in the nation's and the world's greatest financial center, the Federal Reserve Bank of New York is the sole agent of the Federal Reserve System and of the United States Treasury in dealings with other countries. Thus, on its shoulders falls the chief responsibility for operations in defense of the dollar. Those responsibilities were weighing heavily during the great monetary crisis of 1968—and, indeed, since the defense of the dollar sometimes involves the defense of other currencies as well, over the preceding three and a half years.

Charged as it is with acting in the national interest—in fact having no other purpose—the Federal Reserve Bank of New York, together with its brother banks, obviously is an arm of government. Yet it has a foot in the free-enterprise camp; in what some might call characteristic American fashion, it stands squarely astride the chalk line between government and business. Although it functions as a government agency, its stock is privately owned by the member banks throughout the country, to which it pays annual dividends limited by law to six per cent per year. Although its top officers take a federal oath, they are not appointed by the President of the United States, or even by the Federal Reserve Board, but are elected by the bank's own board of directors, and their salaries are paid not out of the federal till but out of the bank's own income. Yet that income—though, happily, always forthcoming—is entirely incidental to the bank's purpose, and if it rises above expenses and dividends the excess is automatically paid into the United States Treasury. A bank that considers profits incidental is scarcely the norm in Wall Street, and this attitude puts Federal Reserve Bank men in a uniquely advantageous social position. Because their bank *is* a bank, after all, and a privately owned, profitable one at that, they can't be dismissed as mere government bureaucrats; conversely, having their gaze fixed steadily above the mire of cupidity entitles them to be called the intellectuals, if not actually the aristocrats, of Wall Street banking.

Under them lies gold—still the bedrock on which all money nominally rests, though in recent times a bedrock that has been shuddering ominously under the force of various monetary earthquakes. As of March, 1968, more than thirteen thousand tons of the stuff, worth more than thirteen billion dollars and amounting to more than a quarter of all the monetary gold in the free world, reposed on actual bedrock seventy-six feet below the Liberty Street level and fifty below sea level, in a vault that would be inundated if a system of sump pumps did not divert a stream that originally wandered through Maiden Lane. The famous nineteenth-century British economist Walter Bagehot once told a friend that when his spirits were low it used to cheer him to go down to his bank and "dabble my hand in a heap of sovereigns." Although it is, to say the least, a stimulating experience to go down and *look* at the gold in the Federal Reserve Bank vault, which is in the form not of sovereigns but of dully gleaming bars about the size and shape of building bricks, not even the best-accredited visitor is allowed to dabble his hands in it; for one thing, the bars weigh about twenty-eight pounds each and are therefore ill-adapted to dabbling, and, for another, none of the gold belongs to either the Federal Reserve Bank or the United States. All United States gold is kept at Fort Knox, at the New York Assay Office, or at the various mints; the gold deposited at the Federal Reserve Bank belongs to some seventy other countries—the largest depositors being European—which find it convenient to store a good part of their gold reserves there. Originally, most of them put gold there for safekeeping during the Second World War. After the war, the European nations—with the exception of France—not only left it in New York but greatly increased its quantity as their economies recovered.

Nor does the gold represent anything like all the foreign deposits at Liberty Street; investments of various sorts brought the March '68 total to more than twenty-eight billion. As a banker for most of the central banks of the non-Communist world, and as the central bank representing the world's leading currency, the Federal Reserve Bank of New York is the undisputed chief citadel of world currency. By virtue of this position, it is afforded a kind of fluoroscopic vision of the insides of international finance, enabling it to detect at a glance an incipiently diseased currency here, a faltering economy there. If, for example, Great Britain is running a deficit in her foreign dealings, this instantly shows up in the Federal Reserve Bank's books in the form of a decline in the Bank of England's balance. In the fall of 1964, precisely such a decline was occurring, and it marked the beginning of a long, gallant, intermittently hair-raising, and ultimately losing struggle by a number of countries and their central banks, led by the United States and the Federal Reserve, to safeguard the existing order of world finance by preserving the integrity of the pound sterling. One trouble with imposing buildings is that they have a tendency to belittle the people and activities they enclose, and most of the time it is reasonably accurate to think of the Federal Reserve Bank as a place where often bored people push around workaday slips of paper quite similar to those pushed around in other banks. But since 1964 some of the events there, if they have scarcely been capable of inspiring reverent obeisance, have had a certain epic quality.

Early in 1964, it began to be clear that Britain, which for several years had maintained an approximate equilibrium in her international balance of payments—that is, the amount of money she had annually sent outside her borders had been about equal to the amount she had taken in—was running a substantial deficit. Far from being the result of domestic depression in Britain, this situation was the result of over-exuberant domestic expansion; business was booming, and newly affluent Britons were ordering bales and bales of costly goods from abroad without increasing the exports of British goods on anything like the same scale. In short, Britain was living beyond her means. A substantial balance-of-payments deficit is a worry to a relatively self-sufficient country like the United States (indeed, the United States was having that very worry at that very time, and it would for years to come), but to a trading nation like Britain, about a quarter of whose entire economy is dependent on foreign trade, it constitutes a grave danger.

The situation was cause for growing concern at the Federal Reserve Bank, and the focal point of the concern was the office, on the tenth floor, of Charles A. Coombs, the bank's vice-president in charge of foreign operations. All summer long, the fluoroscope showed a sick and worsening pound sterling. From the research section of the foreign department, Coombs daily got reports that a torrent of money was leaving Britain. From underground, word rose that the pile of gold bars in the locker assigned to Britain was shrinking appreciably—not through any foul play in the vault but because so many of the bars were being transferred to other lockers in settlement of Britain's international debts. From the foreign-exchange trading desk, on the seventh floor, the news almost every afternoon was that the open-market quotations on the pound in terms of dollars had sunk again that day. During July and August, as the quotation dropped from \$2.79 to \$2.7890, and then to \$2.7875, the situation was regarded on Liberty Street as so serious that Coombs, who would normally handle foreign-exchange matters himself, only making routine reports to those higher up, was constantly conferring about it with his boss, the Federal Reserve Bank's president, a tall, cool, soft-spoken man named Alfred Hayes.

Mystifyingly complex though it may appear, what actually happens in international financial dealings is essentially what happens in private domestic transactions. The money worries of a nation, like those of a family, are the consequence of having too much money go out and not enough come in. The foreign sellers of goods to Britain cannot spend the pounds they are paid in their own countries, and therefore they convert them into their own currencies; this they do by selling the pounds in the foreign-exchange markets, just as if they were selling securities on a stock exchange. The market price of the pound fluctuates in response to supply and demand, and so do the prices of all other currencies—all, that is, except the dollar, the sun in the planetary system of currencies, inasmuch as the United States has, since 1934, stood pledged to exchange gold in any quantity for dollars at the pleasure of any nation at the fixed price of thirty-five dollars per ounce.

Under the pressure of selling, the price of the pound goes down. But its fluctuations are severely restricted. The influence of market forces cannot be allowed to lower or raise the price more than a couple of cents below or above the pound's par value; if such wild swings should occur unchecked, bankers and businessmen everywhere who traded with Britain would find themselves involuntarily engaged in a kind of roulette game, and would be inclined to stop trading with Britain. Accordingly, under international monetary rules agreed upon at Bretton Woods, New Hampshire, in 1944, and elaborated at various other places at later times, the pound in 1964, nominally valued at $2.80, was allowed to fluctuate only between $2.78 and $2.82, and the enforcer of this abridgment of the law of supply and demand was the Bank of England. On a day when things were going smoothly, the pound might be quoted on the exchange markets at, say, $2.7990, a rise of $.0015 from the previous day's closing. (Fifteen-hundredths of a cent doesn't sound like much, but on a round million dollars, which is generally the basic unit in international monetary dealings, it amounts to fifteen hundred dollars.) When that happened, the Bank of England needed to do nothing. If, however, the pound was strong in the markets and rose to $2.82 (something it showed absolutely no tendency to do in 1964), the Bank of England was pledged to—and would have been very happy to—accept gold or dollars in exchange for pounds at that price, thereby preventing a further increase in the price and at the same time increasing its own reserve of gold and dollars, which serve as the pound's backing. If, on the other hand (and this was a more realistic hypothesis), the pound was weak and sank to $2.78, the Bank of England's sworn duty was to intervene in the market and buy with gold or dollars all pounds offered for sale at that price, however deeply this might have cut into its own reserves. Thus, the central bank of a spendthrift country, like the father of a spendthrift family, is eventually forced to pay the bills out of capital. But in times of serious currency weakness the central bank loses even more of its reserves than this would suggest, because of the vagaries of market psychology. Prudent importers and exporters seeking to protect their capital and profits reduce to a minimum the sum they hold in pounds and the length of time they hold it. Currency speculators, whose noses have been trained to sniff out weakness, pounce on a falling pound and make enormous short sales, in the expectation of turning a profit on a further drop, and the Bank of England must absorb the speculative sales along with the straightforward ones.

The ultimate consequence of unchecked currency weakness is something that may be incomparably more disastrous in its effects than family bankruptcy. This is devaluation, and devaluation of a key world currency like the pound is the recurrent nightmare of all central bankers, whether in London, New York, Frankfurt, Zurich, or Tokyo. If at any time the drain on Britain's reserves became so great that the Bank of England was unable, or unwilling, to fulfill its obligation to maintain the pound at $2.78, the necessary result would be devaluation. That is, the $2.78-to-$2.82 limitation would be abruptly abrogated; by simple government decree the par value of the pound would be reduced to some lower figure, and a new set of limits established around the new parity. The heart of the danger was the possibility that what followed might be chaos not confined to Britain. Devaluation, as the most heroic and most dangerous of remedies for a sick currency, is rightly feared. By making the devaluing country's goods cheaper to others, it boosts exports, and thus reduces or eliminates a deficit in international accounts, but at the same time it makes both imports and domestic goods more expensive at home, and thus reduces the country's standard of living. It is radical surgery, curing a disease at the expense of some of the patient's strength and well-being—and, in many cases, some of his pride and prestige as well. Worst of all, if the devalued currency is one that, like the pound, is widely used in international dealings, the disease—or, more precisely, the cure—is likely to prove contagious. To nations holding large amounts of that particular currency in their reserve vaults, the effects of the devaluation is the same as if the vaults had been burglarized. Such nations and others, finding themselves at an unacceptable trading disadvantage as a result of the devaluation, may have to resort to competitive devaluation of their own currencies. A downward spiral develops: Rumors of further devaluations are constantly in the wind; the loss of confidence in other people's money leads to a disinclination to do business across national borders; and international trade, upon which depend the food and shelter of hundreds of millions of people around the world, tends to decline. Just such a disaster followed the classic devaluation of all time, the departure of the pound from the old gold standard in 1931— an event that is still generally considered a major cause of the worldwide Depression of the thirties.

The process works similarly in respect to the currencies of all the hundred-odd countries that are members of the International Monetary Fund, an organization that originated at Bretton Woods. For any country, a favorable balance of payments means an accumulation of dollars, either directly or indirectly, which are freely convertible into gold, in the country's central bank; if the demand for its currency is great enough, the country may revalue it upward—the reverse of a devaluation—as both Germany and the Netherlands did in 1961. Conversely, an unfavorable balance of payments starts the sequence of events that may end in forced devaluation. The degree of disruption of world trade that devaluation of a currency causes depends on that currency's international importance. (A large devaluation of the Indian rupee in June, 1966, although it was a serious matter to India, created scarcely a ripple in the international markets.) And—to round out this brief outline of the rules of an intricate game of which everybody everywhere is an inadvertent player—even the lordly dollar is far from immune to the effects of an unfavorable balance of payments or of speculation. Because of the dollar's pledged relation to gold, it serves as the standard for all other currencies, so its price does, not fluctuate in the markets. However, it can suffer weakness of a less visible but equally ominous sort. When the United States sends out substantially more money (whether payment for imports, foreign aid, investments, loans, tourist expenses, or military costs) than it takes in, the recipients freely buy their own currencies with the newly acquired dollars, thereby raising the dollar prices of their own currencies; the rise in price enables their central banks to take in still more dollars, which they can sell back to the United States for gold. Thus, when the dollar is weak the United States loses gold. France alone—a country with a strong currency and no particular official love of the dollar—required thirty million dollars or more in United States gold regularly every month for several years prior to the autumn of 1966, and between 1958, when the United States began running a serious deficit in its international accounts, and the middle of March 1968, our gold reserve was halved—from twenty-two billion eight hundred million to eleven billion four hundred million dollars. If the reserve ever dropped to an unacceptably low level, the United States would be forced to break its word and lower the gold value of the dollar, or even to stop selling gold entirely. Either action would in effect be a devaluation—the one devaluation, because of the dollar's preeminent position, that would be more disruptive to world monetary order than a devaluation of the pound.

Hayes and Coombs, neither of whom is old enough to have experienced the events of 1931 at first hand as a banker but both of whom are such diligent and sensitive students of international banking that they might as well have done so, found that as the hot days of 1964 dragged on they had occasion to be in almost daily contact by transatlantic telephone with their Bank of England counterparts—the Earl of Cromer, governor of the bank at that time, and Roy A. O. Bridge, the governor's adviser on foreign exchange. It became clear to them from these conversations and from other sources that the imbalance in Britain's international accounts was far from the whole trouble. A crisis of confidence in the soundness of the pound was developing, and the main cause of it seemed to be the election that Britain's Conservative Government was facing on October 15th. The one thing that international financial markets hate and fear above all others is uncertainty. Any election represents uncertainty, so the pound always has the jitters just before Britons go to the polls, but to the people who deal in currencies this election looked particularly menacing, because of their estimate of the character of the Labour Government that might come into power. The conservative financiers of London, not to mention those of Continental Europe, looked with almost irrational suspicion on Harold Wilson, the Labour choice for Prime Minister; further, some of Mr. Wilson's economic advisers had explicitly extolled the virtues of devaluation of the pound in their earlier theoretical writings; and, finally, there was an all too pat analogy to be drawn from the fact that the last previous term of the British Labour Party in power had been conspicuously marked, in 1949, by a devaluation of sterling from the rate of $4.03 to $2.80.

In these circumstances, almost all the dealers in the world money markets, whether they were ordinary international businessmen or out-and-out currency speculators, were anxious to get rid of pounds—at least until after the election. Like all speculative attacks, this one fed on itself. Each small drop in the pound's price resulted in further loss of confidence, and down, down went the pound in the international markets— an oddly diffused sort of exchange, which does not operate in any central building but, rather, is conducted by telephone and cable between the trading desks of banks in the world's major cities. Simultaneously, down, down went British reserves, as the Bank of England struggled to support the pound. Early in September, Hayes went to Tokyo for the annual meeting of the members of the International Monetary Fund. In the corridors of the building where participants in the Fund met, he heard one European central banker after another express misgivings about the state of the British economy and the outlook for the British currency. Why didn't the British government take steps at home to check its outlay and to improve the balance of payments, they asked each other. Why didn't it raise the Bank of England's lending rate—the so-called bank rate—from its current five per cent, since this move would have the effect of raising British interest rates all up and down the line, and would thus serve the double purpose of damping down domestic inflation and attracting investment dollars to London from other financial centers, with the result that sterling would gain a sounder footing?

Doubtless the Continental bankers also put such questions to the Bank of England men in Tokyo; in any event, the Bank of England men and their counterparts in the British Exchequer had not failed to put the questions to themselves. But the proposed measures would certainly be unpopular with the British electorate, as unmistakable harbingers of austerity, and the Conservative Government, like many governments before it, appeared to be paralyzed by fear of the imminent election. So it did nothing. In a strictly monetary way, however, Britain did take defensive measures during September. The Bank of England had for several years had a standing agreement with the Federal Reserve that either institution could borrow five hundred million dollars from the other, over a short term, at any time, with virtually no formalities; now the Bank of England accepted this standby loan and made arrangements to supplement it with another five hundred million dollars in short-term credit from various European central banks and the Bank of Canada. This total of a billion dollars, together with Britain's last-ditch reserves in gold and dollars, amounting to about two billion six hundred million, constituted a sizable store of ammunition. If the speculative assault on the pound should continue or intensify, answering fire would

come from the Bank of England in the form of dollar investments in sterling made on the battlefield of the free market,
and presumably the attackers would be put to rout.

As might have been expected, the assault did intensify after
Labour came out the victor in the October election. The new
British government realized at the outset that it was faced
with a grave crisis, and that immediate and drastic action
was in order. It has since been said that summary devaluation
of the pound was seriously considered by the newly elected
Prime Minister and his advisers on finance—George Brown,
Secretary of State for Economic Affairs, and James Callaghan, Chancellor of the Exchequer. The idea was rejected,
though, and the measures they actually took, in October and
early November, were a fifteen-percent emergency surcharge
on British imports (in effect, a blanket raising of tariffs), an
increased fuel tax, and stiff new capital-gains and corporation
taxes. These were deflationary, currency-strengthening measures, to be sure, but the world markets were not reassured.
The specific nature of the new taxes seems to have discon-
certed, and even enraged, many financiers, in and out of Britain, particularly in view of the fact that under the new budget
British government spending on welfare benefits was actually
to be increased, rather than cut back, as deflationary policy
would normally require. One way and another, then, the sellers—or bears, in market jargon—continued to be in charge
of the market for the pound in the weeks after the election,
and the Bank of England was kept busy potting away at them
with precious shells from its borrowed-billion-dollar arsenal.
By the end of October, nearly half the billion was gone, and
the bears were still inexorably advancing on the pound, a
hundredth of a cent at a time.

Hayes, Coombs, and their foreign-department colleagues
on Liberty Street, watching with mounting anxiety, were as
galled as the British by the fact that a central bank defending
its currency against attack can have only the vaguest idea

of where the attack is coming from. Speculation is inherent in foreign trade, and by its nature is almost impossible to isolate, identify, or even define. There are degrees of speculation; the word itself, like "selfishness" or "greed," denotes a judgment, and yet every exchange of currencies might be called a speculation in favor of the currency being acquired and against the one being disposed of. At one end of the scale are perfectly legitimate business transactions that have specific speculative effects. A British importer ordering American merchandise may legitimately pay up in pounds in advance of delivery; if he does, he is speculating against the pound. An American importer who has contracted to pay for British goods at a price set in pounds may legitimately insist that his purchase of the pounds he needs to settle his debt be deferred for a certain period; he, too, is speculating against the pound. (The staggering importance to Britain of these common commercial operations, which are called "leads" and "lags," respectively, is shown by the fact that if in normal times the world's buyers of British goods were all to withhold their payments for as short a period as two and a half months the Bank of England's gold and dollar reserves would vanish.) At the other end of the scale is the dealer in money who borrows pounds and then converts the loan into dollars. Such a dealer, instead of merely protecting his business interests, is engaging in an out-and-out speculative move called a short sale; hoping to buy back the pounds he owes more cheaply later on, he is simply trying to make a profit on the decrease in value he anticipates—and, what with the low commissions prevailing in the international money market, the maneuver provides one of the world's most attractive forms of high-stakes gambling.

Gambling of this sort, although in fact it probably contributed far less to the sterling crisis than the self-protective measures taken by nervous importers and exporters, was being widely blamed for all the pound's troubles of October and

371

November, 1964. Particularly in the British Parliament, there were angry references to speculative activity by "the gnomes of Zurich"—Zurich being singled out because Switzerland, whose banking laws rigidly protect the anonymity of deposi-tors, is the blind pig of international banking, and conse-quently much currency speculation, originating in many parts of the world, is funnelled through Zurich. Besides low com-missions and anonymity, currency speculation has another attraction. Thanks to time differentials and good telephone service, the world money market, unlike stock exchanges, race tracks, and gambling casinos, practically never closes. London opens an hour after the Continent (or did until Feb-ruary 1968, when Britain adopted Continental time), New York five (now six) hours after that, San Francisco three hours after *that*, and then Tokyo gets under way about the time San Francisco closes. Only a need for sleep or a lack of money need halt the operations of a really hopelessly addicted plunger anywhere.

"It was *not* the gnomes of Zurich who were beating down the pound," a leading Zurich banker subsequently main-tained—stopping short of claiming that there were no gnomes there. Nonetheless, organized short selling—what traders call a bear raid—was certainly in progress, and the defenders of the pound in London and their sympathizers in New York would have given plenty to catch a glimpse of the invisible enemy.

It was in this atmosphere, then, that on the weekend beginning November 7th the leading central bankers of the world held their regular monthly gathering in Basel, Switzerland. The occasion for such gatherings, which have been held regularly since the nineteen-thirties except during the Second World War, is the monthly meeting of the board of directors of the Bank for International Settlements, which was established in Basel in 1930 primarily as a clearing house for the handling of reparations payments arising out of the First World War but has come to serve as an agency of international monetary coöperation and, incidentally, a kind of central bankers' club. As such, it is considerably more limited in resources and restricted as to membership than the International Monetary Fund, but, like other exclusive clubs, it is often the scene of great decisions. Represented on its board of directors are Britain, France, West Germany, Italy, Belgium, the Netherlands, Sweden, and Switzerland—in short, the economic powers of Western Europe—while the United States is a regular monthly guest whose presence is counted on, and Canada and Japan are less frequent visitors. The Federal Reserve is almost always represented by Coombs, and sometimes by Hayes and other New York officers as well.

In the nature of things, the interests of the different central banks conflict; their faces are set against each other almost as if they were players in a poker game. Even so, in view of the fact that international troubles with money at their root have almost as long a history as similarly caused troubles between individuals, the most surprising thing about international monetary coöperation is that it is so new. Through all the ages prior to the First World War, it cannot be said to have existed at all. In the nineteen-twenties, it existed chiefly through close personal ties between individual central bankers, often maintained in spite of the indifference of their governments. On an official level, it got off to a halting start through the Financial Committee of the League of Nations, which was supposed to encourage joint action to prevent monetary catastrophes. The sterling collapse of 1931 and its grim sequel were ample proof of the committee's failure. But better days were ahead. The 1944 international financial conference at Bretton Woods—out of which emerged not only the International Monetary Fund but also the whole structure of postwar monetary rules designed to help establish and maintain fixed exchange rates, as well as the World Bank, designed to ease the flow of money from rich countries to poor or war-devastated ones—stands as a milestone in economic coöperation comparable to the formation of the United Nations in political affairs. To cite just one of the conference's fruits, a credit of more than a billion dollars extended to Britain by the International Monetary Fund during the Suez affair in 1956 prevented a major international financial crisis then.

In subsequent years, economic changes, like other changes, tended to come more and more quickly; after 1958, monetary crises began springing up virtually overnight, and the International Monetary Fund, which is hindered by slow-moving machinery, sometimes proved inadequate to meet such crises alone. Again the new spirit of coöperation rose to the occasion, this time with the richest of nations, the United States, taking the lead. Starting in 1961, the Federal Reserve Bank, with the approval of the Federal Reserve Board and the Treasury in Washington, joined the other leading central banks in setting up a system of ever-ready revolving credits, which soon came to be called the "swap network." The purpose of the network was to complement the International Monetary Fund's longer-term credit facilities by giving central banks instant access to funds they might need for a short period in order to move fast and vigorously in defense of their currencies. Its effectiveness was not long in being put to the test. Between its initiation in 1961 and the autumn of 1964, the swap network had played a major part in the triumphant defense against sudden and violent speculative attacks on at least three currencies: the pound, late in 1961; the Canadian dollar, in June, 1961; and the Italian lira, in March, 1964. By the autumn of 1964, the swap agreements (*"L'accord de swap"* to the French, *"die Swap-Verpflichtungen"* to the Germans) had come to be the very cornerstone of international monetary coöperation. Indeed, the five hundred million American dollars that the Bank of England was finding it necessary to draw on at the very moment the bank's top officers were heading for Basel that November weekend represented part of the swap network, greatly expanded from its comparatively modest beginnings.

As for the Bank for International Settlements, in its capacity as a banking institution it was a relatively minor cog in all this machinery, but in its capacity as a club it had over the years come to play a far from unimportant role. Its monthly board meetings served (and still serve) as a chance for the central bankers to talk in an informal atmosphere—to exchange gossip, views, and hunches such as could not comfortably be indulged in either by mail or over the international telephone circuits. Basel, a medieval Rhenish city that is dominated by the spires of its twelfth-century Gothic cathedral and has long been a thriving center of the chemical industry, was originally chosen as the site of the Bank for International Settlements because it was a nodal point for European railways. Now that most international bankers habitually travel by plane, that asset has become a liability, for there is no long-distance air service to Basel; delegates must deplane at Zurich and continue by train or car. On the other hand, Basel has several first-rate restaurants, and it may be that in the view of the central-bank delegates this advantage outweighs the travel inconvenience, for central banking—or at least European central banking—has a firmly established association with good living. A governor of the National Bank of Belgium once remarked to a visitor, without a smile, that he considered one of his duties to be that of leaving the institution's wine cellar better than he had found it. A luncheon guest at the Bank of France is generally told apologetically, "In the tradition of the bank, we serve only simple fare," but what follows is a repast during which the constant discussion of vintages makes any discussion of banking awkward, if not impossible, and at which the tradition of simplicity is honored, apparently, by the serving of only one wine before the cognac. The table of the Bank of Italy is equally elegant (some say the best in Rome), and its surroundings are enhanced by the priceless Renaissance paintings, acquired as defaulted security on bad loans over the years, that hang on the walls. As for the Federal Reserve Bank of New York, alcohol in any form is hardly ever served there, banking is habitually discussed at meals, and the mistress of the kitchen appears almost pathetically grateful whenever one of the officers makes any sort of comment, even a critical one, on the fare. But then Liberty Street isn't Europe.

In these democratic times, central banking in Europe is thought of as the last stronghold of the aristocratic banking tradition, in which wit, grace, and culture coexist easily with commercial astuteness, and even ruthlessness. The European counterparts of the security guards on Liberty Street are apt to be attendants in morning coats. Until less than a generation ago, formality of address between central bankers was the rule. Some think that the first to break it were the British, during the Second World War, when, it is alleged, a secret order went out that British government and military authorities were to address their American counterparts by their first names; in any event, first names are frequently exchanged between European and American central bankers now, and one reason for this, unquestionably, is the postwar rise in influence of the dollar. (Another reason is that, in the emerging era of coöperation, the central bankers see more of each other than they used to—not just in Basel but in Washington, Paris, and Brussels, at regular meetings of perhaps half a dozen special banking committees of various international organizations. The same handful of top bankers parades so regularly through the hotel lobbies of those cities that one of them thinks they must give the impression of being hundreds strong, like the spear carriers who cross the stage again and again in the triumphal scene of "Aida.") And language, like the manner of its use, has tended to follow economic power. European central bankers have always used French ("bad French," some say) in talking with each other, but during the long period in which the pound was the world's leading currency English came to be the first language of central banking at large, and under the rule of the dollar it continues to be. It is spoken fluently and willingly by all the top officers of every central bank except the Bank of France, and even the Bank of France officers are forced to keep translators at hand, in consideration of the seeming intractable inability or unwillingness of most Britons and Americans to become competent in any language but their own. (Lord Cromer, flouting tradition, speaks French with complete authority.)

At Basel, good food and convenience come before splendor; many of the delegates favor an outwardly humble restaurant in the main railroad station, and the Bank for International Settlements itself is modestly situated between a tea shop and a hairdressing establishment. On that November weekend in 1964, Vice-President Coombs was the only representative of the Federal Reserve System on hand, and, indeed, he was to be the key banking representative of the United States through the early and middle phases of the crisis that was then mounting. In an abstracted way, Coombs ate and drank heartily with the others—true to his institution's traditions, he is less than a gourmet—but his real interest was in getting the sense of the meeting and the private feelings of its participants. He was the perfect man for this task, inasmuch as he has the unquestioning trust and respect of all his foreign colleagues. The other leading central bankers habitually call him by his first name—less, it seems, in deference to changed custom than out of deep affection and admiration. They also use it in speaking of him among themselves; the name "Charliecoombs" (run together thus out of long habituation) is a word to conjure with in central-banking circles. Charliecoombs, they will tell you, is the kind of New Englander (he is from Newton, Massachusetts) who, although his clipped speech and dry manner make him seem a bit cool and detached, is really warm and intuitive. Charliecoombs, although a Harvard graduate

(Class of 1940), is the kind of unpretentious gray-haired man with half-rimmed spectacles and a precise manner whom you might easily take for a standard American small-town bank president, rather than a master of one of the world's most complex skills. It is generally conceded that if any one man was the genius behind the swap network, the man was the New England swapper Charliecoombs.

At Basel, there was, as usual, a series of formal sessions, each with its agenda, but there was also, as usual, much informal palaver in rump sessions held in hotel rooms and offices and at a formal Sunday-night dinner at which there was no agenda but instead a free discussion of what Coombs has since referred to as "the hottest topic of the moment." There could be no question about what that was; it was the condition of the pound—and, indeed, Coombs had heard little discussion of anything else all weekend. "It was clear to me from what I heard that confidence in sterling was deteriorating," he has said. Two questions were on most of the bankers' minds. One was whether the Bank of England proposed to take some of the pressure off the pound by raising its lending rate. Bank of England men were present, but getting an answer was not a simple matter of asking them their intentions; even if they had been willing to say, they would not have been able to, because the Bank of England is not empowered to change its rate without the approval—which in practice often comes closer to meaning the instruction—of the British government, and elected governments have a natural dislike for measures that make money tight. The other question was whether Britain had enough gold and dollars to throw into the breach if the speculative assault should continue. Apart from what was left of the billion dollars from the expanded swap network and what remained of its drawing rights on the International Monetary Fund, Britain had only its official reserves, which had dropped in the previous week to something under two and a half billion dollars—their lowest point in several years.

Worse than that was the frightful rate at which the reserves were dwindling away; on a single bad day during the previous week, according to the guesses of experts, they had dropped by eighty-seven million dollars. A month of days like that and they would be gone.

Even so, Coombs has said, nobody at Basel that weekend dreamed that the pressure on sterling could become as intense as it actually did become later in the month. He returned to New York worried but resolute. It was not to New York, however, that the main scene of the battle for sterling shifted after the Basel meeting; it was to London. The big immediate question was whether or not Britain would raise its bank rate that week, and the day the answer would be known was Thursday, November 12th. In the matter of the bank rate, as in so many other things, the British customarily follow a ritual. If there is to be a change, at noon on Thursday—then and then only—a sign appears in the ground-floor lobby of the Bank of England announcing the new rate, and, simultaneously, a functionary called the Government Broker, decked out in a pink coat and top hat, hurries down Throgmorton Street to the London Stock Exchange and ceremonially announces the new rate from a rostrum. Noon on Thursday the twelfth passed with no change; evidently the Labour Government was having as much trouble deciding on a bank-rate rise after the election as the Conservatives had had before. The speculators, wherever they were, reacted to such pusillanimity as one man. On Friday the thirteenth, the pound, which had been moderately buoyant all week precisely because speculators had been anticipating a bank-rate rise, underwent a fearful battering, which sent it down to a closing price of $2.7829— barely more than a quarter of a cent above the official minimum—and the Bank of England, intervening frequently to hold it even at that level, lost twenty-eight million dollars more from its reserves. Next day, the financial commentator of the London *Times*, under the byline Our City Editor, let himself go. "The pound," he wrote, "is not looking as firm as might be hoped."

The following week saw the pattern repeated, but in exaggerated form. On Monday, Prime Minister Wilson, taking a leaf out of Winston Churchill's book, tried rhetoric as a weapon. Speaking at a pomp-and-circumstance banquet at the Guildhall in the City of London before an audience that included, among many other dignitaries, the Archbishop of Canterbury, the Lord Chancellor, the Lord President of the Council, the Lord Privy Seal, the Lord Mayor of London, and their wives, Wilson ringingly proclaimed "not only our faith but our determination to keep sterling strong and to see it riding high," and asserted that the Government would not hesitate to take whatever steps might become necessary to accomplish this purpose. While elaborately avoiding the dread word "devaluation," just as all other British officials had avoided it all summer, Wilson sought to make it unmistakable that the Government now considered such a move out of the question. To emphasize this point, he included a warning to speculators: "If anyone at home or abroad doubts the firmness of [our] resolve, let them be prepared to pay the price for their lack of faith in Britain." Perhaps the speculators were daunted by this verbal volley, or perhaps they were again moved to let up in their assault on the pound by the prospect of a bank-rate rise on Thursday; in any case, on Tuesday and Wednesday the pound, though it hardly rode high in the marketplace, managed to ride a little less low than it had on the previous Friday, and to do so without the help of the Bank of England.

By Thursday, according to subsequent reports, a sharp private dispute had erupted between the Bank of England and the British government on the bank-rate question—Lord Cromer arguing, for the bank, that a rise of at least one per cent, and perhaps two per cent, was absolutely essential, and Wilson, Brown, and Callaghan still demurring. The upshot was no bank-rate rise on Thursday, and the effect of the inaction was a swift intensification of the crisis. Friday the twentieth was a black day in the City of London. The Stock Exchange, its investors moving in time with sterling, had a terrible session. The Bank of England had by now resolved to establish its last-line trench on the pound at $2.7825—a quarter of a cent above the bottom limit. The pound opened on Friday at precisely that level and remained there all day, firmly pinned down by the speculators' hail of offers to sell; meanwhile, the bank met all offers at $2.7825 and, in doing so, used up more of Britain's reserves. Now the offers were coming so fast that little attempt was made to disguise their places of origin; it was evident that they were coming from everywhere—chiefly from the financial centers of Europe, but also from New York, and even from London itself. Rumors of imminent devaluation were sweeping the bourses of the Continent. And in London itself an ominous sign of cracking morale appeared: devaluation was now being mentioned openly even there. The Swedish economist and sociologist Gunnar Myrdal, in a luncheon speech in London on Thursday, had suggested that a slight devaluation might now be the only possible solution to Britain's problems; once this exogenous comment had broken the ice, Britons also began using the dread word, and, in the next morning's *Times*, Our City Editor himself was to say, in the tone of a commander preparing the garrison for possible surrender, "Indiscriminate gossip about devaluation of the pound can do harm. But it would be even worse to regard use of that word as taboo."

When nightfall at last brought the pound and its defenders a weekend breather, the Bank of England had a chance to assess its situation. What it found was anything but reassuring. All but a fraction of the billion dollars it had arranged to borrow in September under the expanded swap agreements had gone into the battle. The right that remained to it of drawing on the International Monetary Fund was virtually worthless, since the transaction would take weeks to complete, and matters turned on days and hours. What the bank still had—and all that it had—was the British reserves, which had gone down by fifty-six million dollars that day and now stood at around two billion. More than one commentator has since suggested that this sum could in a way be likened to the few squadrons of fighter planes to which the same dogged nation had been reduced twenty-four years earlier at the worst point in the Battle of Britain.

The analogy is extravagant, and yet, in the light of what the pound means, and has meant, to the British, it is not irrelevant. In a materialistic age, the pound has almost the symbolic importance that was once accorded to the Crown; the state of sterling almost *is* the state of Britain. The pound is the oldest of modern currencies. The term "pound sterling" is believed to have originated well before the Norman Conquest, when the Saxon kings issued silver pennies—called "sterlings" or "starlings" because they sometimes had stars inscribed on them—of which two hundred and forty equalled one pound of pure silver. (The shilling, representing twelve sterlings, or one-twentieth of a pound, did not appear on the scene until after the Conquest.) Thus, sizable payments in Britain have been reckoned in pounds from its beginnings. The pound, however, was by no means an unassailably sound currency during its first few centuries, chiefly because of the early kings' unfortunate habit of relieving their chronic financial embarrassment by debasing the coinage. By melting down a quantity of sterlings, adding to the brew some base metal and no more silver, and then minting new coins, an irresponsible king could magically convert a hundred pounds into, say, a hundred and ten, just like that. Queen Elizabeth I put a stop to the practice when, in a carefully planned surprise move in 1561, she recalled from circulation all the debased coins issued by her predecessors. The result, combined with the growth of British trade, was a rapid and spectacular rise in the prestige of the pound, and less than a century after Elizabeth's coup the word "sterling" had assumed the adjectival meaning that it still has—"thoroughly excellent, capable of standing every test." By the end of the seventeenth century, when the Bank of England was founded to handle the government's finances, paper money was beginning to be trusted for general use, and it had come to be backed by gold as well as silver. As time went on, the monetary prestige of gold rose steadily in relation to that of silver (in the modern world silver has no standing as a monetary reserve metal, and only in some half-dozen countries does it now serve as the principal metal in subsidiary coinage), but it was not until 1816 that Britain adopted a gold standard—that is, pledged itself to redeem paper currency with gold coins or bars at any time. The gold sovereign, worth one pound, which came to symbolize stability, affluence, and even joy to more Victorians than Bagehot, made its first appearance in 1817.

Prosperity begat emulation. Seeing how Britain flourished, and believing the gold standard to be at least partly responsible, other nations adopted it one after another: Germany in 1871; Sweden, Norway, and Denmark in 1873; France, Belgium, Switzerland, Italy, and Greece in 1874; the Netherlands in 1875; and the United States in 1879. The results were disappointing; hardly any of the newcomers found themselves immediately getting rich, and Britain, which in retrospect appears to have flourished as much in spite of the gold standard as because of it, continued to be the undisputed monarch of world trade. In the half century preceding the First World War, London was the middleman in international finance, and the pound was its quasi-official medium. As David Lloyd George was later to write nostalgically, prior to 1914 "the crackle of a bill on London"—that is, of a bill of credit in pounds sterling bearing the signature of a London bank—"was as good as the ring of gold in any port throughout the civilized world."

The war ended this idyll by disrupting the delicate balance of forces that had made it possible and by bringing to the fore a challenger to the pound's supremacy—the United States dollar. In 1914, Britain, hard pressed to finance its fighting forces, adopted measures to discourage demands for gold, thereby abandoning the gold standard in everything but name; meanwhile, the value of a pound in dollars sank from $4.86 to a 1920 low of $3.20. In an effort to recoup its lost glory, Britain resumed a full gold standard in 1925, tying the pound to gold at a rate that restored its old $4.86 relation to the dollar. The cost of this gallant overvaluation, however, was chronic depression at home, not to mention the political eclipse for some fifteen years of the Chancellor of the Exchequer who ordered it, Winston Churchill.

The general collapse of currencies during the nineteen-thirties actually began not in London but on the Continent, when, in the summer of 1931, a sudden run on the leading bank of Austria, the Creditanstalt, resulted in its failure. The domino principle of bank failures—if such a thing can be said to exist—then came into play. German losses arising from this relatively minor disaster resulted in a banking crisis in Germany, and then, because huge quantities of British funds were now frozen in bankrupt institutions on the Continent, the panic crossed the English Channel and invaded the home of the imperial pound itself. Demands for gold in exchange for pounds quickly became too heavy for the Bank of England to meet, even with the help of loans from France and the United States. Britain was faced with the bleak alternatives of setting an almost usurious bank rate—between eight and ten per cent—in order to hold funds in London and check the gold outflow, or abandoning the gold standard; the first choice, which would have further depressed the domestic economy, in which there were now more than two and a half million unemployed, was considered unconscionable, and accordingly, on September 21, 1931, the Bank of England announced suspension of its responsibility to sell gold.

The move hit the financial world like a thunderbolt. So great was the prestige of the pound in 1931 that John Maynard Keynes, the already famous British economist, could say, not wholly in irony, that sterling hadn't left gold, gold had left sterling. In either case, the mooring of the old system was gone, and chaos was the result. Within a few weeks, all the countries on the vast portion of the globe then under British political or economic domination had left the gold standard, most of the other leading currencies had either left gold or been drastically devalued in relation to it, and in the free market the value of the pound in terms of dollars had dropped from $4.86 to around $3.50. Then the dollar itself—the potential new mooring—came loose. In 1933, the United States, compelled by the worst depression in its history, abandoned the gold standard. A year later, it resumed it in a modified form called the gold-exchange standard, under which gold coinage was ended and the Federal Reserve was pledged to sell gold in bar form to other central banks but to no one else—and to sell it at a drastic devaluation of forty-one per cent from the old price. The United States devaluation restored the pound to its old dollar parity, but Britain found it small comfort to be tied securely to a mooring that was now shaky itself. Even so, over the next five years, while beggar-my-neighbor came to be the rule in international finance, the pound did not lose much more ground in relation to other currencies, and when the Second World War broke out, the British government boldly pegged it at $4.03 and imposed controls to keep it there in defiance of the free market. There, for a decade, it remained—but only officially. In the free market of neutral Switzerland, it fluctuated all through the war in reflection of Britain's military fortunes, sinking at the darkest moments to as low as $2.

In the postwar era, the pound has been almost continuously in trouble. The new rules of the game of international finance that were agreed upon at Bretton Woods recognized that the old gold standard had been far too rigid and the virtual paper standard of the nineteen-thirties far too unstable; a compromise accordingly emerged, under which the dollar—the new king of currencies—remained tied to gold under the gold-exchange standard, and the pound, along with the other leading currencies, became tied not to gold but to the dollar, at rates fixed within stated limits. Indeed, the postwar era was virtually ushered in by a devaluation of the pound that was about as drastic in amount as that of 1931, though far less so in its consequences. The pound, like most European currencies, had emerged from Bretton Woods flagrantly overvalued in relation to the shattered economy it represented, and had been kept that way only by government-imposed controls. In the autumn of 1949, therefore, after a year and a half of devaluation rumors, burgeoning black markets in sterling, and gold losses that had reduced the British reserves to a dangerously low level, the pound was devalued from $4.03 to $2.80. With the isolated exceptions of the United States dollar and the Swiss franc, every important non-Communist currency almost instantly followed the pound's example, but this time no drying up of trade, or other chaos, ensued, because the 1949 devaluations, unlike those of 1931 and the years following, were not the uncontrolled attempts of countries riddled by depression to gain a competitive advantage at any cost but merely represented recognition by the war-devastated countries that they had recovered to the point where they could survive relatively free international competition without artificial props. In fact, world trade, instead of drying up, picked up sharply. But even at the new, more rational evaluation the pound continued its career of hairbreadth escapes. Sterling crises of varying magnitudes were weathered in 1952, 1955, 1957, and 1961. In its unsentimental and tactless way, the pound—just as by its gyrations in the past it had accurately charted Britain's rise and fall as the greatest of world powers—now, with its nagging recurrent weakness, seemed to be hinting that even such retrenchment as the British had undertaken in 1949 was not enough to suit their reduced circumstances.

And in November, 1964, these hints, with their humiliating implications, were not lost on the British people. The emotional terms in which many of them were thinking about the pound were well illustrated by an exchange that took place in that celebrated forum the letters column of the *Times* when the crisis was at its height. A reader named I. M. D. Little wrote deploring all the breast-beating about the pound and particularly the uneasy whispering about devaluation—a matter that he declared to be an economic rather than a moral issue. Quick as a flash came a reply from a C. S. Hadfield, among others. Was there ever a clearer sign of soulless times, Hadfield demanded, than Little's letter? Devaluation not a moral issue? "Repudiation—for that is what devaluation is, neither more nor less—has become respectable!" Hadfield groaned, in the unmistakable tone, as old in Britain as the pound itself, of the outraged patriot.

In the ten days following the Basel meeting, the first concern of the men at the Federal Reserve Bank of New York was not the pound but the dollar. The American balance-of-payments deficit had now crept up to the alarming rate of almost six billion dollars a year, and it was becoming clear that a rise in the British bank rate, if it should be unmatched by American action, might merely shift some of the speculative attack from the pound to the dollar. Hayes and Coombs and the Washington monetary authorities—William McChesney Martin, chairman of the Federal Reserve Board, Secretary of the Treasury Douglas Dillon, and Under-Secretary of the Treasury Robert Roosa—came to agree that if the British should raise their rate the Federal Reserve would be compelled, in self-defense, to competitively raise *its* rate above the current level of three and a half per cent. Hayes had numerous telephone conversations on this delicate point with his London counterpart, Lord Cromer. A deep-dyed aristocrat—a godson of King George V and a grandson of Sir Evelyn Baring, later the first Earl of Cromer (who, as the British agent in Egypt, was Chinese Gordon's nemesis in 1884–85)—Lord Cromer was also a banker of universally acknowledged brilliance and, at forty-three, the youngest man, as far as anyone could remember, ever to direct the fortunes of the Bank of England; he and Hayes, in the course of their frequent meetings at Basel and elsewhere, had become warm friends.

During the afternoon of Friday the twentieth, at any rate, the Federal Reserve Bank had a chance to show its good intentions by doing some front-line fighting for the pound. The breather provided by the London closing proved to be illusory; five o'clock in London was only noon in New York, and insatiable speculators were able to go on selling pounds for several more hours in the New York market, with the result that the trading room of the Federal Reserve Bank temporarily replaced that of the Bank of England as the command post for the defense. Using as their ammunition British dollars—or, more precisely, United States dollars lent to Britain under the swap agreements—the Federal Reserve's traders staunchly held the pound at or above $2.7825, at ever-increasing cost, of course, to the British reserves. Mercifully, after the New York closing the battle did not follow the sun to San Francisco and on around the world to Tokyo. Evidently, the attackers had had their fill, at least for the time being.

What followed was one of those strange modern weekends in which weighty matters are discussed and weighty decisions taken among men who are ostensibly sitting around relaxing in various parts of the world. Wilson, Brown, and Callaghan were at Chequers, the Prime Minister's country estate, taking part in a conference that had originally been scheduled to cover the subject of national-defense policy. Lord Cromer was at his country place in Westerham, Kent. Martin, Dillon, and Roosa were at their offices or their homes, in and around Washington. Coombs was at his home, in Green Village, New Jersey, and Hayes was visiting friends of his elsewhere in New Jersey. At Chequers, Wilson and his two financial ministers, leaving the military brass to confer about defense policy with each other, adjourned to an upstairs gallery to tackle the sterling crisis; in order to bring Lord Cromer into their deliberations, they kept a telephone circuit open to him in Kent, using a scrambler system when they talked on it, so as to avoid interception of their words by their unseen enemies the speculators. Sometime on Saturday, the British reached their decision. Not only would they raise the bank rate, and raise it two per cent above its current level—to seven per cent—but, in defiance of custom, they would do so the first thing Monday morning, rather than wait for another Thursday to roll around. For one thing, they reasoned, to postpone action until Thursday would mean three and a half more business days during which the deadly drain of British reserves would almost certainly continue and might well accelerate; for another, the sheer shock of the deliberate violation of custom would serve to dramatize the government's determination. The decision, once taken, was communicated by British intermediaries in Washington to the American monetary officials there, and relayed to Hayes and Coombs in New Jersey. Those two, knowing that the agreed-upon plan for a concomitant rise in the New York bank rate would now have to be put into effect as quickly as possible, got to work on the telephone lining up a Monday-afternoon meeting of the Federal Reserve Bank's board of directors, without whose initiative the rate could not be changed. Hayes, a man who sets great store by politeness, has since said, with considerable chagrin, that he fears he was the despair of his hostess that weekend; not only was he on the telephone most of the time but he was prevented by the circumstances from giving the slightest explanation of his unseemly behavior.

What had been done—or, rather, was about to be done—in Britain was plenty to flutter the dovecotes of international finance. Since the beginning of the First World War, the bank rate there had never gone higher than seven per cent and had only occasionally gone that high; as for a bank-rate change on a day other than Thursday, the last time that had occurred, ominously enough, was in 1931. Anticipating lively action at the London opening, which would take place at about 5 A.M. New York time, Coombs went to Liberty Street on Sunday afternoon in order to spend the night at the bank and be on hand when the transatlantic doings began. As an overnight companion he had a man who found it advisable to sleep at the bank so often that he habitually kept a packed suitcase in his office—Thomas J. Roche, at that time the senior foreign-exchange officer. Roche welcomed his boss to the sleeping quarters—a row of small, motel-like rooms on the eleventh floor, each equipped with maple furniture, Old New York prints, a telephone, a clock radio, a bathrobe, and a shaving kit—and the two men discussed the weekend's developments for a while before turning in. Shortly before five in the morning, their radios woke them, and, after a breakfast provided by the night staff, they repaired to the foreign-exchange trading room, on the seventh floor, to man their fluoroscope.

At five-ten, they were on the phone to the Bank of England, getting the news. The bank-rate rise had been announced promptly at the opening of the London markets, to the accompaniment of great excitement; later Coombs was to learn that the Government Broker's entrance into the Stock Exchange, which is usually the occasion for a certain hush, had this time been greeted with such an uproar that he had had difficulty making his news known. As for the first market reaction of the pound, it was (one commentator said later) like that of a race horse to dope; in the ten minutes following the bank-rate announcement it shot up to $2.7869, far above its Friday closing. A few minutes later, the early-rising New Yorkers were on the phone to the Deutsche Bundesbank, the central bank of West Germany, in Frankfurt, and the Swiss National Bank, in Zurich, sounding out Continental reaction. It was equally good. Then they were back in touch with the Bank of England, where things were looking better and better. The speculators against the pound were on the run, rushing now to cover their short sales, and by the time the first gray light began to show in the windows on Liberty Street, Coombs had heard that the pound was being quoted in London at $2.79—its best price since July, when the crisis started.

It went on that way all day. "Seven per cent will drag money from the moon," a Swiss banker commented, paraphrasing the great Bagehot, who had said, in his earthbound, Victorian way, "Seven per cent will pull gold out of the ground." In London, the sense of security was so strong that it allowed a return to political bickering as usual; in Parliament, Reginald Maudling, the chief economic authority of the out-of-office Conservatives, took the occasion to remark that there wouldn't have been a crisis in the first place but for the actions of the Labour Government, and Chancellor of the Exchequer Callaghan replied, with deadly politeness, "I must remind the honorable gentleman that he told us [recently] we had inherited his problems." Everybody was clearly breathing easier. As for the Bank of England, so great was the sudden clamor for pounds that it saw a chance to replenish its depleted supply of dollars, and for a time that afternoon it actually felt confident enough to switch sides in the market, buying dollars with pounds at just below $2.79. In New York, the mood persisted after the London closing. It was with a clear conscience about the pound that the directors of the Federal Reserve Bank of New York could—and, that afternoon, did—carry out their plan to raise their lending rate from three and a half per cent to four per cent. Coombs has since said, "The feeling here on Monday afternoon was: They've done it—they've pulled through again. There was a general sigh of relief. The sterling crisis seemed to be over."

It wasn't, though. "I remember that the situation changed very fast on Tuesday the twenty-fourth," Hayes has said. That day's opening found the pound looking firm at $2.7875. Substantial buying orders for pounds were coming in now from Germany, and the day ahead looked satisfactory. So things continued until 6 A.M. in New York—noon on the Continent. It is around then that the various bourses of Europe—including the most important ones, in Paris and Frankfurt—hold the meetings at which they set the day's rate for each currency, for the purpose of settling transactions in stocks and bonds that involve foreign currency, and these price-fixing sessions are bound to influence the money markets, since they give a clear indication of the most influential Continental sentiment in regard to each currency. The bourse rates set for the pound that day were such as to show a renewed, and pronounced, lack of confidence. At the same time, it appeared subsequently, money dealers everywhere, and particularly in Europe, were having second thoughts about the manner of the bank-rate rise the previous day. At first, taken by surprise, they had reacted enthusiastically, but now, it seemed, they had belatedly decided that the making of the announcement on Monday indicated that Britain was losing its grip. "What would it connote if the British were to play a Cup final on Sunday?" a European banker is said to have asked a colleague. The only possible answer was that it would connote panic in Albion.

The effect of these second thoughts was an astonishingly drastic turnabout in market action. In New York between eight and nine, Coombs, in the trading room, watched with a sinking heart as a tranquil pound market collapsed into a rout. Selling orders in unheard-of quantities were coming from everywhere. The Bank of England, with the courage of desperation, advanced its last-line trench from $2.7825 to $2.7860, and, by constant intervention, held the pound there. But it was clear that the cost would soon become too high; a few minutes after 9 A.M. New York time, Coombs calculated that Britain was losing reserves at the unprecedented, and unsupportable, rate of a million dollars a minute.

Hayes, arriving at the bank shortly after nine, had hardly sat down at his desk before this unsettling news reached him from the seventh floor. "We're in for a hurricane," Coombs told him, and went on to say that the pressure on sterling was now mounting so fast that there was a real likelihood that Britain might be forced either to devalue or to impose a sweeping—and, for many reasons, unacceptable—system of exchange controls before the week was out. Hayes immediately telephoned the governors of the leading European central banks—some of whom, because not all the national markets had yet felt the full weight of the crisis, were startled to hear exactly how grave the situation was—and pleaded with them not to exacerbate the pressure on both the pound and the dollar by raising their own bank rates. (His job was scarcely made easier by the fact that he had to admit that his own bank had just raised *its* rate.) Then he asked Coombs to come up to his office. The pound, the two men agreed, now had its back to the wall; the British bank-rate rise had obviously failed of its purpose, and at the million-a-minute rate of loss Britain's well of reserves would be dry in less than five business days. The one hope now lay in amassing, within a matter of hours, or within a day or so at the most, a huge bundle of credit from outside Britain to enable the Bank of England to survive the attack and beat it back. Such rescue bundles had been assembled just a handful of times before—for Canada in 1962, for Italy earlier in 1964, and for Britain in 1961—but this time, it was clear, a much bigger bundle than any of those would be needed. The central-banking world was faced not so much with an opportunity for building a milestone in the short history of international monetary coöperation as with the necessity for doing so.

Two other things were clear—that, in view of the dollar's troubles, the United States could not hope to rescue the pound unassisted, and that, the dollar's troubles notwithstanding, the United States, with all its economic might, would have to join the Bank of England in initiating any rescue operation. As a first step, Coombs suggested that the Federal Reserve standby credit to the Bank of England ought to be increased forthwith from five hundred million dollars to seven hundred and fifty million. Unfortunately, fast action on this proposal was hampered by the fact that, under the Federal Reserve Act, any such move could be made only by decision of a Federal Reserve System committee, whose members were scattered all over the country. Hayes conferred by long-distance telephone (all around the world, wires were now humming with news of the pound's extremity) with the Washington monetary contingent, Martin, Dillon, and Roosa, none of whom disagreed with Coombs' view of what had to be done, and as a result of these discussions a call went out from Martin's office to members of the key committee, called the Open Market Committee, for a meeting by telephone at three o'clock that afternoon. Roosa, at the Treasury, suggested that the United States' contribution to the kitty could be further increased by arranging for a two-hundred-and-fifty-million-dollar loan from the Export-Import Bank, a Treasury-owned and Treasury-financed institution in Washington. Hayes and Coombs were naturally in favor of this, and Roosa set in motion the bureaucratic machinery to unlock that particular vault—a process that, he warned, would certainly take until evening.

As the early afternoon passed in New York, with the millions of dollars continuing to drain, minute by minute, from Britain's reserves, Hayes and Coombs, along with their Washington colleagues, were busy planning the next step. If the swap increase and the Export-Import Bank loan should come through, the United States credits would amount to a billion dollars all told; now, in consultation with the beleaguered garrison at the Bank of England, the Federal Reserve Bank men began to believe that, in order to make the operation effective, the other leading central banks—spoken of in central-banking shorthand as "the Continent," even though they include the Banks of Canada and Japan—would have to be asked to put up additional credits on the order of one and a half billion dollars, or possibly even more. Such a sum would make the Continent, collectively, a bigger contributor to the cause than the United States—a fact that Hayes and Coombs realized might not sit too well with the Continental bankers and their governments.

At three o'clock, the Open Market Committee held its telephone meeting—twelve men sitting at their desks in six cities, from New York to San Francisco. The members heard Coombs' dry, unemotional voice describing the situation and making his recommendation. They were quickly convinced. In no more than fifteen minutes, they had voted unanimously to increase the swap credit to seven hundred and fifty million dollars, on condition that proportional credit assistance could be obtained from other central banks.

————

By late afternoon, tentative word had come from Washington that prospects for the Export-Import Bank loan looked good, and that more definite word could be expected before midnight. So the one billion dollars in United States credits appeared to be virtually in the bag. It remained to tackle the Continent. It was night now in Europe, so nobody there could be tackled; the zero hour, then, was Continental opening time the next day, and the crucial period for the fate of the pound would be the few hours after that. Hayes, after leaving instructions for a bank car to pick him up at his home, in New Canaan, Connecticut, at four o'clock in the morning, took his usual commuting train from Grand Central shortly after five. He has since expressed a certain regret that he proceeded in such a routine way at such a dramatic moment. "I left the bank rather reluctantly," he says. "In retrospect, I guess I wish I hadn't. I don't mean as a practical matter—I was just as useful at home, and, as a matter of fact, I ended up spending most of the evening on the phone with Charlie Coombs, who stayed at the bank—but just because something like that doesn't happen every day in a banker's life. I'm a creature of habit, I guess. Besides, it's something of a tenet of mine to insist on keeping a proper balance between private and professional life." Although Hayes does not say so, he may have been thinking of something else, too. It can safely be said to be something of a tenet of central-bank presidents or governors not to sleep at their places of business. If word were ever to get out that the methodical Hayes was doing so at a time like this, he may have reasoned, it might well be considered just as much a sign of panic as a British bank-rate rise on a Monday.

Meanwhile, Coombs was making another night of it on Liberty Street; he had gone home the previous night because the worst had momentarily appeared to be over, but now he stayed on after regular work hours with Roche, who hadn't been home since the previous weekend. Toward midnight, Coombs received confirmation of the Export-Import Bank's two-hundred-and-fifty-million-dollar credit, which had arrived from Washington during the evening, as promised. So now everything was braced for the morning's effort. Coombs again installed himself in one of the uninspiring eleventh-floor cubicles, and, after a final marshalling of the facts that would be needed for the job of persuading the Continental bankers, set his clock radio for three-thirty and went to bed. A Federal Reserve man with a literary bent and a romantic temperament was later moved to draw a parallel between the Federal Reserve Bank that night and the British camp on the eve of the Battle of Agincourt in Shakespeare's version, in which King Henry mused so eloquently on how participation in the coming action would serve to ennoble even the vilest of the troops, and how gentlemen safe in bed at home would later think themselves accursed that they had not been at the battle scene. Coombs, a practical man, had no such high-flown opinion of his situation; even so, as he dozed fitfully, waiting for morning to reach Europe, he was well aware that the events he was taking part in were like nothing that had ever happened in banking before.

II

So that evening, Tuesday, November 24, 1964, Hayes arrived at his home, in New Canaan, Connecticut, at about six-thirty, exactly as usual, having inexorably taken his usual 5:09 from Grand Central. Hayes was a tall, slim, soft-spoken man of fifty-four with keen eyes framed by owlish round spectacles, with a slightly schoolmasterish air and a reputation for unflappability. By so methodically going through familiar motions at such a time, he realized with amusement, he must seem to his colleagues to be living up to his reputation rather spectacularly. At his house, a former caretaker's cottage of circa 1840 that the Hayeses had bought and remodelled twelve years earlier, he was greeted, as usual, by his wife, a pretty and vivacious woman of Anglo-Italian descent named Vilma but always called Bebba, who loves to travel, has almost no interest in banking, and is the daughter of the late Metropolitan Opera baritone Thomas Chalmers. Since at that time of year it was completely dark when Hayes got home, he decided to forgo a favorite early-evening unwinding activity of his—walking to the top of a grassy slope beside the house which commands a fine view across the Sound to Long Island. Anyway, he was not really in a mood to unwind; instead, he felt keyed up, and decided he might as well stay that way overnight, since the car from the bank was scheduled to call at his door so early the next morning to take him to work.

During dinner, Hayes and his wife discussed subjects like the fact that their son, Tom, who was a senior at Harvard, would be arriving home the following day for his Thanksgiving recess. Afterward, Hayes settled down in an armchair to read for a while. In banking circles, he is thought of as a scholarly, intellectual type, and, indeed, he *is* scholarly and intellectual in comparison with most bankers; even so, his extra-banking reading tends to be not constant and all-embracing, as his wife's is, but sporadic, capricious, and intensive—everything about Napoleon for a while, perhaps, then a dry period, then a binge on, say, the Civil War. Just then, he was concentrating on the island of Corfu, where he and Mrs. Hayes were planning to spend some time. But before he had got very far into his latest Corfu book he was called to the telephone. The call was from the bank. There were new developments, which Coombs thought President Hayes ought to be kept abreast of.

To recapitulate in brief: drastic action to save the pound, which the Federal Reserve Bank not only would be intimately involved in but would actually join in initiating, was going to be taken by the government banks—or central banks, as they are more commonly called—of the non-Communist world's leading nations as soon as possible after the next morning's opening of the London and Continental financial markets, which would occur between 4 and 5 A.M. New York time. Britain was face to face with bankruptcy, the reasons being that a huge deficit in its international accounts over the previous months had resulted in concomitant losses in the gold and dollar reserves held by the Bank of England; that worldwide fear lest the newly elected Labour Government decide, or be forced, to ease the situation by devaluing the pound from its dollar parity of about $2.80 to some substantially lower figure had caused a flood of selling of pounds by hedgers and speculators in the international money markets; that the Bank of England, fulfilling an international obligation to sustain the pound at a free-market price no lower than $2.78, had been losing millions of dollars a day from its reserves, which now stood at about two billion dollars, their lowest point in many years.

The remaining hope lay in amassing, in a matter of hours before it would be too late, an unheard-of sum in short-term dollar credits to Britain from the central banks of the world's rich nations. With such credits at its disposal, the Bank of England would presumably be able to buy up pounds so aggressively that the speculative attack could be absorbed, contained, and finally beaten back, giving Britain time to set its economic affairs in order. Just what the sum necessary for rescue should be was an open question, but earlier that day the monetary authorities of the United States and Britain had concluded that it would have to be at least two billion dollars, and perhaps even more. The United States, through the Federal Reserve Bank of New York and the Treasury-owned Export-Import Bank, in Washington, had that day committed itself to one billion; the task that remained was to persuade the other leading central banks—habitually spoken of in the central-banking world as "the Continent," even though they include the Banks of Canada and Japan—to lend more than a billion in addition.

Nothing of the kind had ever been asked of the Continent before, through the swap network or any other way. In September, 1964, the Continent had come through with its biggest collective emergency credit so far—half a billion dollars to the Bank of England for use in defending the pound, already embattled then. Now, with this half-billion loan still outstanding and the pound in far worse straits, the Continent was about to be called upon for more than twice that sum— perhaps five times that sum. Obviously, the spirit of coöperation, if not the quality of mercy, was about to be strained. So Hayes' musings that evening may well have run.

With such portentous matters churning around in his head, Hayes found it hard to keep his mind on Corfu. Besides, the prospect of the bank car's arrival at four o'clock made him feel that he should go to bed early. As he prepared to do so, Mrs. Hayes commented that since he would have to get up in the middle of the night, she supposed she ought to feel sorry for him but since he was obviously looking forward with keen anticipation to whatever it was that would get him up at that hour, she envied him instead.

Down on Liberty Street, Coombs slept fitfully until he was awakened by the clock radio in his room at about three-thirty New York time—that is to say, eight-thirty London time and nine-thirty farther east on the European Continent. A series of foreign-exchange crises involving Europe had so accustomed him to the time differential that he was inclined to think in terms of the European day, referring casually to 8 A.M. in New York as "lunchtime," and 9 A.M. as "midafternoon." So when he got up it was, in his terms, "morning," despite the stars that were shining over Liberty Street. Coombs got dressed, went to his office, on the tenth floor, where he had some breakfast provided by the bank's regular night kitchen staff, and began placing telephone calls to the various leading central banks of the non-Communist world. All the calls were put through by one telephone operator, who handles the Federal Reserve Bank's switchboard during off hours, and all of them were eligible for a special government-emergency priority that the bank's officers are entitled to claim, but on this occasion it did not have to be used, because at four-fifteen, when Coombs began his telephoning, the transatlantic circuits were almost entirely clear.

The calls were made essentially to lay the groundwork for what was to come. The morning news from the Bank of England, obtained in one of the first calls from Liberty Street, was that conditions were unchanged from the previous day: the speculative attack on the pound was continuing unabated, and the Bank of England was sustaining the pound's price at $2.7860 by throwing still more of its reserves on the market. Coombs had reason to believe that when the New York foreign-exchange market opened, some five hours later, vast additional quantities of pounds would be thrown on the market on this side of the Atlantic, and more British dollars and gold would have to be spent. He conveyed this alarming intelligence to his counterparts at such institutions as the Deutsche Bundesbank, in Frankfurt; the Banque de France, in Paris; the Banca d'Italia, in Rome; and the Bank of Japan, in Tokyo. (In the last case, the officers had to be reached at their homes, for the fourteen-hour time difference made it already past 6 P.M. in the Orient.) Then, coming to the crux of the matter, Coombs informed the representatives of the various banks that they were soon to be asked, in behalf of the Bank of

England, for a loan far bigger than any they had ever been asked for before. "Without going into specific figures, I tried to make the point that it was a crisis of the first magnitude, which many of them still didn't realize," Coombs has said. An officer of the Bundesbank, who knew as much about the extent of the crisis as anyone outside London, Washington, and New York, has said that in Frankfurt they were "mentally prepared"—or "braced" might be a better word—for the huge touch that was about to be put on them, but that right up to the time of Coombs' call they had been hoping the speculative attack on the pound would subside of its own accord, and even after the call they had no idea how much they might be asked for. In any event, as soon as Coombs was off the wire the Bundesbank's governor called a board of managers' meeting, and, as things turned out, the meeting was to remain in session all day long.

Still, all this was preparatory. Actual requests, in specific amounts, had to be made by the head of one central bank of the head of another. At the time Coombs was making his softening-up calls, the head of the Federal Reserve Bank was in the bank's limousine, somewhere between New Canaan and Liberty Street, and the bank's limousine, in flagrant nonconformity with the James Bond style of high-level international dealings, was not equipped with a telephone.

Hayes, the man being awaited, had been president of the Federal Reserve Bank of New York for a little over eight years, having been chosen for the job, to his own and almost everyone else's bewilderment, not from some position of comparable eminence or from the Federal Reserve's own ranks but from among the swarming legions of New York commercial-bank vice-presidents. Unorthodox as the appointment seemed at the time, in retrospect it seems providential. A study of Hayes' early life and youthful career gives the impression that everything was somehow intended to prepare him for dealing with this sort of international monetary crisis, just as the life of a writer or a painter sometimes seems to have consisted primarily of preparation for the execution of a single work of art. If Divine Providence, or perhaps its financial department, when the huge sterling crisis was imminent, had needed an assessment of Hayes' qualifications for coping with this task and had hired the celestial equivalent of an executive recruiter to report on him, the dossier might have read something like this:

"Born in Ithaca, New York, on July 4, 1910; grew up mostly in New York City. Father a professor of Constitutional law at Cornell, later a Manhattan investment counsellor; mother a former schoolteacher, enthusiastic suffragette, settlement-house worker, and political liberal. Both parents birdwatchers. Family atmosphere intellectual, freethinking, and public-spirited. Attended private schools in New York City and Massachusetts and was usually his school's top-ranking student. Then went to Harvard (freshman year only) *and* Yale (three years: mathematics major, Phi Beta Kappa in junior year, ineffectual oar on class crew, graduated 1930 as top B.A. of class). Studied at New College, Oxford, as Rhodes Scholar 1931–33; there became firm Anglophile, and wrote thesis on 'Federal Reserve Policy and the Working of the Gold Standard in the Years 1923–30,' although he had no thought of ever joining the Federal Reserve. Wishes now he had the thesis, in case it contains blinding youthful illuminations, but neither he nor New College can find it. Entered New York commercial banking in 1933, and rose slowly but steadily (1938 annual salary twenty-seven hundred dollars). Attained title (albeit feeble title) of assistant secretary at New York Trust Company in 1942; after a Navy stint, in 1947 became an assistant vice-president and two years later head of New York Trust's foreign department despite total lack of previous experience in foreign banking. Apparently learned fast; astounded his colleagues and superiors, and gained reputation among them as foreign-exchange wizard by predicting precise amount of 1949 pound devaluation ($4.03 to $2.80) a few weeks before it occurred.

"Was appointed president of Federal Reserve Bank of New York in 1956, to his utter astonishment and that of New York banking community, most of which had never heard of this rather shy man. Reacted calmly by taking his family on a two-month vacation in Europe. The consensus now is that Federal Reserve Bank's directors had almost implausible prescience, or luck, in picking a foreign-exchange expert just when the dollar was weakening and international monetary coöperation becoming crucially important. Is liked by European central bankers, who call him Al (which often comes out sounding more like All). Earns seventy-five thousand dollars a year, making him the second-highest-paid federal official after the President of the United States, Federal Reserve Bank salaries being intended to be more or less competitive in banking terms rather than in government-employee terms. Is very tall and very thin. Tries to observe regular commuting hours and keep his private life sacrosanct, as a matter of principle; considers regular evening work at an office 'outrageous.' Complains that his son has a low opinion of business; attributes this to 'reverse snobbery'—but even then remains calm.

"Conclusion: this is the very man for the job of representing the United States' central bank in a sterling crisis."

And, indeed, Hayes readily fits the picture of a perfectly planned and perfectly tooled piece of machinery to perform a certain complex task, but there are other sides to him, and his character contains as many paradoxes as the next man's. Although hardly anyone in banking ever tries to describe

Hayes without using the words "scholarly" and "intellectual," Hayes tends to think of himself as an indifferent scholar and intellectual but an effective man of action, and on the latter score the events of November 25, 1964, seem to bear him out. Although in some ways he is the complete banker—in conformity with H. G. Wells' notion of such a banker, he seems to "take money for granted as a terrier takes rats," and to be devoid of philosophical curiosity about it—he has a distinctly unbankerlike philosophical curiosity about almost everything else. And although casual acquaintances sometimes pronounce him dull, his close friends speak of a rare capacity for enjoyment and an inner serenity that seem to make him immune to the tensions and distractions that fragment the lives of so many of his contemporaries. Doubtless the inner serenity was put to a severe test as Hayes rode in the bank car toward Liberty Street. When he arrived at his desk at about five-thirty, Hayes' first act was to punch Coombs' button on his interoffice phone and get the foreign-department chief's latest appraisal of the situation. He learned that, as he had expected, the Bank of England's sickening dollar drain was continuing unabated. Worse than that, though; Coombs said his contacts with local bankers who were also on emergency early-morning vigil (men in the foreign departments of the huge commercial banks like the Chase Manhattan and the First National City) indicated that overnight there had accumulated a fantastic pile of orders to unload pounds on the New York market as soon as it opened. The Bank of England, already almost inundated, could expect a new tidal wave from New York to hit in four hours. The need for haste thus became even more urgent. Hayes and Coombs agreed that the project of putting together an international package of credits to Britain should be announced as soon as possible after the New York opening—perhaps as early as ten o'clock. So that the bank would have a single center for all its foreign communications, Hayes decided to forsake his own office—

a spacious one with panelled walls and comfortable chairs grouped around a fireplace—and let Coombs' quarters, down the hall, which were much smaller and more austere but more efficiently arranged, serve as the command post. Once there, he picked up one of three telephones and asked the operator to get him Lord Cromer, at the Bank of England. When the connection was made, the two men—the key figures in the proposed rescue operation—reviewed their plans a final time, checking the sums they had tentatively decided to ask of each central bank and agreeing on who would call whom first.

In the eyes of some people, Hayes and Lord Cromer make an oddly assorted pair. Besides being a deep-dyed aristocrat, George Rowland Stanley Baring, third Earl of Cromer, is a deep-dyed banker. A scion of the famous London merchant bank of Baring Brothers, the third Earl and godson of a monarch went to Eton and Trinity College, Cambridge, and spent twelve years as a managing director of his family's bank and then two years—from 1959 to 1961—as Britain's economic minister and chief representative of his country's Treasury in Washington. If Hayes had acquired his mastery of the arcana of international banking by patient study, Lord Cromer, who is no scholar, acquired his by heredity, instinct, or osmosis. If Hayes, despite his unusual physical stature, could easily be overlooked in a crowd, Lord Cromer, who is of average height but debonair and dashing, would cut a figure anywhere. If Hayes is inclined to be a bit hesitant about casual intimacies, Lord Cromer is known for his hearty manner, and has—doubtless unintentionally—both flattered and obscurely disappointed many American bankers who have been awed by his title by quickly encouraging them to call him Rowley. "Rowley is very self-confident and decisive," an American banker has said. "He's never afraid to barge in, because he's convinced of the reasonableness of his own position. But then he's a reasonable man. He's the kind of man who in a crisis would be able to grab the telephone and do something about it." This banker confesses that until November 25, 1964, he had not thought Hayes was that kind of man.

Beginning at about six o'clock that morning, Hayes did grab the phone, right along with Lord Cromer. One after another, the leading central bankers of the world—among them President Karl Blessing, of the Deutsche Bundesbank; Dr. Guido Carli, of the Bank of Italy; Governor Jacques Brunet, of the Bank of France; Dr. Walter Schwegler, of the Swiss National Bank; and Governor Per Åsbrink, of the Swedish Riksbank—picked up *their* phones and discovered, some of them with considerable surprise, the degree of gravity that the sterling crisis had reached in the past day, the fact that the United States had committed itself to a short-term loan of one billion dollars, and that they were being asked to dig deep into their own nations' reserves to help tide sterling over. Some first heard all this from Hayes, some from Lord Cromer; in either case, they heard it not from a casual or official acquaintance but from a fellow-member of that esoteric fraternity the Basel club. Hayes, whose position as representative of the one country that had already pledged a huge sum cast him almost automatically as the leader of the operation, was careful to make it clear in each of his calls that his part in the proceedings was to put the weight of the Federal Reserve behind a request that formally came from the Bank of England. "The pound's situation is critical, and I understand the Bank of England is requesting a credit line of two hundred and fifty million dollars from you," he would say, in his calm way, to one Continental central-bank governor or another. "I'm sure you understand that this is a situation where we all have to stand together." (He and Coombs always spoke English, of course. Despite the fact that he had recently been taking French refresher lessons, and that at Yale he made one of the most impressive academic records in memory, Hayes doggedly remained a dub at languages and still did not trust himself to carry on an important business conversation in anything but English.) In those cases in which he was on particularly close terms with his Continental counterpart, he spoke more informally, using a central-bankers' jargon in which the conventional numerical unit is a million dollars. Hayes would say smoothly in such cases, "Do you think you can come in for, say, a hundred and fifty?" Regardless of the degree of formality of the approach Hayes made, the first response, he says, was generally cageyness, not unmixed with shock. "Is it really as bad as all that, Al? We were still hoping that the pound would recover on its own" is the kind of thing he recalls having heard several times. When Hayes assured them that it was indeed as bad as all that, and that the pound would certainly not recover on its own, the usual response was something like "We'll have to see what we can do and then call you back." Some of the Continental central bankers have said that what impressed them most about Hayes' first call was not so much what he said as when he said it. Realizing that it was still well before dawn in New York, and knowing Hayes' addiction to what are commonly thought of as bankers' hours, these Europeans perceived that things must be grave the moment they heard his voice. As soon as Hayes had broken the ice at each Continental bank, Coombs would take over and get down to details with his counterparts.

The first round of calls left Hayes, Lord Cromer, and their associates on Liberty and Threadneedle Streets relatively hopeful. Not one bank had given them a flat no—not even, to their delight, the Bank of France, although French policy had already begun moving sharply away from coöperation with Britain and the United States in monetary matters, among others. Furthermore, several governors had surprised them by suggesting that their countries' subscriptions to the loan might actually be bigger than those suggested. With this encouragement, Hayes and Lord Cromer decided to raise their sights. They had originally been aiming for credits of two and a half billion dollars; now, on reconsideration, they saw that there was a chance for three billion. "We decided to up the ante a little here and there," Hayes says. "There was no way of knowing precisely what sum would be the least that would do the job of turning the tide. We knew we would be relying to a large extent on the psychological effect of our announcement—assuming we would be able to make the announcement. Three seemed to us a good, round figure."

But difficulties lay ahead, and the biggest difficulty, it became clear as the return calls from the various banks began to come in, was to get the thing done quickly. The hardest point to convey, Hayes and Coombs found, was that each passing minute meant a further loss of a million dollars or more to the British reserves, and that if normal channels were followed the loans would unquestionably come too late to avert devaluation of the pound. Some of the central banks were required by law to consult their governments before making a commitment and some were not, but even those that were not insisted on doing so, as a courtesy; this took time, especially since more than one Finance Minister, unaware that he was being sought to approve an enormous loan on an instant's notice, with little evidence of the necessity for it beyond the assurance of Lord Cromer and Hayes, was temporarily unavailable. (One happened to be engaged in debate in his country's parliament.) And even in cases where the Finance Minister was at hand, he was sometimes reluctant to act in such a shotgun way. Governments move more deliberately in money matters than central bankers do. Some of the Finance Ministers said, in effect, that upon proper submission of a balance sheet of the Bank of England, along with a formal written application for the emergency credit, they would gladly consider the matter. Furthermore, some of the central banks themselves showed a maddening inclination to stand on ceremony. The foreign-exchange chief of one bank is said to have replied to the request by saying, "Well, isn't this convenient! We happen to have a board meeting scheduled for tomorrow. We'll take the matter up then, and afterward we'll get in touch with you." The reply of Coombs, who happened to be the man on the wire in New York, is not recorded in substance, but its manner is reported to have been uncharacteristically vehement. Even Hayes' celebrated imperturbability was shaken a time or two, or so those who were present have said; his tone remained as calm and even as ever, but its volume rose far above the usual level.

The problems that the Continental central banks faced in meeting the challenge are well exemplified by the situation at the richest and most powerful of them, the Deutsche Bundesbank. Its board of managers was already sitting in emergency session as a result of Coombs' early call when another New York call—this one from Hayes to President Blessing—gave the Bundesbank its first indication of exactly how much it was being asked to put up. The amounts the various central banks were asked for that morning have never been made public, but, on the basis of what *has* become known, it is reasonable to assume that the Bundesbank was asked for half a billion dollars—the highest quota of the lot, and certainly the largest sum that any central bank other than the Federal Reserve had ever been called upon to supply to another on a few hours' notice. Hard on the heels of Hayes' call conveying this jarring information, Blessing heard from Lord Cromer, in London, who confirmed everything that Hayes had said about the seriousness of the crisis and repeated the request. Wincing a bit, perhaps, the Bundesbank managers agreed in principle that the thing had to be done. But right there their problems began. Proper procedure must be adhered to, Blessing and his aides decided. Before taking any action, they must consult with their economic partners in the European Common Market and the Bank for International Settlements, and the key man to be consulted, since he was then serving as president of the Bank for International Settlements, was Dr. Marius W. Holtrop, governor of the Bank of the Netherlands, which, of course, was also being asked to contribute. A rush person-to-person call was put through from Frankfurt to Amsterdam. Dr. Holtrop, the Bundesbank managers were informed, wasn't in Amsterdam; by chance, he had taken a train that morning to The Hague to meet his country's Finance Minister for consultation on other matters. For the Bank of the Netherlands to make any such important commitment without the knowledge of its governor was out of the question, and, similarly, the Bank of Belgium, a nation whose monetary policies are linked inextricably with the Netherlands', was reluctant to act until Amsterdam had given its O.K. So for an hour or more, as millions of dollars continued to drain out of the Bank of England and the world monetary order stood in jeopardy, the whole rescue operation was hung up while Dr. Holtrop, crossing the Dutch lowlands by train, or perhaps already in The Hague and tied up in a traffic jam, could not be found.

All this, of course, meant agonizing frustration in New York. As morning began here at last, Hayes' and Coombs' campaign got a boost from Washington. The leading government monetary authorities—Martin at the Federal Reserve Board, Dillon and Roosa at the Treasury—had all been intimately involved in the previous day's planning for the rescue, and of course part of the planning had been the decision to let the New York bank, as the Federal Reserve System's and the Treasury's normal operating arm in international monetary dealings, serve as campaign headquarters. So the members of the Washington contingent had slept at home and come to their offices at the normal hour. Now, having learned from Hayes of the difficulties that were developing, Martin, Dillon, and Roosa pitched in with transatlantic calls of their own to emphasize the extent of America's concern over the matter. But no number of calls from anywhere could hold back the clock—or, for that matter, find Dr. Holtrop—and Hayes and

Coombs finally had to abandon their idea of having a credit bundle ready in time for an announcement to the world at or near 10 A.M. in New York. And there were other reasons, too, for a fading of the early hopes. As the New York markets opened, the extent of the alarm that had spread around the financial world overnight was only too clearly revealed. The bank's foreign-exchange trading desk, on the seventh floor, reported that the assault on the pound at the New York opening had been fully as terrifying as they had expected, and that the atmosphere in the local exchange market had reached a state not far from panic. From the bank's securities department came an alarming report that the market for United States government bonds was coming under the heaviest pressure in years, reflecting an ominous lack of confidence in the dollar on the part of bond traders. This intelligence served as a grim reminder to Hayes and Coombs of something they knew already—that a fall of the pound in relation to the dollar could quite possibly be followed, in a kind of chain reaction, by a forced devaluation of the dollar in relation to gold, which might cause monetary chaos everywhere. If Hayes and Coombs had been permitting themselves any moments of idle reverie in which to picture themselves simply as good Samaritans, this was just the news to bring them back to reality. And then word arrived that the wild tales flying around Wall Street showed signs of crystallizing into a single tale, demoralizingly credible because it was so specific. The British government, it was being said, would announce a sterling devaluation at around noon New York time. Here was something that could be authoritatively refuted, at least in respect to timing, since Britain would obviously not devalue while the credit negotiations were under way. Torn between the desire to quell a destructive rumor and the need to keep the negotiations secret until they were concluded, Hayes compromised. He had one of his associates call a few key Wall Street bankers and traders to say, as emphatically as possible, that the latest devaluation rumor was, to his firm knowledge, false. "Can you be more specific?" the associate was asked, and he replied, because there was nothing else he could reply, "No, I can't."

This unsupported word was something, but it was not enough; the foreign-exchange and bond markets were only momentarily reassured. There were times that morning, Hayes and Coombs now admit, when they put down their telephones, looked at each other across the table in Coombs' office, and wordlessly exchanged the thought: It isn't going to be done in time. But—in the best tradition of melodrama, which sometimes seems to survive stubbornly in nature at a time when it is dead in art—just when things looked darkest, good news began to arrive. Dr. Holtrop had been tracked down in a restaurant in The Hague, where he was having lunch with the Netherlands' Minister of Finance, Dr. J. W. Witteveen; moreover, Dr. Holtrop had endorsed the rescue operation, and as for the matter of consulting his government, *that* was no problem, since the responsible representative of his government was sitting across the table from him. The chief obstacle was thus overcome, and after Dr. Holtrop had been reached the difficulties began narrowing down to annoyances like the necessity for continually apologizing to the Japanese for routing them out of bed as midnight arrived and passed in Tokyo. The tide had turned. Before noon in New York, Hayes and Coombs, and Lord Cromer and his deputies in London as well, knew that they had agreement in principle from ten Continental central banks—those in West Germany, Italy, France, the Netherlands, Belgium, Switzerland, Canada, Sweden, Austria, and Japan—and also from the Bank for International Settlements.

There remained the wait while each central bank went through the painfully slow process of completing whatever formalities were required to make its action legal and proper. The epitome of orderliness, the Bundesbank, could not act until it had obtained ratification from the members of its board of directors, most of whom were in provincial outposts scattered around Germany. The two leading Bundesbank deputies divided up the job of calling the absent directors and persuading them to go along—a job that was made more delicate by the fact that the absent directors were being asked to approve something that, in effect, the bank's home office had already undertaken to do. At midafternoon by Continental time, while the two deputies were busy at this exercise in doubletalk, Frankfurt got a new call from London. It was Lord Cromer, no doubt sounding as exasperated as his situation permitted, and what he had to say was that the rate of British reserve loss had become so rapid that the pound could not survive another day. Formalities notwithstanding, it was a case of now or never. (The Bank of England's reserve loss that day has never been announced. The *Economist* later passed along a guess that it may have run to five hundred million dollars, or about a quarter of all that remained in Britain's reserve coffers.) After Lord Cromer's call, the Bundesbank deputies tempered their tact with brevity; they got unanimous approval from the directors, and shortly after five o'clock Frankfurt time they were ready to tell Lord Cromer and Hayes that the Bundesbank was in for the requested half-billion dollars.

Other central banks were coming in, or were already in. Canada and Italy put up two hundred million dollars each, and doubtless were glad to do it, inasmuch as their own currencies had been the beneficiaries of much smaller but otherwise similar international bailout operations in 1962 and earlier in 1964, respectively. If a subsequent report in the London *Times* is to be accepted, France, Belgium, and the Netherlands, no one of which ever announced the amount of its participation, each contributed two hundred million dollars, too. Switzerland is known to have come through with a hundred and sixty million dollars and Sweden with a hundred million dollars, while Austria, Japan, and the Bank for International Settlements rounded out the bundle with still undisclosed amounts. By lunchtime in New York, it was all over but the shouting, and the last part of the task was to make the shouting as effective as possible to give it the fastest and most forcible impact on the market.

The task brought to the fore another Federal Reserve Bank man, its vice-president in charge of public information, Thomas Olaf Waage. Waage (his name rhymes with "saga") had been present and active in Coombs' office almost all morning, constantly on the phone as liaison man with Washington. A born-and-bred New Yorker, the son of a Norwegian-born local tug pilot and fishing-boat captain, Waage is a man of broad and unfeigned outside interests— among them opera, Shakespeare, Trollope, and his ancestral heritage, sailing—and one consuming passion, which is striving to convey not only the facts but also the drama, suspense, and excitement of central banking to a skeptical and often glassy-eyed public. In short, a banker who is a hopeless romantic. So now he was overjoyed when Hayes assigned to him the job of preparing a news release that would inform the world, as emphatically as possible, about the rescue operation. While Hayes and Coombs struggled to tie up the loose ends of their package, Waage was busy coördinating timing with his counterparts at the Federal Reserve Board and the Treasury Department in Washington, which would share in the issuing of the American announcement, and at the Bank of England, which, Hayes and Lord Cromer had agreed, would issue a simultaneous announcement of its own. "Two o'clock in the afternoon New York time was the hour we agreed upon for the announcements, when it began to look as if we'd have something to announce by that time," Waage recalls. "That was too late to catch the Continental and London markets that day, of course, but it left the whole afternoon ahead until the New York markets closed, at around five, and if the sterling market could be dramatically reversed here before closing time, chances were the recovery would continue on the Continent and in London next day, when the American markets would be closed for Thanksgiving. As for the amount of the combined credit we were planning to announce, it still stood at three billion dollars. But I remember that a last-minute snag of a particularly embarrassing sort developed. Very late in the game, when we thought the whole package was in hand, Charlie Coombs and I counted up what had been pledged, just to make sure, and we got only two billion eight hundred and fifty million. Apparently, we'd mislaid a hundred and fifty million dollars somewhere. That's just what we'd done—we'd miscalculated. So it was all right."

The package was assembled in time to meet the new schedule, and statements from the Federal Reserve, the Treasury, and the Bank of England duly went out to the news media simultaneously, at 2 P.M. in New York and 7 P.M. in London. As a result of Waage's influence, the American version, though it fell somewhat short of the mood of, say, the last scene of "Die Meistersinger," was nevertheless exceptionally stirring as bank utterances go, speaking with a certain subdued flamboyance of the unprecedented nature of the sum involved and of how the central banks had "moved quickly to mobilize a massive counterattack on speculative selling of the pound." The London release had a different kind of distinction, achieving something of the quintessential Britishness that seems to be reserved for moments of high crisis. It read simply, "The Bank of England have made arrangements under which $3,000M. are made available for the support of sterling."

Apparently, the secrecy of the operation had been successfully preserved and the announcement struck the New York foreign-exchange market all of a heap, because the reaction was as swift and as electric as anyone could have wished. Speculators against the pound decided instantly and with no hesitation that their game was up. Immediately after the announcement, the Federal Reserve Bank put in a bid for pounds at $2.7868—a figure slightly above the level at which the pound had been forcibly maintained all day by the Bank of England. So great was the rush of speculators to get free of their speculative positions by buying pounds that the Federal Reserve Bank found very few pounds for sale at that price. Around two-fifteen, there were a strange and heartening few minutes in which no sterling was available in New York at *any* price. Pounds were eventually offered for sale again at a higher price, and were immediately gobbled up, and thus the price went on climbing all afternoon, to a closing of just above $2.79.

Triumph! The pound was out of immediate danger; the thing had worked. Tributes to the success of the operation began to pour in from everywhere. Even the magisterial *Economist* was to declare shortly, "Whatever other networks break down, it seems, the central bankers [have an] astonishing capacity for instant results. And if theirs is not the most desirable possible mechanism, geared always to short-term support of the status quo, it happens to be the only working one."

So, with the pound riding reasonably high again, the Federal Reserve Bank shut up for Thanksgiving, and the bankers went home. Coombs recalls having drunk a Martini unaccustomedly fast. Hayes, home in New Canaan, found that his son, Tom, had arrived from Harvard. Both his wife and his son noticed that he seemed to be in an unusual state of excitement, and when they asked about it he replied that he had just been through the most completely satisfying day of his entire working career. Pressed for details, he gave them a condensed and simplified account of the rescue operation, keeping constantly in mind the fact that his audience consisted of a wife who had no interest in banking and a son who had a low opinion of business. The reaction he got when his recital was concluded was of a sort that might warm the heart of a Waage, or of any earnest explicator of banking derring-do to the unsympathetic layman. "It was a little confusing at first," Mrs. Hayes has said, "but before you were finished you had us on the edge of our chairs."

Waage, home in Douglaston, told *his* wife of the day's events in *his* characteristic way. "It was St. Crispin's Day," he exclaimed as he burst through his doorway, "and I was with Harry!"

III

Having first become interested in the pound and its perils at the time of the 1964 crisis, I found myself hooked by the subject. Through the subsequent three and a half years, I followed its ups and downs in the American and British press, and at intervals went down to the Federal Reserve Bank to renew my acquaintance with its officers and see what additional enlightenment I could garner. The whole experience was a resounding vindication of Waage's thesis that central banking can be suspenseful.

The pound wouldn't stay saved. A month after the big 1964 crisis, the speculators resumed their assaults, and by the end of that year the Bank of England had used up more than half a billion of its new three-billion-dollar credit. Nor did the coming of the new year bring surcease. In 1965, after a relatively buoyant January, the pound came under pressure again in February. The November credit had been for a term of three months; now, as the term ran out, the nations that had made it decided to extend it for another three months, so that Britain would have more time to put its economy in order. But late in March the British economy was still shaky, the pound was back below $2.79, and the Bank of England was back in the market. In April, Britain announced a tougher budget, and a rally followed, but the rally proved to be short-lived. By early summer, the Bank of England had drawn, and committed to the battle against the speculators, more than a third of the whole three billion. Heartened, the speculators pressed their attack. Late in June, high British officials, let it be known that they now considered the sterling crisis over, but they were whistling in the dark; in July the pound sank again, despite further belt-tightening in the British domestic economy. By the end of July, the world foreign-exchange market had become convinced that a new crisis was shaping up. By late August, the crisis had arrived, and in some ways it was a more dangerous one than that of the previous November. The trouble was the market seemed to believe that the central banks were tired of pouring money into the battle and would now let sterling fall, regardless of the consequences. About that time, I telephoned a leading local foreign-exchange man I know to ask him what he thought of the situation, and he replied, "To my knowledge, the New York market is one hundred per cent convinced that devaluation of sterling is coming this fall—and I don't mean ninety-five per cent, I mean one hundred per cent." Then, on September 11th, I read in the papers that the same group of central banks, this time with the exception of France, had come through with another last-minute rescue package, the amount not being announced at the time—it was subsequently reported to have been around one billion—and over the next few days I watched the market price of the pound rise, little by little, until by the end of the month it was above \$2.80 for the first time in sixteen months.

The central banks had done it again, and somewhat later I went down to the Federal Reserve Bank to learn the details. It was Coombs I saw, and I found him in a sanguine and extraordinarily talkative mood. "This year's operation was entirely different from last year's," he told me. "It was an aggressive move on our part, rather than a last-ditch-defensive one. You see, early this September we came to the conclusion that the pound was grossly oversold—that is, the amount of speculation against it was way out of proportion to what was justified by the economic facts. Actually, during the first eight months of the year, British exports had risen more than five per cent over the corresponding period in 1964, and Britain's 1964 balance-of-payments deficit seemed likely to be cut in half in 1965. Very promising economic progress, and the bearish speculators seemed not to have taken account of it. They had gone right on selling the pound short, on the basis of technical market factors. They were the ones who were in an exposed position now. We decided the time was ripe for an official counterattack."

The counterattack, Coombs went on to explain, was plotted in leisurely fashion this time—not on the telephone but face to face, over the weekend of September 5th in Basel. The Federal Reserve Bank was represented by Coombs, as usual, and also by Hayes, who cut short his long-planned vacation on Corfu to be there. The coup was planned with military precision. It was decided not to announce the amount of the credit package this time, in order to further confuse and disconcert the enemy, the speculators. The place chosen for the launching was the trading room of the Federal Reserve Bank, and the hour chosen was 9 A.M. New York time—early enough for London and the Continent to be still conducting business—on September 10th. At zero hour, the Bank of England fired a preliminary salvo by announcing that new central-bank arrangements would shortly enable "appropriate action" to be taken in the exchange markets. After allowing fifteen minutes for the import of this demurely menacing message to sink in, the Federal Reserve Bank struck. Using, with British concurrence, the new bundle of international credit as its ammunition, it simultaneously placed with all the major banks operating in the New York exchange market bids for sterling totalling nearly thirty million dollars, at the then prevailing rate of $2.7918. Under this pressure, the market immediately moved upward, and the Federal Reserve Bank pursued the movement, raising its bid price step by step. At $2.7934, the bank temporarily ceased operations—partly to see what the market would do on its own, partly just to confuse things. The market held steady, showing that at that level there were now as many independent buyers of sterling as there were sellers, and that the bears—speculators—were losing their nerve. But the bank was far from satisfied; returning vigorously to the market, it bid the price on up to $2.7945 in the course of the day. And then the snowball began to roll by itself—with the results I had read about in my newspapers. "It was a successful bear squeeze," Coombs told me with a certain grim relish, which was easy to sympathize with; I found myself musing that for a banker to rout his opponents, to smite them hip and thigh and drive them to cover, and not for personal or institutional profit but, rather, for the public good, must be a source of rare, unalloyed satisfaction.

I later learned from another banker just how painfully the bears had been squeezed. Margins of credit on currency speculation being what they are—for example, to commit a million dollars against the pound a speculator might need to put up only thirty or forty thousand dollars in cash—most dealers had made commitments running into the tens of millions. When a dealer's commitment was ten million pounds, or twenty-eight million dollars, each change of one-hundredth of a cent in the price of the pound meant a change of a thousand dollars in the value of his account. Between the $2.7918 on September 10th, then, and the $2.8010 that the pound reached on September 29th, such a dealer on the short side of the pound would have lost ninety-two thousand dollars— enough, one might suppose, to make him think twice before selling sterling short again.

An extended period of calm followed. The air of impending crisis that had hung over the exchanges during most of the preceding year disappeared, and for more than six months the world sterling market was sunnier than it had been at any time in recent years. "The battle for the pound sterling is now ended," high British officials (anonymous, and wisely so) announced in November, on the first anniversary of the 1964 rescue. Now, the officials said, "we're fighting the battle for the economy." Apparently, they were winning that battle, too, because when Britain's balance-of-payments position for 1965 was finally calculated, it showed that the deficit had been not merely halved, according to predictions, but *more* than halved. And meanwhile the pound's strength enabled the Bank of England not merely to pay off all its short-term debts to other central banks but also to accumulate in the open market, in exchange for its newly desirable pounds, more than a billion fresh dollars to add to its precious reserves. Thus, between September, 1965, and March, 1966, those reserves rose from two billion six hundred million dollars to three billion six hundred million—a fairly safe figure. And then the pound breezed nicely through a national election campaign—as always, a stormy time for the currency. When I saw Coombs in the spring of 1966, he seemed as cocky and blasé about sterling as an old-time New York Yankee rooter about his team.

I had all but concluded that following the fortunes of the pound was no longer any fun when a new crisis exploded. A seamen's strike contributed to a recurrence of Britain's trade deficit, and in early June of 1966 the quotation was back below $2.79 and the Bank of England was reported to be back in the market spending its reserves on the defense. On June 13th, with something of the insouciance of veteran firemen responding to a routine call, back came the central banks with a new bundle of short-term credits. But these helped only temporarily, and toward the end of July, in an effort to get at the root of the pound's troubles by curing the deficit once and for all, Prime Minister Wilson imposed on the British people the most stringent set of economic restraints ever applied in his country in peacetime—high taxes, a merciless squeeze on credit, a freeze on wages and prices, a cut in government welfare spending, and a limit of a hundred and forty dollars on the annual amount that each Briton could spend on travel abroad. The Federal Reserve, Coombs told me later, helped by moving into the sterling market immediately after the British announcement of the austerity program, and the pound reacted satisfactorily to this prodding. In September, for good measure, the Federal Reserve increased its swap line with the Bank of England from seven hundred and fifty million to one billion three hundred and fifty million dollars. I saw Waage in September, and he spoke warmly of all the dollars that the Bank of England was again accumulating. "Sterling crises have become a bore," the *Economist* remarked at about this time, with the most reassuring sort of British phlegm.

Calm again—and again for just a little more than six months. In April of 1967, Britain was free of short-term debt and had ample reserves. But within a month or so came the first of a series of heartbreaking setbacks. Two consequences of the brief Arab-Israeli war—a huge flow of Arab funds out of sterling into other currencies, and the closing of the Suez Canal, one of Britain's main trade arteries—brought on a new crisis almost overnight. In June, the Bank of England (under new leadership now, for in 1966 Lord Cromer had been succeeded as governor by Sir Leslie O'Brien) had to draw heavily on its swap line with the Federal Reserve, and in July the British government found itself forced to renew the painful economic restraints of the previous year; even so, in September the pound slipped down to $2.7830, its lowest point since the 1964 crisis. I called my foreign-exchange expert to ask why the Bank of England—which in November, 1964, had set its last-line trench at $2.7860, and which, according to its latest statement, now had on hand reserves amounting to more than two and a half billion dollars—was letting the price slide so dangerously near the absolute bottom (short of devaluation) of $2.78. "Well, the situation isn't quite as desperate as the figure suggests," he replied. "The speculative pressure so far isn't anything like as strong as it was in 1964. And the fundamental economic position this year—up to now, at least—is much better. Despite the Middle East war, the austerity program has taken hold. For the first eight months of 1967, Britain's international payments have been nearly in balance. The Bank of England is evidently hoping that this period of weakness of the pound will pass without its intervention."

At about that time, however, I became aware of a disturbing portent in the air—the apparent abandonment by the British of their long-standing taboo against bandying about the word "devaluation." Like other taboos, this one seemed to have been based on a combination of practical logic (talk about devaluation could easily start a speculative stampede and thereby bring it on) and superstition. But now I found devaluation being freely and frequently discussed in the British press, and, in several respected journals, actually advocated. Nor was that all. Prime Minister Wilson, it is true, continued to follow a careful path around the word, even in the very act of pledging, as he did over and over, that his government would abstain from the deed; there would be "no change in existing policy" as to "overseas monetary matters," he said, delicately, on one occasion. On July 24th, though, Chancellor of the Exchequer James Callaghan spoke openly in the House of Commons about devaluation, complaining that advocacy of it as a national policy had become fashionable, declaring that such a policy would represent a breach of faith with other nations and their people and also pledging that his government would never resort to it. His sentiments were familiar and reassuring; his straightforward expression of them was just the opposite. In the darkest days of 1964, no one had said "devaluation" in Parliament.

All through the autumn, I had a feeling that Britain was

being overtaken by a fiendish concatenation of cruel mis-chances, some specifically damaging to the pound and others merely crushing to British morale. The previous spring, oil from a wrecked, and wretched, tanker had defiled the beaches of Cornwall; now an epidemic was destroying tens, and ulti-mately hundreds, of thousands of head of cattle. The economic straitjacket that Britain had worn for more than a year had swelled unemployment to the highest level in years and made the Labour Government the most unpopular government in the postwar era. (Six months later, in a poll sponsored by the *Sunday Times*, Britons would vote Wilson the fourth most vil-lainous man of the century, after Hitler, de Gaulle, and Stalin, in that order.) A dock strike in London and Liverpool that began in mid-September and was to drag on for more than two months decreased still further the already hobbled export trade, and put an abrupt end to Britain's remaining hope of ending the year with its international accounts in balance. Early in November, 1967, the pound stood at $2.7822, its lowest point in a decade. And then things went downhill fast. On the evening of Monday the thirteenth, Wilson took the occasion of his annual appearance at the Lord Mayor of Lon-don's banquet—the very platform he had used for his fiery commitment to the defense of sterling in the crisis three years earlier—to implore the country and the world to disregard, as distorted by temporary factors, his nation's latest foreign-trade statistics, which would be released the next day. On Tuesday the fourteenth, Britain's foreign-trade figures, duly released, showed an October deficit of over a hundred million pounds—the worst ever reported. The Cabinet met at lunch on Thursday the sixteenth, and that afternoon, in the House of Commons, Chancellor Callaghan, upon being asked to con-firm or deny rumors of an enormous new central-bank credit that would be contingent upon still further unemployment-breeding austerity measures, replied with heat, and with what was later called a lack of discretion, "The Government will take what decisions are appropriate in the light of our understanding of the needs of the British economy, and no one else's. And that, at this stage, does not include the creation of any additional unemployment."

With one accord, the exchange markets decided that the decision to devalue had been taken and that Callaghan had inadvertently let the cat out of the bag. Friday the seventeenth was the wildest day in the history of the exchange markets, and the blackest in the thousand-year history of sterling. In holding it at $2.7825—the price decided on this time as the last-line trench—the Bank of England spent a quantity of reserve dollars that it may never see fit to reveal; Wall Street commercial bankers who have reason to know have estimated the amount at somewhere around a billion dollars, which would mean a continuous, day-long reserve drain of over two million per minute. Doubtless the British reserves dropped below the two-billion-dollar mark, and perhaps far below it. Late on a Saturday—November 18th—full of confused alarms, Britain announced its capitulation. I heard about it from Waage, who telephoned me that afternoon at five-thirty New York time. "As of an hour ago, the pound was devalued to two dollars and forty cents, and the British bank rate went to eight per cent," he said. His voice was shaking a little.

On Saturday night, bearing in mind that scarcely anything but a major war upsets world financial arrangements more than devaluation of a major currency, I went down to the capital of world finance, Wall Street, to look around. A nasty wind was whipping papers through empty streets, and there was the usual rather intimidating off-hours stillness in that part-time city. There was something unusual, though: the presence of rows of lighted windows in the otherwise dark buildings—for the most part, one lighted row per building. Some of the rows I could identify as the foreign departments of the big banks. The heavy doors of the banks were locked and barred; foreign-department men evidently ring to gain entrance on weekends, or use invisible side or rear entrances. Turning up my coat collar, I headed up Nassau Street toward Liberty to take a look at the Federal Reserve Bank. I found it lighted not in a single line but—more hospitably, somehow—in an irregular pattern over its entire Florentine façade, yet it, too, presented to the street a formidably closed front door. As I looked at it, a gust of wind brought an incongruous burst of organ music—perhaps from Trinity Church, a few blocks away—and I realized that in ten or fifteen minutes I hadn't seen anyone. The scene seemed to me to epitomize one of the two faces of central banking—the cold and hostile face, suggesting men in arrogant secrecy making decisions that affect all the rest of us but that we can neither influence nor even comprehend, rather than the more congenial face of elegant and learned men of affairs beneficently saving faltering currencies over their truffles and wine at Basel. This was not the night for the latter face.

On Sunday afternoon, Waage held a press conference in a room on the tenth floor of the bank, and I attended it, along with a dozen other reporters, mostly regulars on the Federal Reserve beat. Waage discoursed generally on the devaluation, parrying questions he didn't want to answer, sometimes by replying to them, like the teacher he once was, with questions of his own. It was still far too early, he said, to tell how great the danger was that the devaluation might lead to "another 1931." Almost any prediction, he said, would be a matter of trying to outguess millions of people and thousands of banks around the world. The next few days would tell the story. Waage seemed stimulated rather than depressed; his attitude was clearly one of apprehension but also of resolution. On the way out, I asked him whether he had been up all night. "No, last evening I went to 'The Birthday Party,' and I must say Pinter's world makes more sense than mine does, these days," he replied.

The outlines of what had happened Thursday and Friday began to emerge during the next few days. Most of the rumors that had been abroad turned out to have been more or less true. Britain *had* been negotiating for another huge credit to forestall devaluation—a credit of the order of magnitude of the three-billion-dollar 1964 package, with the United States again planning to provide the largest share. Whether Britain had devalued from choice or necessity remained debatable. Wilson, in explaining the devaluation to his people in a television address, said that "it would have been possible to ride out this present tide of foreign speculation against the pound by borrowing from central banks and governments," but that such action this time would have been "irresponsible," because "our creditors abroad might well insist on guarantees about this or that aspect of our national policies"; he did not say explicitly that they had done so. In any event, the British Cabinet had—with what grim reluctance may be imagined—decided in principle on devaluation as early as the previous weekend, and then determined the exact amount of the devaluation at its Thursday-noon meeting. At that time, the Cabinet had also resolved to help insure the effectiveness of the devaluation by imposing new austerity measures on the nation, among them higher corporate taxes, a cutback in defense spending, and the highest bank rate in fifty years. As for the two-day delay in putting the devaluation into effect, which had been so costly to British reserves, officials now explained that the time had been necessary for conferences with the other leading monetary powers. Such conferences were required by international monetary rules before a devaluation, and, besides, Britain had urgently needed assurances from its leading competitors in world trade that they did not plan to vitiate the effect of the British devaluation with matching devaluations of their own. Some light was now shed, too, on the sources of the panic selling of pounds on Friday. By no means all of it had been wanton speculation by those famous—although invisible and perhaps non-existent—gnomes of Zurich. On the contrary, much of it had been a form of self-protection, called hedging, by large international corporations, many of them American, that made short sales of sterling equivalent to what they were due to be paid in sterling weeks or months later. The evidence of this was supplied by the corporations themselves, some of them being quick to assure their stockholders that through their foresight they had contrived to lose little or nothing on the devaluation. International Telephone & Telegraph, for example, announced on Sunday that the devaluation would not affect its 1967 earnings, because "management anticipated the possibility of devaluation for some time." International Harvester and Texas Instruments reported that they had protected themselves by making what amounted to short sales of sterling. The Singer Company said it might even have accidentally made a profit on the deal. Other American companies let it be known that they had come out all right, but declined to elaborate, on the ground that if they revealed the methods they had used they might be accused of taking advantage of Britain in its extremity. "Let's just say we were smart" was the way a spokesman for one company put it. And perhaps that, if lacking in grace and elegance, was fair enough. In the jungle of international business, hedging on a weak foreign currency is considered a wholly legitimate use of claws for self-defense. Selling short for speculative purposes enjoys less respectability, and it is interesting to note that the ranks of those who speculated against sterling on Friday, and talked about it afterward, included some who were far from Zurich. A group of professional men in Youngstown, Ohio—veteran stock-market players, but never before international currency plungers—decided on Friday that sterling was about to be devalued, and sold short seventy thousand pounds, netting a profit of almost twenty-five thousand dollars over the weekend. The pounds sold had, of course, ultimately been bought with dollars by the Bank of England, thus adding a minuscule drop to Britain's reserve loss. Reading about the little coup in the *Wall Street Journal*, to which the group's broker had reported it, presumably with pride, I hoped the apprentice gnomes of Youngstown had at least grasped the implications of what they were doing.

So much for Sunday and moral speculation. On Monday, the financial world, or most of it, went back to work, and the devaluation began to be put to its test. The test consisted of two questions. Question One: Would the devaluation accomplish its purpose for Britain—that is, stimulate exports and reduce imports sufficiently to cure the international deficit and put an end to speculation against the pound? Question Two: Would it, as in 1931, be followed by a string of competitive devaluations of other currencies, leading ultimately to a devaluation of the dollar in relation to gold, worldwide monetary chaos, and perhaps a world depression? I watched the answers beginning to take shape.

On Monday, the banks and exchanges in London remained firmly closed, by government order, and all but a few traders elsewhere avoided taking positions in sterling in the Bank of England's absence from the market, so the answer to the question of the pound's strength or weakness at its new valuation was postponed; On Threadneedle and Throgmorton Streets, crowds of brokers, jobbers, and clerks milled around and talked excitedly—but made no trades—in a city where the Union Jack was flying from all flagstaffs because it happened to be the Queen's wedding anniversary. The New York stock market opened sharply lower, then recovered. (There was no really rational explanation for the initial drop; securities men pointed out that devaluation just generally sounds depressing.) By nightfall on Monday, it had been announced that eleven other currencies—those of Spain, Denmark, Israel, Hong Kong, Malta, Guyana, Malawi, Jamaica, Fiji, Bermuda, and Ireland— were also being devalued. That wasn't so bad, because the disruptive effect of a currency devaluation is in direct proportion to the importance of that currency in world trade, and none of those currencies were of great importance. The most ominous move was Denmark's, because Denmark might easily be followed by its close economic allies Norway, Sweden, and the Netherlands, and that *would* be pretty serious. Egypt, which was an instant loser of thirty-eight million dollars on pounds held in its reserves at the time of devaluation, held firm, and so did Kuwait, which lost eighteen million.

On Tuesday, the markets everywhere were going full blast. The Bank of England, back in business, set the new trading limits of the pound at a floor of $2.38 and a ceiling of $2.42, whereupon the pound went straight to the ceiling, like a balloon slipped from a child's hand, and stayed there all day; indeed, for obscure reasons inapplicable to balloons, it spent much of the day slightly above the ceiling. Now, instead of paying dollars for pounds, the Bank of England was supplying pounds for dollars, and thereby beginning the process of rebuilding its reserves. I called Waage to share what I thought would be his jubilation, but found him taking it all calmly. The pound's strength, he said, was "technical"—that is, it was caused by the previous week's short sellers' buying pounds back to cash in their profits—and the first objective test of the new pound would not come until Friday. Seven more small governments announced devaluations during the day. In Malaysia, which had devalued its old sterling-backed pound but not its new dollar, based on gold, and which continued to keep both currencies in circulation, the injustice of the situation led to riots, and over the next two weeks more than twenty-seven people were killed in them—the first casualties of devaluation. Apart from this painful reminder that the counters in the engrossing game of international finance are people's livelihoods, and even their lives, so far so good.

But on Wednesday the twenty-second a less localized portent of trouble appeared. The speculative attack that had so long battered and at last crushed the pound now turned, as everyone had feared it might, on the dollar. As the one nation that is committed to sell gold in any quantity to the central bank of any other nation at the fixed price of thirty-five dollars an ounce, the United States is the keystone of the world monetary arch, and the gold in its Treasury—which on that Wednesday amounted to not quite thirteen billion dollars' worth—is the foundation. Federal Reserve Board Chairman Martin had said repeatedly that the United States would under any condition continue to sell it on demand, if necessary down to the last bar. Despite this pledge, and despite President Johnson's reiteration of it immediately after Britain's devaluation, speculators now began buying gold with dollars in huge quantities, expressing the same sort of skepticism toward official assurances that was shown at about the same time by New Yorkers who took to accumulating and hoarding subway tokens. Gold was suddenly in unusual demand in Paris, Zurich, and other financial centers, and most particularly in London, the world's leading gold market, where people immediately began to talk about the London Gold Rush. The day's orders for gold, which some authorities estimated at over fifty million dollars' worth, seemed to come in from everywhere—except, presumably, from citizens of the United States or Britain, who are forbidden by law to buy or own monetary gold. And who was to sell the stuff to these invisible multitudes so suddenly repossessed by the age-old lust for it? Not the United States Treasury, which, through the Federal Reserve, sold gold only to central banks, and not other central banks, which did not promise to sell it at all. To fill this vacuum, still another coöperative international group, the London gold pool, had been established in 1961. Provided by its members—the United States, Britain, Italy, the Netherlands, Switzerland, West Germany, Belgium, and, originally, France—with gold ingots in quantities that might dazzle a Croesus (fifty-nine per cent of the total coming from the United States), the pool was intended to quell money panics by supplying gold to non-governmental buyers in any quantity demanded, at a price effectively the same as the Federal Reserve's, and thereby to protect the stability of the dollar and the system.

And that is what the pool did on Wednesday. Thursday, though, was much worse, with the gold-buying frenzy in both Paris and London breaking even the records set during the Cuban missile crisis of 1962, and many people, high British and American officials among them, became convinced of something they had suspected from the first—that the gold rush was part of a plot by General de Gaulle and France to humble first the pound and now the dollar. The evidence, to be sure, was all circumstantial, but it was persuasive. De Gaulle and his Ministers had long been on record as wishing to relegate the pound and the dollar to international roles far smaller than their current ones. A suspicious amount of the gold buying, even in London, was traceable to France. On Monday evening, thirty-six hours before the start of the gold rush, France's government had let slip, through a press leak, that it intended to withdraw from the gold pool (according to subsequent information, France hadn't contributed anything to the pool since the previous June anyhow), and the French government was also accused of having had a hand in spreading false rumors that Belgium and Italy were about to withdraw, too. And now it was coming out, bit by bit, that in the days just before the devaluation France had been by far the most reluctant nation to join in another credit package to rescue sterling, and that, for good measure, France had withheld until the very last minute its assurance that it would maintain its own exchange rate if Britain devalued. All in all, there was a good case for the allegation that de Gaulle & Co. had been playing a mischievous part, and, whether it was true or not, I couldn't help feeling that the accusations against them were adding a good deal of spice to the devaluation crisis—spice that would become more piquant a few months later, when the franc would be in dire straits, and the United States forced by circumstances to come to its aid.

On Friday, in London, the pound spent the whole day tight up against its ceiling, and thus came through its first really significant post-devaluation test with colors flying. Only a few small governments had announced devaluations since Monday, and it was now evident that Norway, Sweden, and the Netherlands were going to hold firm. But on the dollar front things looked worse than ever. Friday's gold buying in London and Paris had far exceeded the previous day's record, and estimates were that gold sales in all markets over the preceding three days added up to something not far under the billion-dollar mark; there was near pandemonium all day in Johannesburg as speculators scrambled to get their hands on shares in gold-mining companies; and all over Europe people were trading in dollars not only for gold but for other currencies as well. If the dollar was hardly in the position that the pound had occupied a week earlier, at least there were uncomfortable parallels. Subsequently, it was reported that in the first days after devaluation the Federal Reserve, so accustomed to lending support to other currencies, had been forced to *borrow* various foreign currencies, amounting to almost two billion dollars' worth, in order to defend its own.

Late Friday, having attended a conference at which Waage was in an unaccustomed mood of nervous jocularity that made me nervous, too, I left the Federal Reserve Bank half believing that devaluation of the dollar was going to be announced over the weekend. Nothing of the sort happened; on the contrary, the worst was temporarily over. On Sunday, it was announced that central-bank representatives of the gold-pool countries, Hayes and Coombs among them, had met in Frankfurt and formally agreed to continue maintaining the dollar at its present gold-exchange rate with their combined resources. This seemed to remove any doubt that the dollar was backed not only by the United States' thirteen-billion-dollar gold hoard but also by the additional fourteen billion dollars' worth of gold in the coffers of Belgium, Britain, Italy, the Netherland, Switzerland, and West Germany. The speculators were apparently impressed. On Monday, gold buying was much lower in London and Zurich, continuing at a record pace only in Paris—and this in spite of a sulphurous press audience granted that day by de Gaulle himself, who, along with bemusing opinions on various other matters, hazarded the view that the trend of events was toward the decline of the dollar's international importance. On Tuesday, gold sales dropped sharply everywhere, even in Paris. "A good day today," Waage told me on the phone that afternoon. "A better day tomorrow, we hope." On Wednesday, the gold markets were back to normal, but, as a result of the week's doings, the Treasury had lost some four hundred and fifty tons of gold—almost half a billion dollars' worth—in fulfilling its obligations to the gold pool and meeting the demands of foreign central banks.

Ten days after devaluation, everything was quiet. But it was only a trough between succeeding shock waves. From December 8th to 18th, there came a new spell of wild speculation against the dollar, leaching another four hundred tons or so of gold out of the pool; this, like the previous wave, was eventually calmed by reiterations on the part of the United States and its gold-pool partners of their determination to maintain the status quo. By the end of the year, the Treasury had lost almost a billion dollars' worth of gold since Britain's devaluation, reducing its gold stock to below the twelve-billion-dollar mark for the first time since 1937. President Johnson's balance-of-payments program, announced January 1st, 1968 and based chiefly on restrictions on American bank lending and industrial investments abroad, helped keep speculation down for two months. But the gold rush was not to be quelled so simply. All pledges notwithstanding, it had power-ful economic and psychological forces behind it. In a larger sense, it was an expression of an age-old tendency to distrust all paper currencies in times of crisis, but more specifically it was the long-feared sequel to sterling devaluation, and—perhaps most specifically of all—it was a vote of no confidence in the determination of the United States to keep its economic affairs in order, with particular reference to a level of civilian consumption beyond the dreams of avarice at a time when ever-increasing billions were being sent abroad to support a war with no end in sight. The money in which the world was supposed to be putting its trust looked to the gold speculators like that of the most reckless and improvident spendthrift.

When they returned to the attack, on February 29th—choosing that day for no assignable reason except that a single United States senator, Jacob Javits, had just remarked, with either deadly seriousness or casual indiscretion, that he thought his country might do well to suspend temporarily all gold payments to foreign countries—it was with such ferocity that the situation quickly got out of hand. On March 1st, the gold pool dispensed an estimated forty to fifty tons in London (as against three or four tons on a normal day); on March 5th and 6th, forty tons per day; on March 8th, over seventy-five tons; and on March 13th, a total that could not be accurately estimated but ran well over one hundred tons. Meanwhile, the pound, which could not possibly escape a further devalu-ation if the dollar were to be devalued in relation to gold, slipped below its par of $2.40 for the first time. Still another reiteration of the now-familiar pledges, this time from the central-bankers' club at Basel on March 10th, seemed to have no effect at all. The market was in the classic state of chaos, distrustful of every public assurance and at the mercy of every passing rumor. A leading Swiss banker grimly called the situa-tion "the most dangerous since 1931." A member of the Basel club, tempering desperation with charity, said that the gold speculators apparently didn't realize their actions were imperilling the world's money. The *New York Times*, in an editorial, said, "It is quite clear that the international payments system . . . is eroding."

On Thursday, March 14th, panic was added to chaos. London gold dealers, in describing the day's action, used the un-British words "stampede," "catastrophe," and "nightmare." The exact volume of gold sold that day was unannounced, as usual—probably it could not have been precisely counted, in any case—but everyone agreed that it had been an all-time record; most estimates put the total at around two hundred tons, or two hundred and twenty million dollars' worth, while the *Wall Street Journal* put it twice that high. If the former estimate was right, during the trading day the United States Treasury had paid out through its share of the gold pool alone one million dollars in gold every three minutes and forty-two seconds; if the *Journal* figure was right (as a subsequent Treasury announcement made it appear to be), a million every *one* minute and *fifty-one* seconds. Clearly, this wouldn't do. Like Britain in 1964, at this rate the United States would have a bare cupboard in a matter of days. That afternoon, the Federal Reserve System raised its discount rate from four and a half to five per cent—a defensive measure so timid and inadequate that one New York banker compared it to a popgun, and the Federal Reserve Bank of New York, as the System's foreign-exchange arm, was moved to protest by refusing to go along with the token raise. Late in the day in New York, and toward midnight in London, the United States asked Britain to keep the gold market closed the next day, Friday, to prevent further catastrophe and clear the way to the weekend, when face-to-face international consultations could be held. The bewildered American public, largely unaware of the gold pool's existence, probably first sensed the general shape of things when it learned on Friday morning that Queen Elizabeth II had met with her Ministers on the crisis between midnight and 1 A.M.

On Friday, a day of nervous waiting, the London markets were closed, and so were foreign-exchange desks nearly everywhere else, but gold shot up to a big premium in the Paris market—a sort of black market, from the American standpoint—and in New York sterling, unsupported by the firmly locked Bank of England, briefly fell below its official bottom price of $2.38 before rallying. Over the weekend, the central bankers of the gold-pool nations (the United States, Britain, West Germany, Switzerland, Italy, the Netherlands, and Belgium, with France still conspicuously missing and, indeed, uninvited this time) met in Washington, with Coombs participating for the Federal Reserve along with Chairman Martin. After two full days of rigidly secret discussions, while the world of money waited with bated breath, they announced their decisions late on Sunday afternoon. The thirty-five-dollar-an-ounce official monetary price of gold would be kept for use in all dealings among central banks; the gold pool would be disbanded, and the central banks would supply no more gold to the London market, where privately traded gold would be allowed to find its own price; sanctions would be taken against any central bank seeking to profit from the price differential between the central-bank price and the free-market price; and the London gold market would remain closed for a couple of weeks, until the dust settled. During the first few market days under the new arrangements, the pound rallied strongly, and the free-market price of gold settled at between two and five dollars above the central-bank price—a differential considerably smaller than many had expected.

The crisis had passed, or *that* crisis had. The dollar had escaped devaluation, and the international monetary mechanism was intact. Nor was the solution a particularly radical one; after all, gold had been on a two-price basis in 1960, before the gold pool had been formed. But the solution was a temporary, stopgap one, and the curtain was not down on the drama yet. Like Hamlet's ghost, the pound, which had started the action, was offstage now. The principal actors onstage as summer approached were the Federal Reserve and the United States Treasury, doing what they could in a technical way to keep things on an even keel; the Congress, complacent with prosperity, preoccupied with coming elections, and therefore resistant to higher taxes and other uncomfortable retrenching measures (on the very afternoon of the London panic, the Senate Finance Committee had voted down an income-tax surcharge); and, finally, the President, calling for "a program of national austerity" to defend the dollar, yet at the same time carrying on at ever-increasing expense the Vietnam war, which had become as menacing to the health of America's money as, in the view of many, it was to that of America's soul. Ultimately, it appeared, the nation had just three possible economic courses: to somehow end the Vietnam war, root of the payments problem and therefore heart of the matter; to adopt a full wartime economy, with sky-high taxes, wage and price controls, and perhaps rationing; or to face forced devaluation of the dollar and perhaps a depression-breeding world monetary mess.

Looking beyond the Vietnam war and its incredibly broad worldwide monetary implications, the central bankers went on plugging away. Two weeks after the stopgap solution of the dollar crisis, those of the ten most powerful industrial countries met in Stockholm and agreed, with only France dissenting, on the gradual creation of a new international monetary unit to supplement gold as the bedrock underlying all currencies. It will consist (if action follows on resolution) of special drawing rights on the International Monetary Fund, available to nations in proportion to their existing reserve holdings. In bankers' jargon the rights will be called S.D.R.'s; in popular jargon they were at once called paper gold. The success of the plan in achieving its ends—averting dollar devaluation, overcoming the world shortage of monetary gold, and thus postponing indefinitely the threatened mess—will depend on whether or not men and nations can somehow at last, in a triumph of reason, achieve what they have failed to achieve in almost four centuries of paper money: that is, to overcome one of the oldest and least rational of human traits, the lust for the look and feel of gold itself, and come to give truly equal value to a pledge written on a piece of paper. The answer to that question will come in the last act, and the outlook for a happy ending is not bright.

As the last act was beginning to unfold—after the sterling devaluation but before the gold panic—I went down to Liberty Street and saw Coombs and Hayes. I found Coombs looking bone-tired but not sounding disheartened about three years spent largely in a losing cause. "I don't see the fight for the pound as all having been in vain," he said. "We gained those three years, and during that time the British put through a lot of internal measures to strengthen themselves. If they'd been forced to devalue in 1964, there's a good chance that wage-and-price inflation would have eaten up any benefit they derived and put them back in the same old box. Also, over those three years there have been further gains in international monetary coöperation. Goodness knows what would have happened to the whole system with devaluation in 1964. Without that three-year international effort—that rearguard action, you might say—sterling might have collapsed in much greater disorder, with far more damaging repercussions than we've seen even now. Remember that, after all, our effort and the effort of the other central-banks wasn't to hold up sterling for its own sake. It was to hold it up for the sake of preserving the system. And the system has survived."

Hayes, on the surface, seemed exactly as he had when I last saw him, a year and a half earlier—as placid and unruffled as if he had been spending all that time studying up on Corfu. I asked him whether he was still living up to his principle of keeping bankers' hours, and he replied, smiling very slightly, that the principle had long since yielded to expediency—that, as a time consumer, the 1967 sterling crisis had made the 1964 crisis seem like child's play, and that the subsequent dollar crisis was turning out to be more of the same. A side benefit of the whole three-and-a-half-year affair, he said, was that its frequently excruciating melodrama had contributed something to Mrs. Hayes' interest in banking, and even something, if not so much, to the position of business in Tom's scale of values.

When Hayes spoke of the devaluation, however, I saw that his placidity was a mask. "Oh, I was disappointed, all right," he said quietly. "After all, we worked like the devil to prevent it. And we nearly did. In my opinion, Britain could have got enough assistance from abroad to hold the rate. It could have been done without France. Britain chose to devalue. I think there's a good chance that the devaluation will eventually be a success. And the gain for international coöperation is beyond question. Charlie Coombs and I could feel that at Frankfurt in November, at the gold-pool meeting—a sense everyone there had that now is the time to lock arms. But still . . ." Hayes paused, and when he spoke again his voice was full of such quiet force that I saw the devaluation through his eyes—not as just a severe professional reverse but as an ideal lost and an idol fallen. He said, "That day in November, here at the bank, when a courier brought me the top-secret British document informing us of the decision to devalue, I felt physically sick. Sterling would not be the same. It would never again command the same amount of faith around the world."

INDEX